Fiscal Policies and the World Economy

W9-AAO-785

Fiscal Policies and the World Economy

An Intertemporal Approach

Jacob A. Frenkel
and
Assaf Razin

The MIT Press
Cambridge, Massachusetts
London, England

This book was set in Palatino by Asco Trade Typesetting Ltd., Hong Kong, and printed and bound by The Halliday Lithograph in the United States of America.

Library of Congress Cataloging-in-Publication Data

Frenkel, Jacob A.
Fiscal policies and the world economy.

Bibliography: p.
Includes index.
1. Fiscal policy.   2. International economic relations.
I. Razin, Assaf.   II. Title.
HJ141.F74 1987   339.5'2   87-3276
ISBN 0-262-06109-0

To Niza and Shula

Contents

Preface

Recent theoretical developments in closed-economy macroeconomics have not yet been fully incorporated into the main corpus of international macroeconomics. This book aims at filling this void. We develop a unified conceptual framework suitable for the analysis of the effects of government expenditure and tax policies on key macroeconomic aggregates in the interdependent world economy.

The analysis is motivated by stylized facts characterizing recent major developments. These include unsynchronized changes in national fiscal policies resulting in large budgetary imbalances, volatile real rates of interest, sharp changes in real exchange rates, and significant imbalances in national current account positions. Associated with these developments were drastic changes in public-sector debt and in the international allocation of external debt. Although these real-world developments provide the impetus for the analysis, the orientation of the book is theoretical. Its purpose is to identify and clarify the main channels and the pertinent economic mechanisms through which government-spending and tax policies influence the world economic system. We develop a unified coherent theory capable of interpreting the stylized facts and at the same time, provide a framework for the analysis of the normative issues related to the welfare implications of fiscal policies in the world economy.

The main characteristic of the analysis is the detailed attention given to dynamic and intertemporal considerations. In contrast with the more traditional analyses, the modern approach is based on solid microeconomic foundations. These foundations "discipline" the analysis and impose constraints on the modeling of macroeconomic behavior. Specifically, an explicit account of temporal and intertemporal budget constraints and of the forward-looking behavior consistent with these constraints restrict the permissible behavior of households and governments and thereby sharpen the predictive content of the economic theory. Furthermore, by deriving the economic behavior from utility maximization, the modern analytical framework allows for a meaningful treatment of issues in welfare economics.

The resulting macroeconomic model is capable of dealing with new issues in a consistent manner. Among these issues are the effects of various time patterns of government spending and taxes. We can thus distinguish between temporary and permanent, as well as between current and expected future policies. Likewise, the model is capable of analyzing the macroeconomic consequences of alternative specifications of the tax structure, including the effects of different types of taxes (income tax, value-added tax, etc.).

By being grounded on solid microeconomic foundations, this approach to open-economy macroeconomics narrows the gap between the modes of analysis typical to the branch of international economics dealing with the pure theory of international trade and the branch dealing with open-economy macroeconomics.

To provide a self-contained treatment of the subject matter and to motivate the logical progression of the analysis, we devote a part of the book to a review and a synthesis of traditional approaches to open-economy macroeconomics. This part yields the rationale for the developments of the modern treatment which is the key contribution of the book. In addition it also provides the analytical continuity and completeness necessary for the use of this book as a text. Readers familiar with the traditional approach to international macroeconomics may skip part II (chapters 2 through 4).

The focus of this inquiry is the international dimensions of fiscal policies. This instrument of macroeconomic policy is placed at the center stage for two reasons. First, budget deficits in major industrial countries have played a leading role in the world economic scene in recent years. The prominance of, and the complex interactions among, budget policies and key macroeconomic variables in the world economy provide a justification for a book-length study that focuses on various aspects of this policy instrument. Second, even though we touch in various chapters on some issues of monetary policy, we believe that in contrast with fiscal policies, the state of the art of monetary economics is not yet ripe for an analogous unified comprehensive treatment of the international dimensions of monetary policies based on solid microeconomic foundations.

This book was written while J. A. Frenkel was the David Rockefeller Professor of International Economics at the University of Chicago and A. Razin was the Daniel and Grace Ross Professor of International Economics at Tel-Aviv University. Our joint work on the international dimensions of fiscal policies started at Tel-Aviv University in the fall of 1983. During this period, as well as during the summer of 1985, J. A. Frenkel was a fellow at the Sackler Institute of Advanced Studies and a Visiting Professor in the Department of Economics. Our collaboration continued during the winter of 1984 while A. Razin held a visiting professorship at Princeton University. The main work on the book was carried out at the University of Chicago during the spring, summer, and fall of 1986 while A. Razin was a visiting professor in the Department of Economics and the Graduate School of Business. Further work was done in Cambridge, Massachusetts, during our participation in the summer institute sessions of the National Bureau of Economic Research (1984 to 1986), as well as in Washington, D.C., during our visit to the World Bank in the summer of 1986. We wish to thank these institutions for providing a comfortable and stimulating environment which made this research and the preparation of the book possible.

Some of the chapters in this book draw on material contained in our joint articles. Chapter 4 is based on "The Mundell-Fleming Model: A Quarter Century Later" (*IMF Staff Papers*, forthcoming). Chapters 5, 7, and 8 draw on "Spending, Taxes and Deficits: International-Intertemporal Approach" (*Princeton Studies in International Finance*, forthcoming) and on "Deficits with Distortionary Taxes: International Dimensions" (NBER, Working Paper No. 2080, November 1986). Chapter 9 draws on "Fiscal Policies and Real Exchange Rates in the World Economy" (NBER, Working Paper No. 2065, November 1986). Chapters 10 through 13 draw on our articles, "Government Spending, Debt and International Economic Interdependence" (*Economic Journal* 95, September 1985 : 619–636);

"Fiscal Expenditures and International Economic Interdependence" (in W. H. Buiter and R. C. Marston, eds., *International Economic Policy Coordination*, Cambridge: Cambridge University Press, 1985:37–73); "The International Transmission and Effects of Fiscal Policies" (*American Economic Review* 76, May 1986:330–335); "Fiscal Policies in the World Economy" (*Journal of Political Economy* 94, June 1986: 564–594); "Real Exchange Rates, Interest Rates and Fiscal Policies" (*The Economic Studies Quarterly* 37, June 1986:99–113); and "The International Transmission of Fiscal Expenditures and Budget Deficits in the World Economy" (in A. Razin and E. Sadka, eds., *Economic Policy in Theory and Practice*, London: Macmillan, 1987:51–96). Finally, some of the arguments in chapter 15 draw on "The Limited Viability of Dual Exchange-Rate Regimes" (NBER, Working Paper No. 1902, April 1986) and "Exchange-Rate Management Viewed as Tax Policies" (unpublished manuscript, 1987).

During the course of this research we have benefited from useful comments and suggestions by Joshua Aizenman, Alan Auerbach, Olivier Blanchard, William Branson, Willem Buiter, Guillermo Calvo, Avinash Dixit, Rudiger Dornbusch, Martin Feldstein, Stanley Fischer, Robert Flood, John Geweke, Itzhak Gilboa, Jeremy Greenwood, Vittorio Grilli, Koichi Hamada, Elhanan Helpman, Peter Howitt, John Huizinga, Kent Kimbrough, Robert Lucas, Franco Modigliani, Michael Mussa, Maurice Obstfeld, Torsten Persson, Thomas Sargent, Don Schlagenhauf, Alan Stockman, Larry Summers, and Lars Svensson. During the past three years we have also received numerous suggestions in seminars and workshops at the Brookings Institution, the University of Chicago, CEPR (London), CEPREMAP (Paris), Columbia University, Duke University, Harvard University, Hebrew University, International House in Tokyo, the University of Michigan, MIT, NBER (Cambridge), New York University, Princeton University, Stanford University, Tel-Aviv University, University of Washington, University of Western Ontario, the World Bank, and the Latin-American Econometric Society meeting held in Cordoba.

In preparing the book we benefited from comments and efficient research assistance by our graduate students at the University of Chicago, including Ken Kasa, Thomas Krueger, Jonathan Ostry, and Kei-Mu Yi. We owe special thanks to Thomas Krueger who thoroughly read the entire manuscript and provided us with numerous comments and suggestions that improved the presentation and sharpened the arguments.

We wish to thank June Nason of the University of Chicago for her tireless efforts and high efficiency in cheerfully typing successive drafts of the manuscript. Her willingness to work long hours is deeply appreciated. Thanks are also due to Terry Vaughn, the economics editor at the MIT Press, for his remarkable professionalism and dedication in the various stages of this enterprise.

The writing of a jointly authored book under a very tight time schedule always entails complicated arrangements, coordination, and discipline. In our case the need for transatlantic communications added logistical difficulties that could not have been surmounted without the understanding, selflessness, and unfailing support of our wives, Niza Frenkel and Shula Razin. It is only appropriate that we dedicate this book to them.

J. A. F
A. R.
February 1987

I

Prologue

1

Stylized Facts on Fiscal Policies and International Economic Interdependence

This book deals with the international dimensions of fiscal policies. The opening chapter surveys key facts relevant for the analysis of the effects of government spending and tax policies in the world economy. The empirical regularities exhibited by the stylized facts serve to identify the issues and the macroeconomic variables that play central roles in the interdependent world economy. The main purpose of the discussion in this chapter is to motivate the theoretical analysis that follows.

We devote the first section of this chapter to a brief review of major developments related to the effects of public-sector-spending policies and budget deficits during the first quinquennium of the 1980s. Relative to other recent periods this half decade stands out in terms of the major changes taking place in the fiscal policies of the major countries. To identify empirical relations among the key economic variables that are likely to be related to, and influenced by fiscal policies, we present in section 1.2 summary statistics pertaining to comovements among these variables. The summary statistics describe various combinations of temporal, intertemporal, and international correlations among the key variables. These correlations, together with the stylized facts outlined in section 1.1, can be useful in the construction of theoretical models. The final section of this chapter summarizes key characteristics emerging from the data. These characteristics provide a guide to the choice of variables incorporated into the analytical framework, and they highlight issues that need to be addressed by the theory.

1.1 Selected Facts

During the first half of the 1980s the world economy was subject to large and unsynchronized changes in fiscal policies, high and volatile real rates of interest, large fluctuations in real exchange rates and significant variations in private-sector spending. During this period national fiscal policies have exhibited large divergencies. The United States adopted an expansionary course while the other major countries taken together followed a relatively contractionary course. These policies undertaken by the major economies affected the rest of the world through the integrated goods and capital markets, and resulted in increased concern in each country over policy measures undertaken in the rest of the world.

Since the beginning of 1980 short- and long-term real rates of interest exhibited different patterns. As illustrated in figure 1.1, a weighted average of the annual short-term real interest rates in the five major industrial countries (the United States, Japan, France, West Germany, and the United Kingdom) rose from about 2.0 percent at the beginning of 1980 to about 5.0 percent at the end of 1985; the corresponding long-term rates rose from about 0.5 percent in early 1980 to about 6.0 percent at the end of 1985. Both rates peaked and surpassed 8 percent in mid-1982. Thus, during 1980 to 1985, real rates of interest were high (in comparison with early 1980) and the slope of the real yield curve, which was negative until the third quarter of 1981, turned positive starting from mid-1982. Real interest rates fell further in 1986.

The same period also witnessed sharp changes in real exchange rates. In the first quarter of 1985 the real effective value of the U.S. dollar (calculated on the basis of unit labor cost) was about 43 percent above its average value for the decade 1974 to 1983 and 57 percent above its low point of the third quarter of 1980. Likewise, in the last quarter of 1985 the real effective value of the Japanese yen was about 50 percent above its low point in the first quarter of 1980. The other major currencies (especially the French franc and the Italian lira) have also exhibited very large fluctuations. Figure 1.2 illustrates the extent of the changes in the effective nominal exchange rates of the U.S. dollar, Japanese yen, British pound, German mark, French

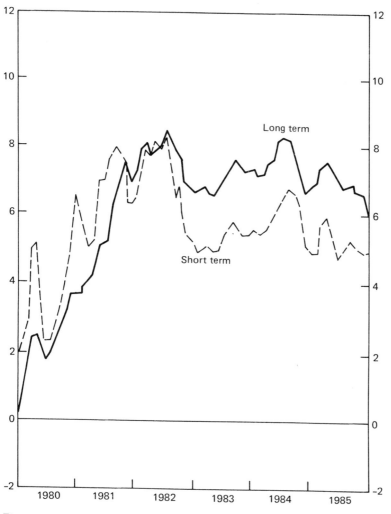

Figure 1.1
Short- and long-term real rates of interest, 1980–1985 (five major industrial
country average)

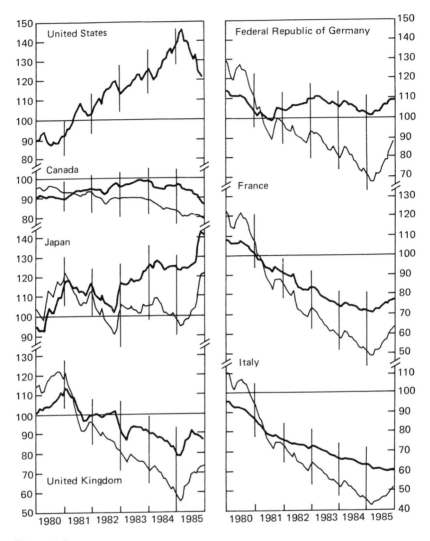

Figure 1.2
Indexes of effective nominal exchange rates (average value for 1974–1983 = 100). The thick lines show the effective exchange rates, and the thin lines show the U.S. dollar exchange rates (measured as the U.S. dollar value of the domestic currency).

franc, Canadian dollar, and Italian lira. The sharp changes in the real exchange rates (as measured by the relative GDP deflators and by the relative unit labor costs) are shown in figure 1.3. As shown by these figures, the U.S. dollar, after several years of consecutive appreciation, depreciated significantly beginning in March 1985. Its depreciation continued throughout 1986. Correspondingly, the currencies of other major industrial countries, especially Japan and West Germany, appreciated in nominal and real terms.

Another key fact characterizing this period is the large and divergent pattern of the current-account positions of the major industrial countries. These divergencies are especially pronounced in the comparison between the developments of the current-account positions of the United States with that of Japan and Germany. For example, the U.S. current-account position switched from a surplus of about 0.25 percent of GNP in 1980 to a deficit of about 3 percent of GNP in 1985. During the same period the current-account position of Japan switched from a deficit of about 0.09 percent of GNP in 1980 to a surplus larger than 3 percent of GNP in 1985. Likewise the current-account position of Germany also switched from a deficit of about 2 percent of GNP in 1980 to a surplus of about 2 percent of GNP in 1985. These developments in the current accounts of the balance of payments reflected themselves in correspondingly large changes in the external debt position of these countries. (The source of the data used in this section is International Monetary Fund: *World Economic Outlook*.)

These developments in real interest rates, real exchange rates, and current-account positions were associated with large and divergent changes in world fiscal policies. The budget deficit of the general U.S. government as a fraction of GNP rose from about 1 percent in 1980 to about 3.5 percent in 1985 (after reaching a peak of 3.8 percent in 1983). At the same time the budget deficit as a fraction of GNP declined in Japan, Germany, and the United Kingdom. Similarly, since 1980 according to IMF measures, the fiscal impulse (which is a more exogenous measure of fiscal policy) has been expansionary for the United States and contractionary for the other major industrial countries taken together. This pattern is shown in figure

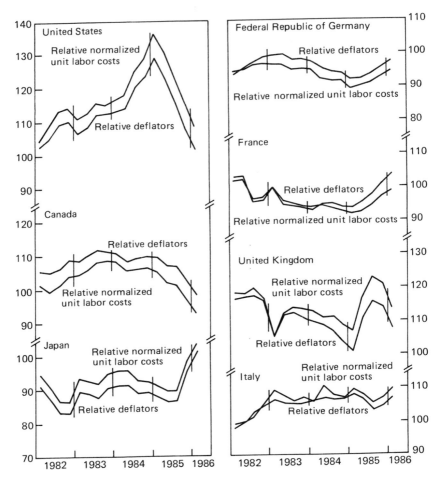

Figure 1.3
Indexes of effective real exchange rates (average value for 1975–1984 = 100)

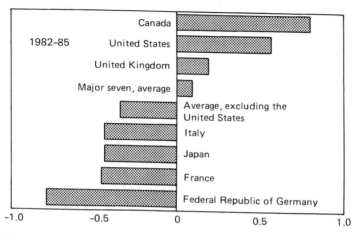

Figure 1.4
Fiscal impulses for the major industrial countries (in percent of GDP at annual rates, 1982–1985)

1.4 in which a positive fiscal impulse indicates injection of stimulus while a negative impulse indicates withdrawal of stimulus.

The cumulative implications of the budgetary imbalances are reflected in the size of public debt. The rapid rise in net public debt as a ratio of GNP in Germany and Japan leveled off toward the end of the first half decade of the 1980s (at around one-quarter of GNP). In the United Kingdom the same quantity remained relatively stable at around one-half of GNP. On the other hand, and in contrast with these countries, the ratio of net government debt to GNP in the United States rose sharply during the same period from about one-fifth of GNP to close to one-third of GNP. These developments are reflected in a relative rise of the debt-service burden imposed on the U.S. government budget.

Another indicator of the levels and divergencies among national fiscal policies is provided by a comparison among annual percentage changes in public-sector consumption. As seen in table 1.1, the percentage annual growth of U.S. public-sector consumption accelerated in the second part of the period, exceeding 4 percent in 1985. During the late 1970s and early 1980s public-sector consumption in Japan and Europe grew faster than in the United States (the difference for Japan reaching 4.3 percent in 1981, and for Europe 1.8

Table 1.1
Differences in private and public consumption: United States, Japan, and Europe, 1977–1985 (annual percentage changes)

	United States		United States minus Japan		United States minus Europe	
	Private	Public	Private	Public	Private	Public
1977	5.0	1.5	+1.2	−2.4	+2.4	−0.1
1978	4.5	2.0	−0.2	−3.1	+1.1	−1.8
1979	2.7	1.3	−3.2	−3.0	−0.8	−1.5
1980	0.5	2.2	−0.8	−0.7	−0.9	0.0
1981	2.0	0.9	+1.2	−4.3	+2.0	−1.0
1982	1.4	2.0	−2.8	+0.2	+0.7	+0.7
1983	4.8	−0.3	+1.5	−3.2	+3.6	−1.9
1984	5.3	3.5	+2.4	+1.2	+4.4	+2.1
1985	4.1	4.5	+0.7	+2.1	+2.3	+3.2

Source: Computed from data in IMF, *World Economic Outlook*, October 1985.

Table 1.2
Differences in real GNP and gross fixed investment: United States, Japan, and Europe (annual percentage changes)

	United States		United States minus Japan		United States minus Europe	
	GNP	Investment	GNP	Investment	GNP	Investment
1977	5.5	13.7	+0.2	+8.9	+3.0	+12.6
1978	5.0	9.9	−0.1	+0.5	+2.1	+8.3
1979	2.8	3.8	−2.4	−2.5	−0.6	+0.2
1980	−0.3	−7.1	−5.1	−8.2	−1.9	−9.5
1981	2.5	3.1	−1.5	−0.5	+2.6	+6.5
1982	−2.1	−6.8	−5.5	−8.7	−2.5	−5.3
1983	3.7	9.7	+0.3	+9.0	+2.3	+9.3
1984	6.8	18.0	+1.0	+12.3	+4.5	+15.7
1985	2.6	6.4	−1.8	+1.9	+0.3	+3.7

Source: Computed from data in IMF, *World Economic Outlook*, October 1985.

percent in 1978), and during 1984–85 public-sector consumption in Japan and Europe grew more slowly (the difference in "favor" of the United States reaching in 1985 2.1 percent in comparison with Japan and 3.2 percent in comparison with Europe).

Concomitantly, the annual percentage changes in real private-sector consumption also displayed large fluctuations that differed across countries. In the United States these changes ranged from 0.5 percent in 1980 to 5.3 percent in 1984, and as seen in table 1.1, the growth of private-sector consumption in Japan and Europe exceeded that in the United States during 1979–80 and fell short of it during 1983–85. As illustrated in table 1.2, the international differentials among growth rates of GNP and of fixed investment also displayed a similar pattern.

1.2 Comovements of Key Economic Variables in the World Economy: Summary Statistics

In this section we present stylized facts concerning the comovements of selected economic variables. These facts are based on data pertaining to the thirty-year period from 1955 to 1984 (obtained from IMF, *International Financial Statistics*). In so doing, we gain insight into some of the empirical regularities characterizing the international transmission mechanism of economic policies and exogenous shocks. We start by presenting figures showing the international comovements of some key variables and proceed with the presentation of summary statistics concerning the temporal, intertemporal, and international correlations among these variables. Throughout, we focus on the seven major industrial countries: Canada, United States, Japan, France, Germany, Italy, and the United Kingdom. We divide these countries into two blocks: the United States and the "rest-of-the-world" (comprised of the other six countries taken together as an aggregate). Our analysis of the stylized facts is based on this "two-country" world economy.

Figures 1.5 and 1.6 show, respectively, the international comovements of the rates of growth of government consumption and of (gross) tax revenue (due to incomplete data on tax revenue, figure 1.6 covers the period up to 1978). The main features exhibited by

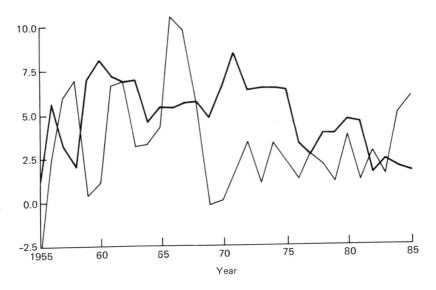

Figure 1.5
Growth rates of government consumption: United States (thin line) versus rest-of-the-world (thick line)

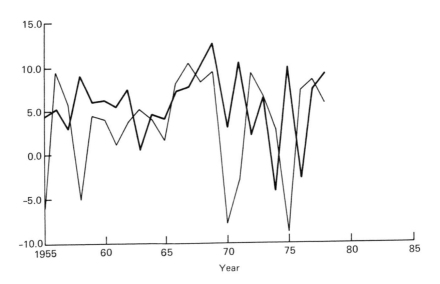

Figure 1.6
Growth rates of tax revenue: United States (thin line) versus rest-of-the-world (thick line) (in percent per annum)

Table 1.3
National and international contemporaneous correlations of growth rates: 1955–1984
(percent per annum)

	Y	I	C	G	Y*	I*	C*	G*	C + C*
Y	1								
I	0.94	1							
C	0.84	0.81	1						
G	0.10	−0.15	0.03	1					
Y*	0.55	0.46	0.56	−0.00	1				
I*	0.32	0.22	0.25	0.02	0.88	1			
C*	0.43	0.35	0.53	0.09	0.85	0.76	1		
G*	0.07	−0.02	0.10	−0.07	0.42	0.44	0.48	1	
C + C*	0.76	0.70	0.90	0.06	0.78	0.54	0.84	0.32	1

Note: Y = GNP, I = private-sector investment, C = private-sector consumption, G = government consumption, and an asterisk(*) denotes "rest of the world" variables, which are constructed as weighted averages of real growth rates. Each country's weight corresponds to the average over the previous three years of the U.S. dollar value of its GNP as a fraction of the six-country sum of the U.S. dollar values of GNP.

these figures are the large amplitude of these series, the low contemporaneous international correlation between growth rates of government consumption, and the somewhat higher correlation between the growth rates of tax revenue (as reported in table 1.3, these correlations are −0.13 and 0.26, respectively). As shown in figure 1.5, the largest changes in the growth rate of U.S. government consumption occurred in the second half of the 1960s in conjunction with the Vietnam War. It is relevant to note, however, that significant variations also took place in other years.

The pattern of tax revenue shown in figure 1.6 reflects in large measure the growth rates of GNP shown in figure 1.7. Indeed, the contemporaneous correlation between the growth rates of GNP and of tax revenue is 0.64 in the United States and 0.44 in the rest-of-the-world. The comovements of GNP growth rates reflect the outcomes of macroeconomic policies, as well as external and internal shocks. All these manifest themselves in the characteristics of the international transmission of business cycles. For example, the high correlation exhibited during the period 1973 to 1976 reflects the common external shock associated with the first oil crisis. On the other hand, the low correlation exhibited during the early part of the 1980s

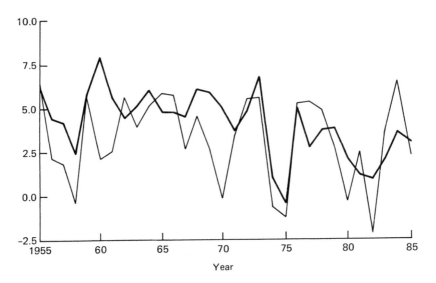

Figure 1.7
Growth rates of GNP: United States (thin line) versus rest-of-the-world (thick line) (in percent per annum)

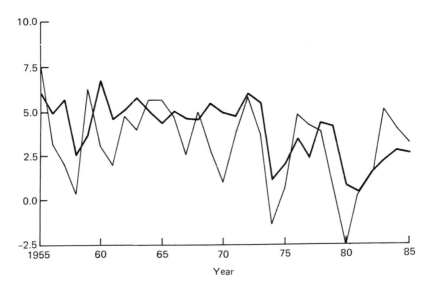

Figure 1.8
Growth rates of private-sector consumption: United States (thin line) versus rest-of-the-world (thick line) (in percent per annum)

reflects the divergencies of internal policies (discussed in section 1.1). On the whole, as indicated in table 1.3, the international correlation between the growth rates over the entire period is 0.55.

Changes in the fiscal stance (government spending and tax revenue) and the induced changes in GNP are associated with corresponding adjustments of private-sector spending (consumption and investment). Figure 1.8 shows the international comovements of the rates of growth of private-sector consumption. As revealed by this figure, in some years (especially during the first half of the period) the growth rates of private-sector consumption were negatively correlated internationally, whereas in other years (especially during the second half of the period) these growth rates were positively correlated. On the whole, as indicated by table 1.3, the international correlation over the entire period was 0.53. We also note that during the second half of the period the amplitude of this series for the United States exceeds that of the rest of the world.

Finally, figure 1.9 shows the comovements of the rates of growth of investment. Typically, the amplitude of these series is very high (exceeding those of the other series), and the United States exhibits higher volatility than the rest-of-the-world. As for the international correlations, table 1.3 indicates that overall there is a (weak) positive correlation between the United States and the rest-of-the-world series. In general (as with tax revenue), the rates of growth of investment in both the United States and the rest-of-the-world are highly correlated with the corresponding growth rates of GNP. As indicated in table 1.3, these correlations are 0.94 for the United States, and 0.88 for the rest-of-the-world.

The bilateral pairwise relations exhibited by figures 1.5 through 1.9 is supplemented by the national and international time-series correlations reported in tables 1.3 and 1.4. Noteworthy among these correlations is the persistence of growth rates of domestic and foreign government consumption as reflected by the magnitudes of the autocorrelation coefficients (0.40 for the United States and 0.54 for the rest-of-the-world). The other feature revealed by these correlations is the relatively high positive association between the growth rates of current (and lagged) government spending of the rest-of-the-

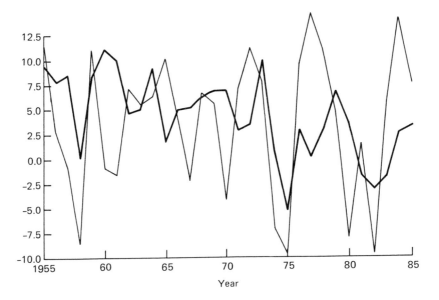

Figure 1.9
Growth rates of private-sector investment: United States (thin line) versus rest-of-the-world (thick line) (percent per annum)

Table 1.4
International and intertemporal correlations of growth rates: autocorrelations with one-year lag, 1955−1984 (percent per annum)

	Y	I	C	G	Y*	I*	C*	G*	C + C*
Y_{-1}	0.13	0.09	−0.01	0.24	0.36	0.41	0.41	0.13	0.21
I_{-1}	0.09	0.12	−0.06	0.08	0.31	0.40	0.40	0.05	0.18
C_{-1}	0.35	0.33	0.29	0.19	0.57	0.56	0.62	0.11	0.50
G_{-1}	0.25	0.09	0.25	0.40	0.18	0.02	0.12	0.05	0.22
Y^*_{-1}	−0.01	−0.07	−0.08	0.24	0.44	0.58	0.47	0.52	0.18
I^*_{-1}	−0.25	−0.31	−0.30	0.25	0.22	0.41	0.30	0.50	−0.04
C^*_{-1}	0.07	−0.03	−0.00	0.31	0.52	0.65	0.56	0.44	0.29
G^*_{-1}	0.01	−0.13	0.03	0.16	0.28	0.23	0.40	0.54	0.29
$C_{-1} + C^*_{-1}$	0.25	0.19	0.17	0.27	0.61	0.67	0.66	0.29	0.45

Note: See table 1.3; the subscript −1 indicates one-year lag.

world and the corresponding growth rates of foreign output, consumption, and investment. The association between the growth rate of current U.S. government spending and the corresponding growth rates of U.S. GNP and private-sector consumption is positive, but relatively weak. However, the (positive) correlation between the growth rates, one-period lagged, of U.S. government spending and the growth rates of U.S. GNP and private-sector consumption are more sizable. Finally, it is relevant to note that the contemporaneous correlation between U.S. government spending and U.S. investment is negative (-0.15).

1.3 Facts and Theory

The selected facts from the 1980s, along with the correlations obtained from the more extended time period, serve as a guide for the selection of variables and for the identification of channels through which the effects of fiscal policy are transmitted throughout the world economy. Accordingly, the discussion in section 1.1 suggests that in modeling the international effects of fiscal policies, allowance should be made for the special role that real exchange rates, short- and long-term interest rates, current-account adjustments, and the size of foreign debt play in the international transmission mechanism. A proper theory of the effects of fiscal policy on the interdependent world economy should be capable of clarifying the mechanisms underlying the varying patterns of responses of these macroeconomic variables to such policies. Furthermore the theory should also illuminate and uncover the economic forces responsible for the large fluctuations and for the varying cross-country correlations of private-sector consumption, investment, and growth rates.

The comovements of the key economic variables discussed in section 1.2 also indicate the significance of an additional consideration that should be incorporated into theoretical modeling of interdependencies. The correlations imply that the timing of the various fiscal measures plays a critical role. In this context the degree of persistence exhibited by the series measuring growth rates of government spending, and the lack of such a persistence in the growth rates of tax revenues suggest that the theory should distinguish between permanent and transitory policies.

The stylized facts reported in this chapter motivate the choice of topics and issues examined in this book. Although the various real-world developments provide the impetus for the analysis, the orientation of the book is theoretical. Its purpose is to identify and clarify the main channels and the pertinent mechanisms through which government-spending and tax policies influence the world economic system. The models that are developed are aimed at providing a coherent theory capable of interpreting the stylized facts, and at the same time, they provide a framework for the analysis of the normative issues related to the desirability of fiscal policies in the interdependent world economy.

In part II of this book we introduce the key issues and concepts within the traditional income-expenditure models of interdependent economies. These models attempt to clarify the factors underlying the patterns of comovements of national outputs, consumption, investment, and fiscal policies observed in the data. Following the presentation of the traditional income-expenditure models, we review their limitations and proceed in parts III through VI to develop an approach that highlights important intertemporal considerations. Factors playing a critical role in this approach include forward-looking behavior, private and public-sectors' intertemporal solvency, and the specification of the precise time pattern of policies. This approach, which rests on solid microeconomic foundations, permits a meaningful analysis of the welfare implications of government-spending and tax policies.

II

Traditional Approaches to Fiscal Policies in the Open Economy

2

The Income-Expenditure Model: Fiscal Policies and the Determination of Output

This chapter, along with chapters 3 and 4, is devoted to the presentation of the traditional income-expenditure approach to open-economy macroeconomics. Its focus on factors underlying the determination of output reflects a Keynesian heritage. The great depression of the 1930s, and the "beggar thy neighbor" policies adopted during that period by many countries, stimulated the development of this approach. Interest in this type of modeling is also stimulated by the observations (reported in tables 1.3 and 1.4 of chapter 1) on the cross-country correlations between private-sector absorption, government spending, and, in particular, national outputs.

In this chapter we outline the analytical framework of the income-expenditure model of the world economy. This framework is employed in the subsequent analysis of fiscal policies and income determination. Here we present a "Keynesian" two-country model in which prices are given while the levels of output and employment adjust in response to changes in aggregate demand. The next chapter presents a "classical" version of the model in which the assumptions concerning the fixity of prices and the flexibility of output and employment are replaced by the assumption that prices are flexible while output is given at the full employment level. The analytical framework outlined in section 2.1 serves both of these analyses.

2.1 The Analytical Framework of the Income-Expenditure Model

Consider a two-country model of the world economy. The two countries are referred to as the home (domestic) country and the foreign country. Each country produces a distinct commodity: the domestic economy produces good x, and the foreign economy produces good m. The domestic level of output is denoted by Y_x, and the foreign level of output by Y_m^*. Throughout the analysis foreign variables are denoted by an asterisk. We assume that there is one noninterest-bearing asset—money, whose domestic and foreign quantities are denoted by M and M^*, respectively. The budget constraint requires that during each period, t, the value of the resources at the disposal of individuals equal the value of the uses of these resources. Accordingly, the domestic and foreign budget constraints are

$$Z_t + M_t = P_t(Y_{xt} - T_t) + M_{t-1},\qquad(2.1)$$

$$Z_t^* + M_t^* = P_t^*(Y_{mt}^* - T_t^*) + M_{t-1}^*,\qquad(2.2)$$

where Z_t and P_t denote, respectively, nominal spending and the GDP deflator, and where Y_{xt} and T_t denote, respectively, real GDP and real taxes—both measured in terms of the domestic good. Equation (1.1) states that the individuals who allocate their resources between spending (Z_t) and asset holding (M_t) are constrained by the total available resources. These resources are the value of disposable income $[P_t(Y_{xt} - T_t)]$ and assets carried over from the previous period (M_{t-1}). As revealed by this formulation, money serves as a store of value facilitating the transfer of purchasing power from one period to the next. Similar notations (with an asterisk) and a similar interpretation apply to the foreign country budget constraint in equation (2.2).

In characterizing the behavior of domestic and foreign individuals, suppose that the desired levels of spending and asset holding depend only on the values of currently available resources. Thus, making use of the budget constraints, the *spending functions* are

$$Z_t = Z(P_t y_{xt}, M_{t-1}),\qquad(2.3)$$

$$Z_t^* = Z^*(P_t^* y_{mt}^*, M_{t-1}^*),\qquad(2.4)$$

where y_{xt} and y_{mt}^* denote, respectively, the values of domestic and foreign real disposable incomes $(Y_x - T$ and $Y_m^* - T^*)$. Analogously, the implied money-demand functions are

$$M_t = M(P_t y_{xt}, M_{t-1}),$$ (2.5)

$$M_t^* = M^*(P_t^* y_{mt}^*, M_{t-1}^*).$$ (2.6)

In this formulation we have specified the spending and the money-demand functions in nominal terms. Naturally the choice of units of measurement should not affect individuals' behavior with respect to real spending and real money demand. It follows that the *nominal* spending and money-demand functions are homogeneous of degree one in their arguments. Accordingly, we can define the *real spending functions* by

$$E_t = E\left(y_{xt}, \frac{M_{t-1}}{P_t}\right),$$ (2.7)

$$E_t^* = E^*\left(y_{mt}^*, \frac{M_{t-1}^*}{P_t^*}\right),$$ (2.8)

where $E_t = Z_t/P_t$ denotes the real value of domestic spending measured in terms of the domestic good, and where $E_t^* = Z_t^*/P_t^*$ denotes the real value of foreign spending, measured in terms of the foreign good.

The marginal propensity to save out of income, s, is assumed to be positive but less than unity, and thus the marginal propensity to spend, $1 - s$, is a positive fraction. Likewise, the marginal propensity to spend out of assets is positive. Similar properties characterize the foreign-spending function.

The domestic private sector is assumed to allocate its spending between domestic goods, C_{xt}, and foreign goods, C_{mt}. Analogously, the foreign private sector also allocates its spending between these two goods, C_{xt}^* and C_{mt}^*. Thus the real values of domestic and foreign spending (each measured in terms of own GDP) are

$$E_t = C_{xt} + p_{mt} C_{mt},$$ (2.9)

$$E_t^* = \frac{1}{p_{mt}} C_{xt}^* + C_{mt}^*,$$ (2.10)

where p_{mt} denotes the *relative* price of good m in terms of good x. This relative price is assumed to be equalized across countries through international trade. The relative share of domestic spending on good m (the foreign good) is denoted by $\beta_m = p_{mt}C_{mt}/E_t$. Likewise, the relative share of foreign spending on good x (the good produced by the home country) is denoted by $\beta_x^* = C_{xt}^*/p_{mt}E_t^*$. Thus β_m and β_x^* are the relative shares of domestic and foreign spending on their corresponding importable good. These expenditure shares are assumed to be constant.

The levels of real government spending in period t in each country (measured in terms of own GDP) are denoted by G_t and G_t^*, respectively. Analogously to the private sectors, the governments also allocate their spending between the two goods. Domestic government spending on importables (good m) is $\beta_m^g G_t/p_{mt}$, and foreign government spending on their importables (good x) is $\beta_x^{g*} p_{mt} G_t^*$, where β_m^g and β_x^{g*} denote, respectively, the domestic and foreign relative shares of government spending on importables.

The surplus in the domestic economy's *trade account* in period t, $(TA)_t$, is defined as the difference between its exports and imports. The economy's export equals the difference between domestic production and national consumption of exportables, where the latter consists of private-sector and government purchases. Here exports are $Y_{xt} - [(1 - \beta_m)E_t + (1 - \beta_m^g)G_t]$. Analogously, the economy's imports equal the difference between national consumption and production of importables. Here, since in the present formulation the importable good is not produced domestically, imports are $\beta_m E_t + \beta_m^g G_t$. It follows that the trade-balance surplus can be expressed as the difference between GDP and national spending (absorption):

$$(TA)_t = Y_{xt} - (E_t + G_t). \tag{2.11}$$

Equation (2.11) can be used together with the budget constraint (2.1) to yield

$$M_t - M_{t-1} = P_t[(TA)_t - (T_t - G_t)]. \tag{2.12}$$

Equation (2.12) expresses private savings (the accumulation of assets by the private sector) as the difference between national savings (indicated by the trade-balance surplus) and government savings (indicated by the surplus in the government budget).

We assume that the economy operates under a fixed exchange-rate regime and that the exchange rate is pegged by the monetary authority. The absence of interest-bearing debt implies that discrepancies between government spending and taxes are met by corresponding changes in the money supply. Thus, abstracting from the commercial-banking system, changes in the money supply reflect two activities of the monetary authorities: those associated with pegging the exchange rate, and those associated with financing government budget deficits. The two terms on the right-hand side of equation (2.12) correspond to these two sources of changes in the money supply. The first is the surplus in the official settlements account of the balance of payments, indicating the official accumulation of international reserves induced by the exchange-rate-pegging operation of the monetary authorities. Since in the present stage of the analysis we do not allow for international borrowing and lending, the official settlements balance equals the trade-balance surplus, $P_t(TA)_t$. The second term on the right-hand side of equation (2.12) is the monetary change induced by the surplus in the government budget, $-P_t(T_t - G_t)$.

Similar considerations apply to the foreign economy. Therefore the foreign-country analogue to the trade-balance and the monetary-flow equations (2.11) and (2.12) is

$$(TA)_t^* = Y_{mt}^* - (E_t^* + G_t^*) \tag{2.13}$$

and

$$M_t^* - M_{t-1}^* = P_t^*[(TA)_t^* - (T_t^* - G_t^*)], \tag{2.14}$$

where the real magnitudes are measured in terms of the foreign good, m.

Equilibrium in the world economy requires that world demand for each good equals the corresponding supply. Accordingly,

$$(1 - \beta_m)E_t + (1 - \beta_m^g)G_t + p_{mt}(\beta_x^* E_t^* + \beta_x^{g*} G_t^*) = Y_{xt}, \tag{2.15}$$

$$\frac{1}{p_{mt}}(\beta_m E_t + \beta_m^g G_t) + (1 - \beta_x^*)E_t^* + (1 - \beta_x^{g*})G_t^* = Y_{mt}^*. \tag{2.16}$$

The two equilibrium conditions (2.15) and (2.16), together with the definitions of the trade balance in equations (2.11) and (2.13), imply that in equilibrium the surplus in the home country's trade account is equal to the foreign country's deficit so that $(TA)_t = -p_{mt}(TA)_t^*$, where $(TA)_t$ is

$$(TA)_t = p_{mt}(\beta_x^* E_t^* + \beta_x^{g*} G_t^*) - (\beta_m E_t + \beta_m^g G_t). \tag{2.17}$$

The relative price of good m in terms of good x, p_{mt}, which is assumed to be equal across countries, can be written as

$$p_{mt} = \frac{e P_t^*}{P_t}, \tag{2.18}$$

where e is the nominal exchange rate expressing the price of the foreign currency in terms of the domestic currency. With this expression the equality between the surplus in the domestic trade balance and the deficit in the foreign trade balance (expressed in common units) states that $(TA)_t = -(e P_t^*/P_t)(TA)_t^*$. This equality together with equations (2.12) and (2.14) implies that

$$(M_t - M_{t-1}) + e(M_t^* - M_{t-1}^*) = P_t(G_t - T_t) + e P_t^*(G_t^* - T_t^*). \tag{2.19}$$

Equation (2.19) indicates that the change in the world money supply is the sum of the deficits in the domestic and the foreign governments' budget (all measured in terms of domestic currency units). This equality reflects the assumed fixity of the world stock of international reserves. As a result of this fixity changes in the foreign-exchange component of the monetary base in any given economy are fully offset by opposite changes in the rest of the world, and changes in the world money supply arise only from public-sector deficit finance.

It should be obvious that the automatic monetization of budget deficits reflects the absence of credit markets. If credit markets existed, then the governments could also finance their budget through borrowing. In chapter 4 we allow for both domestic and international credit markets. For the present analysis, in order to focus only on pure fiscal policies (rather than on monetary policies), we consider only balanced-budget changes in government spending. The analysis of the effects of budget deficits is relegated to chapter 4.

The analytical framework of the income-expenditure model outlined earlier is general in that it encompasses the Keynesian and the classical versions of the model. To simplify the exposition and to highlight the symmetry between the two versions, we conclude this section by presenting a simplified specification of the model. Accordingly, we assume that the marginal propensities to spend and save out of disposable income are the same as the corresponding propensities to spend and save out of assets. With this assumption, the spending and money-demand functions of equations (2.3) through (2.6) become

$$Z_t = Z(P_t Y_t - P_t T_t + M_{t-1}), \quad Z_t^* = Z^*(P_t^* Y_t^* - P_t^* T_t^* + M_{t-1}^*),$$

$$M_t = M(P_t Y_t - P_t T_t + M_{t-1}), \quad M_t^* = M^*(P_t^* Y_t^* - P_t^* T_t^* + M_{t-1}^*),$$

$$(2.20)$$

where we have suppressed the commodity subscripts x and m. With this specification the equilibrium conditions (2.15) and (2.16) become

$$\frac{1 - s - a}{1 - s} Z(P_t Y_t - P_t T_t + M_{t-1}) + (1 - a^g) P_t G_t$$

$$+ \frac{a^*}{1 - s^*} e Z^*(P_t^* Y_t^* - P_t^* T_t^* + M_{t-1}^*) + a^{g*} e P_t^* G_t^* = P_t Y_t, \quad (2.15a)$$

$$\frac{a}{1 - s} Z(P_t Y_t - P_t T_t + M_{t-1}) + a^g P_t G_t$$

$$+ \frac{1 - s^* - a^*}{1 - s^*} e Z^*(P_t^* Y_t^* - P_t^* T_t^* + M_{t-1}^*) + (1 - a^{g*}) e P_t^* G_t^*$$

$$= e P_t^* Y_t^*, \quad (2.16a)$$

where s and a denote, respectively, the domestic marginal propensities to save and import out of income (or assets), a^g denotes the government marginal propensity to import out of government spending, and where similar notations (with an added asterisk) apply to the foreign country. The relations between the propensities to save and spend out of income and the corresponding propensities to save and spend out of expenditures are stated in section 2.3. In the specification of the equilibrium conditions we have used the law-of-one-price according to which $p_{mt} = eP_t^*/P_t$.

The specification of equations (2.15a) and (2.16a) reveals the symmetry between the Keynesian and the classical versions of the income-expenditure model. Specifically, in the absence of government spending and taxes and for given levels of money holdings, the system determines the values of domestic and foreign *nominal* incomes, $P_t Y_t$ and $P_t^* Y_t^*$. In this system the specific values of output and prices generating the equilibrium values of nominal incomes are immaterial. The Keynesian version of the model postulates fixed prices. Thereby the equilibrium changes in nominal incomes are brought about through output adjustments. The classical version postulates fixed outputs and employment. Thereby the equilibrium changes in nominal incomes are brought about through price adjustments. Since both versions of the income-expenditure model generate the same paths of nominal incomes, they also generate the *same* paths of spending and balance-of-payments adjustments. Inspection of equations (2.15a) and (2.16a) also reveals that in the presence of government spending and taxes the relation between the two versions of the model depends on the specification of the paths of government spending and taxes.

2.2 The Keynesian Version

For the remainder of this chapter we analyze the Keynesian version of the income-expenditure model. Under this specification prices are given while the levels of output are determined by aggregate demand. For expository purposes we normalize units so that $e = P_t = P_t^* = p_{mt} = 1$, and accordingly, we suppress the commodity subscripts x and m. In this specification of the model the spending and money-demand functions of equation (2.20) become

$$E_t = E(Y_t - T_t + M_{t-1}), \qquad E_t^* = E^*(Y_t^* - T_t^* + M_{t-1}^*),$$
$$M_t = M(Y_t - T_t + M_{t-1}), \quad M_t^* = M^*(Y_t^* - T_t^* + M_{t-1}^*). \tag{2.20a}$$

In the appendix to this chapter we analyze the more general system which corresponds to equations (2.5) through (2.8).

In the next three sections we analyze the equilibrium levels of output and the balance of payments for the short run, the long run, and the adjustment period characterizing the transition between the short and the long runs.

2.3 Short-Run Equilibrium Levels of Output

In order to characterize the short-run equilibrium of the system, we differentiate the equilibrium conditions (2.15a) and (2.16a) and obtain

$$
\begin{pmatrix} -(s+a) & a^* \\ a & -(s^*+a^*) \end{pmatrix} \begin{pmatrix} dY_t \\ dY_t^* \end{pmatrix}
$$

$$
= \begin{pmatrix} a^g - a - s \\ -(a^g - a) \end{pmatrix} dG + \begin{pmatrix} s - (1 - a - a^*) \\ -s^* + (1 - a - a^*) \end{pmatrix} dM_{t-1}, \qquad (2.21)
$$

where we recall that in this specification $s = 1 - E_y = 1 - E_M$ and $a = \beta_m E_y = \beta_m E_M$ denote, respectively, the domestic marginal propensities to save and to import, $a^g = \beta_m^g$ denotes the government marginal propensity to import out of government spending (E_y and E_M denote the partial derivatives of private real spending, E, with respect to income and assets). In the derivation of the system (2.21) we have assumed that governments run balanced budgets, that the paths of government spending and taxes are stationary (i.e., $G_t = T_t = G = T$ and $G_t^* = T_t^* = G^* = T^*$), and that foreign policies are given. We have also made use of the implication of the balanced-budget assumption, according to which $dM_{t-1} = -dM_{t-1}^*$ (from equation 2.19).

The system shown in (2.21) indicates that changes in the levels of domestic and foreign GDP are induced by two distinct factors. The first corresponds to changes in the level and commodity composition of aggregate demand induced by fiscal policy; the second corresponds to dynamic changes in the distribution of the world money supply. As is evident, the (balanced-budget) changes in the level of government spending induce immediate changes in the levels of domestic and foreign outputs. On the other hand, the effects of redistributions of the world money supply only occur through time.

In what follows, we analyze the effects of balanced-budget changes

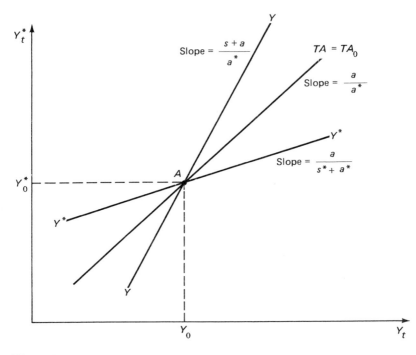

Figure 2.1
Short-run equilibrium outputs

in government spending on the equilibrium of the system. In the short run the international distribution of the world money supply is given. This distribution may change over time through surpluses or deficits in the official-settlements account of the balance of payments. Long-run equilibrium obtains when the dynamic process of the redistribution of world money reaches a halt.

The short-run equilibrium of the system is depicted in figure 2.1. The YY and the Y^*Y^* schedules are, respectively, the domestic and the foreign goods-market equilibrium schedules. Along the YY schedule world demand for domestic output equals domestic GDP, and along the Y^*Y^* schedule world demand for foreign output equals foreign GDP. The domestic schedule YY is positively sloped since a unit rise in domestic GDP raises domestic demand for the domestic good by $1 - s - a$, and thereby creates an excess supply of $1 - (1 - s - a) = s + a$ units. To restore equilibrium, foreign output must rise. A unit rise in foreign output raises foreign demand for the domestic good by a^* units, and therefore, to eliminate the excess supply of $s + a$ units, foreign output must rise by $(s + a)/a^*$. Thus the slope of the YY schedule is

$$\frac{dY^*}{dY} = \frac{s + a}{a^*} \qquad \text{along the } YY \text{ schedule.} \tag{2.22}$$

Analogously, the foreign schedule Y^*Y^* is also positively sloped, and by similar reasoning, its slope is

$$\frac{dY^*}{dY} = \frac{a}{s^* + a^*} \qquad \text{along the } Y^*Y^* \text{ schedule.} \tag{2.23}$$

As is evident, the YY schedule is steeper than the Y^*Y^* schedule. Both of these schedules are drawn for a given level of government spending and for a given distribution of the world money supply.

The equilibrium of the system obtains at point A at which domestic GDP is Y_0 and foreign GDP is Y_0^*; the trade balance associated with these levels of outputs can be inferred from equation (2.17). To complete the characterization of the equilibrium and to set the stage for the analysis of the dynamic effects of government spending, we differentiate the trade-balance equation (2.17) and obtain

$$d(TA)_t = (a^* dY_t^* - a \, dY_t) - (a^g - a) \, dG - (a + a^*) \, dM_{t-1}. \tag{2.24}$$

The three terms on the right-hand side of equation (2.24) correspond to the three factors governing trade-balance adjustments. The first reflects adjustments induced by (endogenous) changes in the levels of output, the second reflects the trade-balance implications of (balanced-budget) changes in government spending, and the third reflects the trade-balance implications of the dynamic process effecting the international distribution of the world money supply.

As seen from equation (2.24), for given values of government spending and the money supply, maintenance of a given level of the trade balance requires that domestic and foreign outputs move in the same direction. These considerations are embodied in the $TA = TA_0$ locus exhibited in figure 2.1. This schedule shows combinations of domestic and foreign outputs along which the balance of trade (which in our case is the official settlements balance) is constant. The

TA locus is positively sloped since a unit rise in domestic GDP worsens the balance of trade by a units, and this worsening can be offset by a rise in foreign output. Since a unit rise in foreign output improves the domestic trade balance by a^* units, it follows that foreign output must rise by a/a^* units. Thus the slope of the $TA = TA_0$ schedule is

$$\frac{dY^*}{dY} = \frac{a}{a^*} \quad \text{along the } TA = TA_0 \text{ schedule.} \quad (2.25)$$

As is evident, by comparison with equations (2.22) and (2.23), this slope falls in between those of the YY and the Y^*Y^* schedules. To the right of the $TA = TA_0$ locus the domestic economy's balance of trade worsens, and to the left of this locus the domestic trade balance improves.

The foregoing analysis implies that for a given level of government spending and for a given distribution of the world money supply, the *short-run* equilibrium is fully characterized by the intersection between the YY and the Y^*Y^* schedules as at point A in figure 2.1. The trade balance, TA_0, associated with this short-run equilibrium, determines the direction of the international redistribution of the world money supply. If TA_0 is negative, the home country's money supply is falling over time while the foreign country's money supply is rising. In the long run, as seen from equations (2.12) and (2.14), with balanced budgets the trade account is balanced (so that $TA = 0$), and as a result the international distribution of the world money supply does not tend to change.

2.4 Long-Run Equilibrium Levels of Output

In this section we analyze the determinants of the long-run equilibrium. As was already indicated, in the long run, the endogenously determined distribution of the world money supply is such that international monetary flows cease and $TA = 0$. Thus in the long run, $M_t = M_{t-1} = M$ and $M_t^* = M_{t-1}^* = M^* = \overline{M} - M$, where $\overline{M}$ is the world money supply which is assumed to be given. Accordingly, using the money-demand equations from (2.20)— omitting the time subscripts of domestic and foreign GDPs and replacing the taxes, T and T^*, by the corresponding levels of government spending, G and G^* (due to the balanced-budget assumption which is necessary for the maintenance of the fixed world money supply)—yield equation (2.26) as the condition for world monetary equilibrium

$$M(Y - G + M) + M^*(Y^* - G^* + \overline{M} - M) = \overline{M}. \qquad (2.26)$$

Similar considerations indicate that in the long run (in which the stocks of assets do not vary over time) the budget constraints (2.1) and (2.2) imply that private spending in each country equals the corresponding level of disposable income; in addition the balanced-budget assumption implies that in each country disposable income equals the level of GDP net of government spending. Hence, using (2.20), the long-run budget constraints are

$$E(Y - G + M) = Y - G, \qquad (2.27)$$

$$E^*(Y^* - G^* + \overline{M} - M) = Y^* - G^*. \qquad (2.28)$$

The system (2.26) through (2.28) yields the combinations of long-run Y and Y^* that are consistent with money-market equilibrium in the world economy. These combinations are depicted by the negatively sloped $\overline{MM}$ schedule in figure 2.2. The schedule is drawn for given levels of government spending and world money supply. The slope of the $\overline{MM}$ schedule is negative since a rise in domestic resources $(dY + dM)$ raises spending by $(1 - s)$ times this quantity, and since in the long run the rise in spending equals the rise in GDP, it follows that $(1 - s)(dY + dM) = dY$. Thus the rise in domestic GDP raises the domestic long-run demand for money by $[s/(1 - s)]\,dY$. Similarly, a fall in foreign output by dY^* induces a decline in foreign money demand by $[s^*/(1 - s^*)]\,dY^*$. With a given world money supply the maintenance of world monetary equilibrium necessitates that the rise in the domestic money demand equals the fall in the foreign demand. Hence

$$\frac{dY^*}{dY} = -\frac{s}{s^*}\frac{(1 - s^*)}{(1 - s)} \qquad \text{along the } \overline{MM} \text{ schedule.} \qquad (2.29)$$

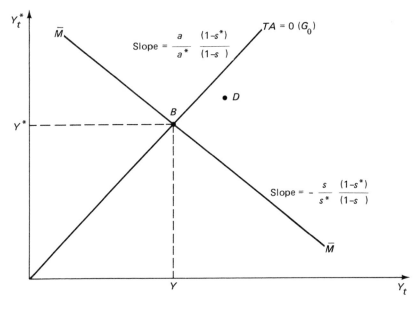

Figure 2.2
Long-run equilibrium outputs

In addition to the requirement of world monetary equilibrium, the conditions for long-run equilibrium also require that the goods market clear. In the long run this requirement implies trade-balance equilibrium. Accordingly, since in the absence of monetary flows $M_t = M_{t-1} = M$ and $M_t^* = M_{t-1}^* = M^* = \overline{M} - M$, it follows that

$$\overline{a}^*E^*(Y^* - G^* + \overline{M} - M) + a^{g^*}G^*$$

$$- [\overline{a}E(Y - G + M) + a^g G] = 0, \tag{2.30}$$

where $\overline{a} = a/(1 - s)$ and $\overline{a}^* = a^*/(1 - s^*)$ are, respectively, the domestic and foreign marginal propensities to import out of *spending* (these propensities should be distinguished from a and a^* which are the corresponding propensities to import out of *income*). Equation (2.30) is the goods-market analogue to the monetary-equilibrium condition (2.26). The system (2.27), (2.28), and (2.30) yield the combinations of long-run values of domestic and foreign outputs that are consistent with goods-market equilibrium in the world economy. Formally, substituting (2.27) and (2.28) into (2.30) yields

$$\bar{a}^*Y^* - \bar{a}Y = (a^g - \bar{a})G - (a^{g*} - \bar{a}^*)G^*. \tag{2.30a}$$

Equation (2.30a) is shown in figure 2.2 by the positively sloped $TA = 0$ schedule. This schedule is drawn for given levels of government spending and world money supply. Its slope is positive since a rise in domestic output worsens the trade balance, whereas a rise in foreign output improves it. Thus, analogously to equation (2.25), the slope of the $TA = 0$ schedule is

$$\frac{dY^*}{dY} = \frac{\bar{a}}{\bar{a}^*} \qquad \text{along the } TA = 0 \text{ schedule.} \tag{2.31}$$

Along the $\overline{MM}$ schedule the stationary distributions of the world money supply, M and $M^* = \overline{M} - M$, and world outputs, Y and Y^* (determined from the system 2.26 through 2.28), generate world demand for money that equals the existing stock, $\overline{M}$. However, the levels of output and the distribution of world money necessary to bring about such a monetary equilibrium may not be consistent with goods-market equilibrium. Analogously, along the $TA = 0$ schedule, the stationary distributions of world money supply and outputs (determined from the system 2.27, 2.28, and 2.30) generate world demand for each output that equals the corresponding supply. However, the levels of output and the distribution of world money necessary to bring about such an equilibrium in the goods market may not generate world money demand that is equal to the existing stock.

The long-run equilibrium obtains at the intersection of the $\overline{MM}$ and the $TA = 0$ schedules. At such an intersection both goods and money markets clear, and the levels of output and money holdings do not change over time. Point B in figure 2.2 depicts the long-run equilibrium. In the next section we complete the characterization of the equilibrium by analyzing the dynamic process that underlies the transition between short- and long-run equilibria.

2.5 Dynamics of Adjustment and the Balance of Payments

The short-run equilibrium depicted by point A in figure 2.1 is associated with an imbalance in the balance of payments equal to

TA_0. The international monetary flows induced by this imbalance disturb the initial short-run equilibrium. As indicated by the goods-market equilibrium conditions (2.21), changes in the international distribution of the world money supply (as measured by dM_{t-1}) alter the positions of the YY and the Y^*Y^* schedules and result in a new short-run equilibrium associated with the prevailing new distribution of the world money supply. In this section we analyze the transition period characterized by a sequence of such short-run equilibria and show that this dynamic process converges to the long-run equilibrium. The impact of a given change in domestic money holdings, dM_{t-1}, on the goods-market equilibrium schedules is shown on the right-hand side of (2.21). Accordingly, a unit rise in the domestic money holdings, accompanied by a unit fall in the foreign money holdings, raises the domestic demand for home output by c units (where c denotes the domestic marginal propensity to spend on domestic goods, $c = 1 - s - a$) and lowers the foreign demand for home output by a^*. Hence, whether at the initial levels of output this change in the distribution of money holdings creates an excess demand or an excess supply of domestic output depends on whether $c - a^*$ is positive or negative. If it is positive, then the rise in domestic money holdings shifts the YY schedule to the right, and vice versa. Similarly, the fall in the foreign money holdings creates an excess supply of foreign output if $c^* - a$ is positive, and it creates an excess demand if $c^* - a$ is negative (where c^* denotes the foreign marginal propensity to spend on foreign goods, $c^* = 1 - s^* - a^*$). If it is positive, then the fall in foreign money holdings shifts the Y^*Y^* schedule downward, and vice versa.

The effects of a redistribution of the world money supply on the short-run equilibrium levels of domestic and foreign outputs are obtained by solving (2.21). Hence

$$\frac{dY_t}{dM_{t-1}} = \frac{s^*c - sa^*}{ss^* + sa^* + s^*a}, \tag{2.32}$$

$$\frac{dY_t^*}{dM_{t-1}} = \frac{s^*a - sc^*}{ss^* + sa^* + s^*a}. \tag{2.33}$$

As seen, the direction of the change in domestic output depends on whether the ratio of the domestic to the foreign saving propensities, s/s^*, exceeds or falls short of the ratio of the domestic to the foreign propensities to spend on *domestic* goods, c/a^*. Analogously, the direction of the change in foreign output depends on whether the ratio of the saving propensities, s/s^* exceeds or falls short of the ratio of the domestic to foreign propensities to spend on *foreign* goods, a/c^*. Thus the direction of the long-run changes in output depends on the saving propensities and on the commodity composition of spending. The role of the saving propensities is clarified by noting that if the domestic saving propensity, s, is small, then a redistribution of the world money supply toward the domestic economy raises the levels of output in both countries. On the other hand, if the foreign saving propensity, s^*, is small, then the same redistribution lowers the levels of output in both countries. The opposite pattern of output changes arises in the other extreme cases in which the corresponding saving propensities are large. The role of the commodity composition of spending is clarified by noting that if the import propensities, a and a^*, are relatively small (i.e., if c and c^* are relatively large so that expenditures in each country are biased toward locally produced goods), then the redistribution of world money toward the domestic economy diverts world demand toward the domestically produced good and away from the foreign-produced goods. This change in the pattern of world demand raises the equilibrium level of domestic output. The opposite holds if each country's demand is biased toward imported goods.

Thus far we have determined the changes in the international *distribution* of world output induced by the dynamic redistribution of world money. The dynamic process is also associated with changes in the *level* of world GDP, $Y_t + Y_t^*$. Accordingly, adding the results in (2.32) and (2.33) yields

$$\frac{d(Y_t + Y_t^*)}{dM_{t-1}} = \frac{s^* - s}{ss^* + sa^* + s^*a}. \tag{2.34}$$

The interpretation of equation (2.34) can be stated in terms of the "transfer-problem" criterion familiar from the theory of international transfers. Accordingly, at the prevailing levels of output the redistribution of the world money supply raises domestic spending by $(1 - s)$ times the rise in the domestic money supply and lowers foreign spending by $(1 - s^*)$ times the same quantity. Hence *world* spending rises if s^* exceeds s, and world spending falls if s^* falls short of s. In the former case the rise in world spending creates an excess demand for world output which, in order to restore equilibrium between world spending and output, necessitates a corresponding rise in world GDP. The opposite holds in the latter case for which s^* falls short of s.

The redistribution of the world money supply and the induced changes in the short-run equilibrium levels of output also alter the initial trade-balance position and bring about additional changes in the money supply. Specifically, substituting equations (2.32) and (2.33) into (2.24) yields

$$\frac{d(TA)_t}{dM_{t-1}} = -\frac{sa^* + s^*a}{ss^* + sa^* + s^*a},$$

and noting that $M_t = M_{t-1} + (TA)_t$, it follows that dM_t/dM_{t-1} is a positive fraction, where

$$\frac{dM_t}{dM_{t-1}} = \frac{ss^*}{ss^* + sa^* + s^*a} < 1. \tag{2.35}$$

Equation (2.35) shows that the additions to the domestic quantity of money induced by the sequence of balance-of-payments surpluses diminish over time. It follows that the dynamic process of the redistribution of the world money supply that is effected through balance-of-payment adjustments converges to the long-run equilibrium.

Figure 2.3 shows the path of adjustment and demonstrates the stability of the dynamic process. In this figure the initial equilibrium is indicated by point A along the M_t schedule at which the level of domestic money holding is M_{-1} and the associated surplus in the balance of payments is TA_0. This initial short-run equilibrium corresponds to the one depicted in figure 2.1, and as before, the M_t schedule in figure 2.3 is drawn for a given level of government spending. The surplus in the balance of payments raises the domestic money supply from M_{-1} to M_0 and results in a new short-run equilibrium at point A' along the M_t schedule. In this equilibrium the trade surplus diminishes to TA_1. The sequence of short-run equilibria is associated with a path along which the positive increments to the money supply (associated with trade surpluses) diminish over time.

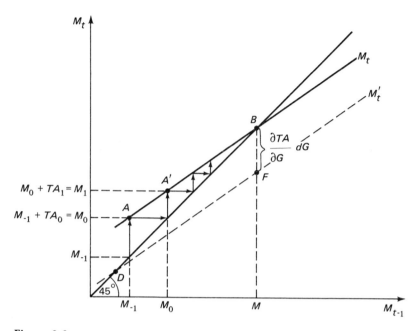

Figure 2.3
Balance-of-payments dynamics

This path converges to the long-run equilibrium at point B at which the long-run money holding by the home country is M. The long-run equilibrium shown in this figure corresponds to the one in figure 2.2.

Before concluding, we note that even though the direction of monetary flows during the adjustment process is clear cut, the directions of changes in domestic and foreign outputs depend on the relations between the marginal saving ratio, s/s^*, and the marginal consumption ratios of domestic goods, c/a^*, and of foreign goods, a/c^*. Independent, however, of the precise pattern of output adjustments, the system characterizing the world economy as a whole (including the level and the international distribution of world output) is dynamically stable.

2.6 Fiscal Policies and Outputs

In this section we use the results of the previous analysis to determine the short- and long-run effects of balanced-budget changes in the domestic government spending. For this purpose suppose that the world economy is initially in a long-run equilibrium, corresponding to point B in figures 2.2 and 2.3. At the prevailing levels of output, a unit rise in government spending raises the demand for domestically produced goods by $1 - a^g$, and the rise in taxes necessary to balance the budget lowers private demand for domestic output by $1 - a - s$. Thus the excess demand for domestic goods induced by this balanced-budget rise in government spending is $s + a - a^g$. By similar reasoning the excess demand for foreign goods induced by the unit rise in government spending is $a^g - a$ (these changes are represented by the coefficients of dG in the system of equations 2.21).

As is evident, the patterns of excess demands generated by the balanced-budget rise in government spending depend critically on the magnitude of the government propensity to import, a^g. For example, in the extreme case for which all government spending falls on domestic goods (so that $a^g = 0$), the excess demand for domestic goods is $(s + a)$, and the excess supply of foreign goods is a. In the other extreme case for which all government spending falls on importables (so that $a^g = 1$), the excess supply of domestic goods is $1 - (s + a)$, whereas the excess demand for foreign goods is $1 - a$.

The relative magnitudes of the government and the private sector marginal propensities to import also determine whether at the prevailing levels of output the trade balance improves or deteriorates. The unit rise in government spending raises imports by a^g, and the corresponding unit rise in taxes lowers private imports by a. Hence (as indicated by equation 2.24) at the prevailing levels of output the trade balance improves if a, the private import propensity, exceeds the government import propensity, a^g, and it deteriorates if a falls short of a^g. If the two import propensities are the same, then at the prevailing levels of output the redistribution of income between the private and the public sectors does not impact on the balance of trade.

In the diagrammatic analysis that follows, we consider the intermediate bench-mark case for which the private and the public sectors have the same marginal propensities to import (so that $a = a^g$). Consider figure 2.4, and let the initial long-run equilibrium be at

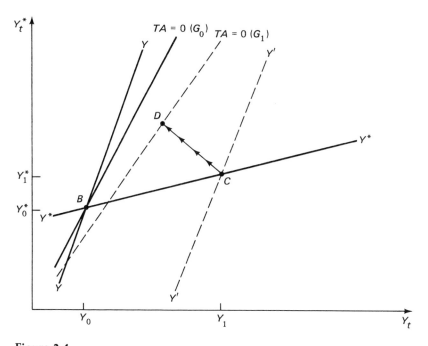

Figure 2.4
The short- and long-run effects of a balanced-budget rise in government spending

point B. The equilibrium schedules YY and Y^*Y^* are drawn for the given initial level of government spending and for the initial distribution of the world money supply. The levels of output associated with this equilibrium are Y_0 and Y_0^*, and since the initial position is that of a long-run equilibrium, point B lies on the $TA = 0$ schedule along which the balance of payments is balanced.

A unit balanced-budget rise in the domestic government spending induces an excess demand for domestic goods by s units (in the bench-mark case for which $a = a^g$) and necessitates an equilibrating rise in domestic output by $s/(s + a)$ units (for a given level of foreign output). In terms of figure 2.4 the balanced-budget rise in government spending shifts the YY schedule rightward by $s/(s + a)$ units times the rise in government spending. This horizontal shift corresponds to the conventional balanced-budget foreign trade multiplier for a small open economy. The new equilibrium schedule is indicated by $Y'Y'$. Since with $a = a^g$ the balanced-budget rise in the domestic government spending does not generate an excess demand or an excess supply of foreign output, the Y^*Y^* schedule remains intact, and the new short-run equilibrium obtains at point C.

In the short-run equilibrium at point C, domestic and foreign outputs are higher than their initial levels. Thus, measured in terms of comovements of domestic and foreign outputs, the domestic fiscal expansion is transmitted positively to the rest of the world. It is also relevant to note that the magnitude of the equilibrium rise in domestic output exceeds the rise implied by the small-country foreign trade multiplier (a rise that is indicated by the rightward shift of the YY schedule).

In the more general case the private and public sectors' marginal propensities to import may differ from each other. In that case the short-run effects of the balanced-budget rise in government spending are obtained from the system in (2.21). Accordingly,

$$\frac{dY_0}{dG} = 1 - \frac{s^* a^g}{ss^* + sa^* + s^* a}, \tag{2.36}$$

$$\frac{dY_0^*}{dG} = \frac{sa^g}{ss^* + sa^* + s^* a}. \tag{2.37}$$

Equation (2.36) illustrates the negative dependence of the short-run equilibrium change in domestic output on the magnitude of the government import propensity. If the government import propensity, a^g, does not exceed the corresponding private-sector propensity, a, then the balanced-budget rise in government spending must raise domestic output. On the other hand, if a^g is relatively large, then domestic output may fall in the short run. This fall stems from the fact that the redistribution of income between the private and the public sectors diverts spending away from domestic output.

Equation (2.37) shows that in general foreign output rises. It also shows that this rise is proportional to the magnitude of the domestic government import propensity, a^g. In the extreme case for which all government spending falls on domestic goods (so that $a^g = 0$), foreign output does not change. In that case the rise in domestic output is maximized, and the balanced-budget multiplier is unity. The comparison between the directions of domestic and foreign output changes reveals that (in contrast with the bench-mark case) *the short-run international transmission of the effects of domestic balanced-budget fiscal policies may be positive or negative.*

Thus far we have characterized the nature of the international transmission mechanism in terms of the sign of the correlation between changes in domestic and foreign *outputs*. The focus on the levels of output reflects concern with respect to resource utilization and employment. An alternative measure characterizes the transmission mechanism in terms of the correlation between domestic and foreign *private-sector spending*. The latter is governed by changes in private disposable incomes. As is evident from equations (2.36) and (2.37), domestic disposable income falls, and foreign disposable income rises (in the limiting case in which $a^g = 0$ both disposable incomes remain unchanged). Thus, measured in terms of comovements of the domestic and the foreign private-sector spending, *the short-run international transmission of the effects of domestic balanced-budget fiscal policies is negative.*

The preceeding analysis examined the short-run effects of fiscal policies on the international *distribution* of world output and spending. The change in the *level* of world output is obtained by adding equations (2.36) and (2.37). Similarly, the change in the level of world private-sector spending reflects changes in each country's disposable income multiplied by the corresponding propensity to spend. Thus using equations (2.36) and (2.37) yields

$$\frac{d(Y_0 + Y_0^*)}{dG} = 1 + \frac{(s - s^*)a^g}{ss^* + sa^* + s^*a}, \tag{2.38}$$

$$\frac{d(E_0 + E_0^*)}{dG} = \frac{(s - s^*)a^g}{ss^* + sa^* + s^*a}. \tag{2.39}$$

Equation (2.38) shows that, in general, the direction of the change in world output depends on the relative magnitudes of the saving and import propensities. If, however, the government propensity to import, a^g, does not exceed the corresponding private-sector propensity, a, then world output must rise. The bench-mark case shown in figure 2.4 illustrates this result. Equation (2.39) shows that the direction of the change in world private-sector spending depends on whether the domestic economy's saving propensity exceeds or falls short of the foreign saving propensity. In the former case world spending rises, and in the latter case world spending falls.

The short-run effects of a balanced-budget rise in government spending are also reflected in the balance of payments. Using equation (2.24) along with the expressions for the equilibrium changes in outputs from equations (2.36) and (2.37) yields

$$\frac{d(TA)_0}{dG} = -\frac{ss^* a^g}{ss^* + sa^* + s^* a}. \tag{2.40}$$

Thus, unless all government spending falls on the domestic goods, the rise in government spending induces a deficit in the home country's balance of payments. This deficit initiates the dynamic process by which the world money supply is redistributed over time from the domestic economy to the rest of the world.

In the bench-mark case shown in figure 2.4 the short-run equilibrium at point C is associated with a deficit in the balance of payments since it lies to the right of the $TA = 0$ schedule. (As seen from equation 2.24, this schedule is invariant with respect to government spending as long as $a = a^g$.) The fall in the domestic money supply, and the corresponding rise in the foreign money supply consequent on the payments imbalances lower domestic spending and raises foreign spending. As a result the $Y'Y'$ schedule shifts leftward, and the Y^*Y^* schedule shifts upward. Their new intersection yields a new short-run equilibrium. This process continues as long as the payments imbalances prevail. The location of this new short-run equilibrium relative to point C depends on whether the ratio of the domestic to the foreign-saving propensities, s/s^*, exceeds or falls short of the ratios of the domestic to the foreign propensities to consume domestic goods, c/a^*, and foreign goods, a/c^*.

Diagrammatically, the slope of the adjustment path characterizing the sequence of short-run equilibria is obtained by dividing equation (2.33) by equation (2.32). Accordingly,

$$\frac{dY_t^*}{dY_t} = \left(\frac{(a/c^*) - (s/s^*)}{(c/a^*) - (s/s^*)}\right)\frac{c^*}{a^*} \qquad \text{along the path of adjustment.} \tag{2.41}$$

As is evident, depending on the relative magnitudes of the parameters, this slope may be positive or negative. In figure 2.4 the path of adjustment is drawn with a negative slope corresponding to the case in which the spending patterns are such that the saving ratio, s/s^*, is bounded by the ratios of the two countries' propensities to spend on the domestic good, c/a^*, and on the foreign good, a/c^*. Accordingly, the sequence of short-run equilibria is described in figure 2.4 by the path connecting the initial short-run equilibrium point C with the long-run equilibrium point D. In general, as seen from equation 2.34, along the path of adjustment world output (and spending) rises or falls depending on whether the domestic saving propensity, s, exceeds or falls short of the foreign saving propensity, s^*.

The dynamics of adjustment can also be illustrated in terms of figure 2.3. In that figure the M_t schedule is drawn for a given level of government spending. The rise in government spending (at the initial distribution of the world money supply) worsens the trade account by $[\partial(TA)/\partial G]\,dG$ and shifts the M_t schedule downward to the position indicated by M_t' (since $M_t = TA_t + M_{t-1}$). This shift sets off the dynamic process (not drawn) that converges to the new long-run equilibrium point D (at which $M_t = M_{t-1}$ along the M_t' schedule). The new equilibrium point corresponds to the new international distribution of the world money supply.

The characteristics of the new long-run equilibrium can be examined with the aid of figure 2.2. The position of the new long-run equilibrium point depends on the effects of the balanced-budget rise in government spending on the world monetary-equilibrium schedule, $\overline{MM}$ and on the balance-of-payments equilibrium schedule, $TA = 0$. It is evident by inspection of equations (2.26) through (2.28) that the $\overline{MM}$ schedule shifts rightward and that the extent of the horizontal shift equals the rise in government spending. The reason for the rightward shift of the $\overline{MM}$ schedule is that given the initial distribution of world money, the rise in domestic output is necessary in order to keep domestic disposable income unchanged for any given level of foreign output (and disposable income). Such a rise ensures the maintenance of world monetary equilibrium since, as long as the initial distribution of world money and the initial levels of disposable incomes do not change, the world demand for money remains intact.

By similar reasoning equation (2.30a) indicates that a unit balanced-budget rise in government spending induces a rightward shift of the $TA = 0$ schedule by $(\bar{a} - a^g)/a$ units. Given the initial distribution of world money, this change in domestic output ensures that the home country's total (private sector plus government) imports are unchanged. With unchanged imports the trade balance is also unchanged since, for a given level of foreign output, domestic exports are given. As is evident, the direction to which the $TA = 0$ schedule shifts depends on whether, at the prevailing situation, the redistribution of income between the domestic private sector and the government (consequent on the balanced-budget rise in government spending) raises or lowers long-run imports. If the private sector's marginal propensity to import out of spending, $\bar{a}$, exceeds the government propensity to import, a^g, then the balanced-budget rise in government spending improves the trade balance. Therefore, ceteris paribus, domestic output must rise in order to restore balanced trade. In this case the $TA = 0$ schedule shifts to the right. The opposite holds if a falls short of a^g.

The long-run equilibrium point D shown in figure 2.2 (as well as in figure 2.4) corresponds to the bench-mark case (used in the short-run analysis) in which the private sector's marginal propensity to import out of *income* equals that of the public sector (so that $a = a^g$). Under such circumstances the private sector's marginal propensity to import out of *spending*, $\bar{a}$, exceeds a^g, and therefore the balanced-budget rise in government spending shifts the $TA = 0$ schedule to the right.

In characterizing the long-run effects of fiscal policies, it is convenient to consider the case in which the initial $TA = 0$ schedule in figure 2.2 goes through the origin. As seen from equation (2.30a), this arises if the initial levels of domestic and foreign government spending are such that $(a^g - \bar{a})G = (a^{g*} - \bar{a}^*)G^*$. This initial configuration is indicated in figure 2.2 by the parameteric value of G_0 which is held constant along the $TA = 0$ schedule. In that case a balanced-budget rise in domestic government spending is *neutral* in its long-run effects on the distribution of world outputs if $\bar{a} = a^g$

since it raises both domestic and foreign outputs equiproportionally. On the other hand, if $\bar{a}$ exceeds a^g, then the long-run output effects of the domestic fiscal expansion are *home-output biased*. In that case (indicated by point D in figure 2.2) the percentage long-run rise in domestic output exceeds the corresponding foreign rise. In the opposite case in which $\bar{a}$ falls short of a^g, the long-run output effects of the domestic fiscal expansion are *foreign-output biased*.

An additional factor determining whether the long-run effects are neutral or biased is the initial level of domestic and foreign government spending. For example, if initially foreign government spending is zero while the level of spending by the domestic government is positive, and if $\bar{a} = a^g$, then the $TA = 0$ schedule intersects the horizontal axis to the right of the origin. In that case a balanced-budget rise in domestic government spending biases the long-run distribution of outputs in favor of the foreign country.

The formal solutions for the long-run effects of the balanced-budget rise in government spending on outputs and on the distribution of the world money supply (as implied by equations A.14 through A.16 of the appendix) are

$$\frac{dY}{dG} = 1 - \frac{s^*(1 - s)a^g}{sa^* + s^*a},$$
(2.42)

$$\frac{dY^*}{dG} = \frac{s(1 - s^*)a^g}{sa^* + s^*a},$$
(2.43)

$$\frac{dM}{dG} = -\frac{ss^*a^g}{sa^* + s^*a},$$
(2.44)

Equation (2.42) indicates that the direction of the long-run effects of the fiscal expansion on domestic output depends on the magnitude of the government import propensity. As is evident, if the government import propensity, a^g, does not exceed the private-sector propensity, a, then domestic output must rise in the long run. Equations (2.43) and (2.44) show that in the long run foreign output rises, and the world money supply is redistributed toward the foreign country (unless government spending falls only on domestic goods).

Finally, we note that in the long run world output changes according to

$$\frac{d(Y + Y^*)}{dG} = 1 + \frac{(s - s^*)a^g}{sa^* + s^*a}.$$ (2.45)

Thus the balanced-budget multiplier of world output exceeds or falls short of unity according to whether the domestic saving propensity exceeds or falls short of the foreign saving propensity.

A comparison between the short-run responses (equations 2.36 through 2.38) and the corresponding long-run responses (equations 2.42, 2.43, and 2.45) reflects the dynamic path of outputs during the adjustment periods. As seen from equations (2.32) and (2.33), the characteristics of the path depend on whether the ratio of the two saving propensities exceeds or falls short of the ratios of the domestic to the foreign propensities to spend on a given good. Accordingly, the long-run level of domestic output falls short of the level obtained in the short run if $s/s^* < c/a^*$, and vice versa. Likewise, the long-run level of foreign output exceeds the level obtained in the short run if $s/s^* > a/c^*$, and vice versa.

So far we have focused mainly on the output effects of fiscal policies. These effects are of interest especially as indicators of employment levels. In order to obtain indicators for private-sector spending, we need to determine the long-run effects of fiscal policies on disposable incomes. Equation (2.42) implies that the balanced-budget rise in the domestic government spending lowers the long-run level of domestic disposable income. Since in the long run private-sector spending equals disposable income, it follows that the domestic private-sector spending also falls in the long run. On the other hand, the foreign private sector, whose taxes have not changed, enjoys (as indicated by equation 2.43) a rise in its long-run disposable income and spending. Finally, using equations (2.42) and (2.43), the effect of the balanced-budget rise in government spending on the long-run level of world spending:

$$\frac{d(E + E^*)}{dG} = \frac{(s - s^*)a^g}{sa^* + s^*a}.$$ (2.46)

As seen, in the long run world private spending rises if the domestic saving propensity, s, exceeds the foreign propensity, s^*, and vice versa. A comparison between equations (2.46) and (2.39) shows that the short-run changes in world private spending (which may be positive or negative) are magnified in the long run.

2.7 Summary

In this chapter we developed the analytical framework underlying the income-expenditure model of the interdependent world economy. Throughout the analysis it was assumed that there is a single noninterest-bearing asset (money) that is held by both countries. The international monentary system was assumed to operate under a fixed exchange-rate regime, and the international distribution of the world money supply was shown to be effected through international payments imbalances.

Following the outline of the analytical framework, we have adapted the extreme version of the Keynesian assumptions by which prices were assumed to be given while output was assumed to be demand determined. To focus on the pure effects of fiscal policies, we have assumed that the government (which in the absence of interesting-bearing debt instruments can not finance its spending through debt issue) finances its spending through taxes rather than through monetary creation. Thus we have analyzed the effects of balanced-budget changes in government spending.

Throughout, we focused on the effects of fiscal policies on domestic output and private-sector spending as well as on foreign output and foreign spending. We drew a distinction between the short-run and long-run effects. In the short run the international distribution of the world money supply is given, whereas in the long run this distribution is endogenously determined so as to yield equality between income and spending in each country. Short-run discrepancies between income and spending yield international payments imbalances and generate a dynamic process by which the world money supply is redistributed internationally. We have demonstrated that the system of the world economy is dynamically stable. Thus the sequence of short-run equilibria converges to the long-run equilibrium.

The short-run and long-run effects of a unit balanced-budget rise in domestic government spending are summarized in table 2.1. It is seen that in the short run foreign output and spending rise while the level of the domestic private-sector spending falls. In the short run the balance of payments (which also equals the trade balance) deteriorates. This deterioration sets off the dynamic process of the redistribution of the world money supply toward the rest of the world. As is also shown in table 2.1, the short-run effects on the level of domestic output depend critically on the spending patterns of the government. If the import propensity of the government does not exceed that of the private sector, domestic output rises in the short run. If, on the other hand, government spending falls heavily on foreign goods, then domestic output may fall.

The second line in table 2.1 shows the long-run effects. A comparison between the two lines reveals that the long-run changes in domestic and foreign output may exceed or fall short of the short-run changes. The key factors determining whether the long-run changes magnify or dampen the corresponding short-run changes are the relations between the ratio of the two countries' saving propensities and the ratios of the two countries' spending propensities on domestic and foreign goods.

The comparison between the long- and the short-run changes in the levels of domestic and foreign private-sector spending shows that the short-run changes are always magnified in the long run. The mechanism responsible for this magnification is the redistribution of the world money supply occurring throughout the adjustment

Table 2.1
The effects of a unit balanced-budget rise in domestic government spending

	Y	Y^*	E	E^*	TA	M
Short run	$1 - \dfrac{s^*a^g}{\Delta}$	$\dfrac{sa^g}{\Delta}$	$-\dfrac{(1-s)s^*a^g}{\Delta}$	$\dfrac{(1-s^*)sa^g}{\Delta}$	$-\dfrac{ss^*a^g}{\Delta}$	—
Long run	$1 - \dfrac{(1-s)s^*a^g}{\Delta - ss^*}$	$\dfrac{(1-s^*)sa^g}{\Delta - ss^*}$	$-\dfrac{(1-s)s^*a^g}{\Delta - ss^*}$	$\dfrac{(1-s^*)sa^g}{\Delta - ss^*}$	—	$-\dfrac{ss^*a^g}{\Delta - ss^*}$

Note: $\Delta = ss^* + sa^* + s^*a > 0$, where s, s^*, a, and a^* are, respectively, the domestic and foreign marginal propensities to save and import out of income and a^g is the domestic government import propensity.

process. This dynamic process of the monetary flows is effected through payments imbalances. The cumulative imbalances characterizing the sequence of short-run equilibria are reflected in the long-run change in each country's money holding. The factor of magnification linking short-run and long-run changes in spending manifests itself in the link between the short-run payments imbalance and the ultimate long-run change in money holdings.

2.8 Appendix

In this appendix we derive the short-run and the long-run solutions for the income-expenditure model of output determination. The equilibrium conditions (2.15) and (2.16) (for fixed $p_{mt} = P_t = P_t^* = e = 1$) are

$$(1 - \beta_m)E(Y_t - G, M_{t-1}) + (1 - \beta_m^g)G$$

$$+ \beta_x^* E^*(Y_t^* - G^*, \overline{M} - M_{t-1}) + \beta_x^{g*}G^* = Y_t, \tag{A.1}$$

$$\beta_m E(Y_t - G, M_{t-1}) + \beta_m^g G + (1 - \beta_x^*)E^*(Y_t^* - G^*, \overline{M} - M_{t-1})$$

$$+ (1 - \beta_x^{g*})G^* = Y_t^*. \tag{A.2}$$

Differentiating this system yields

$$\begin{pmatrix} -(s + a) & a^* \\ a & -(s^* + a^*) \end{pmatrix} \begin{pmatrix} dY_t \\ dY_t^* \end{pmatrix} = \begin{pmatrix} a^g - a - s \\ a - a^g \end{pmatrix} dG$$

$$+ \begin{pmatrix} \dfrac{a^*}{1 - s^*}\gamma_z^* - \left(\dfrac{1 - s - a}{1 - s}\right)\gamma_z \\ \left(\dfrac{1 - s^* - a^*}{1 - s^*}\right)\gamma_z^* - \dfrac{a}{(1 - s)}\gamma_z \end{pmatrix} dM_{t-1}, \tag{A.3}$$

where γ_z and γ_z^* denote, respectively, the domestic and foreign marginal propensities to spend out of assets and where $\beta_m = a/(1 - s)$ and $\beta_x^* = a^*/(1 - s^*)$. In the case analyzed in the text, we have assumed that the marginal propensities to spend out of income and assets are equal to each other so that $\gamma_z = 1 - s$ and $\gamma_z^* = 1 - s^*$.

The Short Run

The *short-run* equilibrium changes in the values of domestic and foreign outputs in response to a balanced-budget change in domestic government spending are

$$\frac{dY_t}{dG} = 1 - \frac{s^* a^g}{\Delta_s},$$ (A.4)

$$\frac{dY_t^*}{dG} = \frac{sa^g}{\Delta_s} > 0,$$ (A.5)

where $\Delta_s = ss^* + sa^* + s^*a > 0$.

The short-run equilibrium responses of domestic and foreign outputs to a redistribution of the world money supply are

$$\frac{dY_t}{dM_{t-1}} = \frac{1}{\Delta_s}\left[a^*(\gamma_z - \gamma_z^*) + s^*\left(\frac{1 - s - a}{1 - s}\gamma_z - \frac{a^*}{1 - s^*}\gamma_z^*\right)\right],$$ (A.6)

$$\frac{dY_t^*}{dM_{t-1}} = \frac{1}{\Delta_s}\left[a(\gamma_z - \gamma_z^*) + s\left(\frac{a}{1 - s}\gamma_z - \frac{1 - s^* - a^*}{1 - s^*}\gamma_z^*\right)\right].$$ (A.7)

The balance-of-trade equation in a differentiated form (corresponding to equation 2.24) is

$$d(TA)_t = (a^* dY_t^* - a\, dY_t) - (a^g - a)\, dG$$

$$- \left(\frac{a^*}{1 - s^*}\gamma_z^* + \frac{a}{1 - s}\gamma_z\right) dM_{t-1}.$$ (A.8)

Substituting equations (A.4) and (A.5) into (A.8) yields

$$\frac{d(TA)_t}{dG} = -\frac{ss^* a^g}{\Delta_s} < 0.$$ (A.9)

Similarly, substituting equations (A.6) and (A.7) into (A.8) yields

$$\frac{d(TA)_t}{dM_{t-1}} = -\left(\frac{a}{1 - s}s^*\gamma_z + \frac{a^*}{1 - s^*}s\gamma_z^*\right)$$ (A.10)

Finally, using equation (A.10) along with the definition $M_t - M_{t-1} = (TA)_t$ yields

$$\frac{dM_t}{dM_{t-1}} = \frac{ss^* + sa^*[1 - \gamma_z^*/(1 - s^*)] + s^*a[1 - \gamma_z/(1 - s)]}{ss^* + sa^* + s^*a}. \quad \text{(A.11)}$$

Equation (A.9) implies that the impact effect of a (balanced-budget) rise in government spending is to worsen the trade account (as long as $a^g > 0$). Equation (A.11) is the stability condition of the system. As is evident for the case analyzed in the text ($\gamma_z = 1 - s$ and $\gamma_z^* = 1 - s^*$), dM_t/dM_{t-1} must be a positive fraction, and stability is ensured. In the general case of equation (A.11) a convergence to long-run stationary equilibrium requires that

$$2ss^* > sa^* \left(\frac{\gamma_z^*}{1 - s^*} - 1 \right) + s^*a \left(\frac{\gamma_z}{1 - s} - 1 \right). \quad \text{(A.12)}$$

Hence, if the spending propensities out of income do not fall short of the spending propensity out of assets, the sequence of short-run equilibria converges to the long-run equilibrium.

The Long Run

Long-run equilibrium requires that in addition to market clearing of domestic and foreign goods, the balance of payments is balanced so that $M_{t-1} = M_t = M$, $M_{t-1}^* = M_t^* = \overline{M} - M$ (where $\overline{M}$ denotes the given world money supply), and the levels of output are stationary so that $Y_t = Y$ and $Y_t^* = Y^*$. Imposing the requirement of trade-balance equilibrium into equation (A.8), and supplementing the system (A.3) with this additional condition, we obtain the differentiated form of the long-run equilibrium conditions. This system is

$$\begin{pmatrix} -(s+a) & a^* & \dfrac{1-s-a}{1-s}\gamma_z - \dfrac{a^*}{1-s^*}\gamma_z^* \\ a & -(s^*+a^*) & \dfrac{a}{1-s}\gamma_z - \dfrac{1-s^*-a^*}{1-s^*}\gamma_z^* \\ -a & a^* & -\left(\dfrac{a}{1-s}\gamma_z + \dfrac{a^*}{1-s^*}\gamma_z^* \right) \end{pmatrix} \begin{pmatrix} dY \\ dY^* \\ dM \end{pmatrix}$$

$$= \begin{pmatrix} a^g - a - s \\ -(a^g - a) \\ a^g - a \end{pmatrix} dG. \quad \text{(A.13)}$$

The *long-run* changes in the values of domestic and foreign outputs and in the domestic money holdings (induced by the cummulative redistribution of the given world money supply) are

$$\frac{dY}{dG} = 1 - \frac{\gamma_z s^* a^g}{\Delta_L}, \tag{A.14}$$

$$\frac{dY^*}{dG} = \frac{\gamma_z^* s a^g}{\Delta_L} > 0, \tag{A.15}$$

$$\frac{dM}{dG} = -\frac{s s^* a^g}{\Delta_L} < 0, \tag{A.16}$$

where

$$\Delta_L = \frac{\gamma_z s^*}{1 - s} a + \frac{\gamma_z^* s}{1 - s^*} a^* > 0.$$

3

Fiscal Policies and Prices in the Income-Expenditure Model

In this chapter we apply the income-expenditure model to the analysis of the effect of fiscal policies on domestic and foreign prices. We replace the Keynesian fixed-price variable-output assumption of chapter 2 with the classical assumption that outputs are given at the full employment levels while prices are flexible. As was already shown, because of the structure of the income-expenditure model, the system that emerges from the flexible-price version is dual to the system emerging from the flexible-output version. The similarity between the basic mechanisms operating in the two alternative versions of the income-expenditure model permits us to use much of the structure developed in chapter 2. By generating the same equilibrium paths of nominal incomes, the two versions of the income-expenditure model yield the same paths of nominal spending and balance-of-payments adjustments. For the sake of completeness we present in this chapter some results that are dual to those shown in the Keynesian version of the model. In addition we analyze issues that are specific to the classical version of the model. In this context we examine the effects of fiscal policies on the terms of trade and real spending. We start with the formal specification of the classical version.

3.1 The Classical Version

In specifying the classical version of the income-expenditure model, we use the analytical framework outlined in section 2.1 and impose the assumptions that the levels of output and employment are fixed while prices adjust freely so as to clear markets. We continue to assume that the exchange rate is set at the level of unity. For expository purposes it is convenient to specify the spending and money-demand functions of equations (2.20) as linear functions. Accordingly, let

$$Z_t = (1 - s)(P_t Y - \tilde{G} + M_{t-1}),$$

$$Z_t^* = (1 - s^*)(P_t^* Y^* - \tilde{G}^* + \overline{M} - M_{t-1}),$$

$$M_t = s(P_t Y - \tilde{G} + M_{t-1}),$$

$$\overline{M} - M_t = M_t^* = s^*(P_t^* Y^* - \tilde{G}^* + \overline{M} - M_{t-1}),$$

(3.1)

where $\tilde{G} = PG$ and $\tilde{G}^* = P^* G^*$ denote, respectively, the *nominal* values of domestic and foreign government spending and where, as before, commodity subscripts are suppressed. The specification of the behavioral functions in (3.1) is analogous to the one in (2.20a) of the fixed-price Keynesian version. It embodies the simplifying assumption that the marginal propensities to spend out of income and assets are equal to each other. In addition the specification in (3.1) presumes that these functions are linear. As before, we assume that the governments run balanced budgets and that the paths of government spending and taxes are stationary. In what follows we normalize units so that $Y = Y^* = 1$.

Goods-market equilibrium requires that world demand for each country's product equals the given world supply. Under the classical specification the equilibrium conditions outlined in equations (2.15a) and (2.16a) become

$$-(s + a)P_t + a^* P_t^* = (a^g - a - s)\tilde{G} + (a^* - c)M_{t-1} - a^* \overline{M}, \quad (3.2)$$

$$aP_t - (s^* + a^*)P_t^* = -(a^g - a)\tilde{G} - (a - c^*)M_{t-1} - c^* \overline{M}, \quad (3.3)$$

where we have used the arbitrage condition by which $P_{mt} = P_t^*/P_t$, and we have assumed for expositional simplicity that the level of foreign government spending, $\tilde{G}^*$, is zero.

The similarity between this equilibrium system and the Keynesian one is evident. In fact the differentiated form of equations (3.2) and (3.3) yields a system like (2.21) except that dY_t and dY_t^* are replaced by dP_t and dP_t^*, and dG is replaced by $d\tilde{G}$.

The nominal trade account associated with the classical version of the income-expenditure model is obtained from equation (2.17) with the specific classical assumptions. Accordingly,

$$(\widetilde{TA})_t = a^* P_t^* - a P_t - (a^g - a)\tilde{G} + a^* \overline{M} - (a + a^*) M_{t-1}, \qquad (3.4)$$

where $(\widetilde{TA})_t = P_t(TA)_t$ denotes the nominal value of the home country's trade balance. The differentiated form of equation (3.4) is the dual to its Keynesian counterpart of equation (2.24).

3.2 Short-Run Equilibrium Prices and the Balance of Payments

The short-run equilibrium of the system is shown in figure 3.1. The PP and the P^*P^* schedules show, respectively, combinations of domestic and foreign prices (GDP deflators) that maintain equilibrium in the domestic and in the foreign goods markets. These schedules

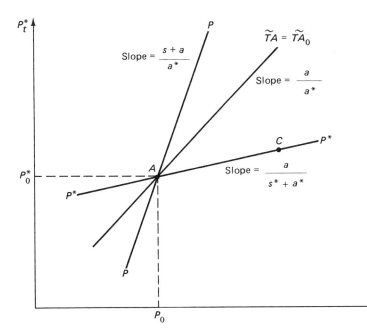

Figure 3.1
Short-run equilibrium prices

represent, respectively, equations (3.2) and (3.3) and are drawn for given levels of nominal government spending $\tilde{G}$ and $\tilde{G}^*$ as well as for a given distribution of the world money supply. The slopes of these schedules reflect identical considerations as those underlying the YY and the Y^*Y^* schedules of chapter 2. The short-run equilibrium obtains at point A at which the (nominal) trade balance is $(\widetilde{TA})_0$.

Using equations (3.2) and (3.3), the short-run equilibrium values of the domestic and foreign prices are

$$P_t = \left(1 - \frac{s^*a^g}{ss^* + sa^* + s^*a}\right)\tilde{G} + \frac{(s^*c - sa^*)M_{t-1} + a^*\overline{M}}{ss^* + sa^* + s^*a}, \qquad (3.5)$$

$$P_t^* = \frac{sa^g\tilde{G} + (s^*a - sc^*)M_{t-1} + [a(1 - s^*)]\overline{M}}{ss^* + sa^* + s^*a}, \qquad (3.6)$$

where, as before, $c = 1 - s - a$ denotes the domestic marginal propensity to spend on domestically produced goods and where $c^* = 1 - s^* - a^*$ is the corresponding foreign propensity to spend on foreign goods. Finally, by dividing equation (3.6) by (3.5), we obtain the short-run equilibrium terms of trade that depend on the level of government spending, $\tilde{G}$, on the level of the world money supply, $\overline{M}$, and on the international distribution of the world money supply as indicated by the domestic money holding, M_{t-1}. Substituting equations (3.5) and (3.6) into the balance-of-payments equation (3.4) yields

$$(\widetilde{TA})_t = \frac{-ss^*a^g\tilde{G} - (sa^* + s^*a)M_{t-1} + a^*s\overline{M}}{ss^* + sa^* + s^*a}. \qquad (3.7)$$

With balanced-budget government spending, payments imbalances induce a redistribution of the world money supply since $(\widetilde{TA})_t = M_t - M_{t-1}$ (see equation 2.12). As shown by equations (3.5) through (3.7), such a redistribution alters the equilibrium trade balance and is also likely to alter the equilibrium values of domestic and foreign prices, and thereby of the terms of trade. The direction of the change in the terms of trade induced by a redistribution of the world money supply depends on differences between domestic and foreign saving propensities as well as on differences between the commodity composition of domestic and foreign spending. For example, if the initial level of government spending is zero (i.e., $\tilde{G} = 0$), then a rise in M_{t-1} (consequent on a trade-balance surplus) worsens the home country's terms of trade (i.e., raises P_t^*/P_t) if the sign of the parameter b is positive, where

$$b = a(s^*a - sc^*) - [a(1 - s^*) + sc^*](s^*c - sa^*). \tag{3.8}$$

On the other hand, if b is negative, then the redistribution of the world money supply toward the home country improves its terms of trade. Obviously, if the two countries do not differ from each other in their saving and spending propensities (so that $s = s^*$, $a = c^*$, and $c = a^*$), then the terms of trade do not change during the adjustment process. Stated in terms of the transfer-problem criterion which is familiar from the analysis of international transfers, the cross-country equalities between the marginal propensities to save and the commodity compositions of marginal spending ensures that the redistribution of the world money supply does not alter the patterns of world spending and saving, and therefore does not necessitate any change in prices.

3.3 Long-Run Equilibrium Prices and Money Holdings

The dynamic process underlying the sequence of short-run equilibria is reflected in the evolution of domestic money holdings. Formally, since $M_t = M_{t-1} + (\widetilde{TA})_t$, we can use equation (3.7) to determine the precise time path of domestic money holdings. Hence

$$M_t = \frac{sa^*\overline{M} - ss^*a^g\tilde{G} + ss^*M_{t-1}}{ss^* + sa^* + s^*a}. \tag{3.9}$$

The stability of the system is governed by identical considerations as those discussed in chapter 2. Accordingly, since the coefficient of M_{t-1} in equation (3.9) is a positive fraction, it follows that the changes in the money supply that occur during the adjustment process eventually come to a halt, and the system converges to its long-run equilibrium. In the long run the money supply is stationary so that $M_t = M_{t-1} = M$. Thus equation (3.9) implies that the long-run domestic money holdings are

$$M = \frac{sa^*}{sa^* + s^*a}\overline{M} - \frac{ss^*a^g}{sa^* + s^*a}\tilde{G}. \tag{3.10}$$

Equation (3.10) expresses the long-run holdings of domestic money in terms of the world money supply and the level of government spending. It reveals that the relative share of domestic money in the world money supply is $sa^*/(sa^* + s^*a)$. In what follows we examine in greater detail the characteristics of the long-run equilibrium.

In the long-run equilibrium private-sector spending in each country equals disposable income. With balanced budgets these long-run conditions are

$$(1 - s)(P - \tilde{G} + M) = P - \tilde{G}, \tag{3.11}$$

$$(1 - s^*)(P^* - \tilde{G}^* + \overline{M} - M) = P^* - \tilde{G}^*. \tag{3.12}$$

In addition the world money-market equilibrium requires that the sum of domestic and foreign long-run demands for money equal the given supply of world money, $\overline{M}$, and that the long-run value of domestic imports equal the corresponding value of foreign imports. These two requirements are expressed by equations (3.13) and (3.14):

$$s(P - \tilde{G} + M) + s^*(P^* - \tilde{G}^* + \overline{M} - M) = \overline{M}, \tag{3.13}$$

$$[a^*(P^* - \tilde{G}^* + \overline{M} - M) + a^{g*}\tilde{G}^*] - [a(P - \tilde{G} + M) + a^g\tilde{G}] = 0. \tag{3.14}$$

Combining equations (3.11) through (3.13) yields the long-run money-market equilibrium schedule $\overline{MM}$ in figure 3.2. Formally, the equation of this schedule is

$$\frac{s}{1-s}P + \frac{s^*}{1-s^*}P^* = \overline{M} + \frac{s}{1-s}\tilde{G} + \frac{s^*}{1-s^*}\tilde{G}^*. \tag{3.15}$$

Analogously, combining equations (3.11), (3.12), and (3.14) yields the long-run goods-market equilibrium schedule $\widetilde{TA} = 0$ in figure 3.2. The equation of this schedule is

$$\overline{a}^*P^* - \overline{a}P = (a^g - \overline{a})\tilde{G} - (a^{g*} - \overline{a}^*)\tilde{G}^*. \tag{3.16}$$

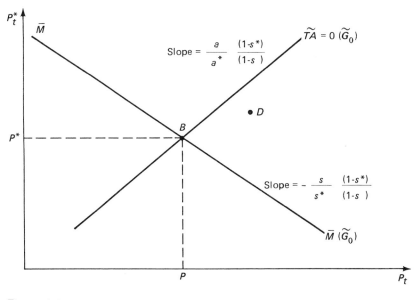

Figure 3.2
Long-run equilibrium prices

The long-run equilibrium of the system is indicated by point B in figure 3.2. At this point the values of domestic and foreign prices are such that both goods markets clear, world money is willingly held, and the international distribution of the existing money stock does not tend to change. Using equations (3.15) and (3.16), the long-run values of domestic and foreign prices are

$$P = \left(1 - \frac{(1-s)s^*}{sa^* + s^*a}\right)\tilde{G} + \frac{(1-s)}{sa^* + s^*a}(a^*\overline{M} + s^*a^{g*}\tilde{G}^*), \qquad (3.17)$$

$$P^* = \frac{(1-s^*)s}{sa^* + s^*a}\tilde{G} + \left(1 - \frac{s(1-s^*)a^{g*}}{sa^* + s^*a}\right)\tilde{G}^* + \frac{(1-s^*)a}{sa^* + s^*a}\overline{M}. \qquad (3.18)$$

The ratio of these prices yields the long-run value of the terms of trade. Finally, since long-run money holdings are linked to the long-run value of disposable income according to $M = [s/(1-s)](P - \tilde{G})$ (where due to our normalization the price P stands for nominal income, and due to the balanced-budget assumption $\tilde{G}$ stands for nominal taxes), we can use equation (3.17) to yield

$$M = \frac{s}{sa^* + s^*a}[a^*\overline{M} + s^*(a^{g*}\tilde{G}^* - a^g\tilde{G})]. \tag{3.19}$$

As should be obvious, this equation is the extension of equation (3.10) for the case in which foreign government spending is not zero. We will return to these expressions in the subsequent analysis of the effects of fiscal policies.

3.4 Fiscal Policies, Prices, and Nominal Spending

In this section we examine the effects of a balanced-budget rise in the domestic government spending on the short-run and long-run equilibrium prices, the terms of trade, and the balance of trade.

Consider the initial equilibrium at point A in figure 3.1. As seen from equation (3.2), a unit balanced-budget rise in government spending induces a horizontal shift of the PP schedule by $(a + s - a^g)/(a + s)$. The schedule shifts to the right if at the prevailing prices the balanced-budget rise in government spending raises the demand for domestic output. Accordingly, if the government propensity to spend on domestic goods, $1 - a^g$, exceeds the corresponding private-sector propensity, $1 - a - s$ (i.e., $a + s - a^g > 0$), the schedule shifts to the right, and vice versa. As seen in equation (3.3), the same rise in government spending also induces a horizontal shift in the P^*P^* by $(a - a^g)/a$ units.

The new short-run equilibrium is specified by equations (3.5) through (3.7), where it is seen that the domestic price changes by $1 - s^*a^g/\Delta$ units, the foreign price rises by sa^g/Δ units, and the trade balance worsens by ss^*c^g/Δ units, where $\Delta = ss^* + sa^* + s^*a > 0$.

As is evident, the effect of the fiscal expansion on the domestic price depends on the relative size of the government import propensity, a^g, but if this propensity does not exceed the corresponding private-sector propensity, a, then the domestic price rises. For example, if we consider (as in chapter 2) the bench-mark case for which $a = a^g$, then the PP schedule shifts to the right, the P^*P^* schedule remains intact, and the new short-run equilibrium in figure 3.1 obtains at point C at which both the domestic and the foreign price levels have risen. Thus, for the case in which the government import propensity does not exceed the corresponding private-sector propensity, the short-run international transmission of balanced-budget fiscal policies (as measured by the comovements of domestic and foreign prices) is positive. In the more general case, if most of government spending falls on imports, then the short-run transmission may be negative.

Turning to the long-run, we note from equation (3.15) that the unit balanced-budget rise in the domestic government spending induces a rightward shift of the money-market equilibrium schedule $\overline{MM}$ by one unit. At the same time, as seen from equation (3.16) the goods-market equilibrium schedule $\widetilde{TA} = 0$ shifts horizontally by $(\bar{a} - a^g)/\bar{a}$ units. The new long-run equilibrium values of P and P^* are inferred from equations (3.17) and (3.18). Accordingly, in the long-run the domestic price changes by $1 - s^*(1 - s)a^g/\Delta_L$ units, where $\Delta_L = sa^* + s^*a > 0$.

Analogously to the previous discussion of the short-run, the long-run effects of the balanced-budget fiscal expansion on the domestic price depend on the relative magnitude of the government import propensity, a^g. If this propensity does not exceed the private-sector propensity to import out of spending, $\bar{a} = a/(1 - s)$, then the long-run value of the domestic price rises. In that case the long-run international transmission of the effects of balanced-budget fiscal policies is positive, as illustrated by point D in figure 3.2. If, however, a^g exceeds $\bar{a}$, then the long-run transmission may be negative.

The equilibrium changes in the levels of output are associated with corresponding changes in the levels of private-sector spending. Specifically, recalling that output is normalized to be unity and that government budgets are balanced, the level of domestic nominal spending, Z_t, is related to income and asset holdings according to $Z_t = (1 - s)(P_t - \tilde{G} + M_{t-1})$. Similar expression applies to the foreign country. It follows from equations (3.5) and (3.6) that in the short run, a unit balanced-budget rise in the domestic government spending lowers domestic private-sector spending by $(1 - s)s^*a^g/\Delta$ units and raises the foreign spending by $(1 - s^*)sa^g/\Delta$ units. Hence, measured in terms of the comovements of domestic and foreign private-sector nominal spending, the short-run international transmission of the effects of balanced-budget fiscal policies is negative.

In order to determine the implications of the balanced-budget fiscal expansion for the long-run levels of private-sector spending, we note that in the long run nominal spending, Z, equals disposable income, $P - \tilde{G}$; similarly, for the foreign country, $Z^* = P^* - \tilde{G}$. Accordingly, using the long-run equations (3.17) and (3.18), a unit balanced-budget rise in the domestic government spending lowers the long-run level of the domestic private-sector nominal spending by $(1 - s)s^*a^g/\Delta_L$ units. The same fiscal expansion raises the corresponding level of foreign spending by $(1 - s^*)sa^g/\Delta_L$ units. Hence the long-run international transmission is also negative.

A comparison between the magnitudes of the short- and the long-run changes in domestic and foreign private-sector spending reveals that *the long-run changes magnify the corresponding short-run changes* (since $\Delta_L = \Delta - ss^*$). The *magnification factor* is Δ/Δ_L. This relation between the size of the short- and long-run spending multipliers reflects the implications of changes in domestic and foreign money holdings occurring during the adjustment process. To clarify this process, we turn next to examine the effects of fiscal policies on the international monetary flows.

Starting from an initial long-run equilibrium, the unit balanced-budget fiscal expansion worsens the home country's balance of payments by ss^*a^g/Δ units (as seen from equation 3.7). This payments imbalance sets off the dynamic process through which the world money supply is redistributed toward the rest of the world. The adjustment process is completed when the international distribution of the world money supply corresponds to the long-run distribution. At that point the international monetary flows cease, and each country's external payments are balanced. The long-run change in the domestic money holdings is the sum of all the payments imbalances during the adjustment process. As seen from equation (3.19), the unit balanced-budget rise in the domestic government spending lowers the domestic long-run money holdings by ss^*a^g/Δ_L units. As is obvious, the cumulative long-run decline in the domestic money holdings exceeds the short-run payments imbalance by the magnification factor Δ/Δ_L. This magnification factor is the same as the one applicable to the comparison between long- and short-run changes in private-sector nominal spending.

3.5 Fiscal Policies, the Terms of Trade, and Real Spending

The foregoing analysis examined the effects of fiscal policies on the *nominal* quantities (income, spending, and monetary flows). We turn next to analyze the implications of these policies on the *real* value of private-sector spending and on the terms of trade. Such an analysis is more appropriate for determining the welfare consequences of fiscal policies. It is relevant to note, however, that since (as typical to the specification of the income-expenditure model) the spending and money-demand functions are not derived explicitly from consumers' utility maximization, the level of real spending is only an imprecise indicator of well-being.

In evaluating real spending, $E_c = Z/P_c$, we employ a consumer price index, P_c, computed by using the private-sector expenditure shares. Accordingly, the relative share of the price of the domestically produced good in the domestic price index is $\bar{c} = (1 - s - a)/(1 - s)$, and the relative share of the price of the foreign good in the domestic price index is $\bar{a} = a/(1 - s)$. Similar considerations underly the computation of the foreign price index, P_c^*, and the level of foreign real spending $E_c^* = Z^*/P_c^*$.

It is convenient to start the analysis by considering the long-run effects of government spending on the terms of trade. For this purpose consider figure 3.3 in which the initial long-run equilibrium is shown by point B. It is assumed that initially the levels of government spending in both countries are zero. In this case the $\widetilde{TA} = 0$ schedule is a ray emerging from the origin. Its slope measures the initial terms of trade. The balanced-budget rise in the domestic government spending induces a rightward shift of the $\overline{MM}$ schedule by the magnitude $\Delta\tilde{G}$ (as seen from equation 3.15). The same fiscal expansion induces a vertical shift of the $\widetilde{TA} = 0$ schedule. As indicated by equation (3.16), the $\widetilde{TA} = 0$ shifts upward if the government propensity to import, a^g, exceeds the domestic private-sector propensity to import out of spending, $\bar{a}$ (the case shown in figure 3.3). In that case, at the prevailing prices, the balanced-budget rise in the domestic government spending raises the national demand for imports and deteriorates the trade balance. In the opposite case in which a^g falls short of $\bar{a}$, the $\widetilde{TA} = 0$ schedule shifts downward. The extent of the

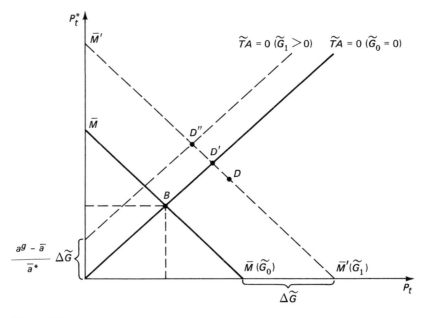

Figure 3.3
The effect of government spending on the terms of trade in the long run.
Data: $a^g - \bar{a} > 0$.

vertical shift is $(a^g - \bar{a})/\bar{a}^*$ times the rise in government spending. As shown in the figure, the new long-run equilibrium obtains at point D''.

The new long-run terms of trade can be measured by the slope of the ray from origin (not drawn) passing through point D''. As is evident, since at D'' the ratio P^*/P rises, the terms of trade move in favor of the foreign country and against the domestic economy. This outcome corresponds to the special case for which a^g exceeds $\bar{a}$. In the opposite case for which a^g falls short of $\bar{a}$, the $\widetilde{TA} = 0$ schedule shifts downward, and the new long-run equilibrium obtains at a point like D in figure 3.3. At point D the terms of trade turn in favor of the domestic economy and against the foreign country. In the intermediate case for which the expenditure shares of the government equal those of the domestic private sector (so that $a^g = \bar{a}$), the balanced-budget rise in government spending does not alter the position of the $\widetilde{TA} = 0$ schedule. In that case the new long-run equilibrium obtains at point D'. In this new equilibrium the terms of trade are not altered.

In general, *the balanced-budget rise in the domestic government spending improves the domestic country's terms of trade if the government import propensity is smaller than the domestic private-sector propensity to import out of spending, and vice versa.* This discussion illustrates the general principles underlying the transfer-problem criterion for determining the long-run effects of government spending on the terms of trade.

We turn next to analyze the effects of the balanced-budget fiscal policies on the long-run values of real private-sector spending. We suppose that initially the levels of spending by both governments are zero and that the world economy is in a long-run equilibrium. The balanced-budget rise in the domestic government spending alters the nominal value of private-sector spending in both countries, and it also alters both GDP deflators, P and P^*. To compute the proportional changes in the real value of private-sector spending (measured in terms of the consumption baskets), we subtract from the proportional changes in nominal spending a weighted average of the proportional change in the GDP deflators, where the weights are the corresponding expenditure shares. Accordingly, by using the long-run equations (3.17) and (3.18), we obtain

$$\frac{d\log E_c}{d\tilde{G}} = \frac{h}{(1-s)a^*}[(\bar{a} - a^g) - 1], \tag{3.20}$$

$$\frac{d\log E_c^*}{d\tilde{G}} = \frac{h}{(1-s^*)a}(a^g - \bar{a}), \tag{3.21}$$

where

$$h = \frac{sa^* + s^*a}{M}.$$

In interpreting these results, we start with equation (3.21) pertaining to changes in foreign real spending. As seen, the balanced-budget rise in the domestic government spending raises the long-run value of foreign real spending if the share of spending on importables by the domestic government, a^g, exceeds the corresponding expenditure share of the domestic private sector, $\bar{a}$, and vice versa. As was shown, this is also the criterion determining the direction of the long-run changes in the terms of trade. Indeed, since in the long-run income equals spending, it is evident that the direction of the change in the terms of trade is the only factor determining the direction of the change in foreign real spending.

The long-run change in the real value of the domestic private-sector spending consequent on a balanced-budget rise in government spending reflects both the effects of changes in the terms of trade and the effects of the rise in taxes. As seen in equation (3.20), the terms-of-trade effect is proportional to $\bar{a} - a^g$, and the (negative) tax effect is proportional to unity. Since $\bar{a} - a^g$ is a fraction, it follows that independent of the spending patterns, the tax effect dominates, and therefore the long-run real value of the domestic private-sector spending must fall.

The foregoing analysis revealed that the key factor underlying the direction of the long-run changes in the terms of trade and in real spending is the import propensities of the *domestic* private sector and government. The foreign spending patterns do not play a role in determining the direction of the change in real spending and the terms of trade. These results imply that the international transmission of balanced-budget fiscal policies, as measured by comovements of long-run private-sector real spending, may be negative or positive depending on whether a^g exceeds or falls short of $\bar{a}$. If a^g exceeds $\bar{a}$, the terms of trade turn in favor of the foreign country, foreign real spending rises, and the transmission is negative. The opposite occurs if a^g falls short of $\bar{a}$.

Up to this point we have analyzed the long-run effects of fiscal policies on the real value of private-sector spending. We turn next to determine the short-run equilibrium changes in real spending. As before, suppose that initially the world economy is in a long-run equilibrium and that the initial levels of government spending are zero. In computing the short-run changes in the real values of private-sector spending, we calculate the changes in nominal spending and in the consumer price indexes from the short-run equilibrium solutions in equations (3.5) and (3.6), and we evaluate these changes around the initial long-run equilibrium (calculated from the long-run equilibrium solutions in equations 3.17 and 3.18). Following this procedure, it can be shown that the short-run effects of the balanced-budget rise in the domestic government spending on the real values of domestic and foreign private-sector spending are

$$
\frac{d\log E_{c0}}{d\tilde{G}} = (1 - s^*)\frac{k}{a^*}\left\{\left[s^*(s - \bar{a}) - s\frac{(1 - s)}{(1 - s^*)}\bar{a}\right]a^g\right.
$$

$$
\left. - (1 - \bar{a})\Delta\right\},
$$
(3.22)

$$
\frac{d\log E_{c0}^*}{d\tilde{G}} = (1 - s)\frac{k}{a}[(s^*\bar{a} + sa^*)a^g - \bar{a}\Delta],
$$
(3.23)

where

$$
k = \frac{sa^* + s^*a}{(ss^* + sa^* + s^*a)\overline{M}(1 - s)(1 - s^*)},
$$

and

$$
\Delta = ss^* + sa^* + s^*a.
$$

As indicated by equations (3.22) and (3.23), the direction of the short-run changes in real spending also depends on the magnitudes of the foreign country's spending and saving patterns. This dependence should be contrasted with our previous discussion of the long-run effects, where it was shown in equations (3.20) and (3.21) that the foreign-country parameters play no role in determining the direction of the long-run change in real spending. As is evident from equations (3.22) and (3.23), if the government import propensity does not exceed the domestic private-sector propensity to import out of spending, both domestic and foreign levels of real spending fall. This means that in this case the short-run international transmission is positive. On the other hand, if the government import propensity is large (e.g., if it is close to unity), then equations (3.22) and (3.23) imply that the real value of the domestic private-sector spending falls while foreign real spending rises. In that case the short-run international transmission of the fiscal policy is negative.

3.6 Summary

In this chapter we have analyzed the classical version of the income-expenditure model of the world economy. The model assumed that the levels of domestic and foreign outputs are given at the full employment level, but prices are flexible to adjust so as to clear markets.

The income-expenditure model builds on the interactions among nominal spending and nominal income of four units: domestic and foreign private sectors and governments. For given government policies, world equilibrium is brought about through the endogenous determination of payments imbalances. The latter in turn determine the international monetary flows that set off the adjustment process. This dynamic process converges to the long-run equilibrium in which payments imbalances vanish and the international distribution of world money is stationary.

The key variables that determine, and are determined by, the mechanisms of the income-expenditure model are the levels of *nominal* income and spending. The income-expenditure model in and of itself does not determine the equilibrium *division* of nominal income and nominal spending between prices and quantities. This division must be determined by additional considerations. Therefore we have analyzed the extreme cases that span the spectrum of such possible divisions. In chapter 2 we have presented the Keynesian version in which changes in nominal income arise from changes in output rather than prices. In the present chapter we have presented the classical version in which the same changes in nominal income arise from changes in prices rather than outputs. Although the two extreme versions of the income-expenditure model are widely apart in terms of their economic structure, they share the same basic payments mechanism. As a result the patterns of nominal income, spending, and payments imbalances predicted by the two versions of the model are similar to each other.

To isolate the pure effects of fiscal policies, we have assumed that government budgets are balanced. Since we have assumed that credit markets are absent, the balanced-budget assumption ensures that the monetary authorities confine themselves to peg the exchange rate and do not monetize budget deficits.

In this chapter we have seen that a balanced-budget rise in the domestic government spending raises foreign prices in both the short and the long runs. The long-run rise in foreign prices exceeds the corresponding short-run rise if the saving ratio s/s^* exceeds the ratio of the domestic fraction of income not spent on domestic goods, $1 - c$, to the fraction of foreign income not spent on imports, $1 - a^*$. On the other hand, if s/s^* *falls short of* $(1 - c)/(1 - a^*)$, then the short-run rise in foreign prices overshoots the corresponding long-run rise.

The effects of the balanced-budget fiscal expansion on the domestic price level depends on the saving and on the spending propensities of the private sectors and the government. The short-run level of domestic prices rises if the saving ratio, s/s^*, exceed the ratio of the domestic net propensity to spend on domestic goods $c - c^g$ to the foreign import propensity, a^* (where $c^g = 1 - a^g$ is the government propensity to spend on domestic goods).

On the other hand, if s/s^* falls short of $(c - c^g)/a^*$, then the domestic price falls in the short run. For example, if government spending falls entirely on domestic goods, $c^g = 1$, and the short-run domestic price rises. In the other extreme case in which government spending falls entirely on imported goods, $c^g = 0$, and the domestic price rises or falls depending on whether s/s^* exceeds or falls short of the spending ratio c/a^*. Regardless of the magnitude of c^g, the same condition determines whether the difference between the long- and the short-run changes in the domestic price is positive or negative. Thus, measured in terms of comovements of domestic and foreign prices, the international transmission of balanced-budget fiscal policies may be positive or negative.

The balanced-budget rise in government spending raises foreign nominal spending in the short and the long runs, lowers domestic private-sector spending in both runs, and worsens the domestic trade balance. The long-run changes in nominal spending magnify the corresponding short-run changes. The common magnification factor equals the ratio of the cumulative payments imbalances (corresponding to the reduction in the long-run domestic money holdings) to the short-run deficit in the balance of payments.

The multipliers corresponding to the short- and long-run changes in domestic and foreign prices, nominal spending, and monetary flows induced by a given balanced-budget rise in nominal government spending are the same as those summarized in table 2.1 of the Keynesian version, with the appropriate relabeling (in relabeling, we replace Y, Y^*, E, E^*, and TA by P, P^*, Z, Z^*, and $\widetilde{TA}$, respectively). This identity between the multipliers reflects the fundamental symmetry between the Keynesian and the classical versions of the income-expenditure model.

To obtain a more appropriate welfare indicator, we have also analyzed the effects of fiscal policies on the *real* value of private-sector spending and on the terms of trade. In computing the real value of spending, we have used the appropriate consumer price indexes based on the relevant expenditure shares. The analysis revealed that the direction of the long-run changes in the terms of trade and in the real value of domestic and foreign private-sector spending depends only on the relative magnitudes of spending patterns of the *domestic* government and private sector. Specifically, the balanced-budget rise in the domestic government spending improves the domestic country's terms of trade if the government import propensity, a^g, is smaller than the private-sector propensity to import out of spending, $\bar{a}$, and vice versa. Since in the long run the real values of spending and income are equal to each other, it follows that the direction of the change in foreign real spending (and welfare) depends exclusively on the change in the long-run terms of trade. Hence foreign real spending falls if a^g falls short of $\bar{a}$, and vice versa.

The long-run change in the real value of the domestic private-sector spending reflects both the change in real income induced by the change in the terms of trade as well as the decline in real income induced by the rise in taxes. The former is proportional to $\bar{a} - a^g$, and the latter, representing the direct absorption of resources by the government, is proportional to unity. However, even though the domestic terms of trade may improve, the effect of the rise in taxes dominates, and therefore the real value of the domestic private-sector spending falls in the long run. Since, depending on the direction of change in the terms of trade, foreign spending may rise or fall, we conclude that if the private-sector share of spending on imports,

$\bar{a}$, exceeds the corresponding government share, a^g, then the international transmission of balanced-budget fiscal-policies, measured in terms of comovements of long-run private-sector real spending, is positive. If, however, $\bar{a}$ falls short of a^g, then this international transmission is negative.

In the short run the factors that determine the effects of balanced-budget fiscal policies on the real value of domestic and foreign private-sector spending include also the foreign saving and spending propensities. This should be contrasted with the long-run situation in which the only factor determining the cross-country correlation between private-sector real spending is the difference between the expenditure shares of the domestic government and private sector.

Throughout our analysis of the income-expenditure model we have focused on the effects of balanced-budget fiscal policies. The analytical framework, however, can be used for other policies such as domestic monetary policies, changes in the world money supply, and changes in the exchange rate. The effects of these policies will also be transmitted internationally through the payments mechanism characterizing the fixed exchange-rate regime.

In both the Keynesian and classical versions of the income-expenditure model we have assumed that the international monetary system is governed by a fixed exchange-rate regime. The deficits or surpluses in the official-settlements account of the balance of payments associated with the maintenance of the fixed exchange-rate regime enable the existence of discrepancies between national income and national expenditure. The fixed exchange-rate regime employed in chapters 2 and 3 facilitates such discrepancies even in the absence of international private credit markets. If, on the other hand, the exchange rate is flexible, then the official-settlements account of the balance of payments must be balanced. Under such circumstances the absence of international private credit markets prevents any discrepancy between income and spending and imposes the requirement of a continuous balance in the trade account of the balance of payments.

Obviously, with continuous trade balance, the flexible exchange-rate regime implies that the levels of nominal income in each country are independent of policies undertaken by the other country. In the

Keynesian version of the income-expenditure model, this lack of interdependence implies that each country's output and employment are insulated from policies undertaken abroad. In the classical version of the model, however, the real value of private-sector spending in each country is not insulated from policies undertaken abroad. The reason for this lack of insulation is that the consumer price index used to compute real spending depends on the equilibrium exchange rate which is determined endogenously so as to equate the values of exports and imports which themselves depend on both countries' policies.

The foregoing discussion of the role that the exchange-rate regime plays in determining the characteristics of the international transmission mechanism, and thereby the patterns of interdependencies in the world economy, highlights the crucial implications of the assumption (adopted in our exposition of the income-expenditure model) that there are no international private credit markets.

The increased integration of the world capital markets motivates the extension of the analytical framework outlined in this chapter and in the preceding one to incorporate the role of international private captial mobility. This extension characterizes the model that is exposited in the next chapter. International private credit markets also play a central role in the intertemporal models of the interdependent world economy. These models, which are developed in detail in subsequent parts of this book, share with the analysis presented in chapter 4 the focus on international capital mobility. But, as will be shown, there are also fundamental differences between the two approaches.

4

Fiscal Policies and International Capital Mobility in the Income-Expenditure Model

In this chapter we extend the analytical framework used in chapters 2 and 3 in two dimensions. First, we expand the menu of assets by adding interest-bearing bonds to the portfolio of assets. Second, we assume that the world capital markets are highly integrated and that all bonds are internationally tradable. The inclusion of interest-bearing bonds permits an analysis of the consequences of debt-financed changes in government spending. These consequences can then be compared with those of tax-financed changes in government spending. In conformity with the analysis in chapter 2 we continue to assume that the prices (GDP deflators) are fixed and that the levels of output are demand determined. In this context we analyze the short- and long-run effects of fiscal policies under fixed and flexible exchange-rate regimes.

As in chapter 2 the fixity of the GDP deflators implies that exchange-rate changes alter the relative prices of the domestically produced goods in terms of the foreign-produced goods (i.e., the terms of trade). Here, due to the expanded menu of assets traded in the integrated world capital market, exchange-rate changes impact on the economic system through two additional channels. First, they alter the real value of existing debts. Second, they influence expectations and thereby impact on the desired composition of the portfolio of assets. Thus the inclusion of interest-bearing assets and international capital mobility introduces new mechanisms governing the effects of fiscal policies and their international transmission.

4.1 The Analytical Framework

In specifying the behavioral functions, it is convenient to focus on the domestic economy. Accordingly, the budget constraint is

$$Z_t + M_t - B_t^p = P_t(Y_t - T_t) + M_{t-1} - R_{t-1}B_{t-1}^p, \tag{4.1}$$

where B_t^p denotes the domestic-currency value of private-sector's one-period debt issued in period t, and R_t denotes one plus the rate of interest. Analogously to equation (2.1) of chapter 2, the right-hand side of equation (4.1) states that in each period, t, the resources available to individuals are composed of disposable income, $P_t(Y_t - T_t)$—where for notational convenience we denote domestic output, Y_{xt}, by Y_t—and the net value of assets carried over from period $t - 1$. The latter consist of money, M_{t-1}, net of debt commitment $R_{t-1}B_{t-1}^p$ (including principal plus interest payments). For subsequent use we denote these assets by A_{t-1}, where

$$A_{t-1} = M_{t-1} - R_{t-1}B_{t-1}^p. \tag{4.2}$$

The left-hand side of equation (4.1) indicates the uses of these resources including nominal spending, Z_t, money holding, M_t, and bond holding, $-B_t^p$.

Throughout this chapter we assume that the GDP deflator, P_t, is fixed and normalized to unity. In that case nominal spending also equals real spending, E_t. Due to the absence of changes in prices we identify the real rate of interest, $r_t = R_t - 1$, with the corresponding nominal rate of interest (we return to this issue later in the chapter where we analyze the implications of exchange-rate changes).

Assuming that the various demand functions depend on the available resources and on the rate of interest, we express the spending and the money-demand function as

$$E_t = E(Y_t - T_t + A_{t-1}, r_t), \tag{4.3}$$

$$M_t = M(Y_t - T_t + A_{t-1}, r_t). \tag{4.4}$$

In specifying these functions, we have used a simplification similar to the one underlying equation (2.20) in chapter 2; we assume that the marginal propensities to spend and to hoard out of disposable income are the same as the corresponding propensities to spend and hoard out of assets. A similar specification underlines the demand for bonds which is omitted due to the budget constraint. We assume that desired spending and money holdings depend positively on available resources and negatively on the rate of interest.

A similar set of demand functions characterizes the foreign economy, where, as before, its variables are denoted by an asterisk and where its fixed GDP deflator, P^*, is normalized to unity. The specification of the equilibrium in the world economy depends on the exchange-rate regime. We start with the analysis of equilibrium under a fixed exchange-rate regime.

4.2 Capital Mobility with Fixed Exchange Rates

Equilibrium in the world economy necessitates that the markets for goods, money, and bonds clear. Under a fixed exchange rate, domestic and foreign money (in their role as assets) are perfect substitutes. Therefore money-market equilibrium can be specified by a single equilibrium relation stating that the world demand for money equals the world supply. Likewise, the assumptions that bonds are internationally tradable assets and that domestic and foreign bonds are perfect substitutes imply that in equilibrium these bonds command the same real return, $r_t = r_{ft}$, and that bond-market equilibrium can also be specified by a single equation pertaining to the unified world bond market. These considerations imply that the world economy is characterized by four markets: the markets for domestic output, foreign output, world money, and world bonds. By Walras's law we omit the bond market from the equilibrium specification of the two-country model of the world economy. Accordingly, the equilibrium conditions are

$$(1 - \beta_m)E(Y_t - T_t + A_{t-1}, r_t) + (1 - \beta_m^g)G$$

$$+ \beta_x^* \bar{e} E^*(Y_t^* + A_{t-1}^*, r_t) = Y_t, \tag{4.5}$$

$$\beta_m E(Y_t - T_t + A_{t-1}, r_t) + \beta_m^g G$$

$$+ (1 - \beta_x^*)\bar{e} E^*(Y_t^* + A_{t-1}^*, r_t) = \bar{e} Y_t^*, \tag{4.6}$$

$$M(Y_t - T_t + A_{t-1}, r_t) + \bar{e}M^*(Y_t^* + A_{t-1}^*, r_t) = \overline{M}, \qquad (4.7)$$

where we continue to assume that foreign government spending and taxes are zero and where $\bar{e}$ denotes the fixed exchange rate expressing the price of foreign currency in terms of domestic currency. The (predetermined) value of foreign assets is measured in foreign-currency units so that $A_{t-1}^* = M_{t-1}^* + R_{t-1}B_{t-1}^p/\bar{e}$. Due to the assumed fixity of the GDP deflators, $\bar{e}$ also measures the relative price of importables in terms of exportables (defined in equation 2.18). As before, $\overline{M}$ denotes the world supply of money, measured in terms of domestic goods (whose domestic-currency price is unity); we continue to assume that the government does not finance its spending through money creation. Here it is relevant to note that in contrast with the analysis in chapters 2 and 3, the presence of capital markets permits discrepancies between spending and taxes which is made up for by debt issue.

The specification of the equilibrium system (4.5) through (4.7) embodies the arbitrage condition by which the yields on domestic and foreign bonds are equal. This equality justifies the use of the same rate of interest in the behavioral functions of the domestic and the foreign economies. The system (4.5) through (4.7) determines the short-run equilibrium values of domestic output, Y_t, foreign output, Y_t^*, and the world rate of interest, r_t, for given (predetermined) values of domestic and foreign net assets, A_{t-1} and A_{t-1}^*, and for given levels of government spending, G_t, and taxes, T_t.

The international distribution of the given world money supply associated with the short-run equilibrium is determined *endogenously* according to the demands. Thus

$$M_t = M(Y_t - T_t + A_{t-1}, r_t), \qquad (4.8)$$

$$M_t^* = M^*(Y_t^* + A_{t-1}^*, r_t). \qquad (4.9)$$

This equilibrium distribution obtains through international asset swaps.

A comparison between this short-run equilibrium system and the one used in chapter 2 reveals the significant role played by international capital mobility. In the absence of such mobility the short-run equilibrium determines the levels of domestic and foreign output from the goods-market equilibrium conditions (2.15) and (2.16) of chapter 2. Associated with these levels of outputs are equilibrium monetary *flows*, as shown by equations (2.12) through (2.14) and (2.19). These flows cease in the long run in which a stationary equilibrium distribution of the world money supply obtains, as indicated by the long-run equilibrium condition (2.26). In contrast, the equilibrium system (4.5) through (4.7) shows that with perfect capital mobility equilibrium in the world money market obtains through instantaneous asset swaps involving exchanges of money for bonds. This instantaneous *stock* adjustments is reflected in equation (4.7).

Fiscal Policies in a Small Country

To illustrate the effects of fiscal policies under a regime of fixed exchange rates with perfect capital mobility, it is convenient to begin with an analysis of a small country facing a given world rate of interest, $\bar{r}_f$, and a given world demand for its goods, $\bar{D}^* = \beta_x^* E^*$. Under these circumstances the equilibrium condition for the small economy reduces to

$$(1 - \beta_m)E(Y_t - T_t + A_{t-1}, \bar{r}_f) + (1 - \beta_m^g)G + \bar{e}\bar{D}^* = Y_t. \qquad (4.5a)$$

This equilibrium condition determines the short-run value of output for the given (predetermined) value of assets and for given levels of government spending and taxes. As before, the money supply, M_t, associated with this equilibrium is obtained from the money-market equilibrium condition (4.8a)

$$M(Y_t - T_t + A_{t-1}, \bar{r}_f) = M_t. \qquad (4.8a)$$

This quantity of money is endogenously determined through instantaneous asset swaps at the prevailing world rate of interest.

　　To analyze the effects of fiscal policies, we differentiate equation (4.5a). Thus

$$\frac{dY_t}{dG} = \frac{1 - a^g}{s + a}, \quad \text{for } dT_t = 0, \qquad (4.10)$$

and

$$\frac{dY_t}{dG} = 1 - \frac{a^g}{s + a}, \quad \text{for } dT_t = dG, \tag{4.11}$$

where, as before, $a^g = \beta^g_m$ is the government marginal propensity to import, and $1/(s + a)$ is the small-country foreign-trade multiplier. Equations (4.10) and (4.11) correspond, respectively, to a bond-financed and a tax-financed rise in government spending. As is evident, if all of government spending falls on domestic goods (so that $a^g = 0$), then the fiscal expansion that is financed by government borrowing raises output by the full extent of the foreign trade multiplier, while the balanced-budget fiscal expansion yields the closed-economy balanced-budget multiplier of unity. If, on the other hand, all of government spending falls on imported goods (so that $a^g = 1$), then the bond-financed multiplier is zero, whereas the balanced-budget multiplier is negative and equal to $(s + a - 1)/(s + a)$.

The changes in output induce changes in the demand for money. The induced changes in money holding can be found by differentiating equation (4.8a) and using (4.10) and (4.11). Accordingly, the debt-financed unit rise in government spending raises money holdings by $(1 - a^g)M_y/(s + a)$ units, and the balanced-budget rise in government spending lowers money holdings by $a^g M_y/(s + a)$.

This analysis is summarized by figure 4.1 in which the IS schedule portrays the goods-market equilibrium condition (4.5a). It is negatively sloped since both a rise in the rate of interest and a rise in output create an excess supply of goods. The initial equilibrium obtains at point A at which the rate of interest equals the exogenously given world rate, $\bar{r}$, and the level of output is Y_0. As indicated, the schedule IS is drawn for given levels of government spending and taxes, G_0 and T_0. The LM schedule passing through point A portrays the money-market equilibrium condition (4.8a). It is positively sloped since a rise in income raises the demand for money, whereas a rise in the rate of interest lowers the money demand. As indicated, the LM schedule is drawn for a given level of (the endogenously determined) money stock, M_0.

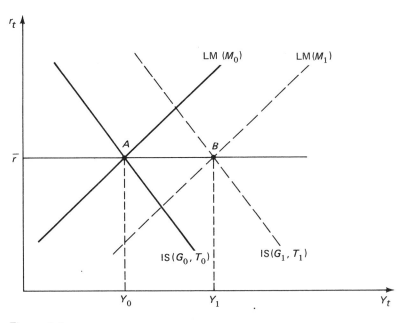

Figure 4.1
The short-run effects of fiscal policy under fixed exchange rates: the small-country case

A unit rise in government spending creates an excess demand for domestic product (at the prevailing level of output). If it is bond financed, then the excess demand is $1 - a^g$ units, and if it is tax financed, then the excess demand is of $s + a - a^g$ units (which, depending on the relative magnitudes of the parameters, may be negative). The excess demand is reflected by a horizontal shift of the IS schedule from $IS(G_0)$ to $IS(G_1)$. As drawn, the IS schedule shifts to the right, reflecting the positive excess demand at the prevailing level of output. The new equilibrium obtains at point B, at which the level of output rises to Y_1. This higher level of output raises the demand for money, which is met instantaneously through an international swap of bonds for money that is effected through the world capital markets. The endogenous rise in the quantity of money from M_0 to M_1 is reflected in the corresponding rightward displacement of the LM schedule from $LM(M_0)$ to $LM(M_1)$.

The foregoing analysis determined the *short-run* consequences of an expansionary fiscal policy. The instantaneous asset swaps induced by the requirement of asset-market equilibrium alter the size of the economy's external debt. Specifically, if initially the economy was in a long-run equilibrium (so that $B_t^p = B_{t-1}^p = B^p$, $M_t = M_{t-1} = M$, $A_t = A_{t-1} = A$, and $Y_t = Y_{t-1} = Y$), then the fiscal expansion, which raises short-run money holdings as well as the size of the external debt, raises the debt-service requirement and (in view of the positive rate of interest) lowers the value of net assets $M_t - (1 + \bar{r}_f)B_t^p$ carried over to the subsequent period. This change sets in motion a dynamic process that is completed only when the economy reaches its new long-run equilibrium. We turn next to determine the long-run consequences of government spending.

The long-run equilibrium conditions can be summarized by the system (4.12) through (4.14):

$$E[Y - T + M - (1 + \bar{r})B^p, \bar{r}_f] = Y - \bar{r}_f B^p - T, \qquad (4.12)$$

$$(1 - \beta_m)E[Y - T + M - (1 + \bar{r}_f)B^p, \bar{r}_f]$$
$$+ (1 - \beta_m^g)G + \bar{e}\bar{D}^* = Y, \qquad (4.13)$$

$$M[Y - T + M - (1 + \bar{r}_f)B^p, \bar{r}_f] = M, \qquad (4.14)$$

where the omission of the time subscripts indicates that in the long run the various variables do not vary over time. Equation (4.12) is obtained from the budget constraint (4.1) by using the spending function from equation (4.3) and by imposing the requirement that in the long run $M_t = M_{t-1}$ and $B_t^p = B_{t-1}^p$. This equation states that in the long run, private-sector spending equals disposable income, so that private-sector savings are zero. Equation (4.13) is obtained from (4.5a) and (4.8a) together with the long-run stationary requirement. This equation is the long-run market-clearing condition for domestic output. Finally, equation (4.14), which is the long-run counterpart to equation (4.8a), is the condition for long-run money-market equilibrium.

Up to this point we have not incorporated explicitly the government budget constraint. In the absence of money creation the long-run government budget constraint states that government outlays on purchases, G, and debt service, $\bar{r}_f B^g$ (where B^g denotes government debt), must equal taxes, T. Accordingly,

$$G + \bar{\tau}_f B^g = T. \tag{4.15}$$

Substituting this constraint into equation (4.12) yields

$$E[Y - G + M - B^p - \bar{\tau}_f(B^p + B^g), \bar{\tau}_f] + G$$

$$= Y - \bar{\tau}_f(B^p + B^g). \tag{4.12a}$$

Equation (4.12a) states that in the long run the sum of private-sector and government spending equals GNP. This equality implies that in the long run the current account of the balance of payments is balanced.

Using equations (4.12), (4.14), and (4.15), we obtain the combinations of output and debt that satisfy the long-run requirement of current-account balance as well as money-market equilibrium. These combinations are portrayed along the $CA = 0$ schedule in figure 4.2. Likewise, using equations (4.13) through (4.15), we obtain the combinations of output and debt that incorporate the requirements

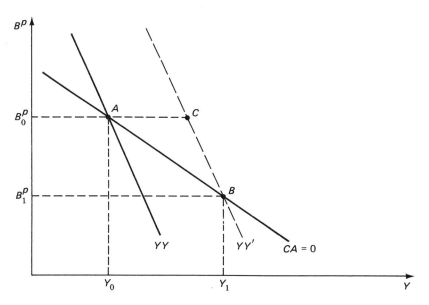

Figure 4.2
The long-run effects of a unit debt-financed rise in government spending under fixed exchange rates: the small-country case

of goods- and money-market equilibrium. These combinations are portrayed along the YY schedule in figure 4.2. The slopes of these schedules are

$$\frac{dB^p}{dY} = -\frac{(s - M_y)}{(1 - s) - \overline{r}_f(s - M_y)} \quad \text{along the } CA = 0 \text{ schedule,} \quad (4.16)$$

$$\frac{dB^p}{dY} = -\frac{(s - M_y) + a}{(1 + \overline{r}_f)(1 - s - a)} \quad \text{along the } YY \text{ schedule.} \quad (4.17)$$

The term M_y is the marginal propensity to hoard (the inverse of the marginal income velocity) and $s - M_y$ represents the marginal propensity to save in the form of bonds. As is evident, the numerators in equations (4.16) and (4.17) are positive. The denominator of equation (4.17) is positive since $1 - s - a > 0$, and the denominator of equation (4.16) is positive on the assumption that $(1 - s) > \overline{r}_f(s - M_y)$. The latter assumption is a stability condition, ensuring that the perpetual rise in consumption $(1 - s)$ made possible by a unit rise in debt exceeds the perpetual return on the saving in bonds $\overline{r}_f(s - M_y)$ made possible by the initial unit rise in debt. If this inequality does not hold, then consumption and debt rise overtime and do not converge to a long-run stationary equilibrium. The foregoing discussion implies that the slopes of both the $CA = 0$ and the YY schedules are negative. Further, since the numerator of (4.17) exceeds the one in (4.16) and the denominator of (4.17) is smaller than the one in (4.16), the YY schedule in figure 4.2 is steeper than the $CA = 0$ schedule. The initial long-run equilibrium is indicated by point A in figure 4.2 in which the levels of output and private-sector debt are Y_0 and B_0^p.

Consider the long-run effects of a *debt-financed* rise in government spending. As is evident by inspection of the system (4.12) through (4.14), as long as taxes remain unchanged, the $CA = 0$, which is derived from equations (4.12) and (4.14), remains intact. On the other hand, the rise in government spending influences the YY schedule, which is derived from equations (4.13) and (4.14). Specifically, to maintain goods-market equilibrium (for any given value of private-sector debt, B^p), a unit rise in government spending must be offset by $(1 - a^g)/(s + a)$ units rise in output. Thus, as long as some portion of government spending falls on domestic goods so that $a^g < 1$, the YY schedule in figure 4.2 shifts to the right. The new equilibrium is indicated by point B at which the level of output rises from Y_0 to Y_1 and private-sector debt falls to B_1^p. The new equilibrium is associated with a rise in money holdings, representing the cumulative surpluses in the balance of payments during the transition period.

A comparison between the short-run multiplier shown in equation (4.10) and the corresponding long-run multiplier (shown in equation A.7 of appendix A) reveals that the latter exceeds the former. In terms of figure 4.2, in the short run the output effect of the debt-financed rise in government spending is indicated by the point C, whereas the corresponding long-run equilibrium is indicated by point B.

Consider next the effects of a *tax-financed* rise in government spending. Such a balanced-budget rise in spending alters the positions of both the $CA = 0$ and the YY schedules. Using equations (4.12) and (4.14) together with the balanced-budget assumption that $dG = dT$, it can be shown that a unit rise in government spending induces a unit rightward shift of the $CA = 0$ schedule. By keeping the value of $Y - T$ intact and holding B^p constant, such a shift maintains the equality between private-sector spending and disposable income, and it also satisfies the money-market equilibrium condition. Likewise, using equations (4.13) and (4.14) together with the balanced-budget assumption, it is shown in appendix A that as long as the government import propensity, a^g, is positive, the YY schedule shifts to the right by less than one unit. The resulting new long-run equilibrium is indicated by point B in figure 4.3. For the case drawn, the long-run level of output falls from Y_0 to Y_1, and private-sector debt rises from B_0^p to B_1^p. Since government debt remains unchanged, the rise in private-sector debt corresponds to an equal rise in the economy's external-debt position. In general, however, depending on the parameters, domestic output may either rise or fall in the long run.

The size of the long-run multiplier of the balanced-budget rise in government spending depends on the government import propensity. At the limit, if all government spending falls on domestic output

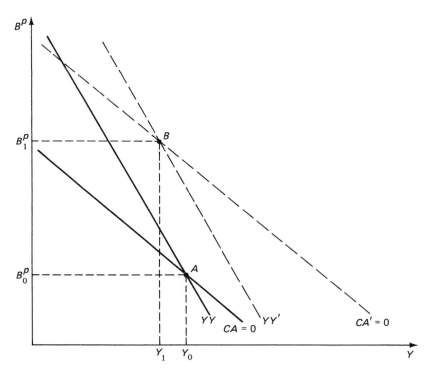

Figure 4.3
The long-run effect of a unit balanced-budget rise in government spending
under fixed exchange rates: the small-country case

so that $a^g = 0$, the long-run balanced-budget multiplier is unity. In
this case the YY schedule in figure 4.3 shifts to the right by one unit,
the long-run level of output rises by one unit, and private-sector debt
(and the economy's external debt) remains unchanged. At the other
limit, if all government spending falls on foreign goods so that
$a^g = 1$, the long-run balanced-budget multiplier is negative. In that
case the rise in the economy's external debt is maximized.

The comparison between the short-run balanced-budget multiplier shown in equation (4.11) with the corresponding long-run
multiplier (shown in equation A.10 of appendix A) highlights the
contrasts between the two. If the government propensity to spend
on domestic goods $(1 - a^g)$ equals the corresponding private-sector
propensity $(1 - s - a)$, then the short-run multiplier is zero while
the long-run multiplier is negative. On the other hand, if the govern-

ment propensity $(1 - a^g)$ exceeds the private-sector propensity $(1 - s - a)$, both the short- and the long-run balanced-budget multipliers are negative, but the absolute-value of the long-run multiplier exceeds the corresponding short-run multiplier. Finally, if government spending falls entirely on domestically produced goods (so that $a^g = 0$), then the short-run and the long-run multipliers are equal to each other, and both are unity.

Fiscal Policies in a Two-Country World

In this section we return to the two-country model outlined in equations (4.5) through (4.7) and analyze the short-run effects of a debt and tax-financed rise in government spending on the equilibrium levels of domestic and foreign outputs as well as on the equilibrium world rate of interest. The endogeneity of the last two variables distinguishes this analysis from the one conducted for the small-country case. To conserve space, we do not analyze here the long-run effects; the formal system applicable to the long-run equilibrium of the two-country world is presented in appendix A.

The analysis is carried out diagrammatically with the aid of figures 4.4 and 4.5. In these figures the YY schedule portrays combinations of domestic and foreign levels of output that yield equality between the levels of production of domestic output and the world demand for it. Likewise, the Y^*Y^* schedule portrays combinations of output that yield equality between the level of production of foreign output and the world demand for it. The two schedules incorporate the requirement of equilibrium in the world money market. It is shown in appendix A that the slopes of these schedules are

$$\frac{dY_t^*}{dY_t} = \frac{1}{\bar{e}} \frac{(s + a)(M_r + \bar{e}M_r^*) + M_y H_r}{a^*(M_r + \bar{e}M_r^*) - M_{y^*}^* H_r} \qquad \text{along the } YY \text{ schedule,}$$

(4.18)

$$\frac{dY_t^*}{dY_t} = \frac{1}{\bar{e}} \frac{a(M_r + \bar{e}M_r^*) - M_y F_r}{(s^* + a^*)(M_r + \bar{e}M_r^*) + M_{y^*}^* F_r} \qquad \text{along the } Y^*Y^* \text{ schedule,}$$

(4.19)

where H_r and F_r denote the partial (negative) effect of the rate of

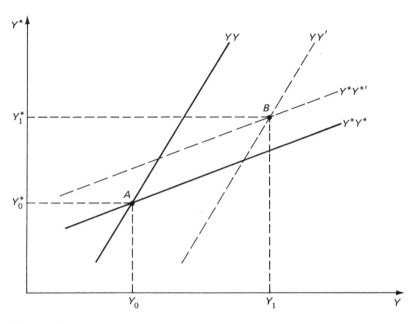

Figure 4.4
A unit debt-financed rise in government spending under fixed exchange rates: the two-country case. Data: $a^*(M_r + \bar{e}M_r^*) - M_y^*.H_r < 0$, $a(M_r + \bar{e}M_r^*) - M_y F_r < 0$.

interest on the world demand for domestic and foreign outputs, respectively, and where E_r, M_r, E_r^*, and M_r^* denote the partial (negative) effects of the world rate of interest on domestic and foreign spending and money demand. As may be seen, the slopes of the two schedules may be positive or negative. To gain intuition, we note that the new element introduced in this chapter, which was absent from the analysis in chapters 2 and 3, is the role played by the market clearing world rate of interest in influencing spending. Indeed, in the special case for which spending does not depend on the rate of interest (so that $H_r = F_r = 0$), the slopes of the schedules indicated in equations (4.18) and (4.19) coincide with the slopes indicated in equations (2.22) and (2.23). Thus in that case both schedules must be positively sloped. If, on the other hand, the rate of interest exerts a strong negative effect on world spending, then the excess supply induced by a rise in one country's output may have to

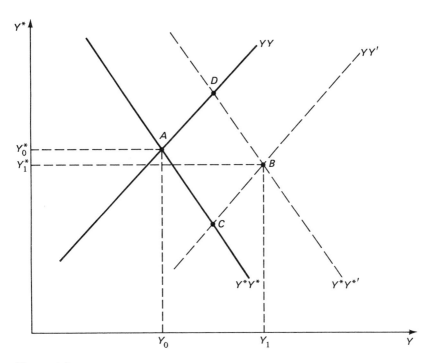

Figure 4.5
A unit debt-financed rise in government spending under fixed exchange rates: the two-country case. Data $a^*(M_r + \bar{e}M_r^*) - M_y^* H_r < 0$, $a(M_r + \bar{e}M_r^*) - M_y F_r > 0$.

be eliminated by a fall in the other country's output. Even though this fall in foreign output lowers directly the foreign demand for the first country's exports, it also induces a decline in the world rate of interest which indirectly stimulates spending and may more than offset the direct reduction in demand. In that case market clearance for each country's output implies that domestic and foreign outputs are negatively related.

Even though the two schedules may be positively or negatively sloped, it may be verified (and is shown in appendix A) that the YY schedule must be steeper than the Y^*Y^* schedule. This restriction leaves four possible configurations of the schedules. The common characteristic of these configurations is that starting from an initial equilibrium, if there is a rightward shift of the YY schedule that exceeds the rightward shift of the Y^*Y^* schedule, then the new equilibrium must be associated with a higher level of domestic output.

Two cases capturing the general pattern of world-output allocations are shown in figures 4.4 and 4.5. The other possible configurations do not yield different qualitative results concerning the effects of fiscal policies. In both figures the initial equilibrium is indicated by point A at which the domestic level of output is Y_0 and the foreign level is Y_0^*.

A debt-financed rise in government spending raises the demand for domestic output and induces a rightward shift of the YY schedule from YY to YY'. On the other hand, the direction of the change in the position of the Y^*Y^* schedule depends on the relative magnitudes of the two conflicting effects influencing world demand for foreign output. On the one hand, the rise in the domestic government spending raises the demand for foreign goods, but on the other hand, the induced rise in the world rate of interest lowers the demand. If the Y^*Y^* schedule is positively sloped, as in figure 4.4, then the rise in the domestic government spending induces a leftward (upward) shift of the Y^*Y^* schedule. The opposite holds if the Y^*Y^* schedule is negatively sloped as in figure 4.5. The formal expressions indicating the magnitudes of the displacements of the schedules are provided in appendix A.

The new equilibrium obtains at point B at which domestic output rises from Y_0 to Y_1. In the case shown in figure 4.4 (for which the interest-rate effect on the world demand for foreign output is relatively weak) foreign output rises. On the other hand, in the case shown in figure 4.5 (for which the interest-rate effect on the world demand for foreign output is relatively strong) foreign output may rise or fall depending on the magnitudes of the parameters, especially the composition of government spending. For example, if government spending falls entirely on domestic output (so that $a^g = 0$), the Y^*Y^* schedule does not shift, and the new equilibrium obtains at a point like point C in figure 4.5 at which foreign output falls. In the other extreme, if government spending falls entirely on foreign goods (so that $a^g = 1$), then the YY schedule does not shift, and the new equilibrium obtains at a point like point D at which foreign output rises.

It is shown in appendix A that independent of the direction of output changes, the debt-financed rise in government spending must raise the world rate of interest. The expressions reported in the appendix also reveal that if the (negative) interest-rate effect on the world demand for domestic output is relatively strong, then domestic output might fall. The balance-of-payments effects of the debt-financed rise in government spending are not clear cut, reflecting transfer-problem criteria. But, if the behavioral parameters of the domestic and foreign private sectors are equal to each other, then the balance of payments must improve, and the domestic money holdings are raised.

A tax-financed rise in government spending also alters the positions of the various schedules, as shown in the appendix A where we also provide the formal expressions for the various multipliers. In general, in addition to the considerations highlighted in the debt-financed case, the effect of a tax-financed fiscal spending also reflects the effects of the reduction in domestic disposable income on aggregate demand. This effect may more than offset the influence of government spending on domestic output. The effect on foreign output is also modified. If the interest-rate effect on world demand for foreign output is relatively weak (the case underlying figure 4.4), then the shift from a debt to a tax finance mitigates the expansion in foreign output. If, on the other hand, the interest-rate effect on the demand for foreign output is relatively strong (the case underlying figure 4.5), then the shift from debt to tax finance exerts expansionary effects on foreign output.

It is shown in appendix A that the direction of the change in the rate of interest induced by the tax-financed rise in government spending depends on a transfer-problem criterion, indicating whether the redistribution of world disposable income consequent on the fiscal policy raises or lowers the world demand for money. Accordingly, the rate of interest rises if the domestic-country ratio, s/M_y, exceeds the corresponding foreign-country ratio, $s^*/M_{y^*}^*$, and vice versa. Independent, however, of the change in the rate of interest, the tax-financed rise in government spending must deteriorate the domestic-country balance of payments and reduce its money holdings.

4.3 Capital Mobility with Flexible Exchange Rates

In this section we assume that the world economy operates under a flexible exchange-rate regime. With this assumption national monies become nontradable assets whose relative price (the exchange rate, e) is assumed to be determined freely in the world market for foreign exchange. We continue to assume that in each country, the GDP deflators, P and P^*, are fixed and equal to unity. Under such circumstances the nominal exchange rates represent the terms of trade, and the nominal rates of interest in each country equal the corresponding (GDP-based) real rates. Further, as was traditionally postulated in the early literature on modeling macroeconomic policies in the world economy, we open the analysis by assuming that exchange-rate expectations are static. Under such circumstances the international mobility of capital brings about equality among national (GDP-based) real rates of interest. We return to the issue of exchange-rate expectations in a subsequent section.

Equilibrium in the world economy requires that world demand for each country's output equal the corresponding supply and that in each country the demand for cash balances equal the supply. Accordingly, the system characterizing the equilibrium in the two-country world economy is

$$(1 - \beta_m)E(Y_t - T_t + A_{t-1}, r_t) + (1 - \beta_m^g)G$$

$$+ e_t \beta_x^* E^*(Y_t^* + A_{t-1}^*, r_t) = Y_t, \tag{4.20}$$

$$\beta_m E(Y_t - T_t + A_{t-1}, r_t) + \beta_m^g G$$

$$+ e_t(1 - \beta_x^*)E^*(Y_t^* + A_{t-1}^*, r_t) = e_t Y_t^*, \tag{4.21}$$

$$M(Y_t - T_t + A_{t-1}, r_t) = M, \tag{4.22}$$

$$M^*(Y_t^* + A_{t-1}, r_t) = M^*. \tag{4.23}$$

Equations (4.20) and (4.21) are the goods-market equilibrium conditions (analogous to equations 4.5 and 4.6), and equations (4.22) and (4.23) are the domestic and foreign money-market equilibrium conditions, where M and M^* denote the supplies of domestic and foreign money. In contrast with the fixed exchange-rate system in which each country's money supply was determined endogenously, here it is determined *exogenously* by the monetary authorities. We also note that by Walras's law the world market equilibrium condition for bonds has been left out.

Finally, it is noteworthy that the value of securities may be expressed in terms of domestic or foreign currency units. Accordingly, the domestic-currency value of private-sector debt, B_t^p, can be expressed in units of foreign currency to yield $B_{ft}^p = B_t^p/e_t$. Arbitrage ensures that the expected rates of return on securities of different currency denomination are equalized. Accordingly, if r_t and r_{ft} are, respectively, the rates of interest on domestic- and foreign-currency-denominated bonds, then $1 + r_t = (\tilde{e}_{t+1}/e_t)(1 + r_{ft})$, where $\tilde{e}_{t+1}$ denotes the expected future exchange rate. By equating r_t to r_{ft}, the system (4.20) through (4.22) embodies the assumption of static exchange-rate expectations and perfect capital mobility. In appendix B we return to the issue of exchange-rate expectations.

Fiscal Policies in a Small Country

Analogously with our procedure in the analysis of fiscal policies under fixed exchange rates, we start the analysis of flexible exchange rates with an examination of the effects of fiscal policies in a small country facing a given world rate of interest, $\overline{r}_f$, and a given foreign demand for its goods, $\overline{D}^*$. The equilibrium conditions for the small country state that world demand for its output equals domestic GDP and that the domestic demand for money equals the supply. In contrast with the situation prevailing under a fixed exchange-rate regime where the monetary authorities, committed to peg the exchange rate, do not control the domestic money supply, under a flexible exchange-rate regime the supply of money is a policy instrument controlled by the monetary authorities.

The goods- and money-market equilibrium conditions are

$$(1 - \beta_m)E(Y_t - T_t + A_{t-1}, \overline{r}_f) + (1 - \beta_m^g)G + e_t\overline{D}^* = Y_t, \quad (4.20a)$$

$$M(Y_t - T_t + A_{t-1}, \overline{r}_f) = M, \quad (4.22a)$$

where

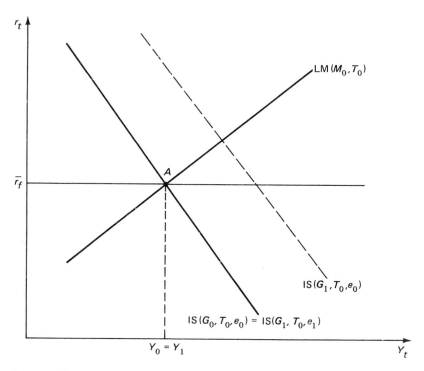

Figure 4.6
The short-run effects of a unit debt-financed rise in government spending under flexible exchange rates: the small-country case. Data: $B^p_{f,-1} = 0$.

$$A_{t-1} = M_{t-1} - (1 + \bar{r}_f)e_t B^p_{f,t-1}.$$

As indicated, the valuation of the foreign-currency-denominated debt commitment, $(1 + \bar{r}_f)B^p_{f,t-1}$, employs the current exchange rate, e_t. These equilibrium conditions determine the short-run values of output and the exchange rate, and for comparison we recall that under the fixed exchange-rate regime the money supply rather than the exchange-rate was endogenously determined.

The equilibrium of the system is exhibited in figure 4.6. The downward-sloping IS schedule shows the goods-market equilibrium condition (4.20a). It is drawn for given values of government spending, taxes, and the exchange rate (representing the terms of trade). The upward-sloping LM schedule portrays the money-market equilibrium condition (4.22a). It is drawn for given values of the money supply, the exchange rate, and taxes. The initial equilibrium obtains at point A at which the rate of interest equals the world rate, $\bar{r}_f$, and the level of output is Y_0. The endogenously determined exchange rate associated with this equilibrium is e_0. It is relevant to note that in this system if the initial debt $B^p_{f,t-1}$ is zero, the LM schedule does not depend on the exchange rate and the level of output is determined exclusively by the money-market equilibrium condition, whereas (given the equilibrium level of output) the equilibrium exchange rate is determined by the goods-market equilibrium condition. This case underlies figure 4.6. Again a comparison with the fixed exchange-rate system is relevant. There, the equilibrium money stock is determined by the money-market equilibrium condition, whereas the equilibrium level of output is determined by the goods-market equilibrium condition.

Consider the effects of a debt-financed unit rise in government spending from G_0 to G_1, and suppose that the initial debt commitment is zero. At the prevailing levels of output and the exchange rate, this rise in spending creates an excess demand for domestic output and induces a rightward shift of the IS schedule by $(1 - a^g)/(s + a)$ units. This shift is shown in figure 4.6 by the displacement of the IS schedule from the initial position indicated by $IS(G_0, T_0, e_0)$ to the position indicated by $IS(G_1, T_0, e_0)$. Since with zero initial debt the LM schedule is unaffected by the rise in government spending, it is clear that given the world rate of interest, the level of output that clears the money market must remain at Y_0, corresponding to the initial equilibrium indicated by point A. To restore the initial equilibrium in the goods market, the exchange rate must fall (i.e., the domestic currency must appreciate). The induced improvement in the terms of trade lowers the world demand for domestic output and induces a leftward shift of the IS schedule. The goods market clears when the exchange rate falls to e_1 so that the IS schedule indicated by $IS(G_1, T_0, e_1)$ also goes through point A. We conclude that under flexible exchange rates with zero initial debt, a debt-financed fiscal policy loses its potency to alter the level of economic activity; its full effects are absorbed by changes in the exchange rate (the terms of trade).

Consider next the effects of a tax-financed unit rise in government

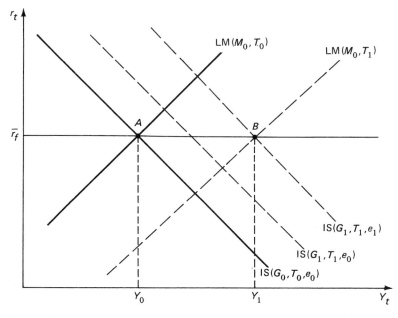

Figure 4.7
The short-run effects of a unit tax-financed rise in government spending under flexible exchange rates: the small-country case. Data: $B^p_{f,-1} = 0$.

spending from G_0 to G_1, shown in figure 4.7. In that case, at the prevailing levels of output and the exchange rate, the excess demand for domestic output induces a rightward displacement of the IS schedule by $1 - a^g/(s + a)$ units to the position indicated by $IS(G_1, T_1, e_0)$. In addition the unit rise in taxes lowers disposable income by one unit and reduces the demand for money. To maintain money-market equilibrium at the given world rate of interest, the level of output must rise by one unit so as to restore the initial level of disposable income. Thus the LM schedule shifts to the right from its initial position indicated by $LM(M_0, T_0)$ to the position indicated by $LM(M_0, T_1)$. With a zero level of initial debt (the case assumed in the figure), the LM schedule does not depend on the value of the exchange rate, and the new equilibrium obtains at point B, where the level of output rises by one unit from Y_0 to Y_1. Since at the initial exchange rate the horizontal displacement of the IS schedule is less than unity (as long as government spending falls in part on imported goods), it follows that at the level of output that clears the money market there is an excess supply of goods. This excess supply is eliminated through a rise in the exchange rate (i.e., a depreciation of the domestic currency) from e_0 to e_1. This deterioration in the terms of trade raises the world demand for domestic output and induces a rightward shift of the IS schedule to the position indicated by IS(G_1, T_1, e_1). We conclude that under flexible exchange rates with zero initial debt, the tax-financed rise in government spending regains its full potency in effecting the level of economic activity.

Up to this point we have assumed that the initial debt position was zero. As a result the only channel through which the exchange rate influenced the system was through altering the domestic-currency value of the exogenously given foreign demand, $\bar{D}^*$. In general, however, with a nonzero level of initial debt, $B^p_{f,t-1}$ (denominated in units of foreign currency), the change in the exchange rate also alters the domestic currency value of the initial debt, and thereby of the initial assets, A_{t-1}. The revaluation of the debt commitment constitutes an additional channel through which the exchange rate influences the economic system. As a result the demand for money, and thereby the LM schedule, also depend on the exchange rate.

To appreciate the role played by debt-revaluation effects, we examine in figure 4.8 the implications of a nonzero level of initial debt. The various IS and LM schedules shown in the figure correspond to alternative assumptions concerning the level of initial debt $B^p_{f,-1}$; the rest of the arguments governing the position of the schedules are suppressed for simplicity. The initial equilibrium is shown by point A, and the solid schedules along which $B^p_{f,-1} = 0$ correspond to the cases analyzed in figures 4.6 and 4.7. With a positive value of initial debt, a rise in the exchange rate lowers the value of assets and lowers the demand for money. Restoration of money-market equilibrium requires a compensating rise in output. As a result in that case the LM schedule is positively sloped. By a similar reasoning, a negative value of initial debt corresponds to a negatively sloped LM schedule. The level of initial debt also

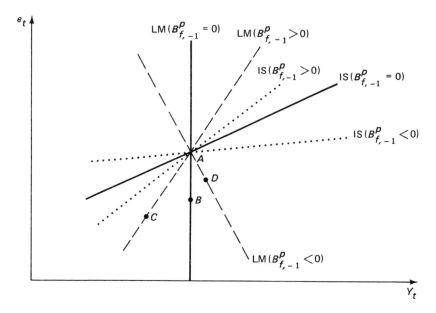

Figure 4.8
The short-run effect of a unit debt-financed rise in government spending under flexible exchange rates: the debt-revaluation effect

influences the slope of the IS schedule. As shown in the figure, using similar considerations, the IS schedule is steeper than the bench-mark schedule (around point A) if $B^p_{f,-1} > 0$, and vice versa.

We can now use this figure to illustrate the possible implications of the initial debt position for the effects of fiscal policy. A debt-financed fiscal expansion induces a rightward shift of the IS schedule and leaves the LM schedule intact. The short-run equilibrium of the system is changed from point A to point B if the level of initial debt is zero, to point C if the level of initial debt is positive, and to point D if this level is negative. Thus the debt revaluation effects critically determine whether a debt-financed rise in government spending is contractionary or expansionary.

Using the system (4.20a) and (4.22a), the changes in the level of output are

$$\frac{dY_t}{dG} = \frac{(1 - a^g)(1 + \bar{r}_f)B^p_{f,t-1}}{(1 + \bar{r}_f)B^p_{f,t-1} - \bar{D}^*}, \quad \text{for } dT_t = 0, \tag{4.24}$$

$$\frac{dY_t}{dG} = 1 - \frac{a^g(1 + \bar{r}_f)B^p_{f,t-1}}{(1 + \bar{r}_f)B^p_{f,t-1} - \bar{D}^*}, \quad \text{for } dT_t = dG. \tag{4.25}$$

Likewise, the induced changes in the exchange rates are

$$\frac{de_t}{dG} = \frac{1 - a^g}{(1 + \bar{r}_f)B^p_{f,t-1} - \bar{D}^*}, \quad \text{for } dT_t = 0, \tag{4.26}$$

and

$$\frac{de_t}{dG} = \frac{-a^g}{(1 + \bar{r}_f)B^p_{f,t-1} - \bar{D}^*}, \quad \text{for } dT_t = dG. \tag{4.27}$$

These results highlight the role played by the debt-revaluation effect of exchange-rate changes. Specifically, as is evident from equations (4.24) and (4.25), a rise in government spending may be contractionary if the initial debt commitment is positive. If, however, the private sector is initially a net creditor, then, independent of its means of finance, government spending must be expansionary. In the benchmark case shown in figures 4.6 and 4.7, the initial debt position is zero, a tax finance is expansionary (yielding the conventional balanced-budget multiplier of unity), and a debt finance is not. The key mechanism responsible for this result is the high degree of capital mobility underlying the fixity of the rate of interest faced by the small country. With the given rate of interest and with a given money supply, there is in the short run a unique value of disposable income that clears the money market as long as the initial debt commitment is zero. Hence in this case a rise in taxes is expansionary, and a rise in government spending is neutral.

A comparison between the exchange-rate effects of government spending also reveals the critical importance of the means of finance and of the debt-revaluation effect. In general, for the given money supply the direction of the change in the exchange rate induced by a rise in government spending depends on whether the government finances its spending through taxes or through debt issue. If the initial debt commitment falls short of the (exogenously given) foreign demand for domestic output, then a debt-financed rise in government spending appreciates the currency, whereas a tax-financed rise in government spending depreciates the currency. The opposite holds if the initial debt commitment exceeds exports.

The foregoing analysis determined the short-run effects of government spending. We proceed to analyze the long-run effects of these policies. The long-run equilibrium conditions are shown in equations (4.28) through (4.30). These equations are the counterpart to the long-run fixed exchange-rate system (4.12) through (4.14). Accordingly,

$$E[Y - T + M - (1 + \bar{r}_f)eB_f^p, \bar{r}_f] = Y - \bar{r}_f eB_f^p - T, \tag{4.28}$$

$$(1 - \beta_m)E[Y - T + M - (1 + \bar{r}_f)eB_f^p, \bar{r}_f]$$
$$+ (1 - \beta_m^g)G + e\bar{D}^* = Y, \tag{4.29}$$

$$M[Y - T + M - (1 + \bar{r}_f)eB_f^p, \bar{r}_f] = M. \tag{4.30}$$

To set the stage for the analysis, consider first the bench-mark case for which the initial equilibrium was associated with a zero private-sector debt. For this case the long run is analyzed in. figure 4.9. The $CA = 0$ schedule portrays combinations of private-sector debt and output that yield equality between spending and income, and thereby satisfy equation (4.28). In view of the government budget constraint shown in equation (4.15), this equality between private-sector income and spending also implies current-account balance. The MM schedule portrays combinations of debt and output that yield money-market equilibrium, and thereby satisfy equation (4.30). Around zero private-sector debt, both of these schedules are independent of the exchange rate. The slope of the $CA = 0$ schedule is $-s/e[1 - s(1 + \bar{r}_f)]$. Analogously to the previous discussion of the long-run equilibrium under fixed exchange rates, this slope is assumed negative for stability. The slope of the MM schedule is $1/(1 + \bar{r}_f)e$. It indicates that a unit rise in long-run private-sector debt raises debt commitment (principal plus debt service) by $(1 + \bar{r}_f)e$ and lowers the demand for money. To offset the reduction in disposable resources and restore the demand for money to its initial level, output must be raised by $(1 + \bar{r}_f)e$ units.

The initial long-run equilibrium is shown by point A, at which the level of private-sector debt is assumed to be zero and the level of

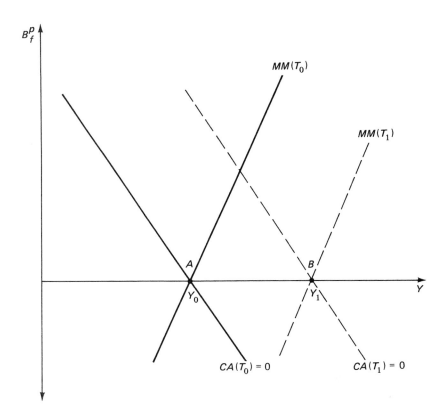

Figure 4.9
The long-run effects of a unit rise in government spending under flexible
exchange rates: the small-country case

output is Y_0. As is evident from equations (4.28) and (4.30), changes in the levels of government spending and government debt do not alter the $CA = 0$ schedule and the MM schedule. It follows that with zero private-sector debt a debt-financed rise in government spending does not alter the long-run equilibrium value of private sector debt indicated by point A in figure 4.9. In this long-run equilibrium the level of output remains unchanged, and the currency appreciates to the level shown in the short-run analysis of figure 4.6.

A rise in taxes alters both the $CA = 0$ and the MM schedules. As is evident from equations (4.28) and (4.30), a rise in output that keeps disposable income unchanged (at the given zero level of private-sector debt) maintains the initial current-account balance as well as money-market equilibrium intact. Thus a tax-financed unit rise in government spending induces a unit rightward displacement of both the $CA = 0$ and the MM schedules and yields a new long-run equilibrium at point B. At this point private-sector debt remains at its initial zero level. Also the level of output rises to Y_1, and the currency depreciates to e_1, as shown in the short-run analysis of figure 4.7.

The preceding discussion shows that under flexible exchange rates with zero initial private-sector debt, the long-run and the short-run effects of fiscal policies coincide. This characteristic is in contrast to the one obtained for fixed exchange rates, where the long-run effects of fiscal policies differ from the corresponding short-run effects. In interpreting these results, we note that due to the nontradability of national monies under a flexible exchange-rate regime, the mechanism of adjustment to fiscal policies does not permit instantaneous changes in the composition of assets through swaps of interest-bearing assets for national money in the world capital markets. As a result the only mechanism by which private-sector debt can change is through savings. Since with zero initial private-sector debt both debt-financed and tax-financed government spending do not alter disposable income (as seen from equations 4.24 and 4.25), it follows that these policies do not affect private-sector saving. Hence, if the initial position was that of a long-run equilibrium with zero savings and zero debt, the instantaneous short-run equilibrium following the rise in government spending is also characterized by zero savings.

This implies that the economy converges immediately to its new long-run equilibrium.

The foregoing analysis of the long-run consequences of government spending abstracted from the debt-revaluation effect arising from exhange-rate changes. In general, if in the initial equilibrium the level of private-sector debt differs from zero, then the debt-revaluation effect breaks the coincidence between the short- and the long-run fiscal policy multipliers. Using the system (4.28) through (4.30), the long-run effects of a debt-financed rise in government spending are

$$\frac{dY}{dG} = 0, \qquad \text{for } dT = 0, \tag{4.31}$$

$$\frac{dB_f^p}{dG} = \frac{(1 - a^g)B_f^p}{e\bar{D}^*}, \quad \text{for } dT = 0, \tag{4.32}$$

$$\frac{de}{dG} = -\frac{(1 - a^g)}{\bar{D}^*}, \quad \text{for } dT = 0. \tag{4.33}$$

Likewise, the long-run effects of a balanced-budget rise in government spending are

$$\frac{dY}{dG} = 1, \qquad \text{for } dT = dG, \tag{4.34}$$

$$\frac{dB_f^p}{dG} = -\frac{a^g B_f^p}{e\bar{D}^*}, \quad \text{for } dT = dG, \tag{4.35}$$

$$\frac{de}{dG} = \frac{a^g}{\bar{D}^*}, \qquad \text{for } dT = dG. \tag{4.36}$$

These results show that independent of the debt-revaluation effects, a rise in government spending does not alter the long-run level of output if it is debt financed, but the same rise in government spending raises the long-run level of output by a unit multiplier if it is tax financed. Thus, in both cases the long-run level of disposable income, $Y - T$, is independent of government spending. The results also show that if government spending is debt financed, and if the initial private-sector debt was positive, then in the long run it rises while the currency appreciates. The opposite holds for the case in which government spending is tax financed.

In comparing the extent of the long-run changes in private-sector debt with the corresponding changes in the exchange rate, we note that the *value* of debt, eB_f^p (measured in units of domestic output) remains unchanged. This invariance facilitates the interpretation of the long-run multipliers. Accordingly, consider the long-run equilibrium system (4.28) through (4.30), and suppose that government spending is debt financed. In that case as is evident from the money-market equilibrium condition (4.30), the equilibrium level of output does not change as long as the money supply, taxes, and the value of the debt commitment are given. Since, however, the rise in government spending creates an excess demand for domestic output, it is seen from equation (4.29) that the currency must appreciate (i.e., e must fall) so as to lower the value of foreign demand, $e\bar{D}^*$, and thereby maintain the same equilibrium output. Obviously, since e falls, (the absolute value of) private sector debt, B_f^p, must rise by the same proportion so as to maintain the product eB_f^p unchanged. Finally, these changes ensure that the zero-saving condition (4.28) is also satisfied. A similar interpretation can be given to the effects of a tax-financed rise in government spending, except that in this case the level of output rises in line with the rise in taxes so as to keep disposable income unchanged.

A comparison between these long-run effects and the corresponding short-run effects shown in equations (4.24) and (4.25) reveals that the relative magnitudes of these multipliers depend on the initial debt position. For example, if the initial debt commitment is positive but smaller than export earnings, then the short-run multiplier of tax finance is positive and larger than unity. In this case the long-run multipliers are more moderate than the corresponding short-run multipliers. If, however, the initial debt commitment exceeds export earnings, then the short-run debt-finance multiplier is positive (in contrast with the long-run multiplier), and the short-run tax-finance multiplier is smaller than unity, and could even be negative (in contrast with the unitary long-run balanced-budget multiplier).

Fiscal Policies in a Two-Country World

In this section we extend the analysis of the small-country case to the two-country model outlined in equations (4.20) through (4.23). To develop a diagrammatic apparatus useful for the analysis of fiscal policies, we proceed in three steps. First, we trace the combinations of domestic and foreign output levels that clear each country's goods market, incorporating the conditions of market clearing in the two national money markets (which under flexible exchange rates are the two nontradable assets). Second, we trace the combinations of domestic and foreign output levels that bring about a money-market equilibrium in each country and, at the same time, yield equality between the domestic and the foreign rates of interest, thereby conforming with the assumption of perfect capital mobility. Finally, in the third step, we find the unique combination of domestic and foreign levels of output that satisfy simultaneously the considerations underlying the first two steps.

Using the domestic money-market equilibrium condition (4.22), we can express the domestic money-market-clearing rate of interest, r_t, as a positive function of disposable resources, $Y_t - T_t + A_{t-1}$, and as a negative function of the domestic money stock, M; that is, $r_t = r(Y_t - T_t + A_{t-1}, M)$. Applying a similar procedure to the foreign country, we can express the foreign money-market-clearing rate of interest, r_t^*, as a function of foreign disposable resources and money stock; that is, $r_t^* = r^*(Y_t^* + A_{t-1}^*, M^*)$, where $A_{t-1}^* = M_{t-1}^* + R_{t-1}B_{t-1}^p/e_t$. By substituting these money-market-clearing rates of interest into the goods-market equilibrium conditions (4.20) and (4.21), we obtain the reduced-form equilibrium conditions (4.37) and (4.38):

$$(1 - \beta_m)\tilde{E}(Y_t - T_t + A_{t-1}, M) + (1 - \beta_m^g)G$$

$$+ e_t\beta_x^*\tilde{E}^*(Y_t^* + A_{t-1}^*, M^*) = Y_t, \qquad (4.37)$$

$$\beta_m\tilde{E}(Y_t - T_t + A_{t-1}, M) + \beta_m^g G$$

$$+ e_t(1 - \beta_x^*)\tilde{E}^*(Y_t^* + A_{t-1}^*, M^*) = e_t Y_t^*, \qquad (4.38)$$

where a tilde (˜) indicates a reduced-form function incorporating the

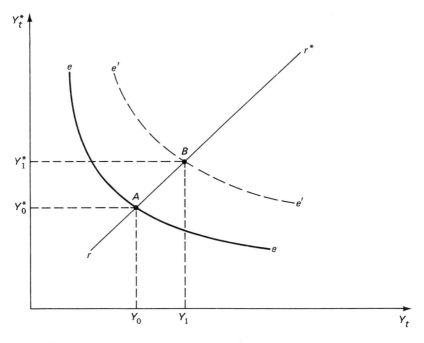

Figure 4.10
A debt-financed unit rise in government spending under flexible exchange
rates: the two-country case. Data: $IM_0 = IM_0^*$, $B_{f,-1}^p = 0$.

money-market equilibrium conditions. For each and every value of
the exchange rate, e_t, equations (4.37) and (4.38) yield the equilibrium
combination of domestic and foreign output that clears the world
market for both goods. The schedule ee in figure 4.10 traces these
equilibrium output levels for alternative values of the exchange rate.
The detailed derivation of this schedule is provided in appendix B,
where it is shown that around balanced-trade equilibria with a zero
initial private-sector debt (so that exchange-rate changes do not
exert revaluation effects), this schedule is negatively sloped. In
general, the ee schedule is negatively sloped if a rise in the exchange
rate (a deterioration in the terms of trade) raises the world demand
for domestic output and lowers the world demand for foreign output, allowing for the proper adjustments in each country's rate of
interest so as to clear the national money market.

So far we have not yet incorporated the constraints imposed by
the perfect international mobility of capital. To incorporate this

constraint, the national money-market-clearing rates of interest, r_t and r_t^*, must be equal. This equally implies that

$$r(Y_t - T_t + A_{t-1}, M) = r^*(Y_t^* + A_{t-1}^*, M^*). \qquad (4.39)$$

The combinations of domestic and foreign output levels conforming with the perfect capital-mobility requirement are portrayed by the rr^* schedule in figure 4.10. With a zero level of initial debt (so that the debt revaluation effects induced by exchange-rate changes are absent) this schedule is positively sloped since a rise in domestic output raises the demand for domestic money and the domestic rate of interest; international interest-rate equalization is restored through a rise in foreign output that raises the foreign demand for money and the foreign rate of interest.

The short-run equilibrium is indicated by point A in figure 4.10. At this point both goods markets clear, both national money markets clear, and the rates of interest are equalized internationally. The levels of output corresponding to this equilibrium are Y_0 and Y_0^*.

A debt-financed unit rise in government spending alters the position of the goods-market equilibrium schedule ee but does not impact on the capital-market equilibrium schedule, rr^*. It is shown in appendix B that for an initial trade-balance equilibrium with zero debt, the ee schedule shifts to the right by $1/\tilde{s}$ units. The new equilibrium is indicated by point B in figure 4.10. Thus (in the absence of revaluation effects) in the new short-run equilibrium both the domestic and the foreign levels of output rise from Y_0 and Y_0^* to Y_1 and Y_1^*, respectively.

For the given supply of money and for the higher level of output (which raises the demand for money), money-market equilibrium obtains at a higher rate of interest (which restores money demand to its initial level). Finally, it is shown in appendix B that the exchange-rate effects of the debt-financed rise in government spending are not clear cut, reflecting transfer-problem criteria. These criteria reflect the relative pressures on the rates of interest in the domestic and foreign money markets induced by the changes in world demands for domestic and foreign outputs. If these pressures tend to raise the domestic rate of interest above the foreign rate, then the domestic currency must appreciate so as to lower the demand for domestic

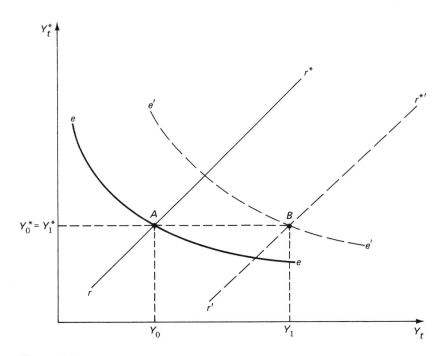

Figure 4.11
A tax-financed unit rise in government spending under flexible exchange rates:
the two-country case. Data: $IM_0 = IM_0^*$, $B_{f,-1}^p = 0$.

output and reduce the upward pressure on the domestic rate of interest. The opposite follows in the converse circumstances. But, if the behavioral parameters of the two private sectors are equal to each other, then the domestic currency must appreciate.

A tax-financed unit rise in government spending alters the positions of both the ee and the rr^* schedules. As is evident by inspection of equations (4.37) through (4.39), both schedules shift to the right by one unit. This case is illustrated in figure 4.11 where the initial equilibrium is indicated by point A and the new short-run equilibrium by point B. At the new equilibrium the domestic level of output rises by one unit so that disposable income remains unchanged. With unchanged levels of disposable income the demand for money is not altered, and the initial equilibrium rate of interest remains intact. As a result the initial equilibrium in the foreign economy is not disturbed, and the foreign level of output remains unchanged. Finally, in order to eliminate the excess supply in the domestic-goods market arising from the rise in domestic output and the unchanged level of disposable income, the currency must depreciate so as to raise the domestic-currency value of the given foreign demand. It follows that in the absence of revaluation effects, the flexible exchange-rate regime permits a full insulation of the foreign economy from the consequences of the domestic tax-financed fiscal policies. The more general results allowing for revaluation effects are provided in the appendix B. Analogously to the procedure adopted in the fixed exchange-rate case, we do not analyze explicitly the long-run equilibrium of the two-country world under the flexible exchange-rate regime. The formal equilibrium system applicable for such an analysis is presented in appendix B.

4.4 Summary and Overview

In this chapter we analyzed the effects of government spending under fixed and flexible exchange-rate regimes. Throughout we have assumed that the world capital markets are highly integrated so that capital is perfectly mobile internationally. To focus on the pure effects of fiscal policies, we assumed that there is no active monetary policy. In particular, we abstracted from money-financed government spending. Accordingly, we analyzed the short- and long-run consequences of debt-financed and of tax-financed changes in government spending. In this context we focused on the effects of fiscal policies on the levels of output, debt, and the rate of interest under the two alternative exchange-rate regimes. In addition, for the fixed exchange-rate regime, we examined the induced changes in the money supply, and for the flexible exchange-rate regime, we determined the induced change in the exchange rate.

The short- and long-run effects of a unit debt and tax-financed rise in government spending for a small country facing a fixed world rate of interest are summarized in table 4.1. In this table we show the various multipliers applicable to the fixed as well as to the flexible exchange-rate regimes. The output multipliers under the fixed exchange-rate regime are the typical simple foreign-trade multipliers. These results are of course expected since the rate of interest is

Table 4.1
The short- and long-run effects of a unit rise in government spending under fixed and flexible exchange rates: the small-country case

	Debt financed		Tax financed	
	Short run	Long run	Short run	Long run
Fixed exchange rates: effects on				
Y	$\dfrac{1-a^g}{s+a}$	$\dfrac{1-a^g}{\Delta}[1-s-\bar{r}_f(s-M_y)]$	$1-\dfrac{a^g}{s+a}$	$1-\dfrac{a^g}{\Delta}[1-s-\bar{r}_f(s-M_y)]$
$B^p_{f,t-1}$	0	$-\dfrac{1-a^g}{\Delta}(s-M_y)$	0	$\dfrac{a^g}{\Delta}(s-M_y)$
M	$\dfrac{(1-a^g)M_y}{s+a}$	$\dfrac{1-a^g}{\Delta}M_y$	$\dfrac{-a^g}{s+a}M_y$	$-\dfrac{a^g}{\Delta}M_y$
Flexible exchange rates: effects on				
Y	$\dfrac{(1-a^g)R_f B^p_{f,t-1}}{R_f B^p_{f,t-1}-\bar{D}^*}$	0	$1-\dfrac{a^g R_f B^p_{f,t-1}}{R_f B^p_{f,t-1}-\bar{D}^*}$	1
$B^p_{f,t-1}$	0	$\dfrac{(1-a^g)B^p_f}{e\bar{D}^*}$	0	$-\dfrac{a^g B^p_f}{e\bar{D}^*}$
e	$\dfrac{(1-a^g)}{R_f B^p_{f,t-1}-\bar{D}^*}$	$-\dfrac{(1-a^g)}{\bar{D}^*}$	$\dfrac{-a^g}{R_f B^p_{f,t-1}-\bar{D}^*}$	$\dfrac{a^g}{\bar{D}^*}$

Note: $\bar{D}^*$ denotes export earnings measured in units of foreign currency, $R_f = 1 + \bar{r}_f$ and $\Delta = a - \bar{r}_f(s-M_y)$. $\Delta > 0$ under the assumption that a rise in income worsens the current account of the balance of payments. The term $1 - s - \bar{r}_f(s-M_y) > 0$ for stability.

exogenously given to the small country. The fixity of the rate of interest implies that the typical crowding-out mechanism induced by changes in the rate of interest are not present.

Under flexible exchange rates the short-run output multipliers of fiscal policies depend crucially on the debt-revaluation effect induced by exchange-rate changes. Indeed, in the absence of such an effect (as would be the case if the initial debt position is zero) fiscal policies lose their capacity to alter disposable income. Accordingly, with debt finance the output multiplier is zero, and with tax finance the corresponding multiplier is unity. In general, however, the signs and magnitudes of the *short-run* output multipliers depend on the size of the initial debt. In contrast, these considerations do not influence the *long-run* output multipliers. As seen in the table, with perfect capital mobility and flexible exchange rates, the long-run value of disposable income cannot be affected by fiscal policies.

One of the important points underscored by the results reported in table 4.1 is the critical dependence of the direction of change in the key variables on the means of fiscal finance. Specifically, a shift from a debt finance to a tax finance reverses the signs of the multipliers of B_f^p, M, and e.

For example, a tax-financed rise in government spending under a fixed exchange-rate regime induces a balance-of-payments deficit and reduces both the short- and the long-run money holdings. On the other hand, a similar rise in government spending that is debt-financed induces a surplus in the balance of payments and raises money holdings in the short run as well as in the long run. Likewise, under a flexible exchange-rate regime the tax-financed rise in government spending depreciates the long-run value of the currency, whereas the debt-financed rise in government spending appreciates the long-run value of the currency. As indicated earlier, a similar reversal in the direction of the change in the exchange rate also pertains to the short-run, but whether the currency depreciates or appreciates in the short run depends on the size of the debt which in turn governs the debt-revaluation effect.

To study the characteristics of the international transmission mechanism, we extended the analysis of the small-country case to a two-country model of the world economy. The new channel of

Table 4.2
The direction of the short-run effects of a rise in government spending under fixed and flexible exchange rates: the two-country world

	Debt financed	Tax financed
Fixed exchange rates: effects on		
Y	+ (for small H_r)	+ (for $a^g \leq a$)
Y^*	+ (for small F_r)	+
r	+	+ (for $A > 0$) − (for $A < 0$)
M	+ (for $B + C < 0$) − (for $B + C > 0$)	−
Flexible exchange rates: effects on		
Y	+	+
Y^*	+	0
r	+	0
e	+ (for $\tilde{B} > 0$) − (for $\tilde{B} < 0$)	+

Note: The signs indicated in the flexible exchange-rate part of the table are applicable to the case of an initial equilibrium with balanced trade and zero initial debt. H_r and F_r denote, respectively, the negative effect of the rate of interest on the world demand for domestic and foreign goods, $A = s/M_y - s^*/M_y^*$, $B = \bar{e}(M_y/M_r)[a^* + s^*(1 - a^g)] - (M_y^*/M_r^*)(a + sa^g)$, and $\tilde{B} = e_t(M_y/M_r)[\tilde{a}^* + \tilde{s}^*(1 - a^g)] - (M_y^*/M_r^*)(\tilde{a} + \tilde{s}a^g)$, correspond, respectively, to the fixed ·and flexible exchange-rate regimes and $C = M_y M_y^* M_r M_r^* [F_r(1 - a^g) - H_r a^g]$.

transmission is the world rate of interest which is determined in the unified world capital market. Table 4.2 summarizes the short-run effects of fiscal policies under the two alternative exchange-rate regimes. To avoid a tedious taxonomy, the summary results for the flexible exchange rates reported in the table are confined to the case in which the twin revaluation effects—debt revaluation and trade-balance revaluation—induced by exchange-rate changes are absent; accordingly, it is assumed that the initial debt is zero and that the initial equilibrium obtains with a balanced trade.

As shown, independent of the exchange-rate regime, a debt-financed rise in government spending raises the world rate of interest. Under the flexible exchange-rate regime the debt-financed rise in government spending stimulates demand for both domestic and foreign goods and results in an expansion of both outputs. Thus in this case the international transmission of the rise in government spending, measured by comovements of domestic and foreign outputs, is positive. On the other hand, under a fixed exchange-rate regime the rise in the world rate of interest may offset the direct effect of government spending on aggregate demand and may result in lower levels of output. But, if the (negative) interest-rate effect on aggregate demand is relatively weak, then both domestic and foreign outputs rise, thereby resulting in a positive international transmission. Finally, we note that there is no presumption about the direction of change in money holdings (under fixed exchange rates) and in the exchange rate (under flexible exchange rates) in response to the debt-financed fiscal expansion. As indicated, depending on the relative magnitudes of the domestic and foreign saving and import propensities, and the domestic and foreign sensitivities of money demand with respect to changes in the rate of interest and income, the balance of payments may be in a deficit or in a surplus, and the currency may depreciate or appreciate.

The results in table 4.2 also highlight the significant implication of alternative means of budgetary finance. Indeed, in contrast with debt finance, a tax-financed rise in government spending under a flexible exchange-rate regime leaves the world rate of interest unchanged. raises domestic output, and depreciates the currency. The reduction in the domestic private-sector demand for foreign output, induced by the depreciation of the currency, precisely offsets the increased demand induced by the rise in government spending. As a result, foreign output remains intact, and the flexible exchange rate regime fully insulates the foreign economy from the domestic tax-financed fiscal policy. In this case the analysis of the two-country world economy reduces to the one carried out for the small-country case. Therefore the long-run multipliers for the two countries operating under flexible exchange rates coincide with the short-run multipliers, the domestic short- and long-run output multipliers are unity, and the corresponding foreign output multipliers are zero.

In contrast with the flexible exchange-rate regime in which the currency depreciates to the extent needed to maintain world demand for (and thereby the equilibrium level of) foreign output, the fixed exchange-rate regime does not contain this insulating mechanism. As a result the tax-financed rise in the domestic government spending raises the world demand for (and thereby the equilibrium level of) foreign output. On the other hand, depending on the relative magnitude of the domestic-government import propensity, the domestic level of output may rise or fall. If, however, the government import propensity does not exceed the corresponding private-sector propensity, then domestic output rises, and the international transmission, measured by comovements of domestic and foreign outputs, is positive. Finally, since at the prevailing rate of interest domestic disposable income falls and foreign disposable income rises (as shown in chapter 2), these changes in disposable incomes alter the world demand for money and necessitate equilibrating changes in the world rate of interest. As shown in table 4.2, the change in the world demand for money (at the prevailing rate of interest) reflects a transfer-problem criterion. If the ratio of the domestic saving to hoarding propensities, s/M_y, exceeds the corresponding foreign ratio, $s^*/M_{y^*}^*$, then the international redistribution of disposable income raises the world demand for money and necessitates a rise in the world rate of interest. The opposite holds if s/M_y falls short of $s^*/M_{y^*}^*$. Independent, however, of the direction of the change in the interest rate, the tax-financed rise in government spending must worsen the balance of payments and lower the short-run equilibrium money holdings.

Throughout this chapter we assume that expectations are static. Since under a flexible exchange-rate regime the actual exchange rates do change, the assumption that exchange-rate expectations are static results in expectation errors during the period of transition toward the long-run equilibrium. The incorporation of a consistent expectations scheme introduces an additional mechanism governing the short-run behavior. Aspects of this mechanism are examined in appendix B.

We conclude this summary with an overview of the income-expenditure model analyzed in chapters 2 through 4. The issues on which we focus are chosen so as to provide the motivation for, and the link to, the formulations and analyses carried out in the subsequent parts of the book.

A key characteristic of the formulation of the income-expenditure model used in this part of the book is the lack of solid micro-economic foundations underlying the behavior of the private and the public sectors, and the absence of an explicit rationale for the holdings of zero interest-bearing money in the presence of safe interest-bearing bonds. The latter issue is of relevance in view of the central role played by monetary flows in the international adjustment mechanism. Furthermore no attention was given to the intertemporal budget constraints, and the behavior of both the private and the public sectors was not forward-looking in a consistent manner. As a result there was no mechanism ensuring that the patterns of spending, debt accumulation, and money hoarding (which are the key elements governing the equilibrium dynamics of the economic system) are consistent with the relevant economic constraints. The implication of this shortcoming is that in determining the level and composition of spending, saving, and asset holdings, the private sector does not incorporate explicitly the intertemporal consequences of government policies.

To illustrate the significance of this issue, consider a debt-financed rise in current government spending. A proper formulation of the government's intertemporal budget constraint must recognize that to service the debt and maintain its solvency, the government must accompany this current fiscal expansion by either cutting down future spending or raising future (ordinary or inflationary) taxes. Furthermore a proper specification of the private sector's behavior must allow for the fact that the forward-looking individuals may recognize the future consequences of current government policies and incorporate these expected consequences into their current as well as planned future spending, saving, and asset holdings.

The neglect of the intertemporal budget constraints and of the consequences of forward-looking behavior consistent with these constraints are among the main deficiencies of the income-expenditure model as formulated in this part of the book. In the subsequent parts of the book we rectify these shortcomings. In doing so, we develop a unified model that is derived from optimizing behavior consistent with the relevant temporal and intertemporal economic constraints. The resulting macroeconomic model, which is grounded upon microeconomic foundations, is capable of dealing with new issues in a consistent manner. Among these issues are the effects of various time patterns of government spending and taxes. We can thus distinguish between temporary and permanent as well as between current and future policies. Likewise, the model is capable of analyzing the macroeconomic consequences of alternative specifications of the tax structure. We can thus distinguish between the effects of different types of taxes (e.g., income taxes, value-added taxes, and international capital flow taxes) used to finance the budget.

In this chapter as in chapter 2 we assumed that producer prices were given and that outputs were demand determined. In this framework nominal exchange-rate changes amounted to changes in the terms of trade. As a result the characteristics of the economic system were drastically different across alternative exchange-rate regimes. Throughout the subsequent parts of the book we relax the fixed-price assumption and allow for complete price flexibility. With this flexibility prices are always at their market-clearing equilibrium levels. Accordingly, changes in the terms of trade induced by equilibrium changes in prices trigger an adjustment mechanism that is analogous to the one triggered by nominal exchange-rate changes in the income-expenditure model. Therefore, except for our analysis in chapters 14 and 15 which deals explicitly with aspects of the nominal exchange-rate regime, we do not consider issues arising from nominal exchange-rate changes, yet we allow for the effects of terms of trade and real exchange-rate changes on the international adjustment mechanism.

Finally, it is noteworthy that an important feature of the intertemporal approach adopted in the rest of this book is its capability of dealing explicitly with the welfare consequences of economic policies and events. This feature reflects the basic attribute of the macroeconomic model: the economic behavior underlying this model is derived from, and is consistent with, the principles of individual utility maximization. Therefore, in contrast with the traditional approach underlying the discussion in this part of the book, the intertemporal optimizing approach to which we turn next provides a framework suitable for the normative evaluation of international macroeconomic policies.

4.5 Appendix A: Fixed Exchange Rates

Long-Run Equilibrium: The Small-Country Case

The long-run equilibrium conditions are specified by equations (4.12) through (4.15) of the text. Substituting the government budget constraint (4.15) into equations (4.12) through (4.14) yields

$$E[Y - G + M - B^p - \bar{r}_f(B^p + B^g), \bar{r}_f] + G$$

$$= Y - \bar{r}_f(B^p + B^g), \tag{A.1}$$

$$(1 - \beta_m)E[Y - G + M - B^p - \bar{r}_f(B^p + B^g), \bar{r}_f]$$

$$+ (1 - \beta_m^g)G + \bar{e}\bar{D}^* = Y, \tag{A.2}$$

$$M[Y - G + M - B^p - \bar{r}_f(B^p + B^g), \bar{r}_f] = M. \tag{A.3}$$

Equations (A.1) and (A.3) yield the combinations of output and private-sector debt underlying the $CA = 0$ schedule, and equations (A.2) and (A.3) yield the combinations of these variables underlying the YY schedule. To obtain the slope of the $CA = 0$ schedule, we differentiate equations (A.1) and (A.3) and obtain

$$\begin{pmatrix} -s & s(1 + \bar{r}_f) - 1 \\ M_y & -(1 + \bar{r}_f)M_y \end{pmatrix} \begin{pmatrix} dY \\ dB^p \end{pmatrix} = \begin{pmatrix} -(1 - s) \\ 1 - M_y \end{pmatrix} dM, \tag{A.4}$$

where $s = 1 - E_y$ and $a = \beta_m E_y$. Solving (A.4) for dY/dM and dividing the resultant solutions by each other yields the expression for dB^p/dY along the $CA = 0$ schedule. This expression is reported in equation (4.16) of the text.

Likewise differentiating equations (A.2) and (A.3) yields

$$\begin{pmatrix} -(s + a) & -(1 + \bar{r}_f)(1 - s - a) \\ M_y & -(1 + \bar{r}_f)M_y \end{pmatrix} \begin{pmatrix} dY \\ dB^p \end{pmatrix}$$

$$= \begin{pmatrix} -(1 - s - a) \\ 1 - M_y \end{pmatrix} dM. \tag{A.5}$$

Following a similar procedure, we obtain the expression for dB^p/dY along the YY schedule. This expression is reported in equation (4.17) of the text.

To obtain the horizontal displacements of the $CA = 0$ schedule following a balanced-budget rise in government spending, we differentiate equations (A.1) and (A.3), holding B^g and B^p constant. Accordingly, equation (A.1) implies that $(1 - s)(dY - dG + dM) = dY - dG$, and equation (A.3) implies that $dM = M_y(dY - dG)/(1 - M_y)$. Susbstituting the latter expression into the former reveals that $dY/dG = 1$. Thus a unit balanced-budget rise in government spending induces a unit rightward shift of the $CA = 0$ schedule.

Analogously, to obtain the horizontal shift of the YY schedule, we differentiate equations (A.2) and (A.3), holding B^g and B^p constant. Equation (A.2) implies that $(1 - s - a)(dY - dG + dM) + (1 - a^g)dG = dY$, where $a^g = \beta_m^g$, and equation (A.3) implies that $dM = M_y(dY - dG)/(1 - M_y)$. Substituting the latter into the former shows that the horizontal shift of the YY schedule is

$$1 - \frac{(1 - M_y)a^g}{s + a - M_y}.$$

Thus, in contrast with the unit rightward displacement of the $CA = 0$ schedule, the unit balanced-budget rise in government spending shifts the YY schedule to the right by less than one unit. These results underly the diagrammatic analysis in figures 4.2 and 4.3.

The long-run effects of fiscal policies are obtained by differentiating the system (4.12) through (4.14) of the text and solving for the endogenous variables. Accordingly,

$$\begin{pmatrix} -s & s(1 + \bar{r}_f) - 1 & 1 - s \\ -(s + a) & -(1 + \bar{r}_f)(1 - s - a) & 1 - s - a \\ M_y & -(1 + \bar{r}_f)M_y & -(1 - M_y) \end{pmatrix} \begin{pmatrix} dY \\ dB^p \\ dM \end{pmatrix}$$

$$= \begin{pmatrix} 0 \\ -(1 - a^g) \\ 0 \end{pmatrix} dG + \begin{pmatrix} -s \\ 1 - s - a \\ M_y \end{pmatrix} dT. \tag{A.6}$$

Using this system, the long-run effects of a debt-financed rise in government spending (i.e., $dT = 0$) are

$$\frac{dY}{dG} = \frac{1 - a^g}{\Delta}[1 - s - \bar{r}_f(s - M_y)] \geq 0, \quad \text{for } dT_t = 0, \tag{A.7}$$

$$\frac{dB^p}{dG} = -\frac{1 - a^g}{\Delta}(s - M_y) \leq 0, \quad \text{for } dT_t = 0, \tag{A.8}$$

$$\frac{dM}{dG} = \frac{1 - a^g}{\Delta}M_y \geq 0, \quad \text{for } dT_t = 0, \tag{A.9}$$

where $\Delta = a - \bar{r}_f(s - M_y) > 0$ under the assumption that a rise in income worsens the current account of the balance of payments. Correspondingly, the long-run effects of a balanced-budget rise in government spending (i.e., $dG = dT$) are

$$\frac{dY}{dG} = 1 - \frac{a^g}{\Delta}[1 - s - \bar{r}_f(s - M_y)] \gtrless 0, \quad \text{for } dG = dT_t, \tag{A.10}$$

$$\frac{dB^p}{dG} = \frac{a^g}{\Delta}(s - M_y) \geq 0, \quad \text{for } dG = dT_t, \tag{A.11}$$

$$\frac{dM}{dG} = -\frac{a^g}{\Delta}M_y \leq 0, \quad \text{for } dG = dT_t. \tag{A.12}$$

Short-Run Equilibrium: The Two-Country World

In this part of the appendix we analyze the short-run equilibrium of the system (4.5) through (4.7). This system determines the short-run equilibrium values of Y_t, Y_t^*, and r_t. The YY and Y^*Y^* schedules in figure 4.4 show combinations of Y_t and Y_t^* that clear the markets for domestic and foreign output, respectively. Both of these schedules incorporate the world money-market equilibrium condition (4.7) of the text. To derive the slope of the YY schedule, we differentiate equations (4.5) and (4.7). This yields

$$\begin{pmatrix} -(s + a) & \bar{e}a^* \\ M_y & \bar{e}M_{y^*}^* \end{pmatrix}\begin{pmatrix} dY_t \\ dY_t^* \end{pmatrix} = -\begin{pmatrix} H_r \\ (M_r + \bar{e}M_r^*) \end{pmatrix}dr_t, \tag{A.13}$$

where H_r denotes the partial (negative) effect a change in the rate of interest on the world demand for domestic output; that is, $H_r = (1 - \beta_m)E_r + \bar{e}\beta_x^*E_r^*$, where E_r, M_r, E_r^*, and M_r^* denote the partial (negative) effects of the rate of interest on domestic and foreign spending and money demand. To eliminate r_t from the goods-market equilibrium schedule, we solve (A.13) for dY_t/dr_t and for dY_t^*/dr_t, and divide the solutions by each other. This yields

$$\frac{dY_t^*}{dY_t} = \frac{1}{\bar{e}} \frac{(s + a)(M_r + \bar{e}M_r^*) + M_y H_r}{a^*(M_r + \bar{e}M_r^*) - M_{y^*}^* H_r} \quad \text{along the } YY \text{ schedule.}$$

(A.14)

Analogously, differentiating equations (4.13) and (4.14) yields

$$\begin{pmatrix} a & \bar{e}(s^* + a^*) \\ M_y & \bar{e}M_{y^*}^* \end{pmatrix} \begin{pmatrix} dY_t \\ dY_t^* \end{pmatrix} = -\begin{pmatrix} F_r \\ M_r + \bar{e}M_r^* \end{pmatrix} dr_t,$$

(A.15)

where $F_r = \beta_m E_r + \bar{e}(1 - \beta_x^*)E_r^*$ denotes the partial (negative) effect of the rate of interest on the world demand for foreign output. Applying a similar procedure as before, the slope of the Y^*Y^* schedule is

$$\frac{dY_t^*}{dY_t} = \frac{1}{\bar{e}} \frac{a(M_r + \bar{e}M_r^*) - M_y F_r}{(s^* + a^*)(M_r + \bar{e}M_r^*) + M_{y^*}^* F_r} \quad \text{along the } Y^*Y^* \text{ schedule.}$$

(A.16)

A comparison of the slopes in (A.14) and (A.16) shows that there are various possible configurations of the relative slopes of the YY and Y^*Y^* schedules. However, two configurations are ruled out: if both schedules are positively sloped, then the slope of the Y^*Y^* cannot exceed the slope of the YY schedule. This can be verified by noting that in the numerator of (A.7) the negative quantity $a(M_r + \bar{e}M_r^*)$ is augmented by additional negative quantities, whereas the same negative quantity in the numerator of (A.16) is augmented by an additional positive quantity. A similar comparison of the denominators of (A.14) and (A.16) shows that the negative quantity $a^*(M_r + \bar{e}M_r^*)$ is augmented by additional negative quantities in (A.16) and by a positive quantity in (A.14). Likewise, if both schedules are negatively sloped, then, by substracting one slope from the other, it can be verified that the Y^*Y^* schedule cannot be steeper than the YY schedule. These considerations imply that for all situations in which there is a rightward shift of the YY schedule exceeding the rightward shift of the Y^*Y^* schedule, the new equilibrium must be associated with a higher level of domestic output.

A rise in the domestic government spending alters the position of both schedules. To determine the horizontal shift of the YY schedule, we use equations (4.5) and (4.7), holding Y^* constant and solving for dY/dG after eliminating the expression for dr/dG. A similar procedure is applied to determine the horizontal shift of the Y^*Y^* schedule from equations (4.6) and (4.7). Accordingly, the horizontal shifts of the schedules induced by a debt-financed rise in government spending are

$$\frac{dY}{dG} = \frac{1 - a^g}{s + a + [M_y H_r/(M_r + \bar{e}M_r^*)]} \geq 0 \qquad \text{for the } YY \text{ schedule,}$$

(A.17)

$$\frac{dY}{dG} = \frac{-a^g}{a - [M_y F_r/(M_r + \bar{e}M_r^*)]} \geq 0 \qquad \text{for the } Y^*Y^* \text{ schedule.}$$

(A.18)

The corresponding shifts for the tax-financed rise in government spending are

$$\frac{dY}{dG} = 1 - \frac{a^g}{s + a + [M_y H_r/(M_r + \bar{e}M_r^*)]} \qquad \text{for the } YY \text{ schedule,}$$

(A.19)

$$\frac{dY}{dG} = 1 - \frac{a^g}{a - [M_y F_r/(M_r + \bar{e}M_r^*)]} \qquad \text{for the } Y^*Y^* \text{ schedule.}$$

(A.20)

Comparisons of (A.17) with (A.18) and of (A.19) with (A.20) reveal the difference between the shifts of the YY and the Y^*Y^* schedules.

To compute the short-run multipliers of fiscal policies, we differentiate the system (4.5) through (4.7). Thus

$$
\begin{pmatrix}
-(s+a) & \overline{e}a^* & H_r \\
a & -\overline{e}(s^*+a^*) & F_r \\
M_y & \overline{e}M_{y^*}^* & M_r + \overline{e}M_r^*
\end{pmatrix}
\begin{pmatrix}
dY_t \\
dY_t^* \\
dr_t
\end{pmatrix}
$$

$$
= - \begin{pmatrix}
1-a^g \\
a^g \\
0
\end{pmatrix} dG +
\begin{pmatrix}
1-s-a \\
a \\
M_y
\end{pmatrix} dT_t.
\tag{A.21}
$$

With a debt-financed rise in government spending $dT_t = 0$, and thus the short-run effects are

$$
\frac{dY_t}{dG} = \frac{1}{\Delta}\{[s^*(1-a^g)+a^*](M_r + \overline{e}M_r^*)
$$

$$
+ M_{y^*}^*[F_r(1-a^g) - a^g H_r]\}, \quad \text{for } dT_t = 0,
\tag{A.22}
$$

$$
\frac{dY_t^*}{dG} = \frac{1}{\overline{e}\Delta}\{(sa^g + a)(M_r + \overline{e}M_r^*)
$$

$$
- M_y[F_r(1-a^g) - a^g H_r]\}, \quad \text{for } dT_t = 0,
\tag{A.23}
$$

$$
\frac{dr_t}{dG} = -\frac{1}{\Delta}\{[s^*(1-a^g)+a^*]M_y
$$

$$
+ (sa^g + a)M_{y^*}^*\} > 0, \quad \text{for } dT_t = 0,
\tag{A.24}
$$

where

$$
\Delta = s[(s^*+a^*)(M_r + \overline{e}M_r^*) + M_{y^*}^* F_r] + a[s^*(M_r + \overline{e}M_r^*)
$$

$$
+ M_{y^*}^*(F_r + H_r)] + M_y[s^* H_r + a^*(F_r + H_r)] < 0.
$$

Differentiating the domestic demand for money function (equation 4.8) and using (A.22) and (A.24) yields the short-run change in the domestic money holdings, that is, the balance of payments:

$$
\frac{dM_t}{dG} = \frac{1}{M_r M_r^* \Delta}\left\{\frac{\overline{e}M_y}{M_r}[a^* + s^*(a - a^g)] - \frac{M_{y^*}^*}{M_r^*}(a + sa^g)\right.
$$

$$
\left. + M_y M_{y^*}^* M_r M_r^*[F_r(1-a^g) - H_r a^g]\right\}, \quad \text{for } dT_t = 0.
\tag{A.25}
$$

With a balanced-budget rise in government spending $dG = dT_t = dT$. Accordingly, the solutions of (A.21) are

$$\frac{dY_t}{dG} = \frac{1}{\Delta}\{s[(s^* + a^*)(M_r + \bar{e}M_r^*) + M_{y^*}^*F_r]$$

$$+ (a - a^g)[s^*(M_r + \bar{e}M_r^*) + M_{y^*}^*(F_r + H_r)]$$

$$+ M_y[s^*H_r + a^*(F_r + H_r)]\}, \quad \text{for } dG = dT_t, \tag{A.26}$$

$$\frac{dY_t^*}{dG} = \frac{a^g}{\bar{e}\Delta}[M_y(F_r + H_r) + s(M_r + \bar{e}M_r^*)] > 0, \quad \text{for } dG = dT_t, \tag{A.27}$$

$$\frac{dr_t}{dG} = \frac{a^g}{\Delta}(s^*M_y - sM_{y^*}^*), \quad \text{for } dG = dT_t. \tag{A.28}$$

Differentiating the domestic money demand function and using (A.26) and (A.28) yields

$$\frac{dM_t}{dG} = -\frac{a^g}{\Delta}[(sM_rM_{y^*}^* + s^*\bar{e}M_r^*M_y)$$

$$+ M_yM_{y^*}^*(F_r + H_r)] < 0, \quad \text{for } dG = dT_t. \tag{A.29}$$

Long-Run Equilibrium: The Two-Country World

The long-run equilibrium of the system is specified by equations (A.30) through (A.36), where the first five equations are the long-run counterpart to the short-run conditions (4.5) through (4.9) and the last two equations are the zero-savings requirements for each country implying (once the government budget constraint is incorporated) current account balances. By employing a common rate of interest, this long-run system embodies the assumption of perfect capital mobility.

$$(1 - \beta_m)E[Y - T + M - (1 + r)B^p, r]$$

$$+ (1 - \beta_m^g)G + \beta_x^*\bar{e}E^*\left[Y^* + M^* + (1 + r)\frac{B^p}{\bar{e}}, r\right] = Y, \tag{A.30}$$

$$\beta_m E[Y - T + M - (1 + r)B^p, r] + \beta_m^g G$$

$$+ (1 - \beta_x^*)\bar{e}E^*\left[Y^* + M^* + (1 + r)\frac{B^p}{\bar{e}}, r\right] = Y^*, \qquad (A.31)$$

$$M[Y - T + M - (1 + r)B^p, r]$$

$$+ \bar{e}M^*\left[Y^* + M^* + (1 + r)\frac{B^p}{\bar{e}}, r\right] = \overline{M}, \qquad (A.32)$$

$$M[Y - T + M - (1 + r)B^p, r] = M, \qquad (A.33)$$

$$M^*\left[Y^* + M^* + (1 + r)\frac{B^p}{\bar{e}}, r\right] = M^*, \qquad (A.34)$$

$$E[Y - T + M - (1 + r)B^p, r] = Y - rB^p - T, \qquad (A.35)$$

$$E^*\left[Y^* + M^* + (1 + r)\frac{B^p}{\bar{e}}, r\right] = Y^* + \frac{rB^p}{\bar{e}}. \qquad (A.36)$$

By Walras's law one of the seven equations can be omitted, and the remaining six equations can be used to solve for the long-run equilibrium values of Y, Y^*, B^p, M, M^*, and r as functions of the policy variables.

4.6 Appendix B: Flexible Exchange Rates

Short-Run Equilibrium: The Two-Country World

In this appendix we analyze the short-run equilibrium of the two-country model under flexible exchange rates. Using the domestic money-market equilibrium condition (4.22), the domestic market-clearing rate of interest is

$$r_t = r(Y_t - T_t + A_{t-1}, M), \qquad (A.37)$$

where a rise in disposable resources raises the equilibrium rate of interest while a rise in the money supply lowers the rate of interest. Similarly, using the foreign money-market-clearing condition (4.23) but not imposing yet an equality between the foreign rate of interest, r_t^*, and the domestic rate, r_t, yields

$$r_t^* = r^*(Y_t^* + A_{t-1}^*, M^*).$$ (A.38)

Substituting (A.37) into the domestic expenditure function (4.3) and substituting (A.38) into the corresponding foreign expenditure function yields

$$E_t = \tilde{E}(Y_t - T_t + A_{t-1}, M),$$ (A.39)

$$E_t^* = \tilde{E}^*(Y_t^* + A_{t-1}^*, M^*).$$ (A.40)

Equations (A.39) and (A.40) are the reduced-form expenditure functions that incorporate the conditions of money-market equilibrium. A rise in disposable resources exerts two conflicting influences on the reduced-form expenditure function. On the one hand, it stimulates spending directly, but on the other hand, by raising the equilibrium rate of interest, it discourages spending. Formally, $\tilde{E}_y = E_y - (E_r/M_r)M_y$. In what follows we assume that the direct effect dominates so that $\tilde{E}_y > 0$. For subsequent use we note that the reduced-form saving propensity $\tilde{s} = 1 - \tilde{E}_y$ exceeds $M_y[1 + (E_r/M_r)]$. This follows from the assumption that bonds are normal goods (so that $1 - E_y - M_y > 0$) together with the former expression linking $\tilde{E}_y$ with E_y.

Substituting the reduced-form expenditure functions (A.39) and (A.40) into the goods-market-clearing conditions yields

$$(1 - \beta_m)\tilde{E}(Y_t - T_t + A_{t-1}, M) + (1 - \beta_m^g)G$$

$$+ e_t\beta_x^*\tilde{E}(Y_t^* + A_{t-1}^*, M^*) = Y_t,$$ (A.41)

$$\beta_m\tilde{E}(Y_t - T_t + A_{t-1}, M) + \beta_m^g G$$

$$+ e_t(1 - \beta_x^*)\tilde{E}^*(Y_t^* + A_{t-1}^*, M^*) = e_t Y_t^*,$$ (A.42)

where we recall that $A_{t-1} = M_{t-1} - (1 + r_{t-1})B_{t-1}^p$ and $A_{t-1}^* = M_{t-1}^* + (1 + r_{t-1})B_{t-1}^p/e_t$. Thus, though A_{t-1} is predetermined, the value of A_{t-1}^* depends on the prevailing exchange rate. Equations (A.41) and (A.42) are the reduced-form goods-market-clearing conditions. These conditions link the equilibrium values of domestic output, foreign output, and the exchange rate. In the first step of the analysis we derive the ee schedule of the text which portrays alternative combinations of Y and Y^* satisfying equations (A.41) and (A.42) for alternative values of the exchange rate (which is treated as a parameter). The slope of this schedule is obtained by differentiating equations (A.41) and (A.42) and solving for dY_t^*/dY_t. Accordingly,

$$
\begin{pmatrix} -(\tilde{s} + \tilde{a}) & e_t\tilde{a}^* \\ \tilde{a} & -e_t(\tilde{s}^* + \tilde{a}^*) \end{pmatrix} \begin{pmatrix} dY_t \\ dY_t^* \end{pmatrix}
$$

$$
= \begin{pmatrix} -IM_t^* + \tilde{a}^*H \\ IM_t + (1 - \tilde{s}^* - \tilde{a}^*)H \end{pmatrix} de_t - \begin{pmatrix} 1 - a^g \\ a^g \end{pmatrix} dG
$$

$$
+ \begin{pmatrix} 1 - \tilde{s} - \tilde{a} \\ \tilde{a} \end{pmatrix} dT_t,
\tag{A.43}
$$

where $H = (1 + r_{t-1})B_{t-1}^P/e_t$ denotes the debt commitment of the home country, the reduced-form saving and import propensities are designated by a tilde ($\tilde{\ }$), and where $IM_t^* = \beta_x^*\tilde{E}^*$ and $IM_t = Y^* - (1 - \beta_x^*)\tilde{E}^*$ are, respectively, the foreign and the domestic values of imports expressed in units of foreign goods. The coefficient matrix in (A.43) is the counterpart of the system (2.21) shown in chapter 2. For given fiscal policies we obtain

$$
\frac{dY_t}{de_t} = \frac{\tilde{s}^*IM_t^* + \tilde{a}^*(IM_t^* - IM_t) - \tilde{a}^*H}{\Delta},
\tag{A.44}
$$

$$
\frac{dY_t^*}{de_t} = -\frac{\tilde{s}IM_t - \tilde{a}(IM_t^* - IM_t) + [\tilde{s}(1 - \tilde{s}^* - \tilde{a}^*) + \tilde{a}(1 - \tilde{s}^*)]H}{e_t\Delta},
$$

$$
\tag{A.45}
$$

where

$$
\Delta = \tilde{s}\tilde{s}^* + \tilde{s}\tilde{a}^* + \tilde{s}^*\tilde{a} > 0.
$$

To obtain the slope of the ee schedule, we divide (A.45) by (A.44), yielding

$$
\frac{dY_t^*}{dY_t} = -\frac{\tilde{s}IM_t - \tilde{a}(IM_t^* - IM_t) + [\tilde{s}(1 - \tilde{s}^* - \tilde{a}^*) + \tilde{a}(1 - \tilde{s}^*)]H}{e_t[\tilde{s}^*IM_t^* + \tilde{a}^*(IM_t^* - IM_t) - \tilde{a}^*H]}
$$

along the ee schedule. (A.46)

Around a trade-balance equilibrium with zero initial debt (i.e., $IM_t = IM_t^*$ and $H = 0$) this slope is negative and is equal to $-\tilde{s}/e_t\tilde{s}^*$. With the negatively sloped ee schedule a downward movement along the schedule (i.e., a rise in Y_t and a fall in Y_t^*) is associated with higher values of e_t.

To determine the effects of changes in government spending, we compute the horizontal shift of the ee schedule by setting $dY_t^* = dT_t = 0$ in the system (A.43) and solving for dY_t/dG. This yields

$$\frac{dY_t}{dG} = \frac{IM_t + a^g(IM_t^* - IM_t) + [(1 - \bar{s}^*)(1 - a^g) - \bar{a}^*]H}{\bar{s}IM_t - \bar{a}(IM_t^* - IM_t) + [\bar{s}(1 - \bar{s}^* - \bar{a}^*) + \bar{a}(1 - \bar{s}^*)]H}$$

for the ee schedule.   (A.47)

Thus around trade-balance equilibrium and zero initial debt, the schedule shifts to the right by $1/\bar{s}$.

By setting $dY_t^* = dG = 0$ and following a similar procedure, the horizontal shift of the ee schedule induced by a unit rise in taxes is

$$\frac{dY_t}{dT_t} = -\frac{\bar{a}(IM_t^* - IM_t) + (1 - \bar{s})IM_t + \{(1 - \bar{s})[1 - \bar{s}^* - \bar{a}^*(1 - \bar{s}^*)]\}H}{-\bar{a}(IM_t^* - IM_t) + \bar{s}IM_t + [\bar{s}(1 - \bar{s}^* - \bar{a}^*) + \bar{a}(1 - \bar{s}^*)]H}$$

for the ee schedule.   (A.48)

Thus around trade-balance equilibrium and zero initial debt, the schedule shifts to the left by $(1 - \bar{s})/\bar{s}$ units.

By combining the results in (A.47) and (A.48), we obtain the effect of a balanced-budget unit rise in government spending. Accordingly,

$$\frac{dY_t}{dG} = \frac{\bar{s}IM_t + (a^g - \bar{a})(IM_t^* - IM_t) + [\bar{s}(1 - \bar{s}^* - \bar{a}^*) + (1 - \bar{s}^*)(\bar{a} - a^g)]H}{\bar{s}IM_t - \bar{a}(IM_t^* - IM_t) + [\bar{s}(1 - \bar{s}^* - \bar{a}^*) + \bar{a}(1 - \bar{s}^*)]H}$$

for the ee schedule with $dG = dT_t$.   (A.49)

Thus around trade-balance equilibrium with zero initial debt, a balanced-budget unit rise in government spending shifts the ee schedule to the right by one unit.

In the second step of the diagrammatic analysis we assume that $H = 0$, and we derive the rr^* schedule portraying combinations of Y and Y^* along which the money-market-clearing rates of interest (under the assumption of static exchange-rate expectations) are equal across countries so that

$$r(Y_t - T_t + A_{t-1}, M) = r^*(Y^* + A^*_{t-1}, M^*). \tag{A.50}$$

The slope of this schedule is $r_y/r^*_{y^*}$ which can also be expressed in terms of the characteristics of the demands for money according to

$$\frac{dY^*_t}{dY_t} = \frac{M_y}{M^*_{y^*}}\frac{M^*_{r^*}}{M_r} > 0 \qquad \text{along the } rr^* \text{ schedule.} \tag{A.51}$$

Obviously, around $r = r^*$, $M^*_{r^*} = M^*_r$. As is evident, the level of government spending does not influence the rr^* schedule, whereas a unit rise in taxes shifts the schedule to the right by one unit.

Formally, the effects of fiscal policies can be obtained by differentiating the system (A.41), (A.42), and (A.50). Thus

$$\begin{pmatrix} -(\tilde{s}+\tilde{a}) & e_t\tilde{a}^* & IM^*_t - \tilde{a}^*H \\ \tilde{a} & -e_t(\tilde{s}^*+\tilde{a}^*) & -IM_t-(1-\tilde{s}^*-\tilde{a}^*)H \\ \dfrac{M_y}{M_r} & -\dfrac{M^*_{y^*}}{M^*_r} & \dfrac{HM^*_{y^*}}{e_tM^*_{r^*}} \end{pmatrix}\begin{pmatrix} dY_t \\ dY^*_t \\ de_t \end{pmatrix}$$

$$= -\begin{pmatrix} 1-a^g \\ a^g \\ 0 \end{pmatrix} dG + \begin{pmatrix} 1-\tilde{s}-\tilde{a} \\ \tilde{a} \\ \dfrac{M_y}{M_r} \end{pmatrix} dT_t. \tag{A.52}$$

Solving (A.52), the short-run effects of a debt-financed rise in government spending are

$$\frac{dY_t}{dG} = \frac{M^*_{y^*}}{\Delta M^*_r}[IM_t(1-a^g)+IM^*_t a^g+(1-a^g)H],$$
$$\text{for } dT_t = 0, \tag{A.53}$$

$$\frac{dY^*_t}{dG} = \frac{M_y}{\Delta M_r}[IM_t + a^g(IM^*_t - IM_t)] + \frac{1}{\Delta}\left\{\frac{M^*_{y^*}}{M^*_r}(\tilde{a}+\tilde{s}a^g)\right.$$
$$+ \frac{M_y}{M_r}[(1-a^g)(1-\tilde{s}^*)-\tilde{a}^*]\}H, \quad \text{for } dT_t = 0, \tag{A.54}$$

$$\frac{de_t}{dG} = \frac{1}{\Delta}\left\{\frac{M^*_{y^*}}{M^*_r}(\tilde{a}+\tilde{s}a^g)-\frac{e_tM_y}{M_r}[\tilde{a}^*+\tilde{s}^*(1-a^g)]\right\}, \quad \text{for } dT_t = 0, \tag{A.55}$$

where

$$\Delta = \frac{M_{y^*}^*}{M_r^*}[(\tilde{s} + \tilde{a})IM_t - \tilde{a}IM_t^*] + \frac{e_t M_y}{M_r}[(\tilde{s}^* + \tilde{a}^*)IM_t^* - a^* IM_t]$$

$$+ \left[(\tilde{s} + \tilde{a})\frac{M_{y^*}^*}{M_r^*} - e_t\tilde{a}^*\frac{M_y}{M_r}\right]H.$$

Thus with an initial balanced trade and with zero initial debt, $\Delta < 0$. Differentiating the money-market equilibrium condition (equation 4.8) and using (A.53), we obtain the equilibrium change in the rate of interest:

$$\frac{dr_t}{dG} = -\frac{M_y M_{y^*}^*}{M_r M_{r^*}^* \Delta}[IM_t + a^g(IM_t^* - IM_t) + (1 - a^g)H], \text{ for } dT_t = 0.$$

$$(A.56)$$

Likewise, the short-run effects of a tax-financed rise in government spending are

$$\frac{dY_t}{dG} = \frac{1}{\Delta}\left\{\frac{M_{y^*}^*}{M_r^*}[\tilde{s}IM_t + (\tilde{a} - a^g)(IM_t - IM_t^*)] + \frac{e_t M_y}{M_r}[\tilde{s}^* IM_t^*\right.$$

$$+ \tilde{a}^*(IM_t^* - IM_t)] + \left[\frac{M_{y^*}^*}{M_r^*}(\tilde{s} + \tilde{a} - a^g) - \frac{e_t M_y}{M_r}\tilde{a}^*\right]H\Big\},$$

$$\text{for } dG = dT_t, \quad (A.57)$$

$$\frac{dY_t^*}{dG} = \frac{a^g}{\Delta}\left\{\frac{M_y}{M_r}(IM_t^* - IM_t) - \left[\frac{M_y}{M_r}(1 - \tilde{s}^*) - \frac{M_{y^*}^*}{M_r^*}\tilde{s}\right]H\right\},$$

$$\text{for } dG = dT_t, \quad (A.58)$$

$$\frac{de_t}{dG} = \frac{a^g}{\Delta}\left(\frac{e_t M_y}{M_r}\tilde{s}^* + \frac{M_{y^*}^*}{M_r^*}\tilde{s}\right), \quad \text{for } dG = dT_t. \quad (A.59)$$

Using the money-market equilibrium condition together with (A.57) yields

$$\frac{dr_t}{dG} = -\frac{M_y}{M_r \Delta}\left\{a^g(IM_t^* - IM_t) + \left[\frac{M_{y^*}^*}{M_r^*}(\tilde{s} + \tilde{a} - a^g) + \frac{e_t M_y}{M_r}\tilde{a}^*\right]H\right\},$$

$$\text{for } dG = dT_t. \quad (A.60)$$

Long-Run Equilibrium: The Two-Country World

The long-run equilibrium of the system is characterized by equations (A.61) through (A.65), where the first three equations are the long-run counterparts to equations (A.41), (A.42), and (A.50) and the last two equations are the requirements of zero savings in both countries implying (once the government budget constraint is incorporated) current-account balances. Embodied in the system are the requirements of money-market equilibria and perfect capital mobility.

$$(1 - \beta_m)\tilde{E}[Y - T + M - (1 + r)B^p, M] + (1 - \beta_m^g)G$$

$$+ e\beta_x^*\tilde{E}^*\left[Y^* + M^* + \left(\frac{1 + r}{e}\right)B^p, M^*\right] = Y, \tag{A.61}$$

$$\beta_m\tilde{E}[Y - T + M - (1 + r)B^p, M] + \beta_m^g G$$

$$+ e(1 - \beta_x^*)\tilde{E}^*\left[Y^* + M^* + \left(\frac{1 + r}{e}\right)B^p, M^*\right] = eY^*, \tag{A.62}$$

$$r[Y - T + M - (1 + r)B^p, M]$$

$$= r^*\left[Y^* + M^* + \left(\frac{1 + r}{e}\right)B^p, M^*\right], \tag{A.63}$$

$$\tilde{E}[Y - T + M - (1 + r)B^p, M] = Y - rB^p - T, \tag{A.64}$$

$$\tilde{E}^*\left[Y^* + M^* + \left(\frac{1 + r}{e}\right)B^p, M^*\right] = Y^* + \frac{rB^p}{e}. \tag{A.65}$$

This system, which determines the long-run equilibrium values of Y, Y^*, e, B^p, and r, can be used to analyze the effects of government spending and taxes on these endogenous variables.

Exchange-Rate Expectations

Up to this point we have assumed that the expectations concerning the evolution of the exchange rate are static. This assumption implied that the rates of interest on securities denominated in different currencies are equalized. Since, however, the actual exchange rate does change over time, it is useful to extend the analysis and allow for exchange-rate expectations that are not static. Specifically, in this part of the appendix we assume that expectations are rational in the sense of being self-fulfilling. We continue to assume that the GDP deflators are fixed. To illustrate the main implication of exchange-rate expectations, we consider a stripped-down version of the small-country flexible exchange-rate model, and for expository convenience, we present the analysis using a continuous-time version of the model.

The budget constraint can be written as

$$E_t + \dot{M}_t - e_t \dot{B}^p_{ft} = Y_t - T_t - \bar{r}_f e_t B^p_{ft}, \qquad (A.66)$$

where a dot over a variable represents a time derivative. The spending and money-demand functions (the counterparts to equations 4.3 and 4.4) are

$$E_t = E(Y_t - T_t - \bar{r}_f e_t B^p_{ft}, M_t - e_t B^p_{ft}, \bar{r}_f), \qquad (A.67)$$

$$M_t = M\left(Y_t - T_t - \bar{r}_f e_t B^p_{ft}, M_t - e_t B^p_{ft}, \bar{r}_f + \frac{\dot{e}_t}{e_t}\right), \qquad (A.68)$$

where the demand for money is expressed as a negative function of the expected depreciation of the currency, $\dot{e}_t/e_t$. In what follows we simplify the exposition by assuming that the world rate of interest, $\bar{r}_f$, is very low (zero), and that the effect of assets ($M_t - e_t B^p_{ft}$) on spending is negligible. With these simplifications the goods and money-market equilibrium conditions (the counterparts to equations 4.20a and 4.22a) are

$$(1 - \beta_m)E(Y_t - T_t) + (1 - \beta^g_m)G + e_t \bar{D}^* = Y_t, \qquad (A.69)$$

$$M\left(Y_t - T_t, M - e_t B^p_{ft}, \frac{\dot{e}_t}{e_t}\right) = M. \qquad (A.70)$$

Equation (A.69) implies that the level of output that clears the goods market depends positively on the level of the exchange rate and on government spending, and negatively on taxes. This dependence can be expressed as

$$Y_t = Y(e_t, G, T_t), \qquad (A.71)$$

where $\partial Y_t / \partial e_t = \bar{D}^* / (s + a)$, $\partial Y_t / \partial G = (1 - a^g) / (s + a)$, and $\partial Y_t / \partial T_t = -(1 - s - a)/(s + a)$ are the conventional foreign-trade multipliers. Substituting the functional relation (A.71) into the money-market equilibrium condition and solving for the (actual and expected) percentage change in the exchange rate yields

$$\frac{\dot{e}_t}{e_t} = f(e_t, B_{ft}^p, G, T_t, M), \tag{A.72}$$

where

$$\frac{\partial f}{\partial e} = \frac{-M_y \bar{D}^*/(s + a) + M_A B_{ft}^p}{M_r},$$

$$\frac{\partial f}{\partial B_{ft}^p} = \frac{e_t M_A}{M_r},$$

$$\frac{\partial f}{\partial G} = -\frac{1 - a^g}{(s + a)M_r},$$

$$\frac{\partial f}{\partial T_t} = \frac{1 - s - a}{(s + a)M_r},$$

and where M_A and M_r denote, respectively, the derivatives of the demand for money with respect to assets $(M - e_t B_{ft}^p)$ and the rate of interest. The former is positive, and the latter negative. The interpretation of the dependence of the percentage change in the exchange rate, representing the money-market-clearing interest rate, on the various variables follows. A rise in the exchange rate raises the goods-market-clearing level of output and raises the demand for money. To restore money-market equilibrium, the rate of interest must rise; that is, $\dot{e}_t / e_t$ must rise. On the other hand, the rise in e raises the domestic-currency value of the debt B_{ft}^p. If the private sector is a net creditor, the depreciation of the currency raises the domestic-currency value of assets and raises the demand for money. This in turn also contributes to the rise in the rate of interest. If, however, the private sector is a net debtor, then the value of assets falls, and the demand for money is reduced, thereby contributing to a downward pressure on the rate of interest. The net effect on the rate of interest depends therefore on the net debtor position of the

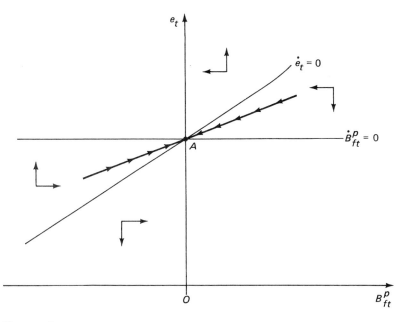

Figure 4A.1
The equilibrium exchange-rate dynamics and debt accumulation

private sector; if, however, B^p_{ft} is zero, then the rate of interest must rise so that $\partial f/\partial e_t > 0$. Analogous interpretations apply to the other derivatives where it is evident that $\partial f/\partial B^p_{ft} < 0$, $\partial f/\partial G \geq 0$, and $\partial f/\partial T_t < 0$.

Equation (A.72) constitutes the first differential equation of the model governing the evolution of the exchange rate over time. The second variable whose evolution over time characterizes the dynamics of the system is the stock of private-sector debt. Substituting the goods-market equilibrium condition (A.71) into the budget constraint (A.66), and using the fact that in the absence of monetary policy $\dot{M}_t = 0$, we can solve for the dynamics of private-sector debt. Accordingly,

$$\dot{B}^p_{ft} = \frac{1}{e_t} h(e_t, G, T_t)$$

$$= \frac{1}{e_t} \{E_t[Y(e_t, G, T_t) - T_t] - Y(e_t, G, T_t) + T_t\}. \qquad \text{(A.73)}$$

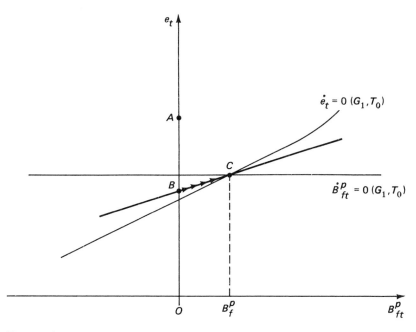

Figure 4A.2
The effects of a debt-financed rise in government spending on the paths of the
exchange rate and private-sector debt

Equation (A.73) expresses the rate of change of private-sector debt
as the difference between private-sector spending and disposable in-
come. The previous discussion implies that $\partial h/\partial e_t = -\bar{D}^*s/(s + a) <$
0, $\partial h/\partial G = -(1 - a^g)s/(s + a) \le 0$, and $\partial h/\partial T_t = s/(s + a) > 0$.

In interpreting these expressions, we note that the function h
represents the negative savings of the private sector. Accordingly, a
unit rise in e_t or G raises savings by the saving propensity times
the corresponding multiplier. Analogously, a unit rise in taxes that
lowers disposable income lowers savings by the saving propensity
times the corresponding disposable-income multiplier.

The equilibrium of the system is exhibited in figure 4A.1. The
positively sloped $\dot{e}_t = 0$ schedule shows combinations of the exchange rate and private-sector debt that maintain an unchanged
exchange rate. The schedule represents equation (A.72) for $\dot{e}_t = 0$. Its
slope is positive around a zero level of private-sector debt, and its
position depends on the policy variables G, T_t, and M. Likewise, the

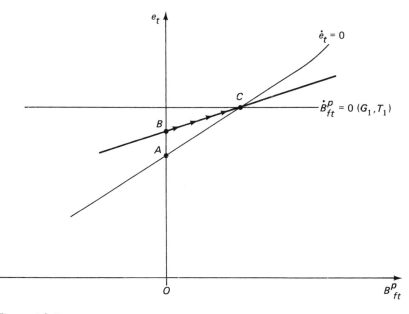

Figure 4A.3
The effects of a tax-financed rise in government spending on the paths of the
exchange rate and private-sector debt. Data: $s + a = a^g$.

$\dot{B}^p_{ft} = 0$ locus represents equation (A.73) for $\dot{B}^p_{ft} = 0$. It is horizontal
since, as specified, the rate of change of private-sector debt does not
depend on the value of debt. The arrows around the schedules indicate the directions in which the variables tend to move, and the solid
curve shows the unique saddle path converging toward a stationary
state. As is customary in this type of analysis, we associate this saddle
path with the equilibrium path. The long-run equilibrium of the system is shown by point A in figure 4A.1, where for convenience we
show a case in which the long-run value of private-sector debt is zero.

The effects of a unit debt-financed rise in government spending
from G_0 to G_1 are shown in figure 4A.2. Starting from an initial
long-run equilibrium at point A, the rise in G shifts the $\dot{B}^p_{ft} = 0$
schedule from point A downward by $-(1 - a^g)/\bar{D}^*$, and it also
shifts the $\dot{e} = 0$ schedule from point A downward by $-(1 - a^g)/$
$M_y\bar{D}^*$. For $M_y < 1$, the vertical displacement of the $\dot{e} = 0$ schedule
exceeds the corresponding displacement of the $\dot{B}^p_{ft} = 0$ schedule,
and the new long-run equilibrium obtains at point C, at which the

domestic currency has appreciated and private-sector debt has risen. The short-run equilibrium obtains at point B along the new saddle path, and transition toward the long run follows along the path connecting points B and C. As is evident, the initial appreciation of the currency overshoots the long-run appreciation.

The effects of a unit tax-financed rise in government spending are shown in figure 4A.3. With $dG = dT$, the $\dot{B}^p_{ft} = 0$ schedule shifts upward by $a^g/\bar{D}^*$ while the $\dot{e} = 0$ schedule shifts vertically by $(s + a - a^g)/M_y\bar{D}^*$. The bench-mark case shown in figure 4A.3 corresponds to the situation in which the private sector and the government have the same marginal propensities to spend on domestic goods (i.e., $s + a = a^g$). In that case the $\dot{e} = 0$ remains intact, the short-run equilibrium is at point B, and the long-run equilibrium is at point C. As seen in this case the domestic currency depreciates, and the short-run depreciation undershoots the long-run depreciation. These results are sensitive to alternative assumptions concerning the relative magnitudes of $(s + a)$ and a^g.

III

Elements of Intertemporal Macroeconomics

5

The Composite-Commodity World

The main characteristic of the modern analysis of fiscal policies is the detailed attention given to dynamic and intertemporal considerations. In contrast with earlier analyses, the modern approach is based on more solid microeconomic foundations. These foundations "discipline" the analysis and impose constraints on the modeling of macroeconomic behavior. Specifically, an explicit account of temporal and intertemporal budget constraints restricts the permissible behavior of households and governments and sharpens the predictive content of the economic model. Furthermore, by deriving the private sector's *aggregate* behavior from the utility maximization behavior of *individuals*, the modern analytical framework allows for a meaningful treatment of normative issues. Hence within this framework a macroeconomic analysis is applicable for both positive economic issues as well as issues in welfare economics.

In this chapter we review basic elements of intertemporal open-economy macroeconomics. In order to motivate the discussion, we start in section 5.1 with a specification of a simple stylized two-period model of a small open economy that has free access to world capital markets and that produces and consumes a single aggregate tradable good. In this context we characterize the maximizing behavior of firms and households and determine the general equilibrium levels of investment, consumption, savings, and the various accounts of the balance of payments.

The intertemporal disparities between the paths of consumption and income are reflected in debt accumulation and decumulation. To highlight the central motives underlying the determination of intertemporal allocations of debt, we introduce in section 5.2 three basic concepts: consumption smoothing, consumption tilting, and consumption augmenting. These concepts are useful for interpreting the role that capital markets play in facilitating the adjustments of consumption paths over time.

In section 5.3 we illustrate the usefulness of the three concepts by applying the stylized model to the analysis of supply shocks. In this context we analyze the effects of temporary (current or anticipated future) and permanent supply shocks on the levels of consumption, investment, and the trade balance.

In section 5.4 we extend the analysis of the small open economy to a two-country model of the world economy. The analysis identifies the factors that determine the equilibrium level of the world rate of interest and the associated international and intertemporal distribution of trade imbalances. The key factors governing the equilibrium are the relation between the domestic and the foreign marginal saving propensities (reflecting differences between marginal rates of time preference), the relation between the domestic and the foreign percentage rates of growth of GDP, the percentage rate of growth of world GDP, and the initial distribution of world debt. The impact of the initial distribution is illustrated through an analysis of the effects of international transfers on the equilibrium level of the world rate of interest.

5.1 A Stylized Model

Consider a small open economy producing and consuming one aggregate tradable good and facing a given world rate of interest. The aggregation of goods into a single aggregate commodity is done in order to focus attention on intertemporal trade, that is, on international borrowing and lending. Obviously, in designing a model that is suitable for intertemporal analysis, we need to extend the single-period perspective into a multi-period setting. In the context of the stylized model we adopt the minimal framework of a two-period model.

We start by specifying the *supply* side of the model. The economy is endowed with an initial sequence of endowments, $\overline{Y}_0$ and $\overline{Y}_1$, where the subscripts zero and one designate the corresponding periods. This initial endowment may be consumed, or alternatively, it may be invested in intertemporal production process. Such an investment process modifies the intertemporal pattern of available outputs (GDP). Formally, output in period one, Y_1, is linked to the initial endowment, $\bar{Y}_0$, through the production function

$$Y_1 = \bar{Y}_1 + F(I_0), \tag{5.1}$$

where I_0 denotes investment (equal to the level of output *not* consumed) in period zero. We assume that the production function exhibits positive and diminishing marginal product and that, in the absence of investment, output cannot be augmented; that is, $F(0) = 0$.

Firms, are assumed to maximize the present value of profits. Formally, the firm's maximization problem is

$$\tilde{\Pi} = \max_{I_0} \, [\alpha_1 F(I_0) - I_0], \tag{5.2}$$

where $\alpha_1 = 1/(1 + r_0)$ denotes the present value factor and r_0 is the world one-period rate of interest. The formulation in (5.2) indicates that the current investment, I_0, bears fruits $F(I_0)$ only in the subsequent period; this is reflected by the discounting in the profit function. Figure 5.1 illustrates the maximization problem and the firm's investment policy. The initial endowment $(\bar{Y}_0, \bar{Y}_1)$ is denoted by point A, and the present value of this endowment is denoted by point D. The (absolute value of the) slope of the dashed line connecting points A and D is the intertemporal price $(1/\alpha_1) = 1 + r_0$. The schedule originating from the initial endowment at point A and passing through point B is the function $F(I_0)$ which specifies the transformation schedule linking current period investment with additions to future period output. Diagrammatically, the level of investment is measured in a leftward direction from $\bar{Y}_0$. In the absence of investment, profits are zero. Thus the dashed line AD is a zero-profit locus. The profit-maximizing firm seeks to reach the highest isoprofit locus subject to its technological constraints. Point B in figure 5.1 represents the outcome of the firm's profit-maximizing investment policy. With such policy profits, $\tilde{\Pi}$, are measured by the distance DE, and the level of investment, I_0, is measured by the distance $G\bar{Y}_0$.

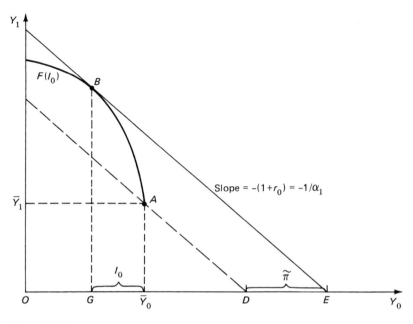

Figure 5.1
The determination of investment and profits

As is evident from figure 5.1, the firm will carry out positive investment only if the transformation function emerging at the initial endowment point, A, is steeper at that point than $1 + r_0$. At point B profits are maximized, and the (absolute value of the) slope of the transformation function $F(I_0)$ equals $1 + r_0$. More formally, we note from equation (5.2) that the first-order condition for profit maximization requires that

$$F'(I_0) = 1 + r_0. \tag{5.3}$$

Diminishing returns on investment, that is, $F''(I_0) < 0$, imply that a higher rate of interest lowers the profit-maximizing level of investment. In terms of figure 5.1, a higher rate of interest steepens the isoprofit loci and slides point B rightward along the $F(I_0)$ schedule toward point A. The new profit-maximization point is associated with a smaller level of investment.

We turn next to an analysis of the *demand* side of the model. Consider a representative consumer maximizing lifetime utility subject to budget constraints. The individual's resources are composed of the initial endowments $\overline{Y}_0$ and $\overline{Y}_1$ and of profits that firms distribute as dividends to share holders. These resources are used in the first period for consumption and saving. During the second (and last) period total income is fully consumed. Hence the first-period budget constraint is

$$C_0 = \overline{Y}_0 + B_0 - I_0 - (1 + r_{-1})B_{-1}, \tag{5.4}$$

and the second-period budget constraint is

$$C_1 = \overline{Y}_1 + F(I_0) - (1 + r_0)B_0. \tag{5.5}$$

In equations (5.4) and (5.5), C_0 and C_1 denote first- and second-period consumption, B_0 denotes first-period borrowing which could be positive or negative, I_0 denotes the initial investment corresponding to the losses of firms (negative dividends), and $(1 + r_{-1})B_{-1}$ is the historically given initial debt commitment of the representative individual corresponding to the economy's external debt. Equation (5.5) indicates that second-period dividends are $F(I_0)$, corresponding to the profits of firms. Finally, the term $-(1 + r_0)B_0$ indicates that in the second-period individuals must repay debts incurred in the previous period. Obviously, in this two-period model the solvency requirement ensures that in the second period the individual does not incur new debt. Thus in the final period all debt commitments are settled.

From national income accounting, the sum of consumption, investment, and the surplus in the current account of the balance of payments equals GNP. In terms of equation (5.4), GDP is $\overline{Y}_0$, external debt payments are rB_{-1}, GNP is $\overline{Y}_0 - r_{-1}B_{-1}$, and the current-account surplus (equal to the capital account deficit) is $-(B_0 - B_{-1})$. Alternatively, the current-account surplus also equals savings $(\overline{Y}_0 - r_{-1}B_{-1} - C_0)$ minus investment (I_0). Hence the specification in equation (5.4) conforms with national income accounting. Similar considerations apply to the second-period budget constraint in equation (5.5).

Since the representative individual has free access to world capital markets, he can lend and borrow freely subject to the world rate of interest r. This access to capital markets implies that rather than facing two separate periodic budget constraints, the individual's choices are constrained by a consolidated present-value budget constraint. To derive the consolidated constraint, we divide equation (5.5) by $(1 + r_0)$, add the resulting equation to equation (5.4), and obtain

$$C_0 + \alpha_1 C_1 = \overline{Y}_0 + \alpha_1 \overline{Y}_1 + \tilde{\Pi} - (1 + r_{-1})B_{-1} \equiv W_0, \qquad (5.6)$$

where $\alpha_1 = 1/(1 + r_0)$ is the present-value factor and where $\tilde{\Pi}$, which is specified in equation (5.2), denotes the present value of dividends stemming from the investment of the profit-maximizing firm. The right-hand side of equation (5.6) also defines the value of wealth in period zero, W_0. The consolidated budget constraint highlights the fact that the key decisions that individuals make concern the choices of C_0 and C_1. Implicit in these decisions is the magnitude of new borrowing, B_0, which appears explicitly in the temporal budget constraints (5.4) and (5.5).

It is relevant to note that intertemporal solvency implies that the discounted sum of the periodic surpluses in the *trade account* must equal the sum of the principal plus interest payments on the historically given initial debt. The trade-balance surplus in each period equals GDP minus domestic absorption (consumption plus investment). Formally, using equations (5.4) and (5.5)—or equivalently using the consolidated equation (5.6)—we note that

$$(TA)_0 + \frac{1}{1 + r_0}(TA)_1 = (1 + r_{-1})B_{-1}, \qquad (5.7)$$

where (TA) denotes the surplus in the trade balance. It follows therefore that the discounted sum of the periodic surpluses in the *current account* must equal the discounted sum of the trade balance surplus plus the discounted sum of the surplus in the *debt-service account*. Formally,

$$(CA)_0 + \frac{1}{1 + r_0}(CA)_1 = (1 + r_{-1})B_{-1} + (DA)_0 + \frac{1}{1 + r_0}(DA)_1,$$

$$(5.7a)$$

where (CA) denotes the surplus in the current account (equal to GNP minus domestic absorption) and DA denotes the surplus in the debt-service account (equal to minus interest payments on previous period debt.) Hence in our two-period model $(DA)_0 = -r_{-1}B_{-1}$ and $(DA)_1 = -r_0 B_0$. Equation (5.7) reveals that in the absence of initial debt, a trade-balance surplus in a given period must equal (in present-value terms) the trade-balance deficits in all other periods taken as a whole. As illustrated by equation (5.7a), a similar property does not apply to the intertemporal pattern of the current account.

The representative individual's utility depends on the levels of consumption, and let his or her lifetime utility function be denoted by $U(C_0, C_1)$. As usual, we assume that the marginal utilities of consumption in each period are positive and that the marginal rate of substitution of consumption between two consecutive periods is diminishing along any given indifference curve. The individual seeks to maximize lifetime utility subject to the consolidated lifetime budget constraint. Formally, the individual's maximization problem is

$$\tilde{U} = \max_{\{C_0, C_1\}} U(C_0, C_1), \tag{5.8}$$

subject to

$$C_0 + \alpha_1 C_1 = W_0.$$

The solution to this maximization problem is shown in figure 5.2, which incorporates the relevant information from the firm's profit maximization problem of figure 5.1. In this figure point E measures the discounted sum of current and future GDP's and W_0 measures the value of wealth in period zero. The horizontal distance between the two corresponds to the initial external debt commitment $(1 + r_{-1})B_{-1}$. The maximized level of utility obtains at point C at the tangency of the indifference curve $\bar{U} = U(C_0, C_1)$ with the budget line. The budget line in turn emerges from point W_0—corresponding to the value of wealth in period zero—and its slope (in absolute terms) equals $1/\alpha_1 = 1 + r_0$. The equilibrium portrayed in figure 5.2 represents the general equilibrium of the small open economy incorporating both the profit maximization by firms and the utility maximization by households. The case shown in the figure

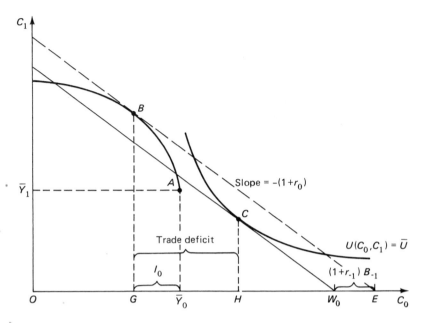

Figure 5.2
The general equilibrium of consumption, investment, and the trade balance

corresponds to a situation in which period zero's absorption (consumption, OH, plus investment, $G\overline{Y}_0$) exceeds that period's GDP, $\overline{Y}_0$. As a result the economy runs in period zero a trade-balance deficit equal to GH. Obviously, the corresponding current-account deficit is obtained by adding the debt service, $r_{-1}B_{-1}$, to the trade-balance deficit.

The foregoing analysis completes the presentation of the stylized model. We turn next to illustrate three basic concepts that are useful in characterizing the intertemporal allocations of debt.

5.2 Three Determinants of Borrowing and Lending

The equilibrium pattern of consumption portrayed in figure 5.2 is associated with discrepancies between the periodic levels of consumption and incomes. The lack of a complete synchronization between the time series of consumption and income is reconciled by a reliance on the world capital markets. Accordingly, in obtaining the optimal time profile of consumption, individuals find it beneficial to incur debt during some periods of their life. In determining the extent of the optimal departure of the path of consumption from that of income, and thereby the optimal reliance on capital markets and debt accumulation, it is useful to identify three separate motives: the consumption-smoothing motive, the consumption-tilting motive and the consumption-augmenting motive. These three motives govern the desired volume of borrowing and lending.

In introducing the three concepts, we need to define the concept of the *subjective discount factor* which plays a critical role in determining the intertemporal allocations. The subjective discount factor, δ, measures the marginal rate of substitution between consumption in two consecutive periods evaluated at the point of a flat time profile of consumption ($C_0 = C_1 = C$). Thus

$$\delta = \frac{\partial U(C, C)/\partial C_1}{\partial U(C, C)/\partial C_0}. \tag{5.9}$$

The subjective discount factor, δ, is related to the subjective marginal rate of time preference, ρ, according to $\delta = 1/(1 + \rho)$.

To facilitate the exposition, suppose that the subjective discount factor is fixed and that the utility function is

$$U(C_0, C_1) = U(C_0) + \delta U(C_1). \tag{5.10}$$

As is evident from the first-order condition of the consumer's maximization problem of equation (5.8), utility maximization implies an equality between the intertemporal marginal rate of substitution and the discount factor. Hence

$$\frac{U'(C_0)}{\delta U'(C_1)} = \frac{1}{\alpha_1}. \tag{5.11}$$

Armed with these preliminaries, we turn now to illustrate the basic concepts. To sharpen the exposition of each concept, we focus on special cases designed to isolate each factor separately. In all cases we assume that there is no initial debt. Consider first the *consumption-smoothing motive*. In figure 5.3 we assume that the subjective and the market discount factors are equal to each other (i.e., $\delta = \alpha_1$),

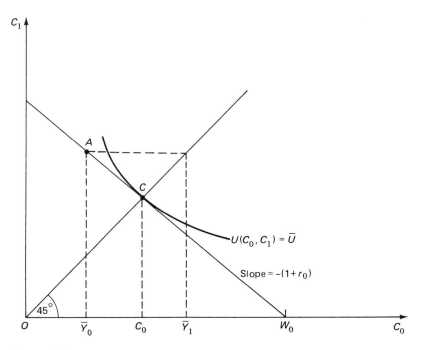

Figure 5.3
The consumption-smoothing effect. Data: $\rho = r_0$, $\overline{Y}_0 < \overline{Y}_1$, $F'(0) \leq 1 + r_0$.

that there is no investment, but that the periodic levels of income (endowments) differ from each other ($\overline{Y}_0 \neq \overline{Y}_1$). In that case equilibrium consumption is described by point C along the 45° ray. As is evident, because of the equality between the subjective and the market discount factors, δ and α_1 (or equivalently, between the subjective rate of time preference, ρ, and the market rate of interest, r_0), individuals wish to *smooth* the time profile of consumption relative to the fluctuating levels of periodic incomes, and as seen in the figure, consumption (which is equal across periods) falls in between $\overline{Y}_0$ and $\overline{Y}_1$. This consumption-smoothing motive is effected through borrowing in period zero and repaying the loan plus interest in the subsequent period.

Consider next the *consumption-tilting motive*. In figure 5.4 we assume that the subjective and the market discount factors differ from each other (i.e., $\alpha_1 \neq \delta$), that there is no investment, and that the periodic levels of income (endowments) equal to each other

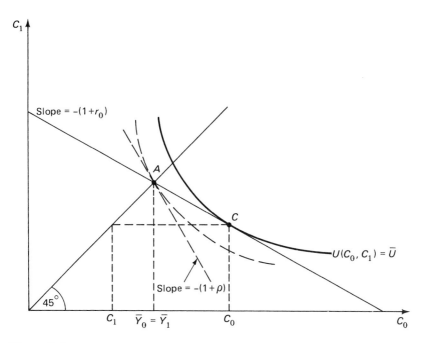

Figure 5.4
The consumption-tilting effect. Data: $\rho > r_0$, $\bar{Y}_0 = \bar{Y}_1$, $F'(0) \leq 1 + r_0$.

$(\bar{Y}_0 = \bar{Y}_1)$. In that case the equilibrium consumption point C does not lie along the 45° ray. In the case drawn, $\delta < \alpha_1$ so that the subjective rate of time preference exceeds the world rate of interest. As a result individuals facing a flat time profile of income wish to *tilt* the time profile of consumption toward period zero. This consumption-tilting motive is also effected through the world capital markets in which the individuals borrow in period zero and settle their debts in period one.

Finally, consider the *consumption-augmenting motive*. In figure 5.5 we assume equality between the subjective and the market discount factors (i.e., $\delta = \alpha_1$) and between the periodic levels of income (endowments) so that $(\bar{Y}_0 = \bar{Y}_1)$; we also assume that there is positive investment (since $F'(0) > 1 + r_0$). In that case equilibrium consumption is at point C. As seen, the investment opportunities, which tilt the time profile of income, *augment* the levels of consumption in each period without introducing variability to its time profile. As

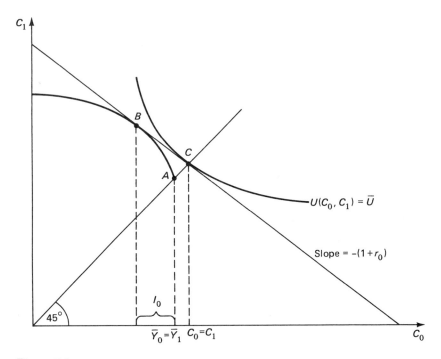

Figure 5.5
The consumption-augmenting effect. Data: $\rho = r_0$, $\bar{Y}_0 = \bar{Y}_1$, $F'(0) > 1 + r_0$.

with the other cases this consumption-augmenting motive is also effected through the world capital markets in which individuals borrow in period zero and repay debt commitment in period one. As is evident, in the absence of international capital markets the investment carried out in period zero would have crowded out private-sector consumption in that period. Access to the world capital markets facilitates the augmentation of consumption at a rate that is uniform over time.

The assumptions needed to generate the *pure* consumption-smoothing, consumption-tilting, and consumption-augmenting effects are summarized in table 5.1. In all cases these motives are expressed through borrowing and lending in the capital market. Although we have isolated each of the three effects, in general, it is likely that the three motives coexist and interact in generating the equilibrium patterns of consumption, investment, and debt accumulation.

Table 5.1
Assumptions generating pure consumption-smoothing, consumption-tilting, and
consumption-augmenting effects

	Smoothing	Tilting	Augmenting
Discount factors	$\delta = \alpha_1$	$\delta \neq \alpha_1$	$\delta = \alpha_1$
Endowments	$\overline{Y}_0 \neq \overline{Y}_1$	$\overline{Y}_0 = \overline{Y}_1$	$\overline{Y}_0 = \overline{Y}_1$
Investment profitability	$F'(0) \leq 1 + r_0$	$F'(0) \leq 1 + r_0$	$F'(0) > 1 + r_0$

5.3 The Intertemporal Adjustment to Supply Shocks

In this section we illustrate the working of the three factors in the context of adjustment to supply shocks. In order to analyze the equilibrium response to supply shocks and to highlight the intertemporal considerations involved in such an adjustment, we distinguish between temporary and permanent shocks and between current and anticipated future shocks. The supply shocks are reflected in either a change in the endowment ($\overline{Y}_0$, $\overline{Y}_1$) or a change in the technology governing investment $F(I_0)$. Throughout we consider positive supply shocks that increase the endowment bundle or improve the technology of investment. To facilitate the exposition in this discussion, we will assume that the utility function $U(C_0, C_1)$ is homothetic. This assumption implies that for a given rate of interest the ratio of consumption in different periods is independent of the level of wealth.

Figure 5.6 illustrates the effects of supply shocks. To focus on the essentials, we assume that the historically given debt, B_{-1}, is zero, that the subjective rate of time preference, ρ, equals the rate of interest, r_0, that initially the endowments are uniformly distributed over time (so that $\overline{Y}_0 = \overline{Y}_1$), and that initially there is no profitable investment. In that case the initial equilibrium is described by point A along the $45°$ ray, and thus consumption in each period equals the corresponding level of the endowment. Hence in the initial equilibrium the trade-balance deficit is zero. Furthermore, since there is no initial debt, the current account of the balance of payments is also balanced.

Consider first a *permanent* supply shock that raises the endowment in each period by the same proportion. In terms of figure 5.6 the new

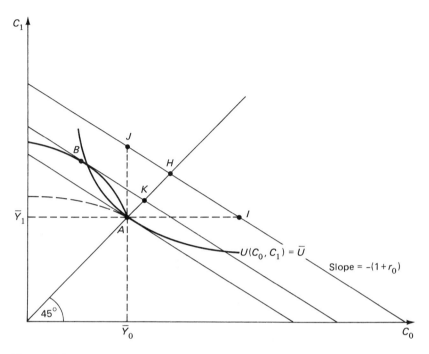

Figure 5.6
Supply shocks

endowment is represented by point H. Since we have assumed that the utility function is homothetic, the consumption-expansion locus is the ray from the origin going through the initial equilibrium point. Hence the new pattern of consumption coincides with the new endowment point H on the new higher budget line. In that case the permanent supply shock results in neither a surplus nor a deficit in the balance of trade. The supply shock yielding this outcome is referred to as a *neutral* supply shock.

Obviously, if the utility function was not homothetic, then the consumption-expansion locus would not have been characterized by the 45° ray in figure 5.6; in that case a permanent supply shock is not neutral with respect to its effect on the current account of the balance of payments. For example, if the rate of time preference is high at low levels of wealth and falls as wealth rises, then the consumption-expansion locus is steeper than the 45° ray (it intersects point A in figure 5.6 from below), and a permanent positive supply shock induces a trade-account surplus in the early period.

Consider next a *temporary* supply shock that raises the endowment only in period zero to point I in figure 5.6. In the figure we have assumed that this temporary supply shock yields the same budget line as the one obtained in the previous case of a permanent shock. Since we are only interested in the qualitative effects of the various shocks, this assumption is made in order to simplify the diagrammatic exposition. With this shock, equilibrium consumption is described by point H. In order to bring about this pattern of consumption, the economy runs a surplus in its balance of trade equal to the difference between the new endowment in period zero (corresponding to point I) and the new consumption in period zero (corresponding to point H). Obviously, the counterpart to this trade surplus is a trade deficit in the subsequent period in which consumption exceeds the endowment level.

Analogously, an expected *future supply shock* that raises the endowment in period one is illustrated by point J in figure 5.6 (which is again designed to yield the same budget as in the previous cases). As before, the consumption point is described by point H, and the economy runs a trade-balance deficit in period zero and a corresponding surplus in period one.

The key factor underlying the consumption response to the various supply shocks is the *consumption-smoothing motive*. Accordingly, the utility-maximizing consumers smooth the time profile of consumption and disregard the variability in the time profile of GDP. The mechanism that facilitates such consumption smoothing operates through the world capital market, and the variability of the stream of GDP is reflected in the time profile of the trade balance. If the (positive) supply shock is temporary, it leads to a trade-balance surplus in the period in which the shock occurs and to trade-balance deficits in all other periods. By analogy with our definition of a neutral (permanent) supply shock, we define a *pro-lending* supply shock as the situation in which the positive temporary shock occurs in the present, and we define a *pro-borrowing* supply shock as the situation in which the positive temporary shock is expected to occur in the future. Obviously, the description of the shocks as being pro-lending or pro-borrowing is valid from the perspective of the current period.

The foregoing analysis examined the response of the economy to supply shocks that take the form of exogenous changes in the levels of GDP. Another possible (positive) supply shock may stem from a technological improvement in the process of investment. In terms of figure 5.6 suppose that under the initial technology the investment opportunities schedule is the dashed schedule emerging from point A. Since the marginal product of investment falls short of the rate of interest, no investment takes place at the initial equilibrium. The technological improvement is represented in figure 5.6 by the higher investment opportunities schedule emerging from point A and passing through point B. In that case, as shown earlier, the level of production is characterized by point B, and the level of consumption by point K. Thus the current level of consumption rises even before the process of investment bears fruit. This represents the consumption-augmenting effect. Following our previous definitions, this type of supply shock may be classified as a pro-borrowing shock.

5.4 The Determination of the World Interest Rate

In the previous sections the analysis of the stylized model treated the world rate of interest as given to the small open economy. In this section we analyze the determination of the equilibrium rate of interest in the world economy. For this purpose we consider a two-country model. All variables pertaining to the foreign economy are designated by an asterisk.

In determining the world equilibrium intertemporal terms of trade (the rate of interest) and the associated patterns of intertemporal trade (trade-account surplus or deficit), it is convenient to separate among the effects of three distinct factors: international differences in subjective rates of time preference, international differences in GDP growth rates, and the growth rate of world output. In the exposition of these three factors we abstract from initial debt and from endogenous investment.

Consider first the role of the subjective rates of time preference.

In order to isolate this factor, suppose that domestic and foreign endowments are stationary and equal to each other; that is, let $\overline{Y}_0 = \overline{Y}_1 = \overline{Y}_0^* = \overline{Y}_1^*$. Also suppose that the domestic subjective rate of time preference exceeds the foreign rate so that $\rho > \rho^*$. The equilibrium of the world economy is portrayed by the Edgeworth box in figure 5.7. In that figure the horizontal axis measures world GDP in period zero ($\overline{Y}_0 + \overline{Y}_0^*$), and the vertical axis measures the corresponding quantity for period one ($\overline{Y}_1 + \overline{Y}_1^*$). By construction the box is squared, and the international and intertemporal distribution of world outputs is specified by point A along the diagonal OO^*. As usual, quantities pertaining to the home country are measured from point O as an origin, and quantities pertaining to the foreign country are measured from point O^* as an origin. At the initial endowment point A the slope of the domestic indifference curve, U, equals one plus the domestic subjective rate of time preference $(1 + \rho)$, whereas the slope of the foreign indifference curve, U^*, equals one plus the foreign subjective rate of time preference $(1 + \rho^*)$.

Since $\rho > \rho^*$, it follows that the equilibrium patterns of international and intertemporal consumption must be located to the southeast of point A at a point like point B on the contract curve (the locus of tangencies between domestic and foreign indifference curves). At the equilibrium point B the rate of interest, r_0, is equalized across countries, and its magnitude must be bounded between the domestic and the foreign subjective rates of time preference; that is, $\rho > r_0 > \rho^*$. As is evident by a comparison between the patterns of consumption at point B with the patterns of GDPs at point A, in period zero the home country runs a deficit in its trade account while the foreign country runs a corresponding surplus of an equal magnitude. In the subsequent period this pattern of trade is reversed so as to ensure that the discounted sum of each country's trade balance is zero. This intertemporal pattern of international trade reflects the consumption-tilting effect operating in each country. Hence *the less patient country (the country with the higher rate of time preference) runs a trade deficit in the early period.*

Consider next the role of international differences in GDP growth rates. In order to isolate this factor, suppose that the domestic and

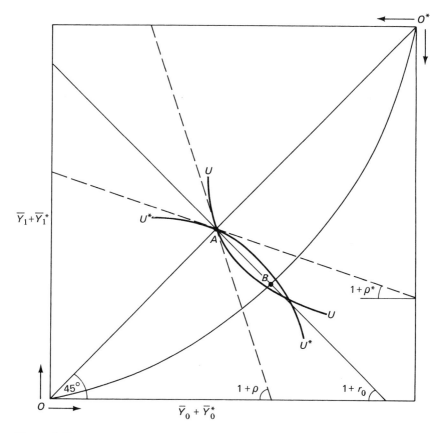

Figure 5.7
International differences in time preferences. Data: $\bar{Y}_0 = \bar{Y}_0^* = \bar{Y}_1 = \bar{Y}_1^*$, $\rho > \rho^*$.

the foreign subjective rates of time preference are equal to each other so that $\rho = \rho^*$. Our previous analysis implies that in equilibrium the rate of interest equals the common value of the subjective rates of time preference; that is, $\rho = r_0 = \rho^*$. Suppose further that *world* output is stationary so that $\overline{Y}_0 + \overline{Y}_0^* = \overline{Y}_1 + \overline{Y}_1^*$, but let the growth rate of the home country GDP exceed the foreign growth rate. We denote the percentage growth of GDP by g, where $g = (\overline{Y}_1 / \overline{Y}_0) - 1$, and a similar definition applies to the foreign growth rate, g^*.

The equilibrium of the world economy is portrayed in figure 5.8. In that figure the international and the intertemporal distributions of GDP is specified by point A. This point lies to the left of the diagonal OO^*, thereby reflecting the assumption that $g > g^*$. The international and intertemporal distribution of world equilibrium consumption is specified by point B. This point lies on the diagonal OO^*, thereby reflecting the assumptions that the *world* output is stationary and that $\rho = \rho^*$. As is evident, in this case the home country runs a trade deficit in the early period while the foreign country runs a corresponding surplus. Obviously, this pattern of trade imbalances is reversed in the subsequent period. This intertemporal pattern of international trade reflects the consumption-smoothing effect operating in each country. Hence *the faster-growing country runs a trade deficit in the early period.*

Finally, consider the role of the rate of growth of *world* output. In order to isolate this factor, we continue to assume that the domestic and the foreign subjective rates of time preference are equal to each other so that $\rho = \rho^*$. We also assume that *world* output is growing at the percentage rate, g, that is common to the percentage growth rate of each country's GDP. Thus let $\overline{Y}_1 / \overline{Y}_0 = \overline{Y}_1^* / \overline{Y}_0^* = 1 + g$. The equalities between the domestic and the foreign marginal rates of time preference and between the domestic and the foreign growth rates imply that in this case the two factors analyzed here do not play a role in determining the rate of interest, nor do they determine the patterns of trade. If we assume that the domestic and the foreign utility functions are identical and homothetic, then we can specify the equilibrium without taking account of international differences in the *levels* of GDP.

The equilibrium of the world economy is shown in figure 5.9 in

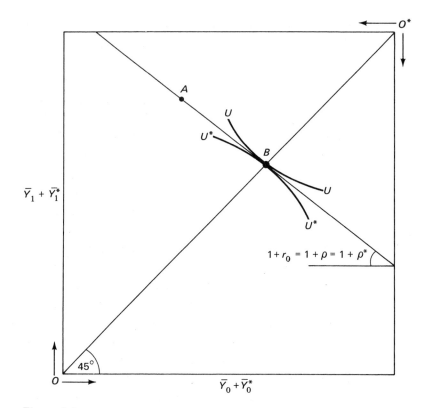

Figure 5.8
International differences in GDP growth rates. Data: $\rho = \rho^*$, $\bar{Y}_0 + \bar{Y}_0^* = \bar{Y}_1 + \bar{Y}_1^*$, $g > g^*$.

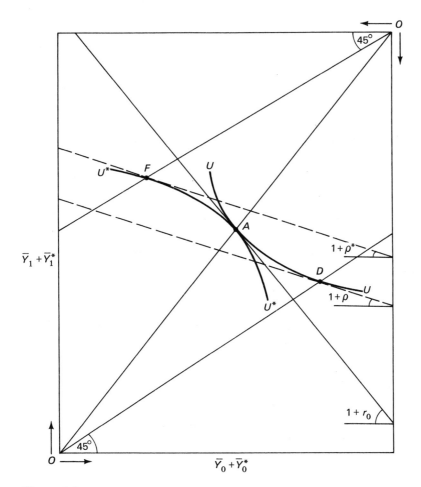

Figure 5.9
Growth of world output. Data: identical homothetic utility functions, $g = g^* > 0$.

which point A describes the international and the intertemporal distributions of both GDP *and* consumption. Obviously, in that case, because of the equality between the patterns of production and consumption in each country, there are no trade imbalances. The main point that is demonstrated by the figure concerns the equilibrium value of the world rate of interest. As shown, the equilibrium rate of interest (corresponding to the common slope of the domestic and the foreign indifference curves at point A) exceeds the domestic and foreign common subjective rates of time preference (corresponding to the slopes of the domestic and the foreign indifference curves at points D and F on the $45°$ lines). The difference between the equilibrium rate of interest and the rates of time preference rises with the growth rate of world GDP. Hence *the higher the growth rate of the world economy, the higher the equilibrium world rate of interest.*

In order to derive the precise relation between the equilibrium rate of interest and the rate of growth of the world economy, we denote the consumption ratio C_1/C_0 by c and the intertemporal elasticity of substitution by σ, where

$$\sigma = \frac{\partial \log c}{\partial \log [(\partial U/\partial C_0)/(\partial U/\partial C_1)]} > 0. \tag{5.12}$$

Assuming that the elasticity of substitution is constant and using these notations, we observe from figure 5.9 that

$$\log c(A) = \log c(D) + \sigma[\log (1 + r_0) - \log (1 + \rho)], \tag{5.13}$$

where $c(A)$ and $c(D)$ are the consumption ratios in figure 5.9 at points A and D, respectively. Since point D lies on the $45°$ line, $c(D) = 1$; further, since point A lies on the diagonal OO^*, it is evident that $c(A) = 1 + g$. It follows that $\log (1 + g) = \sigma \log [(1 + r_0)/(1 + \rho)]$, and therefore

$$(1 + r_0) = (1 + \rho)(1 + g)^{1/\sigma}. \tag{5.14}$$

Hence the positive association between the equilibrium rate of interest and the percentage rate of growth of world GDP increases with the elasticity of substitution between the levels of consumption in two consecutive periods.

The foregoing analysis presumed that the growth of world output stems from an exogenous rise in the levels of the endowments. A similar analysis also applies to the case in which the growth of world output (evenly distributed across countries) arises from an improved availability of investment opportunities. In that case figure 5.9 applies, except the dimensions of the box are endogenous. Specifically, though in the previous case the dimensions of the box reflected the exogenously given growth rate of world GDP, $1 + g = \bar{Y}_1/\bar{Y}_0 = \bar{Y}_1^*/\bar{Y}_0^*$, in the present case they reflect the endogenously determined growth rate of GDP net of investment:

$$1 + g = \frac{\bar{Y}_1 + F[I_0(r_0)]}{\bar{Y}_0 - I_0(r_0)} = \frac{\bar{Y}_1^* + F[I_0^*(r_0)]}{\bar{Y}_0 - I_0^*(r_0)}, \tag{5.15}$$

where $I_0(r_0)$ and $I_0^*(r_0)$ denote desired investment as a function of the rate of interest. The equilibrium rate of interest is determined as the solution to equations (5.14) and (5.15), and as before, in equilibrium there are no trade imbalances.

If investment opportunities are not distributed evenly between the two countries, then the two (endogenous) growth rates of GDP also differ from each other. In that case the total effect exerted by the investment opportunities on the rate of interest and on the patterns of trade reflect the considerations underlying the cases analyzed in figures 5.8 and 5.9. Specifically, suppose that the home country faces a more profitable set of investment opportunities than the foreign country. Then the (endogenously determined) growth rate of the home country's GDP, net of investment, exceeds the corresponding growth rate of the foreign economy, and the world rate of interest exceeds the subjective rate of time preference according to equation (5.14) in which the growth rate g is now interpreted as the weighted average of the two countries' growth rates. The resulting patterns of trade are similar to those portrayed by figure 5.8, reflecting the general principle that the faster-growing country runs a trade deficit in the early period.

Up to now we have abstracted from the role that the historically given initial debt position plays in determining the equilibrium world rate of interest and the patterns of trade. In order to examine the

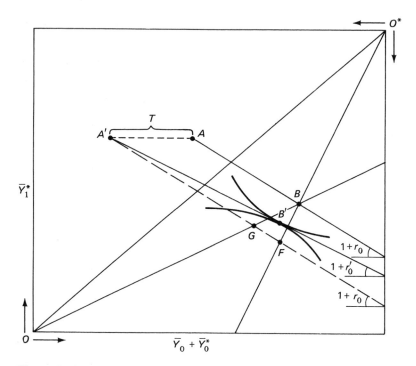

Figure 5.10
The effect of a redistribution of world debt. Data: $\partial C_0/\partial W_0 > \partial C_0^*/\partial W_0^*$, $\rho > \rho^*$.

consequences of the initial debt position, it is useful to compare an equilibrium without an initial debt commitment with another equilibrium in which the initial debt commitment of the home country is positive. Hence consider an initial zero-debt equilibrium that is disturbed by a transfer of $T = (1 + r_{-1})B_{-1}$ units of current output from the home to the foreign country. The effects of such a transfer are examined with the aid of figure 5.10 which is familiar from the famous transfer-problem analysis.

Suppose that at the initial equilibrium the international and intertemporal distributions of GDP are specified by point A and the corresponding distributions of consumption by point B. Analogously to our discussion of figure 5.7, this pattern of consumption reflects the assumption that the domestic marginal propensity to save falls short of the foreign marginal propensity. This difference between the two marginal saving propensities is reflected in the relative slopes of the domestic and foreign consumption-expansion loci OGB and O^*BF, respectively. As shown in figure 5.10, at the initial equilibrium the rate of interest is r_0, and the two expansion loci are drawn for this rate of interest.

As a brief digression we compute now the slopes of the expansion loci. Using the representative individual's maximization problem of equation (5.8), the implied demand functions for current and future consumption are (5.16) and (5.17):

$$C_0 = C_0(\alpha_1, W_0),$$ (5.16)

$$C_1 = C_1(\alpha_1, W_0).$$ (5.17)

Assuming normality, equation (5.16) can be inverted to read:

$$W_0 = h(\alpha_1, C_0).$$ (5.18)

Substituting (5.18) into (5.17) yields

$$C_1 = C_1[\alpha_1, h(\alpha_1, C_0)].$$ (5.19)

The slope of the consumption-expansion locus is obtained by differentiating equation (5.19) and noting that from (5.18) $\partial h/\partial C_0 = 1/(\partial C_0/\partial W_0)$. Thus

$$\frac{dC_1}{dC_0} = \frac{\partial C_1/\partial W_0}{\partial C_0/\partial W_0} = \frac{1 - (\partial C_0/\partial W_0)}{\alpha_1(\partial C_0/\partial W_0)},$$ (5.20)

where the second equality follows from the budget constraint in equation (5.8).

It follows that if the foreign and the domestic residents face the same rate of interest, then the differences between the slopes of their consumption-expansion loci depend only on the relations between their marginal propensities to consume (or save) out of wealth. Our previous analysis of figure 5.7 indicates that in the absence of world output growth there is also a unique relation between the equilibrium pattern of the two countries' consumption ratios (C_1/C_0 and C_1^*/C_0^*) and the difference between their subjective rates of time preference. Specifically, as illustrated by point B in figure 5.7, if $\rho > \rho^*$, then $(C_1/C_0) < (C_1^*/C_0^*)$, and vice versa. Hence in the absence of growth the pattern of consumptions exhibited in figure 5.10, and the analysis of the effects of a redistribution of world debt that is carried out with the aid of the same figure, can also be characterized in terms of differences between the subjective rates of time preference rather than differences between the marginal propensities to save. Finally, we note that if the utility functions are homothetic, then the difference between the domestic and foreign marginal propensities to save depends only on the difference between their subjective rates of time preference. In that case the general-equilibrium configuration exhibited by figure 5.7 is also applicable to a situation in which there is growth.

Consider now the effects of a transfer from the domestic to the foreign country. Following the transfer, the *net* endowments of the two countries are specified in figure 5.10 by point A' where the horizontal distance between A and A' equals the size of the transfer, T. The new endowment alters the patterns of demand in both countries, and since the two subjective rates of time preference differ from each other, the new pattern of demand alters the rate of interest. Specifically, following the transfer at the *initial* rate of interest, the domestic demand for current and future goods is described by point G, and the corresponding foreign demand is described by point F, where points G and F lie on the consumption-expansion loci associated with the initial interest rate. Obviously, this pattern of world demand creates an excess supply of current-period goods and an excess demand for future-period goods. In order to eliminate this disequilibrium, the relative price of current goods in terms of future goods (i.e., the rate of interest) must fall. Put differently, world savings rise because the transfer redistributes wealth from the home country (with the low saving propensity) to the foreign country (with the high saving propensity). The fall in the rate of interest is necessary in order to eliminate excess savings in the world economy. Diagrammatically, the fall in the rate of interest from r_0 to r_0' raises the desired consumption ratios C_0/C_1 and C_0^*/C_1^* and alters accordingly the slopes of both the domestic and the foreign consumption-expansion loci. The new equilibrium obtains at point B' at which the slopes of the two countries' indifference curves are equal to $1 + r_0'$, where $r_0' < r_0$. As is evident, point B' must be located inside the triangle *BGF*. It follows that if the foreign rate of time preference exceeded the domestic rate, the contract curve in figure 5.10 would have been located above the diagonal *OO**, and the transfer from the home to the foreign country would have necessitated a rise rather than a fall in the world rate of interest.

It is relevant to note that as is typical in transfer-problem analyses, the relevant criterion determining the effect of a redistribution of world debt on the rate of interest involves a comparison between the domestic and the foreign *marginal* propensities to save rather than the *average* saving propensities. In fact the initial endowment in figure 5.10 could have been placed to the southeast of point *B* along the extension of the line segment *AB*. The analysis of the effect of the transfer on the rate of interest remains intact as long as the domestic marginal propensity to save is smaller than the foreign marginal propensity, even though in that case the (positive) domestic average propensity to save exceeds the (negative) foreign average propensity to save.

6

The Multiple-Good World

The formulation of the stylized model discussed in the previous chapter adopted a high degree of commodity aggregation; it assumed a single composite-commodity world. With this level of aggregation the only price relevant for individual decision making was the relative price of consumption in different periods. This formulation enabled us to focus on the role played by the intertemporal terms of trade—the rate of interest. In this chapter we extend the stylized model to include multiple goods. This extension introduces the temporal terms of trade (the relative price of different goods in a given period) and facilitates the analysis of the interactions between *temporal* and *intertemporal* relative prices in influencing private-sector behavior and in determining the equilibrium of the system. In extending the model, we introduce the concepts of *consumption-based* real rate of interest and real wealth. We use the extended model to determine the effects of shocks to the commodity terms of trade on saving behavior, and thereby on current account adjustments. These results will prove useful in the subsequent analysis of the intertemporal effects of fiscal policies operating through the induced changes in temporal and intertemporal terms of trade.

6.1 The Analytical Framework

Consider a two-good–two-period model, and suppose that good X is exportable and good M is importable. For simplicity assume that there is no investment. Analogously to equations (5.4) and (5.5), the budget constraints of the representative individual (measured in terms of exportables) are

$$c_{x0} + p_0 c_{m0} = \overline{Y}_{x0} + p_0 \overline{Y}_{m0} + B_0 - (1 + r_{x,-1})B_{-1}, \qquad (6.1)$$

$$c_{x1} + p_1 c_{m1} = \overline{Y}_{x1} + p_1 \overline{Y}_{m1} - (1 + r_{x0})B_0, \qquad (6.2)$$

where c_{xt} and $\overline{Y}_{xt}$ denote, respectively, the levels of consumption and production of exportables in period t, c_{mt} and $\overline{Y}_{mt}$ denote, respectively, the levels of consumption and production of importables in period t, p_t denotes the relative price in period t of importables in terms of exportables, and $t = 0, 1$. The rate of interest, r_{xt}, and the levels of new borrowing, $B_t (t = -1, 0)$, are measured in units of exportables that serve as the numeraire throughout this section.

Before proceeding with the analysis, two points are worth noting. First, using the conventions of national income accounting, the budget constraints can also be expressed by the equality between the current-account surplus, $(CA)_t$, and the capital account deficit $-(KA)_t$. The trade-account surplus, $(TA)_t$, equals the difference between exports (the excess of production over consumption of exportables; i.e., $\overline{Y}_{xt} - c_{xt}$) and imports (the excess of the values of consumption over production of importables; i.e., $p_t[c_{mt} - \overline{Y}_{mt}]$); the current-account surplus is the difference between the surplus in the balance of trade and the deficit in the debt-service account; thus $(CA)_t = (TA)_t - (DA)_t$, where the debt-service account, $(DA)_t = r_{xt-1} B_{t-1}$, and finally, $(KA)_t = B_t - B_{t-1}$. Using these definitions, it can be verified that $(CA)_t + (KA)_t = 0$.

Second, our assumption that the debt commitment is denominated in units of good X may be material when there are unanticipated changes in the terms of trade yielding unanticipated capital gains or losses. Obviously, if all changes in the terms of trade are anticipated, interest-rate parity (across debt instruments denominated in units of different commodities) requires that $1 + r_{xt} = (p_{t+1}/p_t)(1 + r_{mt})$, where r_{mt} denotes the rate of interest in period t on debt denominated in units of importables. In that case the fully anticipated terms of trade changes do not alter the individuals' wealth position. It follows that an unexpected change in p_0 exerts different wealth effects depending on whether the initial debt commitment was $(1 + r_{x,-1})B_{-1}$ (as in equation 6.1) or $p_0/p_{-1}(1 + r_{m,-1})B_{-1}$. We will return to this issue in the subsequent analysis of terms of trade shocks.

The representative individual maximizes lifetime utility subject to the consolidated budget constraint (obtained by dividing equation 6.2 by $(1 + r_{x0})$ and adding the resultant expression to equation 6.1). The utility function is defined over the four goods $(c_{x0}, c_{m0}, c_{x1}, c_{m1})$. We assume that utility can be expressed as a function of two components, C_0 and C_1, which are in turn linearly homogeneous subutility functions of the consumption of goods in period zero (c_{x0}, c_{m0}) and in period one (c_{x1}, c_{m1}), respectively. Formally, the maximization problem is

$$\tilde{U} = \max_{\substack{\{c_{x0}, c_{m0}\} \\ \{c_{x1}, c_{m1}\}}} U[C_0(c_{x0}, c_{m0}), C_1(c_{x1}, c_{m1})], \tag{6.3}$$

subject to

$$c_{x0} + p_0 c_{m0} + \alpha_{x1}(c_{x1} + p_1 c_{m1})$$

$$= \overline{Y}_{x0} + p_0 \overline{Y}_{m0} + \alpha_{x1}(\overline{Y}_{x1} + p_1 \overline{Y}_{m1}) - (1 + r_{x-1})B_{-1}$$

$$= W_0, \tag{6.4}$$

where $\alpha_{x1} = 1/(1 + r_{x0})$ is the discount factor applicable to consumption in period one.

The solution to the maximization problem can be decomposed into two parts. The first involves the *temporal* allocation of spending, $z_t = c_{xt} + p_t c_{mt}$, between the two goods so as to maximize the subutility $C_t(c_{xt}, c_{mt})$, and the second involves the *intertemporal* allocation of lifetime spending $(z_0 + \alpha_{x1} z_1 = W_0)$ so as to maximize the lifetime utility $U(C_0, C_1)$. In the first stage of the temporal maximization the consumer may be viewed as minimizing the cost, z_t, of obtaining a given level of subutility, C_t. The assumption that the subutility functions are linear homogeneous imply that the "cost" function is $z_t = P_t(p_t)C_t$, where $P_t(p_t)$ is the "marginal cost" of obtaining a unit of C_t (and the marginal cost depends on the relative price, p_t). In what follows we refer to P_t as the *consumption-based price index*. This price index exhibits the familiar properties of similar price indexes; in each period the elasticity of the price index, P, with respect to the price of importables, p, equals the expenditure share of this commodity in total spending.

In the second stage the consumer, who has already optimized the temporal allocation of spending, attempts to optimize the inter-temporal allocation. Formally, this maximization problem is

$$\tilde{U} = \max_{\{C_0, C_1\}} U(C_0, C_1), \tag{6.5}$$

subject to

$$P_0(p_0)C_0 + \alpha_{x1} P_1(p_1)C_1 = W_0. \tag{6.6}$$

For subsequent use it is convenient to normalize the budget constraint (6.6) and express it in *real* terms. For this purpose we divide both sides by the price index P_0 and obtain

$$C_0 + \alpha_{c1} C_1 = W_{c0}, \tag{6.6a}$$

where

$$\alpha_{c1} = \frac{P_1}{P_0}\alpha_{x1} \quad \text{and} \quad W_{c0} = \frac{W_0}{P_0}.$$

We refer to α_{c1} as the (consumption-based) *real discount factor* and to W_{c0} as the (consumption-based) *real wealth*. As seen, the real discount factor equals the discount factor expressed in terms of the numeraire (α_{x1}) adjusted by the "rate of inflation," that is, by the percentage change in the consumption-based price index.

The maximization of the utility function (6.5) subject to the normalized budget constraint (6.6a) yields conventional demand functions for the "goods" C_0 and C_1. As usual, these functions depend on the relevant relative price α_{c1}, and on the relevant concept of "income," which in our case is real wealth, W_{c0}. Thus the periodic demand functions (for $t = 0, 1$) are $C_t = C_t(\alpha_{c1}, W_{c0})$. These demand functions are the conventional consumption-based *real spending* functions. Obviously, we could also have used the previous analysis to define and characterize spending in terms of other baskets of goods, such as exportables, importables, or GDP; in these cases spending would have been measured by $P_t(p_t)C_t$, $P_t(p_t)C_t/p_{mt}$, and $P_t(p_t)C_t/(\bar{Y}_{xt} + p_{mt}\bar{Y}_{mt})$, respectively. The choice of units is, of course, of prime importance in circumstances where relative prices change. In the subsequent analysis of the effects of terms of trade changes, we choose to express spending and the current account in terms of the consumption basket. This choice is made in order to obtain indicators useful for welfare evaluations. But first we digress briefly to define the consumption-based real rate of interest.

6.2 The Real Rate of Interest

Corresponding to the concept of the real discount factor, we can define the concept of the (consumption-based) *real rate of interest*. Accordingly, the real interest rate, r_{c0}, is

$$r_{c0} = \frac{1 + r_{x0}}{P_1/P_0} - 1. \tag{6.7}$$

As is evident, this consumption-based real rate of interest, r_{c0}, depends positively on the rate of interest in terms of the numeraire, r_{x0}, and negatively on the rate of "inflation," P_1/P_0, which in turn reflects the path of the relative price of importables, p_0 and p_1. In order to characterize the dependence of the real rate of interest on the path of the temporal terms of trade, p_0 and p_1, we differentiate equation (6.7) and obtain

$$\left(\frac{1}{1 + r_{c0}}\right) dr_{c0} = \left(\frac{1}{1 + r_{x0}}\right) dr_{x0} + \beta_{m0} \frac{dp_0}{p_0} - \beta_{m1} \frac{dp_1}{p_1}, \tag{6.8}$$

where β_{m1} denotes the expenditure share of importables in total spending in period t. Equation (6.8) reveals that, ceteris paribus, a temporary current deterioration in the commodity terms of trade (a rise in p_0) raises the real rate of interest while an expected future deterioration in the commodity terms of trade (a rise in p_1) lowers the real rate of interest. The effect of a permanent deterioration of the commodity terms of trade (so that p_0 and p_1 rise in the same proportion) depends on the intertemporal changes in the expenditure shares. If these shares do not vary over time, a permanent change in the commodity terms of trade is neutral in its effect on the real rate of interest.

6.3 The Terms of Trade and Real Spending

In this section we analyze the effects of transitory and permanent shocks to the commodity terms of trade on real spending, C, measured in terms of the consumption basket. This analysis will aid the subsequent discussion of current-account adjustments. As was shown previously, the periodic spending functions depend on the consumption-based real discount factor and on real wealth. Accordingly, the current-period-spending function is

$$C_0 = C_0(\alpha_{c1}, W_{c0}).$$ (6.9)

We use this function in order to analyze the effects of changes in the terms of trade.

Consider a temporary change in the *current*-period terms of trade. Differentiating the spending function with respect to p_0 and expressing the results in terms of elasticities, it can be shown that

$$\frac{\partial \log C_0}{\partial \log p_0} = \beta_{m0}\left\{-\eta_{c\alpha} + [(1 - \gamma_s)\mu_{m0} - 1]\eta_{cw}\right\},$$ (6.10)

where β_{m0} denotes the relative share of consumption of importables in current-period spending ($p_0 c_{m0}/z_0 = p_0 c_{m0}/P_0 C_0$), $\eta_{c\alpha}$ and η_{cw} denote the elasticities of C_0 with respect to α_{c1} and W_{c0}, respectively, $\gamma_s = \alpha_{c1} C_1/W_{c0}$ is the share of saving in wealth, and $\mu_{m0} = \overline{Y}_{m0}/c_{m0}$ is the ratio of production to consumption of importables, which ranges between zero and one. The two terms on the right-hand side of equation (6.10) reflect the effects of changes in the two variables appearing on the right-hand side of equation (6.19), α_{c1} and W_{c0}, induced by the current change in the commodity terms of trade, p_0. Equation (6.10) can be manipulated further by using the Slutsky decomposition (according to which $\eta_{c\alpha} = \overline{\eta}_{c\alpha} - \gamma_s\eta_{cw}$, where $\overline{\eta}_{c\alpha}$ denotes the compensated demand elasticity) and noting that $\overline{\eta}_{c\alpha} = \gamma_s\sigma$ (where σ, the intertemporal elasticity of substitution, is defined by equation 5.12). Hence

$$\frac{\partial \log C_0}{\partial \log p_0} = \beta_m[-\eta_{cw} + \gamma_s(\eta_{cw} - \sigma) + (1 - \gamma_s)\mu_{m0}\eta_{cw}].$$ (6.11)

In interpreting the bracketed term on the right-hand side of equation (6.11), we note three channels through which changes in current-period terms of trade alter current-period spending. The first term represents the *deflator effect*, which operates through the change in the price index used to deflate wealth; the second term represents the *intertemporal-price effect*, which operates through the change in the real discount factor; and the third term represents the *wealth effect*, which operates through the change in real wealth induced by the change in the valuation of the output of importables.

The deterioration in the terms of trade raises the price index by β_{m0}; this lowers the real value of wealth equiproportionally and (assuming normality) lowers spending according to the elasticity η_{cw}—hence the negative term $-\eta_{cw}$ on the right-hand side of equation (6.11). The intertemporal-price effect depends on the sign of $\eta_{cw} - \sigma$. Finally, the wealth effect is the product of η_{cw} and the percentage rise in wealth due to the appreciation of the output of importables. This can be verified by noting that $\partial \log W_0 / \partial \log p_0 = p_0 \overline{Y}_{m0} / W_0$ and that this can also be written as $(1 - \gamma_s)\beta_{m0}\mu_{m0}$. In interpreting this expression, we note that a given percentage rise in the price of importables appreciates the value of output of importables, but since their consumption exceeds production, the potential rise in the former is only a fraction μ_{m0} of the rise in price. To express the potential rise in consumption of importables in terms of lifetime spending, we need to multiply μ_{m0} by the share of consumption of importables in current spending, β_{m0}, times the share of current spending in lifetime spending $(1 - \gamma_s)$. Hence the last expression on the right-hand side of equation (6.11) is the wealth effect which, by normality, is positive.

The foregoing discussion indicated the signs of the deflator effects, the intertemporal-price effects, and the wealth effect. Combining these effects, we can rewrite equation (6.11):

$$\frac{\partial \log C_0}{\partial \log p_0} = -\beta_{m0}[(1 - \gamma_s)(1 - \mu_{m0})\eta_{cw} + \gamma_s\sigma]. \tag{6.11a}$$

As is evident, since γ_s and μ_{m0} are bound between zero and unity, the deterioration in the current terms of trade must lower current real spending.

To gain further insight into the factors governing the effects of changes in the terms of trade on spending, consider the extreme case in which $\mu_{m0} = 1$, so that in the current-period production and consumption of importables are equal to each other and imports are zero. In that case, as is evident from equation (6.11a), the negative change in spending arises only from the pure intertemporal substitution effect $(-\beta_{m0}\gamma_s\sigma)$. This case is of special interest since it highlights the importance of intertemporal considerations. It demonstrates that even though real income does not change (since net imports are zero), the utility-maximizing individual responds to the rise in the domestic consumption-based real rate of interest (induced by the temporary deterioration in the terms of trade) by substituting away from current spending toward future spending.

Consider next the effect of an expected *future* deterioration in the terms of trade (i.e., a rise in p_1) on current-period spending. Formally, differentiating equation (6.9) with respect to p_1, expressing in terms of elasticities and manipulating as before, yields

$$\frac{\partial \log C_0}{\partial \log p_1} = \beta_{m1}\gamma_s[(\sigma - \eta_{cw}) + \mu_{m1}\eta_{cw}]. \tag{6.12}$$

A comparison between the expressions showing the effects of current and future deteriorations in the terms of trade reveals that the deflator effect, $-\beta_{m0}\eta_{cw}$, which appears in equation (6.11), does not appear in equation (6.12). The other important difference concerns the direction of the intertemporal-price effect. As seen in equation (6.8), a rise in p_0 raises the real rate of interest, whereas a rise in p_1 lowers the real rate of interest. Because of these differences the effect of an anticipated future deterioration on spending is ambiguous. This should be contrasted with the unambiguous response of current spending to a current terms of trade change. The ambiguous effect depends, in part, on whether current consumption, C_0, and future consumption, C_1, are gross substitutes (i.e., $\eta_{c\alpha} > 0$) or gross complements (i.e., $\eta_{c\alpha} < 0$). This is indicated by the term $(\sigma - \eta_{cw})$ in equation (6.12).

The ambiguity of the effects of the expected future deterioration in the terms of trade can be clarified by considering a simple case in which the utility function is homothetic and the level of production of importables in the future is zero. Thus consider the case in which $\eta_{cw} = 1$ and $\mu_{m1} = 0$. Under these circumstances equation (6.12) becomes

$$\frac{\partial \log C_0}{\partial \log p_1} = \beta_{m1} \gamma_s (\sigma - 1). \tag{6.12a}$$

and as is evident, the response of current spending to an anticipated future deterioration in the terms of trade depends only on whether the intertemporal elasticity of substitution, σ, exceeds or falls short of unity.

The foregoing analysis of the effects of temporary (current or future) deteriorations in the terms of trade on current spending provides the ingredients necessary for determining the effects of a *permanent* deterioration. Formally, assuming that the percentage rise in p_0 equals the corresponding rise in p_1 so that $d\log p_0 = d\log p_1 = d\log p$, the effect of the permanent deterioration in the terms of trade on current spending is obtained by adding the expressions in equations (6.11) and (6.12). Hence

$$\frac{\partial \log C_0}{\partial \log p} = -\beta_{m0}\eta_{cw} + \gamma_s(\beta_{m0} - \beta_{m1})(\eta_{cw} - \sigma)$$

$$+ [(1 - \gamma_s)\beta_{m0}\mu_{m0} + \gamma_s\beta_{m1}\mu_{m1}]\eta_{cw}. \tag{6.13}$$

The three terms on the right-hand side of equation (6.13) correspond to the three channels through which a deterioration in the terms of trade affects spending. The first term—the *deflator effect*—represents exclusively the effects of the *current* deterioration in the terms of trade as it operates through the deflation of wealth; the second term—the *intertemporal-price effect*—operates through changes in the real rate of interest that occur only if the shares of expenditure on importables vary through time (as seen in equation 6.8); the third term—the *wealth effect*—operates through changes in the value of output occurring in both periods and stemming from the permanent rise in the price of importables. In general, these three effects exert conflicting influences on current spending.

The relation between the terms of trade and spending can be clarified, however, by considering the special case in which the utility function is homothetic and in which the expenditure shares, the output-consumption ratio of importables, and real spending (in present value) are all constant over time (i.e., let $\eta_{cw} = 1$, $\beta_{m0} = \beta_{m1} =$

β_m, $\mu_{m0} = \mu_{m1} = \mu_m$, and $\gamma_s = 1 - \gamma_s$). In that case equation (6.13) becomes

$$\frac{\partial \log C_0}{\partial \log p} = -\beta_m (1 - \mu_m).$$ (6.13a)

Under these conditions (as long as $\mu_m < 1$) the permanent deterioration in the terms of trade lowers current spending. The fall in current spending arises exclusively from the reduction in real income (by the proportion $\beta_m[1 - \mu_m]$) consequent on the deterioration in the terms of trade. Since this deterioration applies equally to both the current and the future periods, it does not alter the real rate of interest (as seen from equation 6.8), and therefore it does not induce intertemporal substitution. Finally, we note that in the limiting case for which production and consumption of importables are equal to each other (so that $\mu_m = 1$), real income is constant, and the permanent deterioration in the terms of trade does not alter spending.

6.4 The Terms of Trade and the Balance of Trade

The foregoing analysis determined the effects of temporary and permanent shocks to the commodity terms of trade on spending. In this section we use these results to determine the effects of such changes in the terms of trade on the balance of trade. This analysis highlights the principal mechanisms underlying the famous Laursen-Metzler-Harberger effect. Further the results provide the main ingredients necessary to determine the dynamics of the current account and of debt accumulation.

By definition, the balance of trade equals the difference between the value of production and spending. In what follows we express the balance of trade in terms of the consumption basket. Accordingly, we denote the consumption-based real balance of trade in period t by $(TA_c)_t$. Hence $(TA_c)_t = (TA)_t/P_t$, where, as before, $(TA)_t$ denotes the balance of trade in terms of exportables. Using the previous definitions, the consumption-based real balance of trade in the current period is

$$(TA_c)_0 = (GDP)_{c0} - C_0(\alpha_{c1}, W_{c0}),$$ (6.14)

where

$$(\text{GDP})_{c0} = \frac{(\text{GDP})_0}{P_0(p_0)} = \frac{\overline{Y}_{x0} + p_0\overline{Y}_{m0}}{P_0(p_0)}.$$

A given percentage deterioration in the terms of trade influences the balance of trade through its effects on the real value of output and on real spending. The proportional change in $(\text{GDP})_{c0}$ is

$$\frac{\partial \log(\text{GDP})_{c0}}{\partial \log p_0} = \frac{\beta_{m0}}{\mu_{c0}}(\mu_{m0} - \mu_{c0}), \tag{6.15}$$

where $\mu_{c0} = (\text{GDP})_{c0}/C_0$. Thus μ_{c0} exceeds or falls short of unity as the trade balance is in surplus or deficit, respectively; if the balance of trade is balanced, $\mu_{c0} = 1$.

The effects of temporary (current or future) and permanent changes in the terms of trade on the balance of trade can be obtained by differentiating equation (6.14). Substituting equations (6.11), (6.12), and (6.13), respectively, for the change in spending, and substituting equation (6.15) for the change in $(\text{GDP})_{c0}$ yields

$$\frac{\partial(TA_c)_0}{\partial \log p_0} = \beta_{m0}[(\mu_{m0} - \mu_{c0}) + (1 - \gamma_s)(1 - \mu_{m0})\eta_{cw} + \gamma_s\sigma]C_0,$$

$$\tag{6.16}$$

$$\frac{\partial(TA_c)_0}{\partial \log p_1} = -\beta_{m1}\gamma_s[(\sigma - \eta_{cw}) + \mu_{m1}\eta_{cw}]C_0, \tag{6.17}$$

$$\frac{\partial(TA_c)_0}{\partial \log p} = \{\beta_{m0}(\mu_{m0} - \mu_{c0}) + \beta_{m0}\eta_{cw} - (\beta_{m0} - \beta_{m1})\gamma_s(\eta_{cw} - \sigma)$$

$$-[(1 - \gamma_s)\beta_{m0}\mu_{m0} + \gamma_s\beta_{m1}\mu_{m1}]\eta_{cw}\}C_0. \tag{6.18}$$

Equations (6.16) through (6.18) reveal that the response of the balance of trade to current, future, and permanent deteriorations in the terms of trade depends on the key parameters of the economic system. These parameters are the expenditure share of importables (β_m), the ratio of production to consumption of importables (μ_m), the ratio of GDP to spending (μ_c), the average saving propensity (γ_s), the wealth elasticity of spending (η_{cw}), and the intertemporal elasticity of substitution (σ). The ratio of production to ·consumption of importables determines the changes in the real values of GDP and real income consequent on a given percentage deterioration in the terms of trade. The ratio of GDP to spending reflects the imbalance in the balance of trade; if this ratio exceeds unity, then the initial position is that of a trade-balance surplus, and vice versa. The average saving propensity influences both the extent of the intertemporal-price effect as well as the wealth effect consequent on the change in the terms of trade. The wealth elasticity of spending translates direct and indirect changes in wealth into spending. Finally, the inter-temporal elasticity of substitution determines the pure substitution effect induced by changes in the real rate of interest consequent on the terms of trade change.

In order to clarify the precise role played by these parameters, consider the case of a permanent rise in the price of importables. As shown by the four terms on the right-hand side of equation (6.18), there are four effects that operate. The first is the real GDP effect—$\beta_{m0}(\mu_{m0} - \mu_{c0})$. The direction of this effect depends on the difference between two measures of imbalances: the import sector imbalance (μ_{m0}) and the trade-account imbalance (μ_{c0}); this real GDP effect is negative if the trade account is in surplus. The second effect is the deflator effect—$\beta_{m0}\eta_{cw}$. This effect improves the trade balance due to the reduction in spending induced by the β_{m0} percent rise in the price index used to deflate wealth. This change in real wealth is translated into the reduction in spending through the spending elasticity. The third effect is the intertemporal-price effect—$(\beta_{m0} - \beta_{m1})\gamma_s(\eta_{cw} - \sigma)$. The direction of this effect depends on whether the rate of interest rises or falls as well as the response of spending to the change in the rate of interest. As is evident from equation (6.8), the permanent rise in the price of importables raises the rate of interest if β_{m0} exceeds β_{m1}, and vice versa. The change in the rate of interest in turn lowers or raises spending depending on whether the interest elasticity of spending—$\gamma_s(\eta_{cw} - \sigma)$—is positive or negative. Finally, the fourth effect is the wealth effect—which is the product of the wealth elasticity of spending, η_{cw}, and the percentage change in real wealth induced by the appreciated value of the domestic production of importables. This value of the domestic production of importables appreciates in each period t ($t = 0, 1$) by the magnitude $\beta_{mt}\mu_{mt}$. The rise in real wealth associated with each period appreciation is obtained by multiplying this magnitude by the weight of the corresponding period spending in real wealth (these weights are $1 - \gamma_s$ for period zero and γ_s for period one). Hence the percentage change in real wealth is a weighted average of $\beta_{mt}\mu_{mt}$ ($t = 0, 1$).

As is evident from equations (6.16) through (6.18), the net effect of changes in the terms of trade on the balance of trade depend on the relative magnitudes of the four aforementioned effects. To sharpen the analysis, consider the case in which the utility function is homothetic, and the expenditure shares and output-consumption ratios are constant over time (i.e., let $\eta_{cw} = 1$, $\beta_{m0} = \beta_{m1} = \beta_m$, and $\mu_{m0} = \mu_{m1} = \mu_m$). In that case equations (6.16) through (6.18) become

$$\frac{\partial (TA_c)_0}{\partial \log p_0} = \beta_m[(1 - \mu_{c0}) + \gamma_s(\mu_m + \sigma - 1)]C_0, \tag{6.16a}$$

$$\frac{\partial (TA_c)_0}{\partial \log p_1} = -\beta_m\gamma_s(\mu_m + \sigma - 1)C_0, \tag{6.17a}$$

$$\frac{\partial (TA_c)_0}{\partial \log p} = \beta_m(1 - \mu_{c0})C_0. \tag{6.18a}$$

In interpreting these results, consider first equation (6.18a) corresponding to a permanent deterioration in the terms of trade. This equation shows that the key criterion determining the direction of the change in the balance of trade is whether at the initial terms of trade the trade account is in deficit or surplus (i.e., whether μ_{c0} exceeds or falls short of unity). If at the initial terms of trade the trade account is in deficit, then the permanent deterioration in the terms of trade improves the balance of trade, and vice versa. Finally, if initially the trade account is balanced, then the permanent deterioration in the terms of trade is neutral in its effect on the balance of trade. In that case the equiproportional fall in real GDP and in real spending implies that both fall by the same magnitude, and therefore the difference between them (the trade account) remains unchanged.

There are two key differences between the effects of permanent and temporary (current or future) deteriorations in the terms of trade.

First, temporary changes alter the intertemporal pattern of real GDP in a manner similar to that of temporary negative supply shocks (analyzed in section 5.3). This change in the intertemporal pattern of real GDP, taken by itself, induces a trade-account deficit in the case of a current deterioration of the terms of trade and a trade-account surplus in the case of a future deterioration in the terms of trade. These trade-account adjustments are induced by the consumption-smoothing effects and are reflected by the term $\beta_m \gamma_s (1 - \mu_m)$ which appears negatively in equation (6.16a) and positively in equation (6.17a).

The second difference between the effects of permanent and temporary deteriorations in the terms of trade reflects the induced changes in the real rate of interest. If the terms of trade deteriorate permanently, then, with constant expenditure shares, the real rate of interest does not change. This is reflected in equation (6.18a) by the absence of terms relating to intertemporal subsitution. In contrast, a current deterioration raises the rate of interest and induces substitution away from current spending toward future spending. This consumption-tilting effect is reflected by the positive term $\beta_m \gamma_s \sigma$ in equation (6.16a). Analogously, a future deterioration in the terms of trade lowers the real rate of interest and induces substitution toward current spending. This is reflected by the negative term $-\beta_m \gamma_s \sigma$ in equation (6.17a).

The foregoing analysis of the effects of temporary deteriorations in the terms of trade shows that the induced change in the intertemporal pattern of real GDP influences the trade account in a manner opposite to that of the induced change in the real rate of interest. As shown by equations (6.16a) and (6.16b), the net effect depends on whether the intertemporal elasticity of substitution, σ, exceeds or falls short of the ratio of imports to consumption of importables, $1 - \mu_m$. For values of σ smaller than this import-consumption ratio, the qualitative effects of temporary deteriorations in the terms of trade (starting from an initial balance in the trade account) are similar to those exerted by temporary negative supply shocks. On the other hand, for values of σ larger than this import-consumption ratio, the qualitative effects of temporary deteriorations in the terms of trade on the balance of trade are the opposite of those induced by negative supply shocks.

Before concluding, it is worth recalling that throughout the analysis we have expressed the balance of trade in terms of the consumption basket. Since changes in the terms of trade impact on the price index, the choice of the units of measurement is material. As an · example, suppose that the trade account is measured in terms of exportables. By definition, the trade account measured in terms of exportable, TA, is related to its value measured in terms of the consumption basket, TA_c, according to $TA = P_0 TA_c$. Since the price index, P_0, depends only on the current price of importables, p_0, and not on the future price, p_1, it is obvious that changes in the two measures of the trade account may differ from each other only if the current terms of trade change. In that case, using our previous notations, the change in $(TA)_0$ is

$$\frac{\partial(TA)_0}{\partial \log p_0} = \left[\frac{\partial(TA_c)_0}{\partial \log p_0} + \beta_{m0}(\mu_{c0} - 1)C_0\right]P_0. \qquad (6.19)$$

Substituting equation (6.16) into (6.19) yields the expression indicating the effect of a current deterioration of the terms of trade on the trade account measured in terms of exportables. In order to derive the effect of a rise in p_1 on $(TA)_0$, we first note that a future deterioration in the terms of trade does not alter P_0. It follows that the expression (6.17), multiplied by P_0, yields the corresponding effect of a future rise in the price of importables. Obviously, the effect of a permanent deterioration in the terms of trade on the trade account measured in terms of exportables is the sum of these two expressions.

As is evident, changes in the current terms of trade may result in different inferences concerning the direction of the change in the two measures of the trade account only if at the initial terms of trade the trade account is unbalanced. For example, if the current rise in the price of importables worsens the trade account TA_c (measured in terms of the consumption basket), and if at the initial terms of trade there is a relatively large surplus in the trade account ($\mu_{c0} > 1$), then, as seen in equation (6.19), the trade account TA (measured in terms of exportables) improves. Obviously, under such circumstances the trade account measured in terms of importables must worsen. This phenomenon of a *J*-curve effect is exclusively an artifact of the arbitrary choice of units of measurements. As indicated previously, we have chosen to express the values of real spending, real GDP, and thereby the real trade balance in terms of the consumption basket in order to obtain information that is more amenable for a welfare analysis.

Finally, we note that an additional mechanism through which changes in the terms of trade influence the balance of trade operates through the effects of capital gains or losses on external debt commitments. These gains or losses depend on the units in terms of which debt is denominated. Specifically, unless the economy's external debt is fully linked to the consumption-based price index, any change in the terms of trade alters the real value of its initial debt commitment. This alters wealth and exerts an additional independent influence on spending and on the trade balance.

IV

An Intertemporal Approach to Fiscal
Policies in the World Economy

7

Government Spending

Up to now we have disregarded the role of government. In this chapter we extend the analysis by incorporating government into the model. There are various layers through which the introduction of government impacts on the economic system. First, from the perspective of the representative individual the public goods provided by the government enter directly into the utility function. Further the taxes used to finance government spending enter directly into the individual's budget constraint. Second, from the perspective of the economy as a whole, the activities of the government absorb resources and provide public consumer and producer goods. Thereby the government alters the amount of resources available to the private sector, and the availability of public goods may alter the intertemporal pattern of private consumption and production. Third, from the perspective of the rest of the world, the activities of the government are transmitted internationally through its direct and indirect effects on world goods and capital markets. In what follows we examine the implications of government spending as they operate through the various layers. We start with the formal analytical framework.

7.1 The Analytical Framework

In the presence of government the representative individual's utility function, U, is $U(C_0, C_1, G_0, G_1)$, where G_0 and G_1 denote government spending in periods zero and one, respectively. For ease of exposition we assume that the utility function U takes the form of $U(C_0, G_0) + \delta U(C_1, G_1)$, where as before δ denotes the subjective

discount factor. To highlight the pure effects of government spending, we abstract from possible distortionary effects arising from
government finance. Thus throughout this chapter we assume that
the government finances its budget with lump-sum taxes T_0 and T_1.
Hence the individual seeking to maximize lifetime utility solves the
following problem:

$$V(G_0, G_1, T_0, T_1) = \max_{\{C_0, C_1\}} U(C_0, G_0) + \delta U(C_1, G_1), \tag{7.1}$$

subject to

$$C_0 + \alpha_1^p C_1 = (\overline{Y}_0 - T_0) + \alpha_1^p(\overline{Y}_1 - T_1) - (1 + r_{-1}^p)B_{-1}^p = W_0, \tag{7.2}$$

where α_1^p denotes the present-value factor applicable to the private
sector. The formulation in equation (7.1) indicates that, as usual, the
individual who chooses the utility-maximizing path of consumption
$\{C_0, C_1\}$ treats the paths of government spending $\{G_0, G_1\}$, and
taxes $\{T_0, T_1\}$ as given. The function $V(\cdot)$ denotes the maximized
value of utility given the paths of spending and taxes. The lifetime
constraint in equation (7.2) indicates that the discounted sum of lifetime consumption equals the discounted sum of lifetime disposable
income net of initial private debt commitment $(1 + r_{-1}^p)B_{-1}^p$. For
simplicity we assume that there is no investment.

The specification of equation (7.2) indicates that as long as the
discounted sum of taxes $(T_0 + \alpha_1^p T_1)$ remains unchanged, the timing
of taxes does not influence the individual's behavior.

As usual, the first-order condition for utility maximization requires
that the marginal rate of substitution between consumption in two
consecutive periods equals the reciprocal of the market discount
factor applicable to the private sector. It is important to emphasize,
however, that in the present case the marginal rate of substitution
also reflects the interaction between government spending and private consumption. Hence

$$\frac{U_c(C_0, G_0)}{\delta U_c(C_1, G_1)} = \frac{1}{\alpha_1^p}, \tag{7.3}$$

where U_c denotes the marginal utility of consumption. It can also be shown (using the envelope relations obtained by constructing the Lagrangian form associated with equation 7.1 and the implied first-order conditions) that

$$\frac{\partial V(\cdot)}{\partial G_0} = U_G(C_0, G_0), \qquad \frac{\partial V(\cdot)}{\partial G_1} = \delta U_G(C_1, G_1),$$

$$\frac{\partial V(\cdot)}{\partial T_0} = -U_c(C_0, G_0), \qquad \frac{\partial V(\cdot)}{\partial T_1} = -\delta U_c(C_1, G_1). \tag{7.4}$$

These equalities state that the change in the maximized level of utility induced by a marginal change in government spending and by a marginal change in taxes equals, respectively, the marginal utility of public goods and the negative of the marginal utility of ordinary consumption.

The foregoing analysis treated the levels of government spending and taxes as given. The two, however, are linked to each other through the requirement that the government in its various activities must be solvent. The government budget constraints specify that in each period government outlays be financed by taxes or by debt issue, and solvency requires that in the last period all debt be repaid without issuing new liabilities. In our two-period model these constraints are

$$G_0 = B_0^g + T_0 - (1 + r_{-1}^g)B_{-1}^g,$$

$$G_1 = T_1 - \frac{1}{\alpha_1^g}B_0^g, \tag{7.5}$$

where B^g denotes government debt, and thus $(1 + r_{-1}^g)B_{-1}^g$ is the government debt commitment on the historically given initial government debt position. The formulation in (7.5) embodies the possibility that the rate of interest applicable to the government may differ from the one applicable to the private sector. Hence the government budget constraint is specified in terms of the present-value factor applicable to the government, α_1^g, rather than in terms of α_1^p.

Analogously to the procedure applied previously to consolidate the private sector's periodic budget constraints into a single present-value budget constraint, we can also consolidate the government constraints into a single present-value constraint. Applying this procedure to the constraints in (7.5) yields

$$G = G_0 + \alpha_1^g G_1 = T_0 + \alpha_1^g T_1 - (1 + r_{-1}^g)B_{-1}^g, \qquad (7.6)$$

where G denotes the discounted sum of government spending.

The fully informed forward-looking individuals are presumed to "see through" the government budget constraint and thereby to recognize the precise dependence between the levels of government spending and the implied tax liabilities. Hence they incorporate the implications of the government budget constraint into their own. Incorporating the government budget constraint (7.6) into the private-sector constraint (7.2) yields

$$C_0 + \alpha_1^p C_1 = (\overline{Y}_0 + \alpha_1^p \overline{Y}_1) - (G_0 + \alpha_1^p G_1) - (\alpha_1^g - \alpha_1^p)(G_1 - T_1)$$

$$+ (r_{-1}^p - r_{-1}^g)B_{-1}^g - (1 + r_{-1}^p)B_{-1}, \qquad (7.7)$$

where B_{-1} denotes the historically given value of the economy's external debt position, which in turn equals the sum of the corresponding private-sector and government debts (i.e., $B_{-1} = B_{-1}^p + B_{-1}^g$). The right-hand side of equation (7.7) specifies the value of private-sector wealth which incorporates the government budget constraints as perceived (correctly) by the private sector. As may be seen, the value of wealth is composed of three items: the discounted sum of GDP net of government spending (discounted by the private sector's market interest rates), terms that are proportional to the discrepancy between private and government interest rates, and finally the historically given value of the economy's external debt commitment.

Equation (7.7) reveals that changes in taxes that satisfy the government budget constraint and that are not associated with changes in government spending alter private-sector wealth if the discount factors applicable to the private and to the public sectors differ from each other. Likewise, changes in the historical value of government debt that are not associated with corresponding changes in the economy's external debt position or in government spending alter private-sector wealth if there is a discrepancy between the historical rates of interest applicable to the private and to the public sectors.

Consider, for example, the effect of a government budget deficit arising from a current tax cut. Obviously, as indicated by the government budget constraint (7.6), a deficit arising from a fall in T_0, as long as it is not accompanied by a change in government spending, must be accompanied by an equal future surplus (in present-value terms) arising from a rise in future taxes, T_1. Equation (7.7) shows that if for reasons such as finite life the discount factor applicable to the government exceeds the discount factor applicable to the private sector (i.e., $\alpha_1^g - \alpha_1^p > 0$), then the deficit raises private-sector wealth, and thereby influences behavior and alters the real equilibrium of the system. The opposite holds if $\alpha_1^g < \alpha_1^p$. These examples highlight the considerations underlying the famous *Ricardian equivalence* proposition, according to which the timing of taxes and the size of government debt do not influence private sector's behavior and the real equilibrium as long as government spending and the size of foreign debt remain unchanged. In our case the Ricardian proposition emerges if the private and the public rates of interest are equal to each other (i.e., if $\alpha_1^g = \alpha_1^p = \alpha_1$ and $r_{-1}^g = r_{-1}^p = r_{-1}$). With such equalities the private-sector budget constraint (7.7) becomes

$$C_0 + \alpha_1 C_1 = (\overline{Y}_0 - G_0) + \alpha_1(\overline{Y}_1 - G_1) - (1 + r_{-1})B_{-1}. \qquad (7.8)$$

Equation (7.8) shows that if both the private and the public sector can lend and borrow freely in the world capital market (at the same terms) and if all taxes are nondistortionary, then private-sector's wealth consists of the discounted sum of GDP net of government spending and of the initial external debt commitment. This is the case in which the internalization of government activities by the private sector eliminates the influence of the details of public finance.

7.2 Government Spending in a Small Open Economy

The foregoing analysis examined the factors underlying the effects of public finance (with nondistortionary taxes) on private-sector wealth. We turn next to analyze the effects of changes in government spending, starting with the case of a small open economy facing a given world rate of interest. In this context we highlight the role of timing by distinguishing between changes in government spending that are temporary (current or future) and changes that are permanent.

As indicated earlier, government spending influences the private sector through two channels. First, government activities absorb resources that otherwise would have been available to the private sector, and second, government spending may influence the marginal evaluations of private goods. The first channel is reflected in the terms $(\overline{Y}_0 - G_0)$ and $(\overline{Y}_1 - G_1)$ on the right-hand side of the budget constraint (7.8). We refer to this channel as the *resource-withdrawal* channel. The second channel is reflected in equation (7.3) by the dependence of the marginal rate of substitution between consumption in two consecutive periods on the levels of government spending. We refer to this channel as the *consumption-tilting* channel.

In operating through the resource-withdrawal channel, the influence of government spending is similar to that of supply shocks: both alter the size of *net* GDP (GDP net of government spending). Therefore our previous analysis of temporary (current or future) and permanent positive supply shocks (in section 5.3) also applies to the effects of temporary (current or future) and permanent reductions in government spending, operating through the resource-withdrawal channel.

In analyzing the effects of government spending as they operate through the consumption-tilting channel, we note that the dependence of the marginal rate of substitution of consumption in two consecutive periods on the levels of government spending reflects the characteristics of the utility function. If private consumption and government spending are complements (i.e., if the marginal utility of consumption rises with the level of government spending), then a temporary rise in current government spending raises the marginal rate of substitution in equation (7.3), whereas a temporary rise in future government spending lowers the marginal rate of substitution. In the former case the consumption expansion locus tilts toward current consumption, and in the latter case it tilts toward future consumption. The opposite holds if private consumption and government spending are substitutes. In the neutral case the marginal utility of private consumption (and therefore the marginal rate of substitution of consumption between consecutive periods) is independent of the level of government spending. In that case government spending does not induce consumption-tilting effects. Finally, we note that the effect of a permanent change in government spending on the marginal rate of substitution in consumption combines the effects of current and future changes in government spending. As was shown (except for the neutral case), the two effects tend to tilt the intertemporal consumption patterns in opposite directions. In fact, as is evident from equation (7.3), if the initial patterns of consumption and government spending are stationary, then the two effects exactly offset each other. It follows that in that case a permanent change in government spending does not induce a tilt in the intertemporal pattern of consumption. We conclude that the influence of the intertemporal pattern of government spending on the marginal rate of subsitution of consumption are akin to the consumption-tilting effects analyzed in section 5.3.

In summary, the impact of government spending on the equilibrium of the system reflects the combination of the effects operating through the resource-withdrawal channel and through the consumption-tilting channel. In the neutral case, in which the marginal rate of substitution of consumption in two consecutive periods is independent of the level of government spending, the impact of government spending operates only through the resource-withdrawal channel. In that case our analysis of the effects of supply shocks (in section 5.2) is fully applicable to the analysis of the effects of government spending.

7.3 Government Spending and the Rate of Interest

Up to now we considered the case in which the economy is small in the world capital markets. To examine the effects of government spending on the rest of the world, we turn now to an extension of the analysis to a two-country model of the world economy. To simplify exposition, we consider the case in which government spending enters the utility function in a separable way and the utility functions are homothetic. The separability assumption implies that the marginal rate of substitution between consumption in different periods does not depend on the level of government spending. Thus in what follows government spending operates only through the resource-withdrawal channel, and not through the consumption-tilting channel.

Consider, first, the effects of a current transitory rise in the home country's government spending. At the initial rate of interest this rise in spending creates an excess demand for current-period goods. This excess demand arises from the fact that the private sector (whose taxes have risen in order to finance government spending) lowers its demand for current goods by less than the rise in government demand since the private sector's marginal propensity to spend is smaller than unity. This excess demand is eliminated by a rise in the relative price of present goods in terms of future goods, that is, by a rise in the rate of interest. This analysis is illustrated in figure 7.1 in which it is assumed that the home country's propensity to consume

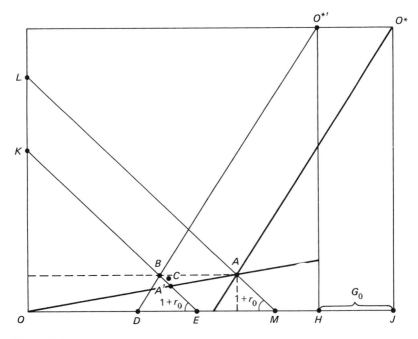

Figure 7.1
The effects of a temporary rise in current government spending on the world rate of interest

present goods relative to future goods exceeds the foreign country's corresponding propensity. As before, the dimensions of the box measure the present and the future levels of world GDP. At the initial equilibrium the international and intertemporal pattern of world consumption is represented by point A which denotes the intersection between the home and the foreign countries' consumption-expansion loci OA and O^*A, respectively. These loci correspond to the equilibrium rate of interest, r_0.

If the level of government spending on present goods is G_0, then the size of the box (corresponding to world GDP net of government spending) diminishes. Accordingly, in figure 7.1 the length of the horizontal axis measuring the supply of current goods net of government spending is reduced from OJ to OH. At the prevailing interest rate foreign demand remains unchanged, as represented in figure 7.1 by point B. This point is located on the foreign consumption-expansion locus displaced to the new origin $O^{*'}$. By construction, the parallel line segments $O^{*'}B$ and O^*A are of equal length. Analogously, as long as the initial rate of interest remains unchanged, the consumption-expansion locus of the domestic residents remains unchanged, but in view of the lower level of wealth (induced by the fall in disposable income), the new level of desired consumption is represented by point A' instead of point A. Diagrammatically, point A' designates the intersection of the domestic consumption-expansion locus and the line KE; the latter is obtained by a leftward (parallel) shift of the initial budget line LM by the magnitude of government spending G_0 (i.e., by construction, $HJ = EM$). As seen, the desired bundles of domestic and foreign consumption (indicated by points A' and B, respectively) represent an excess world demand for current goods and a corresponding excess world supply of future goods. Therefore the rate of interest (the relative price of current goods) must rise. The higher rate of interest induces substitution away from current consumption and toward future consumption. This substitution rotates both countries' consumption-expansion loci toward future goods and results in a new equilibrium (corresponding to their intersection) at a point such as C. Because of this rotation the new equilibrium point must lie to the left of point A' and to the right of point B. It follows that foreign current consumption must fall.

Hence part of the rise in domestic government spending is "financed" through the crowding out of foreign consumption.

If we characterize the international transmission mechanism in terms of the correlations between contemporaneous levels of domestic and foreign private-sector consumption, then the temporary rise in current government spending is transmitted *positively* to the rest of the world. This inference follows since both domestic and foreign private-sector consumption fall. It is also noteworthy that this conclusion concerning the effects of a temporary rise in government spending does not depend on the assumption (implicit in figure 7.1) that the domestic subjective rate of time preference exceeds the foreign rate. Independent of the relation between the domestic and foreign subjective rates of time preference the temporary rise in current government spending must raise the rate of interest and must crowd out both domestic and foreign private-sector consumption of current goods.

The rise in the world rate of interest transmits the effects of the rise in government spending to the rest of the world. The higher rate of interest lowers the discounted sum of foreign disposable incomes, and thereby lowers foreign wealth. These changes in the interest rate and in wealth alter foreign consumption and impact on welfare. In the case shown in figure 7.1, point C indicates a fall in foreign welfare since in the initial equilibrium the bundle of goods represented by point C was affordable but B was chosen. Hence by the principle of revealed preference we conclude that in the case shown, the rise in the home country's government spending lowers foreign welfare. This result, however, is not general since point C could have been located to the southwest of the line segment $A'B$. In that case foreign welfare would have risen. The key factor determining whether the rise in the rate of interest lowers or raises foreign welfare is the initial current account position, reflecting the initial differences between domestic and foreign *average* saving propensities. A rise in the rate of interest lowers foreign welfare if the foreign country was a net borrower in the world economy (i.e., if it ran a current account deficit), and vice versa. In addition to these considerations the impact of government spending on the home country's welfare also depends on both the reduced consumption of private goods and the increased consumption of public goods.

A similar analysis applies to the effects of a transitory rise in *future* government spending. In that case, however, the change in government spending induces an excess world demand for future goods and a corresponding excess supply of current goods. To restore equilibrium, the relative price of current goods—that is, the rate of interest—must fall. The fall in the rate of interest initiates the mechanism that transmits the effects of government spending to the rest of the world. It induces a rise in foreign wealth and impacts on foreign consumption and welfare in a manner opposite to the one discussed earlier when government spending rose in the present.

The analyses of the effects of transitory increases in current or in future government spending provide the ingredients relevant for determining the effects of a *permanent* rise in government spending. Since in that case there is a rise in government demand for both current and future goods, the rate of interest may rise or fall depending on the relative change in private-sector demand for current and future goods. In general, if the extent of the fall in private-sector demand for current goods is large relative to the fall in the demand for future goods, then the rate of interest falls, and vice versa. The key factor determining the relative reductions in private-sector demands for current and future goods is the difference between the domestic and the foreign marginal saving propensities. If the domestic saving propensity falls short of the foreign propensity (i.e., if the domestic subjective rate of time preference exceeds the foreign rate), then, at the prevailing rate of interest, the permanent rise in government spending raises world savings and necessitates a fall in the rate of interest. On the other hand, if the domestic saving propensity exceeds the foreign, the permanent rise in government spending lowers world savings and induces a rise in the rate of interest.

These results are illustrated in figure 7.2a and b. Panel a corresponds to the case in which the domestic subjective rate of time preference exceeds the foreign rate ($\rho > \rho^*$), and panel b corresponds to the opposite case in which $\rho^* < \rho$. The initial equilibrium is specified by point A. The permanent rise in government spending withdraws resources from the world economy in both the present and the future

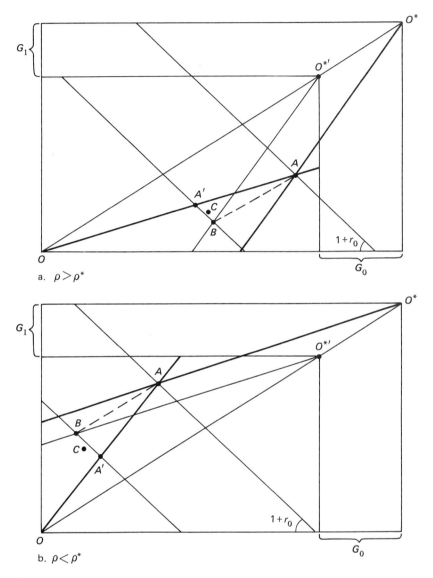

Figure 7.2
The effects of a permanent rise in government spending on the world rate
of interest

periods. Diagrammatically, this rise in the share of world output, which is absorbed by the government, is reflected in an equiproportional decline in the dimensions of the box. Hence, following the permanent rise in domestic government spending, the foreign country's origin shifts along the diagonal of the box from point O^* to point $O^{*\prime}$. At the prevailing rate of interest foreign consumption (measured from $O^{*\prime}$) is represented by point B (where the distance $O^*A = O^{*\prime}B$), and domestic consumption is represented by point A' along the initial consumption-expansion locus. Point A' is obtained by subtracting from the domestic private-sector budget the resources needed to finance the rise in government spending, G_0 and G_1, respectively. Geometrically, we note that by construction the distance $O^*O^{*\prime}$ equals the distance AB and that the slope of the line connecting points A' and B is one plus the prevailing rate of interest. As is evident, the consumption bundles represented by points A' and B indicate an excess supply of current goods in panel a and an excess demand for current goods in panel b. It follows that in the former case the rate of interest must fall, but in the latter case the rate of interest must rise.

As an interpretation of this result, we note that for the case in which $\rho > \rho^*$ (shown in figure 7.2a), the intertemporal pattern of spending of the domestic private sector (relative to the pattern of the foreign private sector) is biased toward current goods. The permanent rise in government spending lowers domestic private disposable income and reduces the relative weight of domestic private spending in world private spending. As a result world private spending is less biased toward current goods, and the rate of interest must fall. An analogous interpretation pertains to the case in which $\rho < \rho^*$ (shown in figure 7.2b) in which the pattern of the intertemporal spending of the domestic private sector is relatively biased toward future goods.

As already indicated, the international transmission mechanism operates through the integrated world capital market, and the change in the rate of interest serves to transmit the effects of the rise in government spending to the rest of the world. The change in the rate of interest induced by the permanent rise in government spending rotates both countries' consumption-expansion loci and brings about a new equilibrium at a point like point C. This new equilibrium point must lie inside the rectangle whose opposite vertexes are A' and B, implying a rise in foreign current consumption and a fall in foreign future consumption; the opposite holds in panel b in which point C must lie to the southeast of point B.

The effects of changes in domestic government spending on the level of foreign private-sector consumption are summarized in table 7.1 (which also contains a summary of the other results). As may be seen, depending on its timing and on the relation between the domestic and the foreign marginal propensities to save (which is governed by the relation between ρ and ρ^*), the rise in government spending may crowd out or crowd in foreign private consumption. Since domestic private consumption must always be crowded out, it follows that the sign of the correlation between changes in domestic and foreign private-sector consumption induced by changes in domestic government spending also depends on the time pattern of government spending and on the difference between the two private sectors' subjective rates of time preference.

7.4 Government Spending and the Terms of Trade in a Two-Country World

The preceding analysis of government spending was conducted under the assumption of a single composite-commodity world. As a result government spending influenced the world economy only through its impact on the *intertemporal* terms of trade (the rate of interest). In general, of course, if the economy is large enough in the world markets for goods, then changes in the level and commodity composition of government purchases also alter the *temporal* terms of trade (the relative price of importables in terms of exportables). Such changes in the temporal terms of trade provide an additional mechanism through which the effects of government spending are transmitted internationally.

In this section we extend the analysis by considering the effects of government spending on both the temporal and the intertemporal terms of trade. In order to identify the key principles, we first analyze the effects that government spending exert on the commodity terms

Table 7.1
Effects of a rise in domestic government spending on the world rate of interest, levels of consumption, and the trade account

Rates of time perference	Effects of a current rise in Government spending on				Effects of a future rise in government spending on				Effects of a permanent rise in government spending on			
	r_0,	C_0,	C_0^*,	$(TA)_0$	r_0,	C_0, •	C_0^*,	$(TA)_0$	r_0,	C_0,	C_0^*,	$(TA)_0$
$\rho > \rho^*$	+	−	−	−	−	−	+	+	−	−	+	+
$\rho < \rho^*$	+	−	−	−	−	−	+	+	+	−	−	−

Note: The case in which $\rho > \rho^*$ indicates that the domestic marginal propensity to save out of wealth falls short of the foreign propensity, and vice versa.

of trade in isolation from the intertemporal repercussions induced by possible changes in the rate of interest. We then consider the other extreme by reexamining the effects that government spending exerts on the intertemporal terms of trade in isolation from the temporal repercussions induced by possible changes in the commodity terms of trade. Finally, we consider some aspects of the interactions between the temporal and the intertemporal terms of trade.

We start by focusing on the relation between the temporal terms of trade and the commodity composition of government spending. For this purpose consider a bench-mark case in which the transmission mechanism operates exclusively through the commodity terms of trade and not through the rate of interest. Accordingly, we assume that the utility functions are homothetic, that in each country the composition of outputs (net of government purchases) does not vary over time, and that the domestic and foreign subjective rates of time preference are equal to each other. Also we assume that the time profiles of government and private consumption spendings are identical. These assumptions ensure (as implied by the analysis in chapter 6) that the domestic and the foreign (consumption-based) real rates of interest are equal to each other and that both are equal to the common rate of time preference (adjusted for growth, as in equation 5.14). As a result, in each country income equals spending. Thus in this bench-mark case a *permanent* rise in government spending does not impact on the world rate of interest, and its effects are absorbed exclusively by induced changes in the (temporal) relative price of goods.

The diagrammatic analysis of the effects of a rise in government spending in this bench-mark case can be carried out with the aid of a relabeled version of figure 7.2. The relabeling replaces the two periods by the two commodities, the intertemporal terms of trade by the temporal terms of trade, and the international differences between the marginal propensities to spend out of wealth in the two periods (indicated by the difference between the domestic and the foreign marginal rates of time preference) by the international differences in the marginal shares of expenditures on the two goods. Thus in figure 7.2 the dimensions of the box correspond to the world supply of the two goods net of government spending on these goods. The vertical axis measures good x—the home country's exportables—and the horizontal axis measures good m—the home country's importables. In the initial equilibrium the commodity composition of the domestic and foreign private-sector demands are indicated by the slopes of the rays OA and O^*A, respectively. The initial equilibrium obtains at point A, at which the relative price of importables, p_m, is the common slope of the domestic and foreign indifference curves at point A (not drawn). Thus the angle indicated by $1 + r_0$ in figure 7.2 now measures the relative price of goods, p_m. The case shown in panel a differs from the one shown in panel b. Panel a corresponds to a situation in which the domestic pattern of the commodity composition of spending is relatively biased toward importables so that the domestic expenditure share β_m exceed the foreign share, β_m^*, whereas panel b corresponds to the opposite case in which the domestic spending patterns are relatively biased toward exportables so that $\beta_m < \beta_m^*$. (In that case the composition of domestic output is even more biased in favor of good x, which therefore is the export good.)

Consider first the case of an equiproportional rise in government spending on both goods (indicated in figure 7.2 by G_0 on importables and G_1 on exportables). This lowers world output net of government spending and reduces the dimensions of the box. It changes the foreign-country origin along the diagonal from point O^* to point $O^{*\prime}$. At the initial terms of trade the desired domestic consumption basket is indicated by point A', and the corresponding foreign consumption basket (measured from the origin $O^{*\prime}$) is indicated by point B. As is evident, if β_m exceeds β_m^* (as in panel a), this configuration represents excess supply of importables and a corresponding excess demand for exportables, and vice versa if β_m falls short of β_m^* (as in panel b). In the former case p_m falls so that the terms of trade of the domestic country improve, and in the latter case p_m rises so that the domestic terms of trade worsen. These changes in the terms of trade bring about a new equilibrium pattern of world consumption as indicated in figure 7.2 by a point located within the square whose opposite vertexes are points B and A', such as point C.

This example of the terms-of-trade effects of an equiproportional rise in government spending indicates the analogy between the intertemporal analysis of the effects of permanent government spending and the temporal analysis of an equiproportional rise of government purchases of goods. In order to derive the general principle governing the effects of government spending on the terms of trade, we define the marginal share of government expenditure on importables by $\beta_m^g = p_m G_m / (p_m G_m + G_x) = 1/[1 + (G_x/p_m G_m)]$, where G_m and G_x denote the rise in government purchases of importables and exportables, respectively. With this definition the basic criterion determining the effects of a rise in government spending on the terms of trade involves a comparison between the expenditure shares of the private sector and of the government. *If β_m^g exceeds β_m, then the rise in government spending induces a deterioration of the terms of trade, and conversely if β_m^g falls short of β_m.*

The dependence of the change in the terms of trade on the relative magnitudes of β_m and β_m^g is shown in figure 7.3 which illustrates the

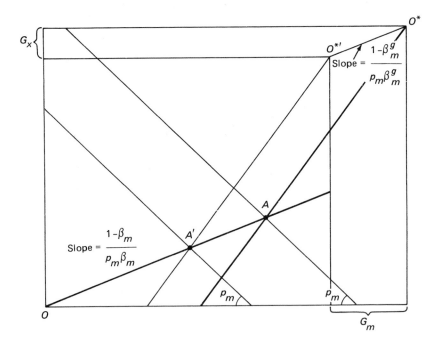

Figure 7.3
The effects of the commodity-composition of government spending on the terms of trade. Data: $\beta_m > \beta_m^*$, $G_x/G_m \equiv (1 - \beta_m^g)/p_m \beta_m^g = C_x/C_m \equiv (1 - \beta_m)/p_m \beta_m$.

case of a borderline situation in which the change in government spending does not alter the terms of trade. In the case shown, the government expenditure share β_m^g is assumed to be equal to the domestic expenditure share β_m. The rise in government spending shifts the origin O^* to $O^{*\prime}$ and alters the equilibrium point from point A to point A'. In the figure the rays OA and $O^*O^{*\prime}$ are drawn parallel to each other due to the assumed equality between β_m^g and β_m. As is evident, in the move from the initial equilibrium point, A, to the new equilibrium point, A', the terms of trade have not changed.

The interpretation of this result is given in terms of the transfer-problem criterion. In the present case the transfer of income from the domestic private sector to the government (a transfer associated with the taxes levied to finance the rise in government spending) does not alter the commodity composition of the domestic *national* spending (private sector plus government) since it involves a transfer of income between units with identical spending patterns. Therefore the transfer does not alter the levels of world demand and supply, and the terms of trade do not change. This borderline case implies that if β_m^g exceeds β_m, then the rise in government spending tilts the composition of national spending toward importables and results in a deterioration of the domestic terms of trade. Conversely, if $\beta_m^g < \beta_m$, the rise in government spending tilts the composition of national spending toward exportables, and the terms of trade improve.

We turn next to reexamine the effects of the time profile of government spending on the intertemporal terms of trade, and we consider another bench-mark case in which the transmission mechanism operates exclusively through the intertemporal terms of trade and not through the commodity terms of trade. For that reason we assume that the composition of output (net of government purchases) does not vary over time and that the government as well as the domestic and the foreign expenditure shares are equal to each other. These assumptions ensure that the commodity terms of trade are fixed and do not depend on the time pattern of government spending. Under these assumptions we can aggregate the two goods into a single composite commodity. This aggregation reduces the multiple good model to its single-good counterpart of section 7.3.

As in the previous analysis of the effects of government spending on the temporal terms of trade, there is a general principle that governs the effects of government spending on the intertemporal terms of trade. This principle can also be stated in terms of a transfer-problem criterion; it involves a comparison between the saving propensities of the private sector and the government. For this we define the government marginal propensity to save out of government "wealth" (the discounted sum of government spending) by $\gamma_s^g = \alpha_{x1} G_1 / (G_0 + \alpha_{x1} G_1)$; we recall that the private sector marginal propensity to save out of wealth is $\gamma_s = \alpha_{x1} z_1 / (z_0 + \alpha_{x1} z_1)$, where z_t ($t = 0, 1$) denotes private-sector spending in terms of good x. The effect of a rise in government spending on the rate of interest depends on whether the time profile of the rise in government spending is such that the implied saving propensity, γ_s^g, exceeds or falls short of the private saving propensity, γ_s. *If γ_s^g exceeds γ_s, then a rise in government spending lowers the rate of interest (raises α_{x1}), and conversely if γ_s^g falls short of γ_s.* As with the analysis of the temporal terms of trade, the transfer-problem criterion provides the interpretation of this result. Accordingly, if γ_s^g exceeds γ_s, the rise in government spending transfers wealth from a low saver (the private sector) to a higher saver (the government), and thereby raises *national* (private-sector plus government) saving. This induces excess world savings and necessitates a fall in the rate of interest. The opposite holds if $\gamma_s^g < \gamma_s$. Finally, in the borderline case in which $\gamma_s^g = \gamma_s$, the rise in government spending redistributes wealth between economic units with identical saving propensities. Therefore in that case national and world saving do not change, and the rate of interest remains intact.

Before proceeding, it is relevant to note that the definitions of saving used in the preceding analysis, which provided the key criterion for determining the effect of government spending on the intertemporal terms of trade, differ from those used in the national income accounts. In particular, we have defined the government-saving propensity as the ratio of future government spending (in present value) to the discounted sum of current and future taxes. In contrast, the national income accounts define government saving in terms of the difference between contemporaneous taxes and spending. A similar remark applies to the definition of private saving.

It is noteworthy that the analysis of the effects of temporary (current or future) and permanent changes in government spending (conducted in the previous sections) can be viewed as specific illustrations of the general principle. Accordingly, a transitory current rise in government spending corresponds to the case $\gamma_s^g = 0$ (and hence $\gamma_s > \gamma_s^g$). An anticipated future rise in government spending corresponds to the case $\gamma_s^g = 1$ (and hence $\gamma_s < \gamma_s^g$). Finally, a permanent rise in government spending (which raises permanently the relative share of government spending in world output) corresponds to the case in which the government-saving propensity, γ_s^g, equals the world private-sector-saving propensity, γ_s^w, which is defined as the ratio of the discounted sum of future net world output to the discounted sum of current and future world net output. Thus

$$\gamma_s^w = \frac{\alpha_1(\overline{Y}_1 - G_1 + \overline{Y}_1^* - G_1^*)}{[(\overline{Y}_0 - G_0) + (\overline{Y}_0^* - G_0^*)] + \alpha_1[(\overline{Y}_1 - G_1) + (\overline{Y}_1^* - G_1^*)]}.$$

We further note that γ_s^w is a weighted average of the saving propensities of the domestic and foreign private sectors, γ_s and γ_s^*. It follows that if $\gamma_s^* > \gamma_s$, then $\gamma_s^g > \gamma_s$—and conversely, if $\gamma_s^* < \gamma_s$, then $\gamma_s^g < \gamma_s$. Our previous analysis showed that the effects of a permanent change in government spending depend on differences between the saving propensities of the domestic and the foreign private sectors. This dependence, however, reflects the more general principle stated in terms of the relation between the saving propensities of the domestic government and the *domestic* private sector, since with a permanent change in government spending the relation between γ_s^g and γ_s can be cast in terms of the relation between γ_s^* and γ_s.

The foregoing analysis isolated the two mechanisms through which the effects of government spending are transmitted to the rest of the world. These two mechanisms operate through the induced changes in the temporal terms of trade (the relative price of exportables in terms of importables) and through the induced changes in the intertemporal terms of trade (the rate of interest). The two bench-mark cases were designed to distinguish between the two mechanisms of adjustment. In general, however, if the subjective rates of time preference and the expenditure shares differ across countries, changes in government spending alter both the temporal and the intertemporal terms of trade. In that case the generalization of the transfer-problem analysis implies that the changes in the two terms of trade are governed by a multitude of transfer-problem criteria involving comparisons between the private-sector and the government temporal spending propensities—indicated by the expenditure shares β_m and β_m^g—and intertemporal spending propensities—indicated by the saving ratios γ_s and γ_s^g.

To illustrate the interactions between the temporal and the intertemporal terms of trade, consider the logarithmic utility function

$$U = [\beta_{m0} \log c_{m0} + (1 - \beta_{m0}) \log c_{x0}]$$

$$+ \delta[\beta_{m1} \log c_{m1} + (1 - \beta_{m1}) \log c_{x1}]. \tag{7.9}$$

With this utility function it is shown in the appendix that for each period the consumption-based temporal price index (defined in section 6.1) can be written as

$$P_0 = (p_{m0})^{\beta_{m0}} \quad \text{and} \quad P_1 = (p_{m1})^{\beta_{m1}}. \tag{7.10}$$

Using these price indexes, the (consumption-based) real discount factor $\alpha_{c1} = \alpha_{x1}(P_1/P_0)$ is

$$\alpha_{c1} = \frac{1}{1 + r_{c0}} = \frac{1}{1 + r_{x0}} \frac{P_1}{P_0}, \tag{7.11}$$

and the (consumption-based) wealth deflator, P_w (the intertemporal "true" price index) is defined by

$$P_w = P_0^{(1-\gamma_s)}(\alpha_{x1} P_1)^{\gamma_s}. \tag{7.12}$$

In general, government spending influences both the temporal and the intertemporal terms of trade, and thereby alters both the (consumption-based) real discount factor and the real wealth deflator. In the appendix we show that, in general, the effects of government spending can be characterized in terms of a multitude of transfer-problem criteria. Accordingly, at the prevailing prices a rise in government spending alters the temporal and the intertemporal pattern of the domestic national demand (private sector plus government) only if the saving propensity and the expenditure shares of the government differ from the corresponding magnitudes of the domestic private sector. In the absence of such differences, changes in government spending do not create an excess demand or supply and do not necessitate a change in the initial equilibrium prices.

It is shown in the appendix that the rise in government spending creates excess demands only if the government's marginal propensities to spend on importables out of government wealth (i.e., government lifetime spending) differ from that of the domestic private sector. Formally, the rise in government spending does not create excess demands only if

$$\beta_{m0}(1 - \gamma_s) = \beta_{m0}^g(1 - \gamma_s^g) \qquad (7.13)$$

and

$$\beta_{m1}\gamma_s = \beta_{m1}^g\gamma_s^g. \qquad (7.14)$$

In the absence of such equalities, the induced excess demands must alter the prevailing prices. The precise changes in the equilibrium prices depend on differences among the saving propensities of the domestic and foreign private sectors, on differences among the temporal expenditure shares of the two private sectors, and on the relative shares of the two private sectors in world demands and supplies.

As is evident, the complex structure of the model implies that, in general, the effects of government spending on the temporal and the intertemporal terms of trade—and thereby on the (consumption-based) real rates of interest and wealth deflator—depend on numerous transfer-problem criteria involving comparisons among the value of parameters characterizing the behavior of the domestic government, the domestic private sector, and the foreign private sector. In order to focus on the differences between the private and the public sectors, we examine the special case in which in the initial equilibrium the domestic and the foreign economies are identical in terms of production and consumption patterns. In this case the effects of the rise in the domestic government spending reflect only the differences in the behavioral patterns of the domestic private and public sectors.

Table 7.2 summarizes the effects of government spending on the (consumption-based) real rate of interest, r_{c0}, and on the real wealth deflator, P_w. The results reported in the table are based on the analysis in the appendix. It shows that if the government propensity to spend on exportables in the current period, $(1 - \gamma_s^g)(1 - \beta_m^g)$, falls short of the corresponding private-sector saving propensity, $(1 - \gamma_s)(1 - \beta_m)$, then the rise in the domestic government spending raises the real wealth deflator (which is the "true" price of lifetime spending). Conversely, if the government propensity to spend on exportables in the current period exceeds the corresponding private sector's propensity, then the rise in government spending lowers the real wealth deflator. If the two spending propensities are equal to each other, then the transfer-problem criterion implies that the rise in government spending does not alter the real wealth deflator.

The second row (r_{c0}) in table 7.2 shows the effects of the rise in government spending on the (consumption-based) real rate of interest. As is evident, in this multicommodity world the key factor governing the direction of the induced change in the real rate of interest remains the transfer-problem criterion applied to a comparison between the saving propensities of the domestic government and the domestic private sector. Accordingly, if the private-sector-saving propensity, γ_s, exceeds the government-saving propensity, γ_s^g, then (at the prevailing prices) a rise in government spending redistributes wealth from the private to the public sectors and lowers national savings. To restore equilibrium, the level of savings must be raised. The necessary rise in savings is brought about through changes in the temporal and in the intertemporal prices. These price changes yield a higher (consumption-based) real rate of interest. The opposite holds if the saving propensity of the private sector falls short of the corresponding propensity of the domestic government. In the borderline case for which the two saving propensities are equal to each other so that $\gamma_s = \gamma_s^g$, the transfer-problem criterion implies

Table 7.2
The effects of a rise in government spending on the (consumption-based) real rate of interest and real wealth deflator

Effects on	Relation between private and public spending propensities		
	$(1 - \beta_m)(1 - \gamma_s) > (1 - \beta_m^g)(1 - \gamma_s^g)$	$(1 - \beta_m)(1 - \gamma_s) = (1 - \beta_m^g)(1 - \gamma_s^g)$	$(1 - \beta_m)(1 - \gamma_s) < (1 - \beta_m^g)(1 - \gamma_s^g)$
P_w	+	0	−
	$\gamma_s > \gamma_s^g$	$\gamma_s = \gamma_s^g$	$\gamma_s < \gamma_s^g$
r_{c0}	+	0	−

Note: r_{c0} is the (consumption-based) real rate of interest, and P_w is the (consumption-based) real wealth deflator (the intertemporal price index). The symbols $+$, 0, and $-$ indicate, respectively, that the rise in the domestic government spending raises, leaves unchanged, or lowers P_w or r_{c0}. The underlying assumption is that the private sectors in the two countries are identical, that the initial equilibrium is autarkic, and that initially government spending in both countries is zero.

that the rise in government spending does not alter national savings, and therefore the (consumption-based) real rate of interest remains intact.

Finally, it is relevant to note that the assumed similarity between the two countries' private sectors implies that the changes in the foreign (consumption-based) real rate of interest and real wealth deflator are the same as those occurring in the domestic economy.

7.5 Government Spending and Investment

Up to this point our analysis of the effects of government spending on the world economy abstracted from investment. The stylized facts, on the other hand, suggest a close correlation between public-sector spending and investment. In what follows we extend the analysis and allow for endogenous investment. In order to focus on the essentials, we return to the single composite-commodity world. As seen earlier, government spending influences the level of the equilibrium rates of interest. These changes in interest rates alter the profitability of domestic and foreign investment and influence the evolution of world output.

The analysis is conducted with the aid of figure 7.4, in which the upward-sloping schedule, S^w, describes the ratio, z, of current to future world GDP net of investment and government spending as an increasing function of the rate of interest. Formally, using the previous notation,

$$z = \frac{\overline{Y}_0 - I_0(r_0) + \overline{Y}_0^* - I_0^*(r_0) - G_0 - G_0^*}{\overline{Y}_1 + F[I_0(r_0)] + \overline{Y}_1^* + F^*[I_0^*(r_0)] - G_1 - G_1^*}. \qquad (7.15)$$

The positive dependence of z on the rate of interest reflects the fact that investment falls when the rate of interest rises.

The downward-sloping schedules in figure 7.4 plot the desired ratio of current to future consumption as a decreasing function of the rate of interest. The assumption that the utility functions are homothetic enables us to express the various demand schedules in terms of desired consumption ratios. The domestic and foreign private-sector relative demands are denoted by D and D^*, and their values at the point in which $(C_0/C_1) = (C_0^*/C_1^*) = 1$ indicate,

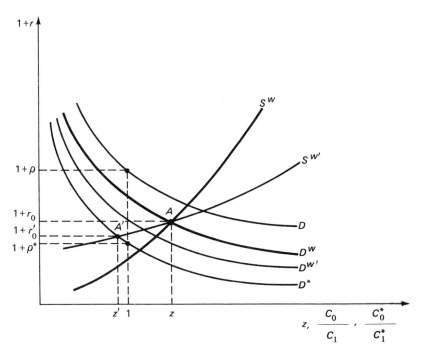

Figure 7.4
The effects of a permanent rise in domestic government spending on the
rate of interest and investment. Data: $\rho > \rho^*$.

respectively, the subjective rates of time preference ρ and ρ^*. The
elasticities of the relative demand schedules are the corresponding
intertemporal elasticities of substitution in consumption. The world
relative demand, D^w, is a weighted average of the two private
sectors' relative demands, D and D^*. That is,

$$\frac{C_0 + C_0^*}{C_1 + C_1^*} = \mu \frac{C_0}{C_1} + (1 - \mu)\frac{C_0^*}{C_1^*}, \tag{7.16}$$

where

$$\mu = \frac{C_1}{C_1 + C_1^*}.$$

The initial equilibrium is described by point A in figure 7.4, at which
the rate of interest is r_0.

Consider the effect of a permanent rise in domestic government spending. This permanent rise alters both the supply schedule and the world demand schedule in figure 7.4. We define a permanent rise in government spending as an equal rise in the relative share of the domestic government in world net output in both the present and the future. It follows that such a change in current and future government spending does not alter the initial ratio on the supply schedule. As a matter of arithmetic it is obvious that this rise in government spending rotates the supply schedule around the initial equilibrium of point A. As a result the supply schedule associated with the permanently higher level of government spending is $S^{w'}$ instead of S^w. The rise in government spending also alters the world demand schedule. Specifically, since at the prevailing rate of interest domestic disposable income must fall (in order to finance the growth of government), it follows that the relative weight μ attached to the domestic schedule D falls. This change in relative weights shifts the world (weighted-average) demand schedule closer to D^* and results in a new world demand schedule $D^{w'}$.

The new equilibrium obtains at point A'. The equilibrium rate of interest falls from r_0 to r_0', and as may be seen, in the new equilibrium the world rate of interest is closer to the foreign rate of time preference ρ^*. In the new equilibrium aggregate private spending is less biased toward present goods, reflecting the lower weight attached to the lower saving pattern of the home country's private demand. The lower rate of interest encourages investment in both countries according to the properties of the investment functions $I_0(r_0)$ and $I_0^*(r_0)$. This rise in investment raises future outputs according to the properties of the investment opportunity functions $F(\cdot)$ and $F^*(\cdot)$.

It is relevant to note that the effect of the permanent rise in government spending on the balance of trade is ambiguous since it reflects the possibly different responses of domestic and foreign investment and future outputs. This should be contrasted with the situation analyzed earlier in figure 7.2a in which investment was absent. In that case the permanent rise in government spending lowered interest rates and induced a deficit in the first-period balance of trade.

The foregoing analysis of the effects of permanent changes in government spending was conducted under the assumption that (in

Table 7.3
The effects of a rise in domestic government spending on the levels of investment

Rates of time preference	Current rise	Future rise	Permanent rise
$\rho > \rho^*$	−	+	+
$\rho < \rho^*$	−	+	−

Note: The case in which $\rho > \rho^*$ indicates that the domestic marginal propensity to save out of wealth falls short of the foreign propensity, and vice versa.

comparison with the rest of the world) the home country's spending patterns are biased toward the consumption of present goods. This relative bias reflected the assumption that the domestic rate of time preference, ρ, exceeds the corresponding foreign rate, ρ^*. In the opposite case, for which $\rho < \rho^*$, the permanent rise in government spending raises the (weighted-average) world relative demand curve in figure 7.4 and results in a higher world rate of interest and in lower levels of investment.

Similar principles can be applied to the analysis of the effects of transitory (current or future) changes in the levels of government spending. Corresponding to our previous analysis, it follows that a transitory rise in current government spending lowers domestic and foreign investment since it raises the rate of interest, whereas a transitory rise in future government spending raises domestic and foreign investment since it lowers the rate of interest. These results are summarized in table 7.3. The key point underscored by this table is that whether government spending crowds out or crowds in private investment depends on the timing of government spending and on the difference between the domestic and the foreign private sectors' marginal propensities to save. Alternatively, cast in terms of the general rule, if γ_s exceeds γ_s^g, then, by raising the world rate of interest, government spending crowds out domestic and foreign private-sector investment, and conversely if γ_s falls short of γ_s^g.

7.6 The Optimal Size of Government

Throughout the previous analysis we have treated the level of government spending as exogenous, and we have examined the effects of various changes in the time profile of spending. In this section we extend the analysis and examine the optimal path of government spending. This extension facilitates a more complete analysis of the welfare implications of fiscal policies.

In order to determine the optimal size of government, we use the private sector's utility function and recognize that the provision of public goods influences the level of welfare. Thus we use the maximized level of utility (defined in equation 7.30) together with the government budget constraint (defined in equation 7.35). In order to focus on the determination of the optimal path of government spending and abstract from issues concerning the optimal path of taxes, we assume that the private and the public sectors face the same world rate of interest so that $\alpha_1^g = \alpha_1^p = \alpha_1$. This assumption introduces the Ricardian irrelevance property into the model. Formally, the government maximization problem is

$$\tilde{V} = \max_{\{G_0, G_1, T_0, T_1\}} V(G_0, G_1, T_0, T_1) \tag{7.17}$$

subject to

$$G_0 + \alpha_1 G_1 = T_0 + \alpha_1 T_1 - (1 + r_{-1})B^g_{-1}.$$

Carrying out the maximization and using the conditions specified in equation (7.4) yields the first-order conditions:

$$\frac{U_G(C_0, G_0)}{U_C(C_0, G_0)} = \frac{U_G(C_1, G_1)}{U_C(C_1, G_1)} = 1. \tag{7.18}$$

As usual for a two-good economy, equation (7.18) states the requirement that in each period the marginal rate of substitution between the two goods equals the marginal rate of transformation (which in the present specification equals unity). Since the two goods are a private good and a public good, the equality between the marginal rate of substitution and the marginal rate of transformation reflects the implicit assumption of a single-consumer economy; in general, the Samuelson condition requires equality between the *sum* of the individual marginal rates of substitution and the economy's marginal rate of transformation.

The formal specification of the government maximization problem embodies the utility-maximizing conditions of the private sector. Hence in addition to the *temporal* condition (7.18) the solution contains the intertemporal condition (7.3) stating the *intertemporal* marginal rate of substitution between consumption of private goods as well as between consumption of public goods equals one plus the rate of interest. These equilibrium conditions along with the economy's consolidated budget constraint (6.3) determine the optimal path of government spending as part of the general equilibrium solution of model.

The symmetric treatment of private and public goods suggests that the question of the optimal size of government can also be cast in terms of the utility-maximizing demand functions for current and future consumption of private and public goods. As usual, these demand functions are expressed as functions of prices and wealth. In our case the relevant temporal price of public goods in terms of private goods is unity, the intertemporal price is α_1, and the relevant concept of wealth is the discounted sum of GDP net of the historically given initial external debt commitment; that is, $\overline{Y}_0 + \alpha_1 \overline{Y}_1 - (1 + r_{-1})B_{-1}$. Formally, these demand functions are

$$C_t = C_t[\alpha_1; \overline{Y}_0 + \alpha_1 \overline{Y}_1 - (1 + r_{-1})B_{-1}],$$
$$G_t = G_t[\alpha_1; \overline{Y}_0 + \alpha_1 \overline{Y}_1 - (1 + r_{-1})B_{-1}], \quad t = 0, 1, \tag{7.19}$$

where we have suppressed the temporal prices that are equal to unity.

The equations in (7.19) can be used to analyze the effects of supply shocks on the optimal path of government spending. For this purpose we assume that the private and the public goods are normal goods. Consider the effect of a temporary supply shock that raises the value of current GDP, $\overline{Y}_0$. Since all goods (including future goods) are normal, it is obvious that in order to "finance" a rise in future consumption (C_1 and G_1), the induced rise in current consumption of both goods (C_0 and G_0) must be smaller than the rise in $\overline{Y}_0$. Thus, since not all new output is absorbed by current consumption, it follows that the current-period supply shock induces an improvement in the economy's balance of trade. Analogously, if the temporary supply shock is expected to occur in the future, normality implies that the rise in $\overline{Y}_1$ raises consumption of all four goods, including current goods. In that case the economy's trade balance deteriorates in the early period. The foregoing examples demonstrate that the consumption-smoothing motive that characterizes private consumption in the absence of public goods also extends to the broader concept of consumption that includes both private and public goods, if the supply of the latter is optimal. Consequently the qualitative trade-balance effects of temporary supply shocks also remain intact.

Finally, consider the effects of a permanent supply shock. For ease of exposition suppose that the historically given initial external debt position, B_{-1}, is zero, that the utility function over all four goods is homothetic, and that the level of GDP is stationary. In that case the initial trade balance is zero, and an equiproportional rise in current and future GDP raises the consumption of all goods (including public goods) by the same proportion and leaves the trade balance unchanged. This outcome is the analogue to the neutral-supply shock analyzed in figure 5.3 for the case in which public goods were absent.

A key proposition of the foregoing analysis is that in the presence of both private and public goods, supply shocks induce a positive correlation between the levels of consumption of private and public goods if the latter are optimally supplied. The symmetric treatment of private and public goods reveals that the optimal supply of public goods (as reflected by the level of government spending) responds to expected future events in a manner similar to that of the consumption of private goods. Therefore the optimal level of government spending need not be synchronized with supply shocks, and as a result the contemporaneous correlation between government spending and GDP may be low. This property reflects the role of government as a supplier of public goods and not as an instrument of stabilization policies. Allowance for the latter role would introduce countercyclical elements to the path of government spending and would thereby contribute to a negative correlation between contemporaneous changes in GDP and government spending.

7.7 Summary

In this chapter we incorporated the government into the model. For this purpose we extended the specification of the utility function and the budget constraints so as to include public goods and taxes. We showed that there are two channels through which government spending influences the equilibrium of the economic system: the resource-withdrawal channel and the consumption-tilting channel. The former reflects the combination of changes in net output (induced by government purchases of goods and services) and in private-sector wealth (induced by the nondistortionary taxes used for government finance). The latter reflects the temporal-intertemporal substitution—complementarity relations between public and private consumption and production.

In analyzing the effects of domestic government spending on the two-country world economy, we focused on the induced changes in the temporal and intertemporal terms of trade and on the cross-country comovement of private sectors' spending. We cast the analysis in terms of various transfer-problem criteria familiar from the theory of international transfers. In the present context these criteria involve comparisons between the domestic country's private and public sector's saving and spending propensities. Accordingly, if the government's propensity to spend on importables (out of expenditure) exceeds the corresponding private-sector propensity, then a rise in the domestic government's spending raises the relative price of importables, and thereby worsens the domestic country's temporal terms of trade, and vice versa. Likewise, if the domestic government's saving propensity exceeds the corresponding private-sector propensity, then the rise in the domestic government's spending lowers the world rate of interest—the intertemporal terms of trade, and vice versa. In this context both the private and the public sector's saving propensities reflect the relation between the present value of future consumption and the discounted sum of current and future consumption. This transfer-problem criterion underscores the significance of the timing of government spending, being transitory or permanent.

In our multicommodity world there is a complex interaction between the temporal and the intertemporal terms of trade. To allow for this interaction, we defined the appropriate (consumption-based) real rate of interest and real wealth deflator, and applied the transfer-problem criterion to determine the effects of the commodity composition and the time pattern of government spending on these variables.

In regards to investment, we showed that the key factor determining whether government spending crowds in or crowds out private-sector investment at home and abroad is again the relation between the domestic private and public sector's saving propensities.

The chapter concluded with a brief analysis of the optimal size of government. In this context we showed that the consumption-smoothing motive characterizing private consumption in the absence of public goods extends to the broader concept of consumption that includes both private and public goods, if the supply of the latter is optimal. A key proposition emerging from this consumption-smoothing feature is that with an optimal provision of public goods, supply shocks induce a positive correlation between the levels of consumption of private and public goods.

7.8 Appendix

In this appendix we provide a formal analysis of the effects of government spending on the temporal and the intertemporal terms of trade. Throughout we assume logarithmic utility functions. We start with a derivation of the consumption-based price indexes corresponding to the specific utility function.

The maximization problem is

$$\tilde{U} = \max_{\substack{\{c_{m0}, c_{x0}\} \\ \{c_{m1}, c_{x1}\}}} \beta_{m0} \log c_{m0} + (1 - \beta_{m0}) \log c_{x0}$$

$$+ \delta[\beta_{m1} \log c_{m1} + (1 - \beta_{m1}) \log c_{x1}] \tag{A.1}$$

subject to

$$z_0 + \alpha_{x1} z_1 = W_0,$$

where

$$z_0 = (p_{m0} c_{m0} + c_{x0}),$$

$$z_1 = (p_{m1} c_{m1} + c_{x1}).$$

The solution to this maximization problem yields the following demand functions:

$$c_{m0} = \frac{\beta_{m0} W_0}{(1 + \delta)P_{m0}}, \qquad c_{m1} = \frac{\delta\beta_{m1} W_0}{(1 + \delta)\alpha_{x1} P_{m1}},$$

$$c_{x0} = \frac{1}{1 + \delta}(1 - \beta_{m0}) W_0, \quad c_{x1} = \frac{\delta(1 - \beta_{m1}) W_0}{(1 + \delta)\alpha_{x1}}. \tag{A.2}$$

Substitution of the demand functions into the utility function yields the indirect utility function

$$\tilde{U} = a + \log\left(\frac{W_0^{(1+\delta)}}{p_{m0}^{\beta_{m0}} p_{m1}^{\beta_{m1}\delta} \alpha_{x1}^{\delta}}\right), \tag{A.3}$$

where a is a constant.

Recalling the definition of γ_s—the private sector propensity to save out of wealth—and using the definitions of spending and the demand functions from (A.2) yields

$$\gamma_s = \frac{\alpha_{x1} z_1}{z_0 + \alpha_{x1} z_1} = \frac{\delta}{1 + \delta}. \tag{A.4}$$

Substituting (A.4) for δ into (A.3) yields

$$\tilde{U} = a + \log\frac{W_0^{1/(1-\gamma_s)}}{P_w^{1/(1-\gamma_s)}} = a + \left(\frac{1}{1 - \gamma_s}\right)\log\left(\frac{W_0}{P_w}\right), \tag{A.5}$$

where

$$P_w = (P_0)^{1-\gamma_s}(\alpha_{x1} P_1)^{\gamma_s} \tag{A.6}$$

and where

$$P_0 = p_{m0}^{\beta_{m0}}, \quad P_1 = p_{m1}^{\beta_{m1}}.$$

Equation (A.6) defines the "true" utility-based *temporal* price indexes P_0 and P_1 and the "true" utility-based *intertemporal* price index P_w. As seen from (A.5), P_w is the price index relevant for welfare analysis.

Equilibrium in the world economy requires that in each period world private-sector demand for the two goods equals the corresponding supply net of government purchases. Thus

$$\beta_{m0}\frac{1}{1 + \delta} W_0 + \beta_{m0}^* \frac{1}{1 + \delta^*} W_0^*$$

$$= p_{m0}[\overline{Y}_{m0} - G_{m0}) + (\overline{Y}_{m0}^* - G_{m0}^*)], \tag{A.7}$$

$$(1 - \beta_{m0})\frac{1}{1 + \delta} W_0 + (1 - \beta_{m0}^*)\frac{1}{1 + \delta^*} W_0^*$$

$$= (\overline{Y}_{x0} - G_{x0}) + (\overline{Y}_{x0}^* - G_{x0}^*), \tag{A.8}$$

$$\beta_{m1}\frac{\delta}{1 + \delta} W_0 + \beta_{m1}^*\frac{\delta^*}{1 + \delta^*} W_0^*$$

$$= \alpha_{x1} p_{m1}[(\overline{Y}_{m1} - G_{m1}) + (\overline{Y}_{m1}^* - G_{m1}^*)], \tag{A.9}$$

$$(1 - \beta_{m1})\frac{\delta}{1 + \delta} W_0 = (1 - \beta_{m1}^*)\frac{\delta^*}{1 + \delta^*} W_0^*$$

$$= \alpha_{x1}[(\overline{Y}_{x1} - G_{x1}) + (\overline{Y}_{x1}^* - G_{x1}^*)], \tag{A.10}$$

where

$$W_0 = p_{m0}(\overline{Y}_{m0} - G_{m0}) + (\overline{Y}_{x0} - G_{x0})$$

$$+ \alpha_{x1}[p_{m1}(\overline{Y}_{m1} - G_{m1}) + (\overline{Y}_{x1} - G_{x1})]$$

and

$$W_0^* = p_{m0}(\overline{Y}_{m0}^* - G_{m0}^*) + (\overline{Y}_{x0}^* - G_{x0}^*)$$

$$+ \alpha_{x1}[p_{m1}(\overline{Y}_{m1}^* - G_{m1}^*) + (\overline{Y}_{x1}^* - G_{x1}^*)].$$

By Walras's law we omit, in what follows, equation (A.10).

Differentiating totally the system (A.7) through (A.9) around $G = 0$ yields

$$[\lambda_{m0}(1 - \gamma_s)\beta_{m0}\mu_{m0} + \lambda_{m0}^*(1 - \gamma_s^*)\beta_{m0}^*\mu_{m0}^* - 1]\hat{p}_{m0}$$

$$+ [\lambda_{m0}\gamma_s\beta_{m1}\mu_{m1} + \lambda_{m0}^*\gamma_s^*\beta_{m1}^*\mu_{m1}^*]\hat{p}_{m1}$$

$$+ [\lambda_{m0}\gamma_s\mu_1 + \lambda_{m0}^*\gamma_s^*\mu_1^*]\hat{\alpha}_{x1}$$

$$= g_{m0}[\beta_{m0}(1 - \gamma_s) - \beta_{m0}^g(1 - \gamma_s^g)]\,dG, \tag{A.11}$$

$$[\lambda_{x0}(1 - \gamma_s)\beta_{m0}\mu_{m0} + \lambda_{x0}^*(1 - \gamma_s)\beta_{m0}^*\mu_{m0}^*]\hat{p}_{m0}$$

$$+ [\lambda_{x0}\gamma_s\beta_{m1}\mu_{m1} + \lambda_{x0}^*\gamma_s^*\beta_{m1}^*\mu_{m1}^*]\hat{p}_{m1}$$

$$+ [\lambda_{x0}\gamma_s\mu_1 + \lambda_{x0}^*\gamma_s^*\mu_1^*]\hat{\alpha}_{x1}$$

$$= g_{x0}[(1 - \beta_{m0})(1 - \gamma_s) - (1 - \beta_{m0}^g)(1 - \gamma_s^g)]\,dG, \tag{A.12}$$

$$[\lambda_{m1}(1 - \gamma_s)\beta_{m0}\mu_{m0} + \lambda_{m1}^*(1 - \gamma_s^*)\beta_{m0}^*\mu_{m0}^*]\hat{p}_{m0}$$

$$+ [\lambda_{m1}\gamma_s\beta_{m1}\mu_{m1} + \lambda_{m1}^*\gamma_s^*\beta_{m1}^*\mu_{m1}^* - 1]\hat{p}_{m1}$$

$$+ [\lambda_{m1}\gamma_s\mu_1 + \lambda_{m1}^*\gamma_s^*\mu_1^* - 1]\hat{\alpha}_{x1}$$

$$= g_{m1}[\beta_{m1}\gamma_s - \beta_{m1}^g\gamma_s^g]\,dG, \tag{A.13}$$

where λ denotes the share of spending on a given good by the corresponding unit in world net output of the given good (net of governments purchases). For example, λ_{m0} denotes the share of domestic private-sector spending on good m (in period zero) in world net output of good m in period zero; that is, $\lambda_{m0} = c_{m0}/[(\overline{Y}_{m0} - G_{m0}) + (\overline{Y}_{m0}^* - G_{m0}^*)]$. Initially, with $G = 0$, $\lambda_{m0} = c_{m0}/(\overline{Y}_{m0} + \overline{Y}_{m0}^*)$, and in this case $\mu_{m1} = \overline{Y}_{m1}/c_{m1}$. The terms g_{m0}, g_{x0}, and g_{m1} denote, respectively, the reciprocals of the world production of good m_0, x_0, m_1 (net of government purchases of the good). The rest of the variables are defined in the text.

The system (A.11) through (A.13) can be solved to yield the effects of G on p_{m0}, p_{m1}, and α_{x1}. As is obvious by inspection of the coefficients of dG in equations (A.11) through (A.13), changes in the level of domestic government spending influence the temporal and the intertemporal terms of trade according to the principles known from the analysis of transfers. Thus changes in government spending influence the equilibrium only if the various spending propensities of the private sector differ from the corresponding propensities of the government. Indeed, in the special case in which these propensities are equal to each other so that $\beta_{m0} = \beta_{m0}^g$, $\beta_{m1} = \beta_{m1}^g$, and $\gamma_s = \gamma_s^g$, changes in government spending do not influence the equilibrium temporal and intertemporal prices.

As is evident, the complex structure of the model implies that, in general, the effects of government spending on the temporal and intertemporal terms of trade depend on a multitude of transfer-problem criteria, involving comparisons among the marginal propensities to save of the private sector and of the government as well as comparisons among the periodic expenditure shares of the domestic and the foreign private sectors and the government.

In order to focus on differences between the private and the public sectors, suppose that the various shares do not vary over time and that the domestic and the foreign private sectors are identical in their marginal propensities to save, in their expenditure shares, and in their relative shares in world private demand. In that case $\lambda_m = \lambda_m^*$, $\beta_m = \beta_m^*$, and $\gamma_s = \gamma_s^*$, where the time subscript is omitted due to the assumption that the various propensities and shares are constant over time. We further assume that initially the ratios of output to private-sector spending are equal across countries so that $\mu_m = \mu_m^*$ and $\mu_1 = \mu_1^*$. This implies that the initial equilibrium is autarkic, so that $\mu_1 = \mu_m = 1$. With these assumptions the solution for the effect of government spending on the consumption-based intertemporal price index (the utility-based wealth deflator), P_w, is

$$\frac{d\log P_w}{dG} = \frac{1}{\overline{Y}_x + \overline{Y}_x^*}[(1 - \beta_m)(1 - \gamma_s) - (1 - \beta_m^g)(1 - \gamma_s^g)]. \quad \text{(A.14)}$$

Equation (A.14) shows that, as usual, the direction of the effect of a rise in government spending on the utility-based wealth deflator depends only on the various transfer-problem criteria.

Similarly, under the same assumptions the effect of a rise in government spending on the consumption-based real discount factor, $\alpha_{c1} = \alpha_{x1}P_1/P_0$, is

$$\frac{d\log \alpha_{c1}}{dG} = \frac{\beta_m}{\gamma_s p_m(\overline{Y}_m + \overline{Y}_m^*)}[\beta_m(1 - \gamma_s) - \beta_m^g(1 - \gamma_s^g)]$$

$$+ \frac{(1 - \beta_m)c_m}{\gamma_s c_x(\overline{Y}_m + \overline{Y}_m^*)}[(1 - \beta_m)(1 - \gamma_s) + (1 - \beta_m^g)(1 - \gamma_s^g)].$$

Using the equality $p_m c_m/c_x = \beta_m/(1 - \beta_m)$ yields

$$\frac{d\log \alpha_{c1}}{dG} = \frac{\beta_m}{\gamma_s p_m(\overline{Y}_m + \overline{Y}_m^*)}(\gamma_s^g - \gamma_s). \quad \text{(A.15)}$$

Equations (A.14) through (A.15) underlie the results reported in table 7.2 of the text.

8

Budget Deficits with Distortionary Taxes

Up to this point we have assumed that all taxes are lump sum and nondistortionary. As a result we have focused on the effects of government spending rather than on the means of government finance; in fact we have used a model in which budget deficits arising from changes in the timing of taxes do not affect the real equilibrium. The assumption that all taxes are nondistortionary may, however, miss important features characterizing actual taxes. In this chapter we replace this assumption with the assumption that taxes are distortionary. Under these circumstances the real equilibrium is sensitive to alternative specifications of the time profile of taxes and public-debt issue. Hence the equilibrium is not invariant with respect to budget deficits.

In the analysis that follows we examine the effects of budget deficits under alternative assumptions about the taxes that are reduced. We consider consumption taxes, taxes on income from domestic investment, taxes on income from foreign lending, and taxes on labor income.

The analysis reveals that the various taxes may exert different quantitative and qualitative effects on the real equilibrium, and therefore the impact of a budget deficit and its international transmission may depend critically on the mix of taxes used to generate the deficit. Furthermore in the presence of distortionary taxes the wealth effects, which traditionally serve as the principal mechanism through which budget deficits influence the equilibrium, are supplemented by another important mechanism operating through intertemporal substitution. In fact it is shown that there are circumstances under which the wealth effects are weak and of ambiguous sign while the intertemporal substitution effects of distortionary taxes are the main driving force of budget deficits.

8.1 Taxes on Consumption, Capital Income, and International Borrowing: The Analytical Framework

In order to incorporate the effects of non-lump-sum taxes, we start with the one-good stylized model of section 5.1 and extend it to allow for taxes on consumption, international borrowing, and capital income. (In a subsequent section the stylized model is extended to allow for taxes on labor income.) With this modification the private sector's periodic budget constraints are

$$(1 + \tau_{c0})C_0 = (1 - \tau_{k0})(\overline{Y}_0 - I_0) + (1 - \tau_{b0})B_0^p$$

$$- (1 + r_{-1} - \tau_{b0})B_{-1}^p, \tag{8.1}$$

$$(1 + \tau_{c1})C_1 = (1 - \tau_{k1})(\overline{Y}_1 + F(I_0)) - (1 + r_0 - \tau_{b1})B_0^p, \tag{8.2}$$

where τ_{ct}, τ_{kt}, and τ_{bt} ($t = 0, 1$) denote, respectively, the advalorem tax rates in period t on consumption, capital income, and new borrowing. In equation (8.1) the coefficient of C_0 indicates that the unit cost of consumption is one plus the corresponding advalorem tax. The coefficient of the level of capital income ($\overline{Y}_0 - I_0$) is one minus the corresponding advalorem tax, reflecting taxes on income from existing capital ($\overline{Y}_0$) and a tax rebate on negative income from current investment. This tax is a cash-flow capital income tax (with full expensing of investment). Our formulation of the tax on international borrowing assumes that the tax applies to new net private-sector borrowing, that is, ($B_0^p - B_{-1}^p$). This could be verified by noting that the last two terms on the right-hand side of equation (8.1) could also be written as $(1 - \tau_{b0})(B_0^p - B_{-1}^p) - r_{-1}B_{-1}^p$. In this formulation debt service is exempt from the tax. An analogous interpretation applies to the second budget constraint in equation (8.2). We note that in the second period there is negative new net borrowing (since past debt is repaid and no new debt is issued); therefore the term $\tau_{b1}B_0^p$ corresponds to a tax rebate. As is evident from the formulation of equations (8.1) and (8.2), the three taxes are linked through an equivalence relation. This equivalency implies that the effect on the real equilibrium of any combination of the three taxes can be duplicated by a policy consisting of any two of them. Our formulation reveals that although in a closed-economy context consumption and income taxes are equivalent, they do not remain equivalent if the economy is open to international trade.

With these taxes the periodic budget constraints of the government are

$$G_0 = B_0^g + \tau_{c0} C_0 + \tau_{k0}(\overline{Y}_0 - I_0) + \tau_{b0}(B_0^p - B_{-1}^p)$$

$$- (1 + r_{-1})B_{-1}^g, \tag{8.3}$$

$$G_1 = \tau_{c1} C_1 + \tau_{k1}[\overline{Y}_1 + F(I_0)] - \tau_{b1} B_0^p - (1 + r_0)B_0^g. \tag{8.4}$$

In this formulation we have implicitly assumed that aside from domestically imposed taxes, the private sector and the government can borrow at the same rate of interest in the world capital market. We also note that in conformity with the national income identities, in each period the sum of the private sector's and the government budget constraints implies that the difference between aggregate absorption and GNP equals the net accumulation of external debt.

Finally, it is noteworthy that according to the specification in equations (8.1) through (8.4), the government does not sell bonds to the domestic private sector. This simplifying assumption does not affect the analysis. To verify this point, let $-B^p$ and $-B^g$ denote foreign bonds purchased by the domestic private sector and the domestic government, respectively, and let A^g denote domestic-goverment bonds purchased by the domestic private sector. In the presence of a tax on international borrowing, arbitrage between government bonds and foreign bonds implies that $(1 - r_0 - \tau_{b1})/(1 - \tau_{b0}) = 1 + r_0^g$ and $(1 - r_{-1} - \tau_{b0})/(1 - \tau_{b, -1}) = 1 + r_{-1}^g$, where r_t^g ($t = -1, 0$) denotes the market rate of interest on government bonds sold to the domestic private sector. These considerations can be incorported into the various budget constraints by subtracting the term $[A_0^g - (1 + r_{-1}^g)A_{-1}^g]$ from the right-hand side of equation (8.1) and adding it to the right-hand side of equation (8.3), and by adding the term $[(1 + r_0^g)A_0^g]$ to the right-hand side of equation (8.2) and subtracting it from the right-hand side of equation (8.4). The reader may verify that these modifications do not affect the results, and for ease of exposition, we henceforth set $A_{-1}^g = A_0^g = 0$.

The private-sector periodic budget constraints can be combined in order to yield the consolidated lieftime constraint. Adding equation (8.2), multiplied by $(1 - \tau_{b0})/(1 + r_0 - \tau_{b1})$, to equation (8.1) and dividing the resulting equation by $(1 + \tau_{c0})$ yields

$$C_0 + \alpha_{\tau 1} C_1 = \frac{(1 - \tau_{k0})}{(1 + \tau_{c0})} \overline{Y}_0 + \frac{(1 - \tau_{k1})(1 - \tau_{b0})}{(1 + \tau_{c0})(1 + r_0 - \tau_{b1})} \overline{Y}_1$$

$$+ \frac{(1 - \tau_{k0})}{(1 + \tau_{c0})} [\alpha_{I1} F(I_0) - I_0] - \frac{(1 + r_{-1} - \tau_{b0})}{(1 + \tau_{c0})} B^p_{-1},$$

$$(8.5)$$

where

$$\alpha_{\tau 1} = \frac{(1 - \tau_{b0})(1 + \tau_{c1})}{(1 + r_0 - \tau_{b1})(1 + \tau_{c0})}, \quad \alpha_{I1} = \frac{(1 - \tau_{b0})}{(1 + r_0 - \tau_{b1})} \frac{(1 - \tau_{k1})}{(1 - \tau_{k0})}.$$

For subsequent use we recall that the world discount factor is denoted by $\alpha_1 = \dfrac{1}{(1 + r_0)}$.

Equation (8.5) is the private-sector consolidated budget constraint which incorporates the role of taxes. The key point to emphasize is that the discount factors applicable to the quantities pertaining to the future period (period one) are the tax-inclusive discount factors. These are the *effective discount factors* relevant for private-sector decisions. Accordingly, $\alpha_{\tau 1}$ measures the effective intertemporal price of C_1 in terms of C_0. This price reflects the prevailing tax structure. It is governed by the time profiles of the consumption tax—reflected by the ratio $(1 + \tau_{c1})/(1 + \tau_{c0})$—and of the international borrowing tax—reflected by the ratio $(1 - \tau_{b0})/(1 + r_0 - \tau_{b1})$.

Analogously, the effective discount factor applicable for investment decisions is α_{I1}. This effective discount factor is governed by the time profiles of the taxes on international borrowing and on capital income. It does not depend on the time profile of the tax on consumption.

This dependence of the effective discount factors on the time profiles of the various taxes reflects the non-Ricardian feature of the model. A budget deficit arising from a current tax cut (for a given path of government spending) must be followed by a future tax hike (to ensure government solvency). This change in the time profile of taxes alters the effective discount factors. This provides for the principal channel through which budget deficits affect the intertemporal allocation of consumption and investment.

Finally, we note that if the time profile of any given tax is flat— so that $\tau_{c0} = \tau_{c1}$, $\tau_{k0} = \tau_{k1}$, or $\tau_{b0} = \tau_{b1}/(1 + r_0) = \alpha_1 \tau_{b1}$—then this tax is nondistortionary, and its impact is similar to that of a lump-sum tax. This convenient property underlies our choice of the cash-flow formulation of the capital-income tax.

8.2 Effects of Cuts in Taxes on Consumption

Consider the effects of a budget deficit induced by a cut in the tax on consumption. We note in passing that this consumption tax is equivalent to a value-added tax system (VAT) under which investment and exports are exempt. In order to isolate the effect of this tax cut, we assume that all other taxes are zero. We also assume that the paths of foreign taxes are flat (so that the foreign tax system does not introduce a distortion) and that the foreign government runs a balanced budget (so that changes in the world rate of interest do not impact on the foreign government's solvency). In order to determine the effects of this change in taxes on the real equilibrium of the world economy, it is convenient to employ a diagrammatic device similar to the one used in figure 7.4. Accordingly, suppose that the utility functions are homothetic.

The initial equilibrium is described in figure 8.1 by point A. In this figure the vertical axis measures the (tax-free) world rate of interest which is initially r_0. The schedules pertaining to the initial equilibrium $(D, D^*, D^w, \text{and } S^w)$ are drawn for the given initial configuration of taxes. A reduction in the current tax on consumption from τ_{c0} to τ'_{c0}, and a corresponding rise in the future tax from τ_{c1} to τ'_{c1} (necessary to restore government solvency) raises the effective discount factor applicable to consumption, $\alpha_{\tau 1}$ (i.e., lowers the effective rate of interest) and induces a substitution toward current consumption. Thus for each and every value of the world rate of interest, the domestic (relative) demand schedule shifts to the right from D to D'. The proportional vertical displacement of the schedule equals the

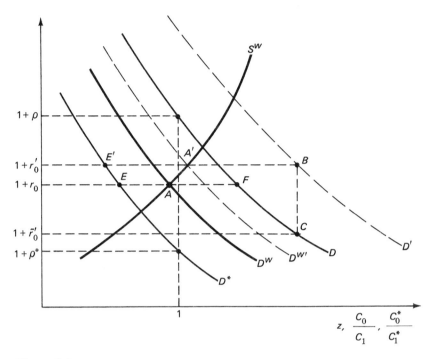

Figure 8.1
The effects of a budget deficit arising from a cut in consumption taxes

proportional rise in the effective discount factor. This proportion is $[(1 + \tau_{c1}')/(1 + \tau_{c1})][(1 + \tau_{c0})/(1 + \tau_{c0}')]$. Associated with the new domestic relative demand, the new world relative demand also shifts to the right from D^w to $D^{w'}$. Being a weighted average of the domestic and foreign relative demands, the vertical displacement of D^w is smaller than that of D.

The rise in the effective discount factor applicable to consumption decisions, from $\alpha_{\tau 1}$ to $\alpha_{\tau 1}'$, does not affect the effective discount factor applicable to investment decisions. Therefore the relative supply schedule in figure 8.1 remains intact. Hence the equilibrium world rate of interest rises from r_0 to r_0'. This higher world rate of interest discourages domestic investment as well as investment in the foreign country and results in a positive cross-country correlation of investment.

To determine the incidence of this change in the time profile of taxes on the domestic effective rate of interest, we recall that the percentage vertical displacements of the D schedule equals the tax-induced percentage change in the effective discount factor. This change is represented by the distance BC in figure 8.1. Accordingly, in order to determine the new equilibrium value of the domestic effective rate of interest, we subtract from $1 + r'_0$ the distance BC. This yields $1 + \tilde{r}'_0$ in figure 8.1. Evidently, the new equilibrium effective rate of interest $\tilde{r}'_0$ is lower than the initial rate r_0 since the vertical displacement of D^w is smaller than BC, and since the percentage fall in the world discount factor is even smaller than the vertical displacement of D^w.

Since in the new equilibrium the world rate of interest rises, it induces intertemporal substitution in foreign consumption toward future consumption and thereby results in a higher growth rate of foreign consumption (represented by the move from point E to point E' in figure 8.1). By similar reasoning, the fall in the domestic effective rate of interest induces intertemporal substitution in domestic consumption toward current consumption which lowers the growth rate of domestic consumption (represented by the move from point F to point B in figure 8.1). Finally, we note that even though the growth rate of foreign consumption rises, the growth rate of world consumption falls (as represented by the move from point A to point A' in figure 8.1). This decline reflects the fall in world investment.

The unambiguous inference concerning the effects of this cut in taxes on domestic and foreign investment, and on the growth rates of consumption (indicated by the ratios C_1/C_0 and C_1^*/C_0^*), does not generally carry over to the level of domestic consumption. In order to determine the effect of the tax cut on the level of consumption, we need to take account of the induced changes in the value of the budget constraint relevant for the economy as a whole and the changes in the rate of interest relevant for private-sector decisions. The budget constraint relevant for the economy as a whole is obtained by combining the private sector lifetime budget constraint (8.5) with the corresponding government present-value budget constraint, which is obtained by dividing equation (8.4) by $(1 + r_0)$ and adding to equation (8.3). This consolidated budget constraint is

$$C_0(\alpha_{\tau 1}, W_0) + \alpha_1 C_1(\alpha_{\tau 1}, W_0)$$

$$= (\overline{Y}_0 - G_0) + \alpha_1(\overline{Y}_1 - G_1) + \alpha_1 F[I_0(\alpha_1)] - I_0(\alpha_1)$$

$$- (1 + r_{-1})B_{-1} = V_0, \tag{8.6}$$

where B_{-1} denotes the historically given initial external debt ($B_{-1} = B^p_{-1} + B^g_{-1}$). The left-hand side of equation (8.6) is the discounted sum of lifetime consumption, and the right-hand side (defined as V_0) is the discounted sum of GDP net of government spending, investment, and initial debt commitment. Both discounted sums are evaluated by using the discount factor, α_1, applicable to the economy in the world capital markets. Thus V_0 is the value of the constraint relevant for the economy as a whole. However, as reflected in the arguments of the consumption functions $C_t(\alpha_{\tau 1}, W_0)$, the decisions concerning the intertemporal allocation of consumption are governed by the effective (tax-inclusive) discount factor, $\alpha_{\tau 1}$.

At the initial world rate of interest, a cut in the current tax on consumption, τ_{c0}, accompanied by a future rise in the tax, τ_{c1}, raises the effective discount factor, $\alpha_{\tau 1}$. As seen from equation (8.6), for a given value of α_1, this rise in $\alpha_{\tau 1}$ does not alter the value of the constraint, V_0. The change in the world rate of interest, however, does alter the constraint according to

$$\frac{\partial V_0}{\partial \alpha_1} = F[I_0(\alpha_1)] + (\overline{Y}_1 - G_1). \tag{8.7}$$

Hence it follows that the budget deficit, which raises the world rate of interest, must lower the value of V_0 by an amount equal to (period-one) GDP net of government spending.

In what follows we use these considerations concerning the induced changes in α_1, $\alpha_{\tau 1}$, and V_0 in order to analyze the effects of the budget deficit on the level of domestic consumption. Points A and B in figure 8.2 describe the patterns of consumption and investment prevailing in the initial equilibrium in which the world rate of interest is r_0. The assumption that the tax on capital income is zero implies that the initial level of investment is undistorted (hence the tangency at point B between the investment opportunity schedule and the world "price line" with the slope of $1 + r_0$) and that the consump-

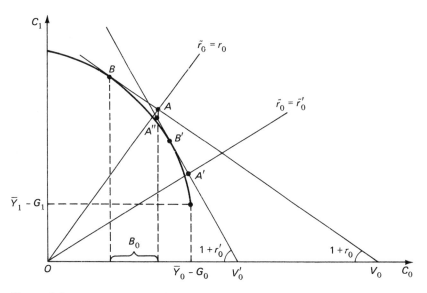

Figure 8.2
The effects of a budget deficit arising from a cut in consumption taxes on the level of domestic consumption. Data: $B_{-1} = 0$, $r_0 < r_0'$, $r_0 > \tilde{r}_0'$, $B_0 > 0$.

tion expansion locus, OA, corresponds to the situation in which the initial effective rate of interest, $\tilde{r}_0$, equals the world rate, r_0. The rise in the world rate of interest from r_0 to r_0' shifts the domestic investment point to B' (lowering investment), alters the economywide budget constraint from BV_0 (with the slope $1 + r_0$) to $B'V_0'$ (with the steeper slope $1 + r_0'$), and rotates the consumption-expansion locus from OA (corresponding to $\tilde{r}_0$) to OA' (corresponding to the lower effective rate, $\tilde{r}_0'$).

The new pattern of consumption is described by point A' in figure 8.2. In the case drawn, current consumption rises, but this result is not general. For example, if the intertemporal elasticity of substitution is low, then the rotation of the consumption-expansion locus is relatively small, and the new equilibrium can be obtained at a point such as A'' at which current consumption falls. A key factor determining the effects of the budget deficit on the level of domestic consumption is whether, in the current period, the entire country lends or borrows internationally. The case shown in figure 8.2 corresponds to a situation in which the domestic economy borrows abroad (the amount B_0). Alternatively, if the economy is a net lender (if the consumption point lies to the left of the investment point), then both the rise in the world rate of interest and the fall in the effective rate of interest operate to raise the level of domestic current consumption.

This ambiguity of the effects of the budget deficit on the level of consumption is enhanced in the more general situation in which the initial time profile of taxes is not flat. In that case the initial equilibrium is distorted, and the change in the level of consumption also reflects the influence of the change in the magnitude of the initial distortion.

By influencing the world rate of interest, the domestic budget deficit is transmitted internationally. In general, due to possible conflicts between income and substitution effects, induced by the tax policy and by the interest-rate changes, the effects of the budget deficit on the *level* of consumption and trade balance is not clear cut. However, if the foreign economy has a flat tax profile, then, ruling out a backward-bending saving function, the rise in the world rate of interest operates to reduce current foreign consumption. In this case, since world investment falls while output is unchanged, the market-clearing condition for world output implies that domestic consumption rises. We conclude that if the intertemporal elasticities of substitution between current and future consumption are relatively low, then the correlation between changes in domestic and foreign consumption consequent on the budget deficit may be positive or negative. On the other hand, if the elasticities of substitution are relatively high, then the budget deficit results in a negative correlation between domestic and foreign levels of consumption.

Finally, in the case for which the foreign saving function does not bend backward, foreign absorption (consumption plus investment) falls, and therefore the foreign economy's trade account improves. This improvement is mirrored by a corresponding deterioration in the domestic balance of trade.

8.3 Effects of Cuts in Taxes on Capital Income

We now consider the effects of a deficit arising from a current cut in taxes on income from capital. Assuming that all other taxes are zero, this tax cut must be accompanied by a corresponding rise in future

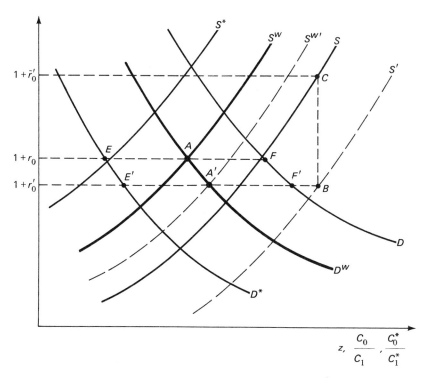

Figure 8.3
The effects of a budget deficit arising from a cut in capital income tax

taxes. Accordingly, suppose that the time profile of taxes is changed from (τ_{k0}, τ_{k1}) to a steeper profile (τ'_{k0}, τ'_{k1}). The initial equilibrium is described by point A in figure 8.3. Since the taxes τ_{k0} and τ_{k1} do not influence the effective discount factor applicable to consumption decisions, $\alpha_{\tau 1}$, changes in the time profile of this tax do not alter the desired ratio of intertemporal consumption. Therefore the relative demand schedules in figure 8.3 remain intact.

Turning to the supply side, we note that, in analogy with the construction of the world relative demand schedule, the world relative supply schedule is also a weighted average of the two countries' schedules, S and S^*. Accordingly, $S^w = \mu_s S + (1 - \mu_s)S^*$, where the domestic-country weight is

$$\mu_s = \frac{\overline{Y}_1 + F(I_0) - G_1}{\overline{Y}_1 + F(I_0) - G_1 + \overline{Y}_1^* + F^*(I_0^*) - G_1^*} = \frac{\overline{Y}_1 + F(I_0) - G_1}{C_1 + C_1^*}.$$

By lowering the effective discount factor relevant to investment decisions, α_{I1}, the budget deficit displaces the domestic relative supply schedule downward from S to S'. The proportional displacement is equal to $(1 - \tau'_{k1})(1 - \tau_{k0})/(1 - \tau_{k1})(1 - \tau'_{k0})$ which measures the percentage change in α_{I1}. The proportional downward displacement of the *world* relative supply schedule is smaller than this quantity since the weight μ_s is smaller than unity.

The new equilibrium obtains at the intersection between the (unchanged) world relative demand schedule, D^w, and the new world relative supply schedule, $S^{w'}$. This equilibrium is indicated by point A' at which the world rate of interest falls, from r_0 to r'_0, and (one plus) the effective interest rate applicable to domestic investment rises by the proportion $(1 + \tilde{r}'_0)/(1 + r_0)$. This rise is indicated by the distance BC corresponding to the vertical displacement of the domestic relative supply schedule. In the new equilibrium the rates of growth of domestic and foreign consumption fall. This is indicated by the respective moves from points F to F' and E to E'. As a result the rate of growth of world consumption must also fall. In view of the fall in the world rate of interest from r_0 to r'_0, foreign investment rises, and in view of the rise in the effective domestic rate of interest from r_0 to $\tilde{r}'_0$, domestic investment falls. Thus a deficit arising from a cut in taxes on income from capital crowds out domestic investment and crowds in foreign investment. These changes result in a negative correlation between domestic and foreign investment and in a positive correlation between domestic and foreign rates of growth of consumption.

In contrast with the ambiguity concerning the effects of a cut in consumption taxes on the level of domestic consumption, the consumption effects of a cut in taxes on income from capital are unambiguous if the initial equilibrium is undistorted (i.e., the initial tax profile is flat). This is because the fall in the world rate of interest raises current consumption by increasing wealth (through the increased value of the discounted sum of GDPs) and by inducing intertemporal substitution. Similarly, if the time profile of foreign taxes is also flat, the fall in the world rate of interest raises foreign consumption for the same reasons. It follows that under these circumstances the domestic budget deficits crowds in domestic and foreign private-sector consumption and results in a positive cross-country correlation between the levels of consumption.

It is also noteworthy that in contrast with the effects of a cut in consumption taxes, the reduction in taxes on income from capital improves the domestic-country trade balance. This improvement of the domestic balance of trade is the counterpart to the deterioration in the foreign-trade account consequent on the rise in foreign absorption (consumption plus investment).

Finally, we note that if the initial tax profile is not flat, then the effects of the cut in capital-income tax on the level of domestic consumption are not clear cut. In this case the reason is that the budget constraint relevant for the economy as a whole is the same as in equation (8.6) except·for one modification: in the present case the discount factor relevant for investment decisions is the effective discount factor, α_{I1}, rather than the world discount factor, α_1. With this modification, for a given value of α_1, the rise in the effective domestic discount factor induced by the change in the time profile of taxes on capital income alters the value of the constraint, V_0, by

$$\frac{\partial V_0}{\partial \alpha_{I1}} = \{\alpha_1 F'[I_0(\alpha_{I1})] - 1\} I_0'(\alpha_{I1}), \quad \text{for given } \alpha_1. \tag{8.8}$$

Since investment depends positively on the effective discount factor and since the marginal product of investment diminishes with the rate of investment, it follows that whether V_0 rises, remains unchanged, or falls, depends on whether α_{I1} is smaller than, equal to, or larger than α_1. If initially taxes are zero, then $\alpha_1 = \alpha_{I1}$, and therefore for given α_1 the value of V_0 stays intact. Hence the change in taxes does not exert a first-order effect on V_0, and as implied by equation (8.7), the rise in the world rate of interest lowers the value of V_0 by the amount $F(I_0) + \bar{Y}_1 - G_1$.

8.4 Effects of Cuts in Taxes on International Borrowing

The foregoing analysis demonstrated that consumption-tax policies influence the equilibrium in the world economy by altering the relative demand schedules, whereas capital-income tax policies influence the equilibrium by altering the relative supply schedules. With fixed labor supply, as evident from the budget constraints (8.1) and (8.2), a tax on international borrowing is equivalent to a combination of consumption and capital-income taxes. It follows that such a tax policy influences the equilibrium by altering both the relative demand and the relative supply schedules. In this section we analyze such a tax policy by examining the effects of a budget deficit arising from a current cut in taxes on international borrowing. In order to focus on this tax, we assume that all other taxes are zero, and for convenience, we assume that the initial taxes on international borrowing are also zero. As seen from the government budget constraints, taxes on international borrowing induce both government revenue from tax collections and government expenditures from tax rebates. Therefore we need to determine first whether the deficit arises from a current cut in tax rates or from a current rise in tax rebates. Then we need to determine what changes in future tax rates are necessary to maintain the discounted sum of tax revenue unchanged.

The first-period government budget constraint (8.3) implies that if during the first period the private sector is a net borrower (i.e., $B_0^p - B_{-1}^p$ is positive), then obviously a cut in the current tax rate τ_{b0} induces a budget deficit. The second-period government budget constraint (8.4) indicates that the tax rebate is $\tau_{b1} B_0^p$. Hence, with positive borrowing, the maintenance of a given government revenue (in present-value terms) implies that the tax rate τ_{b1} must also fall according to

$$\frac{d\tau_{b1}}{d\tau_{b0}} = \frac{B_0^p - B_{-1}^p}{\alpha_1 B_0^p}. \tag{8.9}$$

These changes in the time profile of taxes on international borrowing influence the effective discount factors that are applicable to both consumption and investment decisions. As is evident from equation (8.5), in the absence of other taxes, the two effective discount factors, $\alpha_{\tau 1}$ and α_{I1}, are both equal to $(1 - \tau_{b0})/(1 + r_0 - \tau_{b1})$. Using equation (8.9) and the definition of $\alpha_{\tau 1}$, it can be shown that for a given world rate of interest and for zero initial taxes the change in the effective domestic discount factor is

An Intertemporal Approach to Fiscal Policies in World Economy   237

$$\frac{d\log \alpha_{\tau 1}}{d\tau_{b0}} = -\frac{B^p_{-1}}{B^p_0}, \quad \text{for a given } \alpha_1. \tag{8.10}$$

Thus, with positive borrowing, the current cut in taxes on international borrowing raises the effective domestic discount factor and correspondingly lowers the effective domestic rate of interest.

The analysis of the effects of the budget deficit on the equilibrium values of the world rate of interest and on the growth rates of domestic and foreign consumption is carried out with the aid of figure 8.4, in which the initial equilibrium is shown by point A. The reduction in the domestic tax on international borrowing, τ_{b0}, raises the effective discount factor applicable to consumption, $\alpha_{\tau 1}$ (i.e., lowers the effective rate of interest) and induces a substitution toward

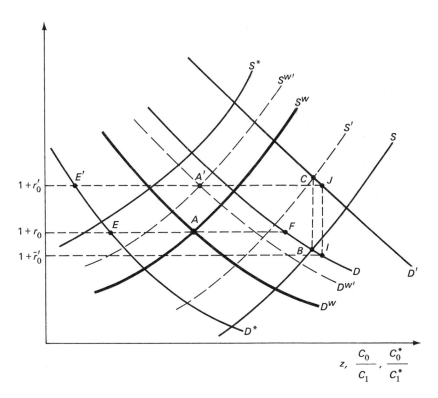

Figure 8.4
The effect of a budget deficit arising from a cut in taxes on international borrowing. Data: $B^p_{-1} > 0$, $B^p_0 > B^p_{-1}$.

current consumption. Thus for each and every value of the world rate of interest, the domestic (relative) demand schedule shifts to the right from D to D'. As argued earlier, the vertical displacement of the schedule equals the proportional change in α_{t1} (represented by the distance BC in figure 8.4). Associated with the new domestic relative demand, the new world relative demand (the weighted average of domestic and foreign relative demands) also shifts to the right from D^w to $D^{w'}$, and its proportional rightward displacement is equal to the fraction μ—representing the domestic-country weight, $C_1/(C_1 + C_1^*)$—times the percentage rightward displacement of the D schedule. Since the weight, μ, is smaller than unity, the D^w schedule shifts upward by a proportion smaller than the change in α_{t1}.

The rise in the effective discount factor, α_{t1}, is associated with an equiproportional rise in the effective discount factor applicable to domestic investment decisions or, equivalently, a fall in the corresponding effective rate of interest. At the prevailing world interest rate this stimulates current investment and results in an upward displacement of the domestic relative supply schedule from S to S'. This proportional displacement equals the percentage rise in the effective discount factor (represented by the distance BC in figure 8.4). As a result the world relative supply schedule shifts to the left from S^w to $S^{w'}$ by a proportion that is equal to the fraction μ_s times the percentage leftward displacement of the S schedule. Since μ_s is smaller than unity, the S^w schedule shifts upward by a proportion smaller than the percentage rise in α_{I1}. Hence the new equilibrium obtains at point A', at which the world rate of interest rises from r_0 to r_0'. This higher world rate of interest discourages investment in the foreign country.

To determine the incidence of the change in the tax on the equilibrium value of the domestic effective rate of interest, we subtract from the new equilibrium value $1 + r_0'$, the tax-induced rise in the effective discount factor. Diagrammatically, this subtraction is indicated by the distance IJ in figure 8.4, measuring the vertical displacement of the domestic relative demand schedule. As seen, in the new equilibrium the domestic effective rate of interest falls to $\tilde{r}_0'$, and the new equilibrium is associated with higher domestic investment. We thus conclude that the budget deficit arising from a cut in taxes on international borrowing results in a negative correlation between domestic and foreign investment.

The rise in the world rate of interest raises the equilibrium growth rate of foreign consumption (as indicated by the move from point E to E'). At the same time the fall in the effective domestic rate of interest lowers the equilibrium growth rate of domestic consumption (as indicated by the move from point F to J). Thus, as in the case of budget deficits arising from a cut in consumption taxes, the cut in taxes on international borrowing also results in a negative correlation between the growth rates of domestic and foreign consumption.

The effect of the tax cut on the growth rate of world consumption depends on the relative vertical displacements of the world relative demand and relative supply schedules. These two displacements are equal to each other if μ, the domestic-country weight in the world relative demand schedule, D^w, equals its weight, μ_s, in the world relative supply schedule, S^w. Recalling that $\mu = C_1/(C_1 + C_1^*)$ and that $\mu_s = [\overline{Y}_1 + F(I_0) - G_1]/(C_1 + C_1^*)$, it follows that if $\mu = \mu_s$, then the (second-period) trade account is balanced. In that case the new equilibrium point, A', lies vertically above the previous equilibrium point, A, and the growth rate of world consumption remains unchanged. If, on the other hand, μ_s exceeds μ, then the (second-period) trade account is in a surplus, and point A' lies to the left of point A. In this case the growth rate of world consumption rises. The opposite holds if μ_s falls short of μ (the case illustrated in figure 8.4).

As with consumption taxes, the unambiguous inference concerning the changes in domestic and foreign investment and in the growth rates of consumption that are induced by the tax change does not carry over to the level of domestic consumption. The effect of the tax cut on the level of consumption reflects both the induced changes in the value of the budget constraint relevant for the economy as a whole and the induced changes in the rate of interest relevant for private-sector decisions.

From this point onward the analysis of the effects of the change in taxes on international borrowing on the levels of domestic and foreign consumption and on the trade balance follows similar lines to the previous analysis of the effects of changes in consumption taxes. Accordingly, the budget deficit that raises the world rate of interest lowers foreign consumption (ruling out a backward-bending saving function), and since foreign investment also falls, it follows that foreign absorption (consumption plus investment) falls and the foreign trade balance improves. The counterpart to this improvement is a deterioration in the domestic balance of trade. Finally, the direction of the change in the level of domestic consumption is not clear cut. It depends on the initial level of international borrowing as well as on the extent of the rise in domestic investment induced by the fall in the effective domestic rate of interest.

8.5 Taxes on Labor Income: The Analytical Framework

In this section we extend the stylized model to allow for a variable labor supply and for taxes on labor income. We consider the effects of a budget deficit arising from a cut in current taxes on labor income. In order to focus on this effect, we abstract from other taxes. Further, in order to allow for endogenous labor supply and variable output, we modify the utility function and the production function.

Normalizing total endowment of time in each period t to unity, let the fraction of time spend on labor be l_t. Correspondingly, the fraction of time left for leisure is $1 - l_t$. We assume that lifetime utility is a function of four "goods": ordinary consumption (C_0, C_1), and leisure consumption ($1 - l_0$, $1 - l_1$). To facilitate the exposition, suppose that the utility function is separable between ordinary consumption and leisure, and let each subutility be homothetic. These assumptions imply that the utility-maximizing ratio of consumption in the two consecutive periods depends only on the rate of interest; likewise, the utility-maximizing ratio of leisure in the two consecutive periods depends only on the ratio of wages (net of tax).

As in the previous sections the individual who has access to the world capital market maximizes his or her lifetime utility subject to a consolidated lifetime budget constraint. With variable labor supply it is convenient to include in the definition of lifetime spending the imputed spending on leisure. Correspondingly, the definition of wealth includes the imputed value of labor endowment. Thus the lifetime budget constraint is

$$C_0 + (1 - \tau_{l0})(1 - l_0)w_{l0} + \alpha_1[C_1 + (1 - \tau_{l1})(1 - l_1)w_{l1}]$$

$$= (1 - \tau_{l0})w_{l0} + r_{k0}K_0 - I_0$$

$$+ \alpha_1\{(1 - \tau_{l1})w_{l1} + r_{k1}[K_0 + K(I_0)]\}$$

$$- (1 + r_{-1})B^p_{-1} = W_0, \tag{8.11}$$

where τ_{lt}, w_{lt}, and r_{kt} denote, respectively, the tax on labor income, the wage rate, and the rental rate on capital in period t ($t = 0, 1$), and where K_0 denotes the initial endowment of capital. As indicated in (8.11), the individual lifetime (full) income—that is, the individual wealth (W_0)—is the discounted sum of the value of time endowment (net of taxes) and of capital income (net of initial debt commitment). Capital income in the current period is the rental on existing capital, $r_{k0}K_0$, minus investment, I_0; correspondingly, the stock of capital in the subsequent period is $K_0 + K(I_0)$.

Maximization of the utility function subject to the lifetime budget constraint yields the demand functions for ordinary consumption and for leisure in each period. These demand functions depend on the three relative prices (net wages in each of the two periods and the discount factor) and on wealth. Accordingly, the labor supply functions (which are inversely related to the leisure demand functions) can be written as

$$l_0 = l_0[(1 - \tau_{l0})w_{l0}, \alpha_1, \alpha_1(1 - \tau_{l1})w_{l1}; W_0], \tag{8.12}$$

$$l_1 = l_1[(1 - \tau_{l0})w_{l0}, \alpha_1, \alpha_1(1 - \tau_{l1})w_{l1}; W_0]. \tag{8.13}$$

The assumption that leisure is not a Giffen good implies that a rise in the current period net wage raises l_0 and a rise in the (discounted value of) future net wage raises l_1. Assuming that the amounts of leisure consumed in two consecutive periods are gross substitutes implies that for a given level of wealth, a current tax cut lowers future labor supply while a future tax cut lowers current labor supply. This specification will be useful in the subsequent analysis of the effects of changes in the time profile of taxes on labor income.

In each period the level of outputs Y_0 and Y_1 depends on labor and capital inputs. In order to simplify the exposition, we assume linear production functions. Thus let

$$Y_0 = a_0 l_0 + b_0 K_0, \tag{8.14}$$

$$Y_1 = a_1 l_1 + b_1 [K_0 + K(I_0)]. \tag{8.15}$$

The assumption that factor markets are competitive implies that in equilibrium the wage rates and the rental rate equal the corresponding marginal productivities of labor and capital, respectively. Thus

$$w_{l0} = a_0, \quad w_{l1} = a_1, \quad r_{k0} = b_0, \quad r_{k1} = b_1. \tag{8.16}$$

As usual, profit-maximizing investment implies equality between the marginal cost of capital $(1 + r_0)$ and the marginal return on the investment, which is the product of the marginal product of investment in capital formation and the discounted sum of the rental rates on capital. Hence in the present two-period model, profit maximization requires that

$$r_{k1} K'(I_0) = 1 + r_0. \tag{8.17}$$

In order to close the model, we note that the present-value budget constraint of the government is

$$G_0 + \alpha_1 G_1 = \tau_{l0} w_{l0} l_0 + \alpha_1 \tau_{l1} w_{l1} l_1 - (1 + r_{-1}) B^g_{-1}. \tag{8.18}$$

Combining the private sector lifetime constraint (8.11) with the government present-value constraint (8.18), and making use of the supply-side equations (8.13) through (8.15), yields the economy's consolidated budget constraint in which the discounted sum of consumption equals V_0, where

$$C_0 + \alpha_1 C_1 = (a_0 l_0 + b_0 K_0 - G_0 - I_0)$$

$$+ \alpha_1 \{ a_1 l_1 + b_1 [K_0 + K(I_0)] - G_1 \} - (1 + r_{-1}) B_{-1}$$

$$= V_0. \tag{8.19}$$

The right-hand side of equation (8.19) measures the value of the constraint, V_0, relevant for the economy as a whole. As with the previous case a key property of the specification of this constraint is that it is evaluated by using undistorted prices. Thus in comparison with the private-sector constraint (8.11), the wages used in (8.19) for evaluating leisure and income are the tax-free wages. Obviously the

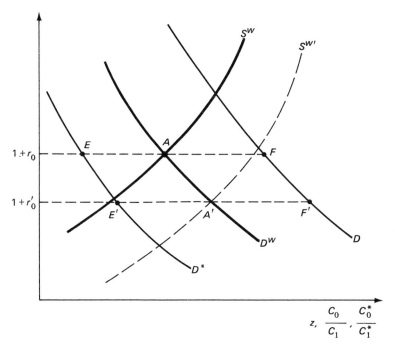

Figure 8.5
The effects of a budget deficit arising from a cut in taxes on labor income

wages that appear as arguments in the consumption and leisure demand (labor supply) functions, C_0, C_1, l_0, and l_1 are the aftertax wages.

To analyze the equilibrium of the system, we assume that the foreign economy has a similar structure of production, consumption, and taxes. The initial equilibrium of the system is described by point A in figure 8.5. As before, the downward-sloping schedules D and D^* denote the domestic and foreign relative demands for (ordinary goods) consumption in the two periods, and the schedule D^w is the weighted average of the domestic and foreign relative demands. The negative slopes of the schedules reflect the intertemporal substitution arising from changes in the rate of interest. The positively sloped schedule, S^w, reflects the response of z to the rate of interest, where, as before, z measures the ratio of world GDP net of investment and government spending in the two consecutive periods.

That is,

$$z = \frac{(a_0 l_0 + b_0 K_0 - I_0 - G_0) + (a_0^* l_0^* + b_0^* K_0^* - I_0^* - G_0^*)}{\{a_1 l_1 + b_1 [K_0 + K(I_0)] - G_1\} + \{a_1^* l_1^* + b_1^* [K_0^* + K^*(I_0^*)] - G_1^*\}}.$$

(8.20)

The S^w schedule is drawn with a positive slope for convenience. In fact changes in the rate of interest affect the intertemporal prices of leisure and of ordinary goods as well as wealth. These changes may alter the supply of labor in a way that more than offsets the effect of the induced changes in investment on z. In that case the S^w schedule is negatively sloped, but as long as it is steeper than the world relative demand schedule, our subsequent analysis remains intact.

8.6 Effects of Cuts in Taxes on Labor Income

Consider the effect of a budget deficit arising from a current reduction in the tax (τ_{l0}) on labor income (accompanied by a future rise in the tax, τ_{l1}). Implicit in this formulation is the assumption that there is a negative relation between the tax rate and the budget deficit so that the tax system operates on the "efficient" portion of the Laffer curve. The assumption that the homothetic utility functions are separable between leisure and ordinary consumption implies that for a given rate of interest the change in the time profile of wages (net of taxes) does not alter the desired ratios of ordinary consumption in the two consecutive periods. Thus the budget deficit does not alter the position of the relative demand schedules in figure 8.5.

On the other hand, the assumption that the amounts of leisure consumed in the two periods are gross substitutes ensures that the rise in the current net wage and the fall in the future net wage raises the current labor supply, l_0, and lowers the future labor supply, l_1. As a result the domestic relative supply schedule (not drawn) shifts to the right. Therefore, as seen from equation (8.20), this change in the time profile of taxes raises the value of z for any given rate of interest. This is shown by the rightward shift of the world relative supply schedule from S^w to $S^{w'}$ in figure 8.5.

The new equilibrium shifts from point A to A', the world rate of interest falls from r_0 to r_0', and the rates of growth of domestic, foreign, and world consumption fall. The lower rate of interest induces a positive correlation between growth rates of consumption. It also stimulates investment in both countries and therefore induces a positive correlation between domestic and foreign rates of investment.

The budget deficit arising from the change in the time profile of taxes on labor income also alters the levels of consumption in both countries. In the domestic economy the changes in the level of consumption reflect the combination of the induced changes in labor supply, the wealth and substitution effects induced by changes in the world rate of interest, and the response of investment. To illustrate the first two, we abstract for the moment from domestic investment. Consider figure 8.6. Points A and B describe the initial pattern of domestic consumption and production. The change in the time profile of taxes and the lower rate of interest alter the pattern of GDP

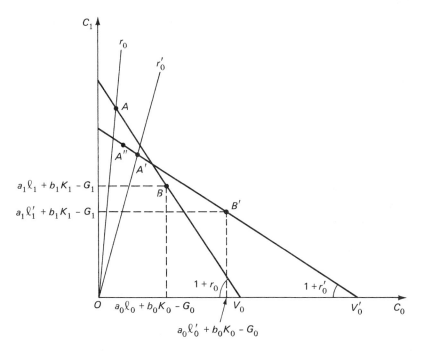

Figure 8.6
The effects of a budget deficit arising from a cut in taxes on labor income on the level of domestic consumption. Data: $B_{-1} = 0$, $r_0' < r_0$.

from point B to B', it shifts the economy's budget line from BV_0 to $B'V_0'$, and rotates the consumption-expansion locus from OA to OA'. The assumption implicit in the construction and rotation of the consumption-expansion loci is that consumption and leisure are separable in the utility function, and therefore the indifference map between C_0 and C_1 (underlying these loci) is independent of labor supply.

The new equilibrium pattern of consumption is described by point A' which, in the case shown in figure 8.6, corresponds to a higher level of current consumption. This result, however, is not general. For example, if the intertemporal elasticity of substitution is relatively low, then the extent of the rotation of the consumption-expansion locus is small, and the new equilibrium obtains at a point such as A''. In that case current consumption falls. As with taxes on international borrowing, a key factor governing the direction of the change in the level of consumption is whether the economy as a whole is a lender or borrower in the world capital market. In the case shown in figure 8.6 the economy is a lender; in that case a fall in the rate of interest exerts conflicting effects on current consumption. If, on the other hand, the economy is a borrower (so that the consumption point lies to the right of the production point), then both the wealth and the substitution effects induced by the fall in the rate of interest operate to raise the level of current consumption.

The exposition up to this point abstracted from the role of investment. With investment the fall in the rate of interest contributes positively to wealth by raising the profits on investment $[\alpha_1 K(I_0) - I_0]$. Furthermore the increased profitability of investment encourages borrowing (or discourages lending). This diminishes the weight of the factor contributing to a negative wealth effect associated with a fall in the rate of interest.

To determine the effects of the domestic budget deficit on the level of foreign consumption, we note that the fall in the world rate of interest raises the discounted sum of foreign GDP (provided that the foreign labor supply is not greatly reduced by the fall in the rate of interest). In addition (ruling out a backward-bending saving function) the fall in the rate of interest induces substitution of current consumption for future consumption. Hence, if the intertemporal elasticities of substitution are relatively large, the budget deficit results in a positive correlation between domestic and foreign consumption.

Finally, in the present framework the budget deficit may cause an improvement in the balance of trade. For example, if the foreign labor supply does not respond appreciably (positively) to the fall in the rate of interest, and correspondingly if the foreign GDP (net of government spending) does not rise much, then the rise in foreign absorption (consumption plus investment) worsens the foreign trade balance and correspondingly improves the domestic balance of trade. Thus, in contrast with the previous examples, the budget deficit causes an improvement in the trade account. This improvement reflects the rise in current period output induced by the stimulative policy of the lower taxes on labor income.

8.7 Summary

The foregoing analysis examined the effects of budget deficits on the world rates of interest, investment, and consumption and on the trade balance. We have analyzed the implications of four kinds of tax cuts: a cut in consumption taxes (valued-added taxes), a cut in taxes on income from capital, a cut in taxes on international borrowing, and a cut in taxes on labor income. Throughout we have assumed that the path of government spending is given, that the initial paths of domestic and foreign taxes are flat (or zero), and that the foreign government runs a balanced budget. The cut in current taxes results in a budget deficit and necessitates a tax hike in future periods in order to restore solvency. We have shown that the effects of such a deficit depend critically on the precise tax that is altered.

The formulation of the various taxes also suggests that they are interrelated through equivalence relationships. For example, as indicated by equations (8.1), (8.2), and the periodic budget constraints underlying (8.11), a consumption (VAT) tax is equivalent to a cash-flow income tax (capital income tax with expensing, plus a labor income tax) plus a tax on foreign borrowing. The inclusion of the tax on foreign borrowing in this tax-equivalence proposition is the special feature arising from the openness of the economy. Obviously this feature is absent from the various tax-equivalence propositions developed in the context of closed-economy analyses.

The mechanism through which the budget deficit impacts on the world economy operates through wealth effects and through temporal and intertemporal substitution effects. The latter are of central importance under circumstances in which taxes are distortionary. In such cases the substitution effects induced by tax cuts may operate in opposite directions to the wealth effects and as a result may yield outcomes opposite to those predicted by models (e.g., the Keynesian or the overlapping generations models) in which the wealth effects serve as the principal mechanism through which budget deficits influence the economy.

The important role attached to the intertemporal substitution effects suggests that the various distortionary taxes can be usefully divided according to whether they induce excess demand for current goods or for future goods or, equivalently, whether they stimulate current external borrowing (national dissaving) or lending (national saving). Tax policy that induces an excess demand for current goods by raising current consumption or investment or by lowering current GDP relative to future GDP is classified as a *pro-borrowing* policy, and tax policy that creates an excess supply of current goods by discouraging current consumption or investment, or by raising current GDP relative to future GDP, is classified as a *pro-lending* policy. Alternatively, the various tax policies associated with the budget deficit can be classified into expansionary *supply-shift* policies and expansionary *demand-shift* policies. Accordingly, a deficit arising from a cut in taxes on income from capital or labor (i.e., a cut in income tax) reflects supply-shift policies, whereas a deficit arising from a cut in consumption tax (value-added tax) reflects demand-shift policy and the latter is a pro-borrowing policy. With this classification we note that a budget deficit arising from a cut in taxes on international borrowing contains elements of both supply- and demand-shift policies. Since, however, the demand-shift component dominates, this tax cut is a pro-borrowing policy.

The results of the analysis are summarized in table 8.1. It is seen that the effects of the budget deficit on the world rate of interest, r_0, depend on whether the deficit arises from a pro-borrowing or a

Table 8.1
The effects of domestic budget deficits arising from a cut in taxes on international borrowing, capital income, and labor income

Tax cut on	g_c^w	r_0	$\tilde{r}_0$	g_c	g_c^*	I_0	I_0^*	C_0	C_0^*	$(TA)_0$
Consumption	−	+	−	−	+	−	−	+	−	−
International borrowing	+ if $\mu_s > \mu$									
	− if $\mu_s < \mu$	+	−	−	+	+	−	?	−	−
Capital income	−	−	+	−	−	−	+	+	+	+
Labor income	−	−	−	−	−	+	+	?	+	+

Note: g_c^w, g_c, and g_c^* denote, respectively, the world, domestic, and foreign growth rates of consumption. $\tilde{r}_0$ denotes the effective domestic rate of interest applicable to consumption decisions (except for the case of a capital income tax for which consumption depends on the world rate, r_0). This effective rate also governs domestic investment decisions (except for the case of consumption taxes for which domestic investment depends on the world rate of interest r_0). If $\mu_s > \mu$, then the (second-period) domestic trade account is in a surplus, and vice versa. The ambiguities in the effects of taxes on domestic consumption reflect conflicting substitution and wealth effects. Domestic consumption rises if the substitution effect dominates the wealth effect. The latter depends on the initial borrowing needs position. The assumption underlying the direction of the changes in the *levels* of consumption and the trade account is the absence of backward-bending saving functions.

pro-lending tax cut. A cut in current taxes on consumption and international borrowing is a pro-borrowing tax policy that raises the world rate of interest. On the other hand, a cut in current taxes on capital income and labor income is a pro-lending tax policy that lowers the world rate of interest.

The table also shows that in the case of consumption and capital-income taxes domestic investment falls, while in the case of taxes on international borrowing and labor income investment rises.

The results reported in the table show that independent of whether the tax cut is pro-borrowing or pro-lending, the budget deficit always lowers the growth rate of domestic consumption, $g_c = (C_1/C_0) - 1$. On the other hand, the international transmission of the effects of the deficit depends on whether the deficit arises from a pro-borrowing or pro-lending tax policy. If the tax policy is a pro-borrowing policy, then the growth rate of foreign consumption rises and foreign investment falls, and conversely if the tax policy is a pro-lending policy.

Table 8.1 also reports the changes in the growth rates of world consumption, $g_c^w = (1/z) - 1$ (which is equal to the growth rate of world GDP net of investment and government spending). As seen, the direction of the change in the growth rate of world consumption depends on the characteristics of the taxes that are changed. Since the various taxes influence the levels of current and future consumption, investment, and GDP, the net effects reflect the interactions among these changes. Accordingly, the growth rate of world consumption rises if the (second-period) domestic trade account is in a surplus, and the budget deficit arises from a cut in taxes on international borrowing. On the other hand, the growth rate of world consumption falls if the tax cut on international borrowing occurs in the presence of a (second-period) domestic trade-account deficit, or if the budget deficit stems from a cut in the other taxes.

Expressed in terms of correlations, table 8.1 reveals that a budget deficit arising from a pro-borrowing tax policy results in *negative* cross-country correlations between growth rates of consumption. On the other hand, a budget deficit arising from a pro-lending tax policy results in *positive* cross-country correlations between the growth rates of consumption. As for the cross-country correlations between levels of investment, table 8.1 shows that this correlation is positive if the deficit arises from a cut in taxes on consumption or labor income, and the correlation is negative if the budget deficit stems from a cut in taxes on international borrowing and capital income.

The effects of the budget deficit on the *levels* of domestic and foreign consumption and on the balance of trade generally depend on the shape of the initial time profile of taxes, the initial borrowing needs of the country (being positive or negative), and the size of the intertemporal elasticity of substitution. The signs of the effects indicated in the last three columns in table 8.1 are based on the assumption that the initial tax profile is flat and that the saving functions are not backward bending. With these assumptions a budget deficit arising from a pro-borrowing tax policy lowers foreign consumption and worsens the domestic balance of trade, whereas a budget deficit arising from a pro-lending tax policy raises foreign consumption improves the domestic balance of trade.

9

Fiscal Policies and the Real
Exchange Rate

Up to this point we have assumed that all goods are internationally tradable in world markets. This characteristic implies that fiscal policies that alter the relative price of goods impact directly on the rest of the world. In this section we extend the analysis by allowing for goods that are nontradable internationally, and whose relative prices are determined exclusively in the domestic economy. In that case the domestic effects of fiscal policies and their international transmission also operate through changes in the relative price of nontradable goods (the inverse of the real exchange rate). In what follows we examine the role of the real exchange rate in the analysis of fiscal policies. After introducing the analytical framework, we study the effects of government spending and then analyze the implications of budget deficits arising from tax cuts.

9.1 The Analytical Framework

In order to focus on the essentials relevant for the analysis of government spending, we simplify the exposition by abstracting from investment and from distortionary taxes. In section 9.3 we extend the analysis and allow for distortionary taxes. Throughout this chapter we assume that there are two composite goods: an internationally tradable good, denoted by x, and a nontradable good, denoted by n. The relative price of the nontradable good (the inverse of the real exchange rate) is denoted by p_{nt}, the output of that good is $\bar{Y}_{nt}$, government purchases of the nontradable good are G_{nt}, and private-sector demand is c_{nt} ($t = 0, 1$). We rely in this section on the general structure of the multiple-good model of chapter 6 modified to the special circumstances arising when some of the goods are nontradable.

In what follows we use the budget constraints from the previous chapters and interpret the various expressions so as to allow for the fact that output, consumption, and government spending are composed of tradable and nontradable goods. Accordingly, the disaggregated analogue to the private-sector lifetime budget constraint (8.5) from chapter 8 is

$$(c_{x0} + p_{n0}c_{n0}) + \alpha_{x1}(c_{x1} + p_{n1}c_{n1})$$

$$= (\overline{Y}_{x0} + p_{n0}\overline{Y}_{n0}) + \alpha_{x1}(\overline{Y}_{x1} + p_{n1}\overline{Y}_{n1}) - (T_0 + \alpha_{x1}T_1)$$

$$- (1 + r_{x,-1})B^p_{-1} = W_0, \qquad (9.1)$$

where, as before, $\alpha_{x1} = 1/(1 + r_{x0})$ denotes the effective discount factor and where T_t, c_{xt}, and $\overline{Y}_{xt}$ denote, respectively, lump-sum taxes and the levels of consumption and production of tradable goods, in period t ($t = 0, 1$), W_0 denotes wealth, and r_{xt} ($t = -1, 0$) denotes the world rate of interest. The values of wealth, taxes, and the rates of interest as well as the units of debt are measured in terms of tradable goods.

In addition to the private-sector lifetime budget constraint (9.1), the economy's overall constraint incorporates the government budget constraint. Rewriting the periodic government constraints (8.3) and (8.4) from chapter 8 by allowing for the disaggregation of commodities and consolidating into a present-value constraint yields

$$(G_{x0} + p_{n0}G_{n0}) + \alpha_{x1}(G_{x1} + p_{n1}G_{n1})$$

$$= T_0 + \alpha_{x1}T_1 - (1 + r_{x,-1})B^g_{-1}. \qquad (9.2)$$

Finally, consolidating the private sector lifetime constraint (9.1) with that of the government (9.2), and imposing equality between consumption and production of nontradable goods in each period, yields the economy's consolidated constraint:

$$c_{x0} + \alpha_{x1}c_{x1} = (\overline{Y}_{x0} - G_{x0}) + \alpha_{x1}(\overline{Y}_{x1} - G_{x1}) - (1 + r_{x,-1})B_{-1}.$$
$$(9.3)$$

The individual maximizes lifetime utility subject to the consolidated budget constraint (9.1). Formally, the individual's maximization problem is analogous to the problem outlined in chapter 6 with one modification. The goods are labeled as x and n (tradables and nontradables) instead of x and m (exportables and importables). As before, we assume that the lifetime utility function can be expressed as a function of two linearly homogeneous subutility functions $C_0(c_{x0}, c_{n0})$ and $C_1(c_{x1}, c_{n1})$. Hence lifetime utility is $U(C_0, C_1)$. Following the same procedure as in chapter 6 the maximization of this utility function subject to the lifetime constraint (9.1) is carried out in two stages—where the first stage optimizes the composition of spending within each period and the second stage optimizes the intertemporal allocation of spending between periods.

The optimization of the intertemporal allocation of (consumption-based) real spending (the analogue to equations 6.5 and 6.6a of chapter 6) yields the demand functions for each period real spending $C_t = C_t(\alpha_{c1}, W_{c0})$, where α_{c1} is the (consumption-based) real discount factor and where W_{c0} is (the consumption-based) real wealth. Expressed in terms of tradable goods, the level of spending in each period is $P_t C_t$, where P_t is the consumption-based price index (the "true" price deflator). Thus $\alpha_{c1} = \alpha_{x1} P_1/P_0$ and $W_{c0} = W_0/P_0$. Obviously, the price index in each period depends on the temporal relative price p_{nt} with an elasticity that equals the relative share of expenditure on nontradable goods, β_{nt}. Within each period the (sub)utility-maximizing allocation of spending between goods depends on the relative price p_{nt}.

The market for nontradable goods must clear in each country during each period. Accordingly, the market-clearing conditions for the domestic nontradable goods are

$$c_{n0}[p_{n0}, P_0 C_0(\alpha_{c1}, W_{c0})] = \bar{Y}_{n0} - G_{n0}, \tag{9.4}$$

$$c_{n1}[p_{n1}, P_1 C_1(\alpha_{c1}, W_{c0})] = \bar{Y}_{n1} - G_{n1}, \tag{9.5}$$

where the left-hand sides of these equilibrium conditions show the demand functions and the right-hand sides show the supply net of government purchases. As seen, the demand function depends on the relative price, p_{nt}, and on spending, $P_t C_t$, where P_t is the (consumption-based) price index, and C_t is (the consumption-based) real spending. As indicated, the level of real spending depends on the (consumption-based) real discount factor, α_{c1}. We assume that the utility function is homothetic so that the elasticity of consumption demand with respect to spending as well as the elasticity of spending with respect to wealth are unity.

Market clearing requires that in each period changes in the demand for nontradable goods (induced by various shocks) are equal to changes in the supply net of government purchases. Accordingly, differentiating equations (9.4) and (9.5) and evaluating around $G = 0$ (reflecting the assumption that the initial level of government spending is zero) yields

$$(\eta_{n_0 p_{n0}} + \eta_{P_0 p_{n0}})\hat{p}_{n0} + \eta_{C_0 \alpha}\hat{\alpha}_{c1} + \hat{W}_{c0} = \mu_{n0}\hat{Y}_{n0} - \varphi_{n0}\beta_{n0}^g(1 - \gamma_s^g)\,dG,$$
$$(9.6)$$

$$(\eta_{n_1 p_{n1}} + \eta_{P_1 p_{n1}})\hat{p}_{n1} + \eta_{C_1 \alpha}\hat{\alpha}_{c1} + \hat{W}_{c0} = \mu_{n1}\hat{Y}_{n1} - \varphi_{n1}\beta_{n1}^g\gamma_s^g\,dG,$$
$$(9.7)$$

where, as usual, η denotes the elasticity of the variable indicated by the first subscript with respect to the variable indicated by the second subscript, $\mu_{nt} = (\overline{Y}_{nt}/c_{nt}) \geq 1$, where φ_{nt} denotes the inverse of the value of private consumption of nontradable goods in period t, that is, $\varphi_{nt} = 1/p_{nt}c_{nt}$ ($t = 0, 1$), and where a circumflex denotes a logarithmic derivative. The intertemporal and the temporal allocations of government spending are governed by the government saving propensity, γ_s^g, and by the relative share of government spending on nontradables, β_{nt}^g. The left-hand sides of equations (9.6) and (9.7) show that private-sector demand is altered through changes in temporal prices (p_{nt}), intertemporal prices (α_{c1}), and real wealth (W_{c0}). The right-hand sides of these equations show that the net supply of nontradable goods is altered through changes in output (supply shocks) and through changes in government purchases.

In what follows we abstract from supply shocks and use the market-clearing conditions to analyze the international transmission of fiscal policies. In general, such a transmission is effected only through changes in international prices. In the present case, since the only tradable good is a single composite commodity, the international price that effects the transmission mechanism is the world rate of interest. Our analysis proceeds in two stages. In the first, we determine the effects of fiscal policies on the time paths of the real exchange rate and of private consumption of tradable goods under the assumption that the world rate of interest is given. Similarly, we also determine the effects of changes in the world rate of interest on the paths of the real exchange rate and of private consumption of tradable goods under the assumption that fiscal policies are given. In the second stage we use a two-country framework and combine these partial results in order to determine the equilibrium relations between fiscal policies, the world rate of interest, and the time paths of the domestic and foreign real exchange rates.

9.2 Government Spending, the Rate of Interest, and the Real Exchange Rate

In this section we analyze the effects of government spending on the world rate of interest and on the paths of the domestic and foreign real exchange rates. This analysis identifies the precise mechanism of the international transmission of the effects of government spending on both tradable and nontradable goods. The equilibrium value of wealth, W_0, is obtained by substituting the government present-value budget constraint (9.2) into the corresponding private-sector budget constraint. Accordingly,

$$W_0 = [p_{n0}(\overline{Y}_{n0} - G_{n0}) + (\overline{Y}_{x0} - G_{x0})] + \alpha_{x1}[p_{n1}(\overline{Y}_{n1} - G_{n1})$$

$$+ (\overline{Y}_{x1} - G_{x1})] - (1 + r_{x,-1})B_{-1}. \tag{9.8}$$

Starting from a zero level of initial government spending, consider a rise in the discounted sum of government spending by dG. This change in aggregate government spending falls in part on nontradable goods as indicated by the relevant terms on the right-hand side of equations (9.6) and (9.7). For a given value of the world rate of interest (measured in terms of tradable goods) the effect of the rise in government spending on the time path of the real exchange rate, p_{n0}/p_{n1}, is found by subtracting equation (9.7) from (9.6) and using the Slutsky decomposition. As shown in the appendix, if the expenditure shares of the private sector do not vary over time, this yields

$$\frac{d\log(p_{n0}/p_{n1})}{dG} = \frac{\varphi_{n0}\beta_n(1-\gamma_s)}{\beta_n\sigma + (1-\beta_n)\sigma_{nx}}\left[\frac{\beta_{n0}^g(1-\gamma_s^g)}{\beta_n(1-\gamma_s)} - \frac{\beta_{n1}^g\gamma_s^g}{\beta_n\gamma_s}\right] \quad (9.9)$$

where σ and σ_{nx} denote the intertemporal and the temporal elasticities of substitution and where γ_s denotes the private-sector-saving propensity.

Equation (9.9) reveals that the direction of the change in the path of the real exchange rate depends on the temporal and the intertemporal allocations of government demand for nontradable goods relative to the corresponding allocations of private-sector demand. If the ratio of the relative share of government spending on nontradable goods in the current period, $\beta_{n0}^g(1-\gamma_s^g)$, to the private-sector share, $\beta_n(1-\gamma_s)$, exceeds the corresponding ratio in the future period, $\beta_{n1}^g\gamma_s^g/\beta_n\gamma_s$, then a rise in government spending raises the percentage rate of change of the real exchange rate, and vice versa.

This result can be interpreted in terms of a transfer-problem criterion relating the temporal and the intertemporal spending patterns of the government and the domestic private sector. Accordingly, the rise in government spending raises the current price of nontradable goods relative to its future price, if the pattern of government spending is biased toward current nontradable goods in comparison with the pattern of private-sector spending.

We turn next to determine the effects of government spending on the path of private-sector consumption of tradable goods. Analogously to the previous specification, the demand functions for tradable goods are

$$c_{x0} = c_{x0}[p_{n0}, P_0 C_0(\alpha_{c1}, W_{c0})], \quad (9.10)$$

$$c_{x1} = c_{x1}[p_{n1}, P_1 C_1(\alpha_{c1}, W_{c0})]. \quad (9.11)$$

Obviously, in contrast to the markets for nontradable goods, the consumption of tradable goods in any given period is not limited by the available domestic supply. In determining the percentage change in the ratio c_{x0}/c_{x1}, we differentiate equations (9.10) and (9.11) and use the Slutsky decomposition. It is shown in the appendix that

$$\frac{d\log(c_{x0}/c_{x1})}{d\log(p_{n0}/p_{n1})} = \beta_n(\sigma_{nx} - \sigma). \quad (9.12)$$

Equation (9.12) shows that the qualitative effects of a rise in the price ratio p_{n0}/p_{n1} on the tradable-good consumption ratio, c_{x0}/c_{x1}, depends only on whether the temporal elasticity of substitution, σ_{nx}, exceeds or falls short of the intertemporal elasticity of substitution, σ. A rise in the relative price of nontradable goods, p_{nt}, induces substitution of consumption of tradable goods for nontradable goods *within* the period. The magnitude of this temporal substitution is indicated by σ_{nx}. Further, if p_{n0} rises by more than p_{n1} (so that the ratio p_{n0}/p_{n1} rises), then the extent of the temporal substitution within the current period exceeds the corresponding substitution within the future period. As a result the ratio of current to future consumption of tradable goods rises. This is reflected by the positive term $\beta_n \sigma_{nx}$ in equation (9.12). The same rise in the intertemporal price ratio p_{n0}/p_{n1} raises the (consumption-based) real rate of interest (and lowers the corresponding real discount factor, α_{c1}). This rise in the real rate of interest induces substitution of spending *between* periods: from the present to the future period. The magnitude of this intertemporal substitution is indicated by the negative term $-\beta_n \sigma$ in equation (9.12). Finally, we note that the change in the intertemporal consumption ratio does not depend on private wealth. This reflects the homotheticity assumption which implies that the tax-induced fall in wealth lowers current and future demand for tradable goods by the same proportion.

Combining equations (9.9) with (9.12) yields

$$\frac{d\log(c_{x0}/c_{x1})}{dG} = \frac{\beta_n^2 \varphi_{n0}(1 - \gamma_s)(\sigma_{nx} - \sigma)}{\beta_n \sigma + (1 - \beta_n)\sigma_{nx}} \left[\frac{\beta_{n0}^g(1 - \gamma_s^g)}{\beta_n(1 - \gamma_s)} - \frac{\beta_{n1}^g \gamma_s^g}{\beta_n \gamma_s} \right].$$
(9.13)

Equation (9.13) shows that the direction of the effect of a rise in government spending on the path of tradable-goods consumption, c_{x0}/c_{x1}, depends on the product of two factors. First, the government-induced temporal-intertemporal bias in demand relative to the private sector (indicated by the term in the squared brackets in equation 9.13), and second, the temporal-intertemporal substitution bias in private-sector demand (indicated by $\sigma_{nx} - \sigma$). The first determines the effect of the rise in G on the price ratio, and the second translates the change in the price ratio into changes in the consumption ratio.

We turn next to determine the effects of changes in the world rate of interest (or equivalently the world discount factor) under the assumption that government spending remains intact. Using equations (9.6) and (9.7), it is shown in the appendix that the percentage changes in the periodic price of nontradable goods arising from a given percentage change in the world discount factor are

$$\hat{p}_{no} = \left[\frac{\gamma_s \sigma}{\beta_n \sigma + (1 - \beta_n)\sigma_{nx}} + \frac{\gamma_s(\mu_1 - 1)}{(1 - \beta_n)\sigma_{nx}} \right] \hat{\alpha}_{x1}, \tag{9.14}$$

$$\hat{p}_{n1} = \left[\frac{-(1 - \gamma_s)\sigma}{\beta_n \sigma + (1 - \beta_n)\sigma_{nx}} + \frac{\gamma_s(\mu_1 - 1)}{(1 - \beta_n)\sigma_{nx}} \right] \hat{\alpha}_{x1}, \tag{9.15}$$

where $\mu_1 = [p_{n1}(\overline{Y}_{n1} - G_{n1}) + (\overline{Y}_{x1} - G_{x1})]/(p_{n1}c_{n1} + c_{x1})$ denotes the ratio of future net output to private consumption and where γ_s denotes the private-sector relative share of saving out of wealth.

It is seen that the link between p_{nt} and α_{x1} operates through two channels. The first channel (indicated by the first term) is the intertemporal substitution effect which is positive in its effect on the current price and negative in its effect on the future price. Accordingly, a rise in the world discount factor (i.e., a fall in the rate of interest) induces substitution of spending from the future toward the present. Part of the rise in current aggregate demand falls on the nontradable goods and drives up their current price. Likewise, the decline in future demand reduces the future price of nontradable goods.

The second channel (indicated by the second term in equations 9.14 and 9.15) is the wealth effect. As is evident, the wealth effect induced by changes in the world rate of interest may be positive or negative depending on whether the country is a borrower or lender. Accordingly, if $\mu_1 > 1$, that is, if in the future period GDP net of government spending exceeds private spending (so that in the future period the private sector runs a trade account surplus), then the rise in the world discount factor (the fall in the rate of interest) induces a positive wealth effect. On the other hand, if $\mu_1 < 1$, the same rise in the discount factor induces a negative wealth effect. In this context it is relevant to note that the influence of the wealth effect on p_{n0} is identical to its influence on p_{n1}; this reflects the assumption that the wealth elasticity of spending is unitary and that the expenditure share, β_n, and the temporal elasticity of substitution, σ_{nx}, do not vary over time.

The dependence of the wealth effect on whether the *future* value of GDP net of government spending exceeds or falls short of future private spending (i.e., on whether μ_1 exceeds or falls short of unity) is interpreted by reference to the economy's consolidated budget constraint (9.3). This constraint implies that the discounted sum of the trade account surpluses, $(TA)_0 + \alpha_{x1}(TA)_1$, equals the historically given external debt commitment, $(1 + r_{x,-1})B_{-1}$. If $\mu_1 > 1$, then $(TA)_1 > 0$, and therefore the sum of the present-period current account deficit $[-(TA)_0 + r_{x,-1}B_{-1}]$ and the amortization of the historical debt B_{-1} must be positive. This sum is the private sector's present-period *borrowing needs*, to which the current rate of interest applies. Thus the direction of the wealth effect induced by the fall in the current rate of interest depends on whether the borrowing needs (current account deficit plus amortization) are positive or negative.

Equations (9.14) and (9.15) show that if the current borrowing needs are positive ($\mu_1 > 1$), then the fall in the world rate of interest must raise p_{n0} since in that case both the substitution and the wealth effects operate in the same direction. The two effects exert, however, conflicting influences on the future price, p_{n1}. If the current borrowing needs are negative ($\mu_1 < 1$), then the fall in the world rate of interest lowers the future price p_{n1} (since both the wealth and substitution effects operate in the same direction), but its impact on the current price depends on the relative magnitudes of the (negative) wealth and (positive) substitution effects. If the current borrowing needs are zero (so that $\mu_1 = 1$), then the fall in the rate of interest does not exert any wealth effect, and therefore it must induce a rise in p_{n0} and a fall in p_{n1} through a pure intertemporal substitution.

The multitude of possibilities arising from alternative assumptions about the sign and magnitude of the wealth effect does not impact on the analysis of the time profile of the real exchange rate, nor does it influence the analysis of changes in the (consumption-based) real rate of interest. The homotheticity assumption, together with the assumption that the expenditure share, β_n, and the temporal elasticity of substitution, σ_{nx}, do not vary over time, implies that the intertemporal ratio, p_{n0}/p_{n1}, is independent of wealth. Therefore we proceed by analyzing the effects of changes in the world rate of interest on the time path of the real exchange rate.

Subtracting equation (9.15) from (9.14) yields

$$\frac{d\log(p_{n0}/p_{n1})}{d\log\alpha_{x1}} = \frac{\sigma}{\beta_n\sigma + (1 - \beta_n)\sigma_{nx}}. \tag{9.16}$$

Equation (9.16) indicates that changes in the world rate of interest influence the path of the real exchange rate only through the intertemporal substitution effect. Accordingly, a rise in the world rate of interest (a fall in α_{x1}) induces intertemporal substitution of spending toward the future and thereby lowers the current price of nontradable goods relative to the future price (i.e., decelerates the rate of increase of the real exchange rate between period zero and period one). As before, wealth effects do not influence the price ratio p_{n0}/p_{n1}.

The induced change in the price ratio of nontradable goods together with the change in the world rate of interest influence the intertemporal-consumption ratio of tradable goods, c_{x0}/c_{x1} according to

$$\frac{d\log(c_{x0}/c_{x1})}{d\log\alpha_{x1}} = \frac{\sigma_{nx}\sigma}{\beta_n\sigma + (1 - \beta_n)\sigma_{nx}}. \tag{9.17}$$

Equation (9.17), which is derived in the appendix, shows that the only factors governing the change in this intertemporal-consumption ratio are pure temporal and intertemporal substitution effects. In this case, however (and in contrast with the effects of the rise in government spending analyzed in equation 9.13), both the temporal and the intertemporal elasticities of substitution operate in the same direction. This is evident by noting from the definition of the (consumption-based) real discount factor and from equation (9.16) that

$$\frac{d\log\alpha_{c1}}{d\log\alpha_{x1}} = 1 - \beta_n\frac{d\log(p_{n0}/p_{n1})}{d\log\alpha_{x1}} = \frac{(1 - \beta_n)\sigma_{nx}}{\beta_n\sigma + (1 - \beta_n)\sigma_{nx}}. \tag{9.18}$$

Thus a rise in the world discount factor raises the (consumption-based) real discount factor (but by a smaller proportion in view of the rise in p_{n0}/p_{n1}). This rise induces intertemporal substitution of spending toward the present and raises the consumption ratio c_{x0}/c_{x1}. Further a rise in the price of nontradable goods induces within each period substitution in consumption toward tradable goods. Since the rise in the discount factor raises p_{n0}/p_{n1}, the temporal substitution in consumption is stronger in the current period and therefore also operates to raise the ratio c_{x0}/c_{x1}.

Finally, notice that a rise in government spending induces a change in the world relative demand for tradable goods due to both the change in domestic relative demand and the change in the domestic weight in the world relative demand, μ. The latter effect is given by

$$\frac{d\log(c_{x0} + c_{x0}^{*})/(c_{x1} + c_{x1}^{*})}{dG}$$

$$= \frac{(1 - \mu)(1 - \beta_n)\gamma_s}{(c_{x0} + c_{x0}^{*})\{[(1 - \gamma_s^{*})/\gamma_s^{*}] - [(1 - \gamma_s)/\gamma_s]\}},$$

while maintaining relative demands constant. Note that this effect vanishes if $\gamma_s = \gamma_s^{*}$.

Equations (9.13) and (9.17) summarize the results of the first stage of the analysis. To determine the equilibrium in the world economy, we need to consider also the factors governing world supply of tradable goods. The foreign economy is assumed to be characterized by a structure of demand and supply similar to that of the domestic economy. Thus the relative world supply of tradable goods net of government purchases, z, is

$$z = \frac{(\overline{Y}_{x0} - G_{x0}) + (\overline{Y}_{x0}^{*} - G_{x0}^{*})}{(\overline{Y}_{x1} - G_{x1}) + (\overline{Y}_{x1}^{*} - G_{x1}^{*})}. \tag{9.19}$$

The analysis of the equilibrium in the world economy is carried out with the aid of figure 9.1. Panel I of figure 9.1 shows the *relative* intertemporal world supply, S^w, and the *relative* intertemporal domestic, D, foreign, D^{*}, and world, D^w, demands for tradable goods. As before, the world relative demand and relative supply are,

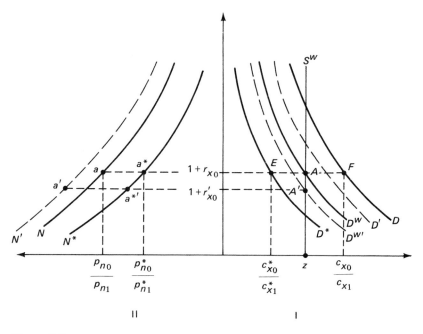

Figure 9.1
The effects of government spending on the world rate of interest and on the
paths of the real exchange rates. Data: $\sigma > \sigma_{nx}$, $\gamma_s > \gamma_s^g$, $\beta_n^g = 1$, $I_0 = 0$.

respectively, weighted averages of the domestic and foreign relative
demands and relative supplies. The relative demand schedules relate
the desired consumption ratio of tradable goods to the rate of interest. Their slope reflects the negative relation embodied in equation
(9.17). These demand schedules are drawn for a given level of
government spending. The relative supply schedule is drawn with
a zero interest elasticity since we abstract from investment. This
schedule is also drawn for a given level of government spending.

The schedules N and N^* in panel II of figure 9.1 show the relation
between the world rate of interest and the internal relative price
structure (the path of the real exchange rate) in each country. The
negative slope of these schedules reflects the relation embodied in
equation (9.16).

The initial equilibrium is described in panel I by point A in which
the world rate of interest is r_{x0}. The domestic and foreign intertemporal consumption ratios are indicated by points F and E. The
periodic percentage changes of the domestic and the foreign real

exchange rates associated with the initial equilibrium are shown in panel II by points a and a^*.

Consider the effects of a rise in the level of the domestic government spending. This change alters the domestic relative demand (and thereby the world relative demand), as well as the world relative supply. As shown in equation (9.13), the direction of the change in the relative demand schedules depend on the government-induced bias in the intertemporal net supply of nontradable goods and on the bias in the temporal-intertemporal substitution in private-sector demand. To determine the direction of the change in the relative supply schedule, we differentiate equation (9.19). Accordingly,

$$\frac{d\log z}{dG} = \lambda_{x1}^{g}(1 - \beta_{n1}^{g})\gamma_{s}^{g} - \lambda_{x0}^{g}(1 - \beta_{n0}^{g})(1 - \gamma_{s}^{g}), \tag{9.20}$$

where λ_{xt}^{g} denotes the reciprocal of the world output of tradable goods net of government purchases of these goods in period t ($t = 0, 1$). Thus $\lambda_{xt}^{g} = 1/(\bar{Y}_{xt} - G_{xt} + \bar{Y}_{xt}^{*} - G_{xt}^{*})$. Equation (9.20) indicates that the direction of the change in the relative supply reflects the bias in the intertemporal allocation of government spending on tradable goods.

Since the direction of the shift of the world relative demand and supply depends on the assumed magnitude of the various parameters, we cannot determine on a priori grounds whether the rise in government spending raises or lowers the equilibrium world rate of interest. Similar considerations apply to the effects of government spending on the paths of the domestic and foreign real exchange rates. As indicated by equation (9.9), depending on the temporal and intertemporal pattern of government spending, the rise in government spending may induce a rightward or leftward shift of the N schedule in panel II of figure 9.1.

To illustrate the working of the model, consider the case in which the various expenditure shares of both the private sector and the government do not vary over time (i.e., suppose that $\beta_{nt}^{g} = \beta_{n}^{g}$, $\beta_{nt} = \beta_{n}$, $\varphi_{n0}/\varphi_{n1} = \gamma_{s}/(1 - \gamma_{s})$, $\lambda_{xt}^{g} = \lambda_{x}^{g}$, for $t = 0, 1$). Figure 9.1 shows the effects of government spending for a bench-mark case in which the intertemporal elasticity of substitution, σ, exceeds the temporal elasticity, σ_{nx}, the ratio of the shares of government spending to private spending in the current period, $(1 - \gamma_s^g)/(1 - \gamma_s)$ exceeds the corresponding ratio of future spending, γ_s^g/γ_s, so that γ_s exceeds γ_s^g, and government spending falls entirely on nontradable goods (so that $\beta_n^g = 1$). As indicated by equation (9.13), in this bench-mark case the domestic and thereby the world relative demand schedules shift leftward from the position indicated by D and D^w to the position indicated by D' and $D^{w'}$, respectively. Further, as indicated by equation (9.20) with $\beta_n^g = 1$, the relative supply of world tradable goods does not change. It follows that in this case the equilibrium point shifts from point A to A' in panel I of figure 9.1, and the world rate of interest falls from r_{x0} to r'_{x0}.

In panel II of figure 9.1 we show the effects of the rise in government spending on the paths of the domestic and foreign real exchange rates. As indicated by equation (9.9), in this bench-mark case, the N schedule shifts leftward, and given the new lower world rate of interest, the domestic and foreign equilibrium points shift from a and a^* to a' and $a^{*'}$, respectively. Accordingly, the percentage change (per unit of time) of the real exchange rates increases in both countries. In concluding the presentation of this bench-mark case, we note that since the world rate of interest (measured in terms of tradable goods) falls and since in both countries the time paths of the real exchange rates steepen, it follows that in both countries the consumption-based real rates of interest fall (even though, in general, the magnitude of this decline need not be the same for both countries).

It is important to note that we chose this specific bench-mark case in which the rise in government spending lowers the world rate of interest in order to highlight the implications of government spending on nontradable goods. In fact, if government spending falls entirely on tradable goods, so that $\beta_n^g = 0$, then the rise in spending does not alter the relative demand schedules in figure 9.1 (as seen from equation 9.13 with $\beta_n^g = 0$), but it induces a leftward shift of the relative supply schedule (as seen from equation 9.20) for the case in which $\beta_n^g = 0$ and $\gamma_s > \gamma_s^g$. Thus under such circumstances the rise in government spending raises the equilibrium rate of interest. This outcome is analogous to the one obtained in section 6.3 for the case of a transitory rise in current government spending in a model in which all goods are internationally tradable.

Table 9.1
The effects of a rise in government spending on the world rate of interest in a model with nontradable goods

Relation between temporal and inter-temporal elasticities of substitution	Intertemporal and temporal allocations of government spending			
	$\gamma_s > \gamma_s^g$		$\gamma_s < \gamma_s^g$	
	$\beta_n^g = 0$	$\beta_n^g = 1$	$\beta_n^g = 0$	$\beta_n^g = 1$
$\sigma_{nx} > \sigma$	$+$	$+$	$-$	$-$
$\sigma_{nx} = \sigma$	$+$	0	$-$	0
$\sigma_{nx} < \sigma$	$+$	$-$	$-$	$+$

Note: The world rate of interest is measured in terms of internationally tradable goods. The table assumes that initially $\gamma_s = \gamma_s^*$.

The more general configurations of the effects of government spending on the world rate of interest, as implied by equations (9.13) and (9.19), are summarized in table 9.1, which assumes that initially $\gamma_s = \gamma_s^*$. The table demonstrates that if the commodity composition of government spending is strongly biased toward goods that are internationally tradable (so that β_n^g is small), then the key factor determining the direction of the change in the world rate of interest is the intertemporal allocation of government and private-sector spending. If government spending is biased toward the current period relative to private-sector spending, so that γ_s exceeds γ_s^g, then the world rate of interest rises, and vice versa. On the other hand, if the commodity composition of government spending is strongly biased toward nontradable goods (so that β_n^g is close to unity), then the direction of the change in the interest rate depends on the interaction between the intertemporal allocation of government spending relative to the private sector and the difference between the temporal and the intertemporal elasticities of substitution of the domestic private sector. In fact, since in this case the effects of government spending operate only through changes in the relative demand schedules, the rate of interest rises if $(\sigma_{nx} - \sigma)[(1 - \gamma_s^g)/(1 - \gamma_s) - \gamma_s^g/\gamma_s]$ is positive, and vice versa.

The various possibilities concerning the relative magnitudes of the key parameters also imply that the effects of government spending on the time path of the domestic and foreign real exchange rates are not clear cut. The possible outcomes are summarized in table 9.2.

Table 9.2
The effects of a rise in government spending on the paths of domestic and foreign real exchange rates

Relation between temporal and intertemporal elasticities of substitution	Real exchange rate in the	Intertemporal and temporal allocations of government spending			
		$\gamma_s > \gamma_s^g$		$\gamma_s < \gamma_s^g$	
		$\beta_n^g = 0$	$\beta_n^g = 1$	$\beta_n^g = 0$	$\beta_n^g = 1$
$\sigma_{nx} > \sigma$	Domestic economy	−	?	+	?
	Foreign economy	−	−	+	+
$\sigma_{nx} = \sigma$	Domestic economy	−	+	+	−
	Foreign economy	−	0	+	0
$\sigma_{nx} < \sigma$	Domestic economy	−	+	+	−
	Foreign economy	−	+	+	−

Note: The paths of the real exchange rates are measured by p_{n0}/p_{n1} and p_{n0}^*/p_{n1}^*. The table assumes that initially $\gamma_s = \gamma_s^*$.

The results in the table show that if the commodity composition of government spending is strongly biased toward internationally tradable goods (so that β_n^g is about zero), then, as implied by equation (9.9), the change in government spending does not displace the N schedule in panel II of figure 9.1. Therefore the induced change in the path of the domestic real exchange rate mirrors only the change in the rate of interest since it involves a movement along the given N schedule. It follows that, with β_n^g small, the change in the domestic time path of the real exchange rate is inversely related to the change in the world rate of interest. This inverse relation is verified from a comparison between the entries appearing in tables 9.1 and 9.2 in the columns corresponding to the case of $\beta_n^g = 0$.

In the other extreme case, in which government spending falls mainly on nontradable goods (so that β_n^g is close to unity), then, as long as the temporal elasticity of substitution, σ_{nx}, does not exceed the intertemporal elasticity of substitution, σ, the key factor determining whether the path of the real exchange rate steepens or flattens is the intertemporal allocation of government spending. If government spending is biased toward the current period relative to private-sector spending, so that γ_s exceeds γ_s^g, then the rise in spending accelerates the time path of the real exchange rate, and vice versa. On the other hand, if σ_{nx} exceeds σ, then the time path of the real exchange rate is influenced by two conflicting forces, the one operating through a movement along the N schedule (induced by the change in the rate of interest) and the other operating through a shift of the N schedule (induced by the direct effect of government spending on the relative supply of nontradable goods).

Finally, we note that since the foreign schedule, N^*, is not affected by domestic government spending, the time path of the foreign real exchange rate, p_{n0}^*/p_{n1}^*, is always related negatively to the world rate of interest. On the other hand, since the correlation between the time path of the domestic real exchange rate and the world rate of interest may be positive, zero, or negative (as may be verified by comparing the results reported in tables 9.1 and 9.2), it follows that the cross-country correlations between the paths of the real exchange rates and between the (consumption-based) real rates of interest may also be negative, zero, or positive. The analysis underlying tables 9.1 and 9.2 identifies the main factors governing the signs of the various cross-country correlations.

9.3 Tax Policies, Interest Rates, and the Real Exchange Rate

In the previous section we analyzed the effects of government spending under the assumption that taxes are nondistortionary. We turn next to examine the effects of changes in taxes under the assumption that government spending remains intact. Thus we analyze the effects of a budget deficit arising from a change in the time profile of taxes. Such a tax policy influences the effective (tax-adjusted) rate of interest and impacts on private-sector behavior. The altered behavior influences the equilibrium of the world economy and thereby transmits the effects of the domestic tax policy to the rest of the world. In this section we analyze these mechanisms using an extension of the formulation outlined in section 9.1.

Since the key mechanism through which the tax policy influences private-sector behavior operates through alterations of the effective (tax-adjusted) discount factor, we start by incorporating taxes into the definition of the discount factor using the analytical framework developed in chapter 8. We illustrate the mechanism by focusing on a specific tax: a consumption tax, that is, a value-added tax system (VAT) under which export is exempt. In the presence of such a tax the effective (tax-adjusted) discount factor is denoted by α_{xt1} which is related to the undistorted world discount factor, α_{x1}, according to

$$\alpha_{x\tau 1} = \frac{1 + \tau_{c1}}{1 + \tau_{c0}}\alpha_{x1},$$

where τ_{ct} is the advalorem consumption tax rate in period t ($t = 0, 1$). Correspondingly the effective (consumption-based) real discount factor is denoted by $\alpha_{c\tau 1}$, where

$$\alpha_{c\tau 1} = \alpha_{x\tau 1}\frac{P_1}{P_0}.$$

With such taxes, as discussed in chapter 8, private-sector demands depend on $\alpha_{c\tau 1}$ rather than on α_{c1}, and therefore changes in the time profile of taxes alter private-sector behavior. To simplify, we assume that foreign-government spending and taxes are zero.

A budget deficit arising from a current-period tax cut (a reduction in τ_{c0}) must be accompanied by a corresponding rise in future taxes (a rise in τ_{c1}) so as to maintain government solvency as long as government spending policies remain intact. The effects of such a

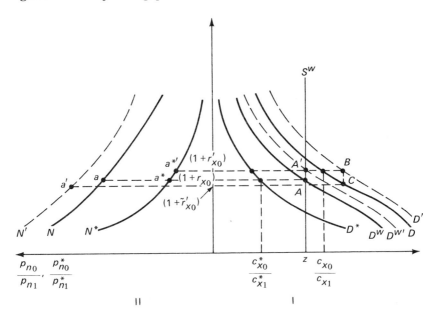

Figure 9.2
The effects of a budget deficit arising from a cut in a value-added tax on the world rate of interest and on the paths of the real exchange rates. Data: $I_0 = 0$.

change in the time profile of taxes are analyzed with the aid of figure 9.2. The initial equilibrium is described in panel I by point A in which the world rate of interest is r_{x0}. For convenience of exposition we assume that in the initial situation the time profile of taxes is "flat" (i.e., $\tau_{c0} = \tau_{c1}$) so that initially the domestic and foreign rates of interest (in terms of tradable goods) are equal to each other. The time paths of the domestic and foreign real exchange rates associated with the initial equilibrium is indicated in panel II by points a and a^* along the N and the N^* schedules. Thus the initial equilibrium is identical to the one portrayed in figure 9.1.

Consider the effects of a budget deficit arising from a tax cut. Given the initial value of the world rate of interest, r_{x0}, the reduction in τ_{c0} and the increase in τ_{c1} (implied by the government budget constraint) raise the domestic effective discount factor, $\alpha_{x\tau1}$, and induce an upward displacement of the domestic relative demand schedule from D to D'. The proportional vertical displacement of the schedule equals the proportional change in the effective discount factor. This displacement is necessary to offset the effect of the tax-induced reduction in the effective rate of interest on the desired domestic consumption ratio. Corresponding to the new domestic schedule D', the world relative demand schedule shifts from D^w to $D^{w'}$. The new equilibrium is described by point A' in panel I of figure 9.2. Hence the world rate of interest rises from r_{x0} to r'_{x0}. The proportional vertical displacement of the world relative demand schedule, D^w (indicated by the distance AA'), is smaller than the corresponding displacement of the domestic schedule, D (indicated by the distance BC) since the world schedule is a weighted average of the domestic and the given foreign schedules. It follows that the domestic effective rate of interest must fall from r_{x0} to a lower level such as $\tilde{r}'_{x0}$.

The change in the time profile of taxes, which (for any given level of the world rate of interest) raises the effective discount factor, also alters the position of the domestic schedule N in panel II of figure 9.2. In analogy to the previous analysis of the displacement of the relative demand schedule, the proportional vertical displacement of the N schedule equals the percentage change in the effective discount factor. As indicated by equation (9.16), this displacement is necessary to offset the effects of the tax-induced reduction in the effective rate of interest on the time path of the domestic real exchange rate. Hence, given the new domestic effective rate of interest $\tilde{r}'_{x0}$, the rate of increase of the domestic real exchange rate from period zero to period one accelerates (as p_{n0}/p_{n1} rises). Likewise, given the new world rate of interest, r'_{x0}, the rate of increase of the foreign real exchange rate decelerates (as p^*_{n0}/p^*_{n1} falls). These changes are indicated in panel II of figure 9.2 by the displacement of the equilibrium points a^* and a to $a^{*\prime}$ and a', respectively.

The foregoing analysis implies that the budget deficit arising from a cut in consumption taxes raises the world rate of interest and lowers the domestic effective rate of interest (both measured in terms of tradable goods). Further the deficit raises the periodic percentage change of the domestic real exchange rate and lowers the corresponding foreign percentage change. These changes in the time paths of relative prices imply from equation (9.18) that the foreign (consumption-based) real rate of interest rises and that the domestic (consumption-based) effective real rate of interest falls. Further the magnitudes of the changes in the rates of interest are smaller if the rates of interest are measured in terms of the consumption baskets than if they are measured in terms of internationally tradable goods (the absolute difference between the two magnitudes rises with the ratio of the temporal to the intertemporal elasticities of substitution, σ_{nx}/σ). We conclude that this budget deficit results in a negative cross-country correlation between changes in the domestic and the foreign (consumption-based) real rates of interest.

The analysis of the effects of the budget deficits on the levels of domestic and foreign spending, and thereby on the cross-country correlations among private-sector spending, is very similar to the one conducted in the context of a single-commodity world. This similarity reflects the fact that the direction of the changes in the (consumption-based) real effective rates of interest does not depend on whether or not the model contains nontradable goods. It follows that, as shown in the first line in table 8.1, with high intertemporal elasticities of substitution the domestic budget deficit raises domestic real spending, lowers foreign real spending, and worsens the domestic balance of trade. The rise in current domestic spending lowers the current domestic real exchange rate (the inverse of p_{n0}), and the fall in foreign current spending raises the foreign real exchange rate.

Hence, under such circumstances, the budget deficit results in negative correlations between domestic and foreign real spending and real exchange rates.

9.4 Summary

In this chapter we extended the analytical framework to incorporate nontradable goods into the analysis of fiscal policies. We showed that the effects of government spending depend critically on two biases: the bias in the intertemporal allocation of government spending relative to the domestic private sector and the bias in the commodity composition of government purchases relative to the domestic private sector. If government spending is strongly biased toward purchases of tradable goods, then the effects of such purchases are similar to those analyzed in chapter 7 in which all goods were internationally tradable. In that case the key factor determining whether the world rate of interest rises or falls is the intertemporal pattern of government spending relative to the private sector: if the latter is biased toward current spending, then the rate of interest rises, and vice versa. These adjustments in the rate of interest reflect the changes in the country's borrowing needs that arise from the intertemporal pattern of government spending.

The extended framework also provides information about the time paths of the domestic and foreign real exchange rates. If the relative share of government spending on tradable goods is high, then a rise in government spending decelerates the rate of change of the domestic and foreign real exchange rates if the intertemporal allocation of government spending (relative to the private sector) is biased toward the present. On the other hand, if the intertemporal allocation of government spending (relative to the private sector) is biased toward the future, then the rates of change of the real exchange rates accelerate. It follows that in this case government spending induces positive cross-country correlations between the time paths of the real exchange rates as well as between the (consumption-based) real rates of interest.

In contrast, if the commodity composition of government spending is strongly biased toward purchases of nontradable goods, then the qualitative results of chapter 7 concerning the interest-rate effects need not hold any more. Specifically, we showed that in this case the interest-rate effects depend on the interaction between the bias in the intertemporal allocation of government spending relative to the private sector and the temporal-intertemporal substitution bias of the domestic private sector. Accordingly, in the absence of knowledge of the magnitudes of the saving propensities of the government and of the private sector, as well as of the private-sector temporal and intertemporal elasticities of substitution, there is no presumption as to whether a rise in government spending raises or lowers world rates of interest.

The lack of an apriori presumption is even more pronounced when we consider the effects of government spending (which are strongly biased toward nontradable goods) on the time paths of the real exchange rates. We showed that the correlation between the domestic and foreign paths of the real exchange rates is positive if the intertemporal elasticity of substitution exceeds the temporal elasticity, and is zero if the temporal and intertemporal elasticities of substitution are equal to each other. This correlation may be positive, zero, or negative if the temporal elasticity of substitution exceeds the intertemporal elasticity. Since there is no presumption about the cross-country correlations between the paths of the real exchange rates, it follows that there is also no presumption about the cross-country correlation between the (consumption-based) real rates of interest.

The sharpest contrast between the implications of alternative biases in the commodity-composition of government spending arises in situations in which the intertemporal elasticity of substitution of the domestic private sector exceeds the temporal elasticity of substitution. In that case the direction of the effects of government spending on the world rate of interest and on the time paths of the domestic and foreign real exchange rates is reversed as the commodity composition of government spending changes from one extreme to the other. For example, if the intertemporal allocation of government spending relative to the domestic private sector is biased toward the present, then a rise in government spending on tradable goods raises the world rate of interest and decelerates the rates of change of the domestic and foreign real exchange rates. On the other hand, if the rise in government spending falls on nontradable goods, then it lowers the world rate of interest and accelerates the rates of change of the domestic and foreign real exchange rates.

It is important to emphasize that even though there is no apriori presumption concerning the precise effects of government spending on the world rate of interest and on the time paths of the real exchange rates, our analysis identified the key parameters whose relative magnitudes determine these effects.

In contrast with the analysis of the effects of government spending, for which the inclusion of nontradable goods led to significant modifications of some of the previous results (obtained under the assumption that all goods are tradable), the effects of budget deficits arising from a current cut in consumption taxes are very similar to those obtained in the absence of nontradable goods. Specifically, the budget deficit raises the world rate of interest and lowers the domestic effective rate. In addition the deficit accelerates the rate of change of the domestic real exchange rate and decelerates the corresponding foreign rate of change. Thereby the deficit lowers the domestic (consumption-based) effective real rate of interest and raises the corresponding foreign real rate of interest. These changes result in a negative cross-country correlation between the (consumption-based) real effective rates of interest. We also saw that with high intertemporal elasticities of substitution the budget deficit raises domestic spending and lowers the contemporaneous domestic real exchange rate; at the same time the deficit lowers foreign spending and raises the contemporaneous foreign real exchange rate. These effects result in negative cross-country correlations between spending as well as between real exchange rates.

In conclusion we note that the analytical framework, which allows for tradable and nontradable goods can be reinterpreted and applied to the analysis of the effects of fiscal policies on real wages in a model with variable labor supply. The reinterpretation of the model treats leisure as the nontradable good, the real wage as the real exchange rate, and the temporal elasticity of substitution as the elasticity of labor supply. With this interpretation, government hiring of labor is viewed as government purchases of nontradable goods, and the relative share of government expenditure on non-tradable goods, β_n^g, corresponds to the relative share of wages in the government budget. Likewise, the private-sector expenditure share, β_n, is viewed as the relative share of leisure in private-sector total spending (inclusive of the imputed value of leisure). This interpretation suggests that the effects of government spending on the rate of interest and on the time path of real wages depend critically on the relative importance of wages in the government budget. Our analysis implies that this dependence is especially pronounced in cases in which labor is inelastically supplied.

9.5 Appendix

In this appendix we analyze the effects of changes in government spending and changes in the world rate of interest on the equilibrium path of the real exchange rate and on the intertemporal ratio of tradable goods consumption.

Using equations (9.4) and (9.5), the market-clearing conditions for nontradable goods are

$$c_{n0}[p_{n0}, P_0 C_0(\alpha_{c1}, W_{c0})] = \overline{Y}_{n0} - G_{n0}, \tag{A.1}$$

$$c_{n1}[p_{n1}, P_1 C_1(\alpha_{c1}, W_{c0})] = \overline{Y}_{n1} - G_{n1}, \tag{A.2}$$

and the demand functions for tradable goods are

$$c_{x0} = c_{x0}[p_{n0}, P_0 C_0(\alpha_{c1}, W_{c0})], \tag{A.3}$$

$$c_{x1} = c_{x1}[p_{n1}, P_1 C_1(\alpha_{c1}, W_{c0})], \tag{A.4}$$

where G_{nt} denote government purchases of nontradable goods in period t, ($t = 0, 1$), where $P_0 = P_0(p_{n0})$, $P_1 = P_1(p_{n1})$, $\alpha_{c1} = \alpha_{x1} P_1 / P_0$, $W_{c0} = W_0 / P_0$, and where

$$W_0 = p_{n0}(\overline{Y}_{n0} - G_{n0}) + (\overline{Y}_{x0} - G_{x0})$$

$$+ \alpha_{x1}[p_{n1}(\overline{Y}_{n1} - G_{n1}) + (\overline{Y}_{x1} - G_{x1})].$$

Evidently, in contrast with the market for nontradable goods, discrepancies between production and total consumption (private sector plus government) of tradable goods are reflected in periodic trade imbalances.

We assume that the utility function is homothetic, and thus the elasticities of the demand for each good with respect to total spending and of spending with respect to wealth are unity. Prior to carrying out the formal analysis, we provide explicit expressions for some of the elasticities that will be employed in the subsequent derivations:

$$\eta_{n_t p_{nt}} = -(1 - \beta_{nt})\sigma_{nx} - \beta_{nt},$$

$$\eta_{x_t p_{nt}} = \beta_{nt}(\sigma_{nx} - 1), \quad \text{for } t = 0, 1,$$

$$\eta_{c_0 \alpha} = \gamma_s(\sigma - 1),$$

$$\eta_{c_1 \alpha} = -[(1 - \gamma_s)\sigma + \gamma_s],$$

(A.5)

where $\eta_{n_t p_{nt}}$ and $\eta_{x_t p_{nt}}$ denote, respectively, the elasticities of the demand for nontradable and for tradable goods with respect to the price of nontradable goods in period t, and where $\eta_{c_0 \alpha}$ and $\eta_{c_1 \alpha}$ denote, respectively, the elasticities of real spending in period zero and period one with respect to the discount factor α_{c1}. The various expressions follow from the Slutsky decomposition.

The Effect of a Rise in Government Spending

In this part of the appendix we use the system (A.1) through (A.4) in order to analyze the effects of a rise in a government spending. We assume throughout this analysis that the world discount factor, α_{x1}, is given. Let G, G_{nt}, and G_{xt} ($t = 0, 1$) be the discounted sum of total government spending, government spending on nontradable goods in period t, and government spending on tradable goods in period t ($t = 0, 1$), respectively. By definition, the periodic government purchases of each good are related to the discounted sum of total government spending, G, according to

$$G_{n0} = \frac{\beta_{n0}^g (1 - \gamma_s^g) G}{p_{n0}}, \quad G_{x0} = (1 - \beta_{n0}^g)(1 - \gamma_s^g) G,$$

$$G_{n1} = \frac{\beta_{n1}^g \gamma_s^g G}{p_{n1}}, \qquad G_{x1} = (1 - \beta_{n1}^g)\gamma_s^g G,$$

(A.6)

where β_{nt}^g and γ_s^g denote, respectively, the share of government spending on nontradable goods in period t ($t = 0, 1$) and the government-saving propensity.

Differentiating equations (A.1) and (A.2) and evaluating around $G = 0$ yields

$$\eta_{n_0 p_{n0}}\hat{p}_{n0} + \beta_{n0}\hat{p}_{n0} + \eta_{c_0\alpha}\hat{\alpha}_{c1} + \hat{W}_{c0} = -\varphi_{n0}\beta_{n0}^g(1 - \gamma_s^g)\,dG, \quad (A.7)$$

$$\eta_{n_1 p_{n1}}\hat{p}_{n1} + \beta_{n1}\hat{p}_{n1} + \eta_{c_1\alpha}\hat{\alpha}_{c1} + \hat{W}_{c0} = -\varphi_{n1}\beta_{n1}^g\gamma_s^g\,dG, \quad (A.8)$$

$$\hat{W}_{c0} = -\gamma_s(\beta_{n0}\hat{p}_{n0} - \beta_{n1}\hat{p}_{n1}) - a\,dG, \quad (A.9)$$

where $\varphi_{nt} = 1/p_{nt}c_{nt}$, ($t = 0, 1$), and $a = 1/W_0$, and where the levels of output are assumed to be exogenous so that $\hat{Y}_{n0} = \hat{Y}_{n1} = 0$. The circumflex ($\hat{}$) is used to denote a logarithmic derivative.

In deriving equation (A.9) we have used (A.6) along with the following expressions for the elasticities of wealth with respect to the relative price of nontradable goods:

$$\eta_{wp_{n0}} = \beta_{n0}(1 - \gamma_s), \quad \eta_{wp_{n1}} = \beta_{n1}\gamma_s. \quad (A.10)$$

We have also used the assumption that α_{x1} is given, and therefore the (consumption-based) real discount factor changes according to $\hat{\alpha}_{c1} = \beta_{n1}\hat{p}_{n1} - \beta_{n0}\hat{p}_{n0}$.

Substituting (A.5) for the various elasticities in (A.7) and (A.8) yields

$$-[(1 - \beta_{n0})\sigma_{nx} + \beta_{n0}]\hat{p}_{n0} + \beta_{n0}\hat{p}_{n0} + \gamma_s(\sigma - 1)(\beta_{n1}\hat{p}_{n1} - \beta_{n0}\hat{p}_{n0})$$
$$+ \hat{W}_{c0} = -\varphi_{n0}\beta_{n0}^g(1 - \gamma_s^g)\,dG, \quad (A.11)$$

$$-[(1 - \beta_{n1})\sigma_{nx} + \beta_{n1}]\hat{p}_{n1} + \beta_{n1}\hat{p}_{n1} - [(1 - \gamma_s)\sigma$$
$$+ \gamma_s](\beta_{n1}\hat{p}_{n1} - \beta_{n0}\hat{p}_{n0}) + \hat{W}_{c0} = -\varphi_{n1}\beta_{n1}^g\gamma_s^g\,dG. \quad (A.12)$$

Substituting (A.9) for $\hat{W}_{c0}$ into (A.11) and (A.12) and collecting terms yields

$$-[\beta_{n0}\gamma_s\sigma + (1 - \beta_{n0})\sigma_{nx}]\hat{p}_{n0} + \beta_{n1}\gamma_s\sigma\hat{p}_{n1}$$
$$= [a - \varphi_{n0}\beta_{n0}^g(1 - \gamma_s^g)]\,dG, \quad (A.13)$$

$$\beta_{n0}(1 - \gamma_s)\sigma\hat{p}_{n0} - [\beta_{n1}(1 - \gamma_s)\sigma + (1 - \beta_{n1})\sigma_{nx}]\hat{p}_{n1}$$
$$= (a - \varphi_{n1}\beta_{n1}^g\gamma_s^g)\,dG. \quad (A.14)$$

Equation (A.13) and (A.14) can be solved to yield the effects of changes in G on p_{n0} and p_{n1}.

To simplify the exposition, suppose that the expenditure shares do not vary overtime so that $\beta_{n0} = \beta_{n1} = \beta_n$. In that case equations (A.13) and (A.14) can be easily solved for the effects of changes in G on the *ratio* p_{n0}/p_{n1}. This ratio indicates the path of the real exchange rate. Accordingly, the elasticity of this price ratio with respect to G is

$$\frac{d\log(p_{n0}/p_{n1})}{dG} = \frac{\varphi_{n0}\beta_n(1 - \gamma_s)}{\beta_n\sigma + (1 - \beta_n)\sigma_{nx}} \left[\frac{\beta_{n0}^g(1 - \gamma_s^g)}{\beta_n(1 - \gamma_s)} - \frac{\beta_{n1}^g \gamma_s^g}{\beta_n\gamma_s} \right],$$
(A.15)

where we have used the fact that $(\varphi_{n0}/\varphi_{n1}) = [\beta_{n1}\gamma_s/\beta_{n0}(1 - \gamma_s)]$ and that with constant expenditure shares this ratio equals $\gamma_s/(1 - \gamma_s)$. As is seen, the sign of this elasticity depends only on the difference between the temporal-intertemporal spending patterns of the government and the domestic private sector.

To determine the effects of government spending on the intertemporal ratio of tradable-goods consumption c_{x0}/c_{x1}, we differentiate equations (A.3) and (A.4) and obtain

$$\hat{c}_{x0} - \hat{c}_{x1} = \eta_{x_0 p_{n0}}\hat{p}_{n0} + \beta_{n0}\hat{p}_{n0} + \eta_{c_0\alpha}\hat{\alpha}_{c1} + \hat{W}_{c0}$$
$$- (\eta_{x_1 p_{n1}}\hat{p}_{n1} + \beta_{n1}\hat{p}_{n1} + \eta_{c_1\alpha}\hat{\alpha}_{c1} + \hat{W}_{c0}).$$
(A.16)

Substituting (A.5) for the various elasticities, and assuming that $\beta_{n0} = \beta_{n1} = \beta_n$, yields

$$\hat{c}_{x0} - \hat{c}_{x1} = \beta_n(\sigma_{nx} - \sigma)(\hat{p}_{n0} - \hat{p}_{n1}).$$
(A.17)

Thus a rise in the price ratio p_{n0}/p_{n1} lowers the consumption ratio c_{x0}/c_{x1} if the temporal elasticity of substitution, σ_{nx}, exceeds the intertemporal elasticity of substitution, σ, and vice versa.

Finally, substituting (A.15) into (A.17) yields

$$\frac{d\log(c_{x0}/c_{x1})}{dG} = \frac{\beta_n^2 \varphi_{n0}(1 - \gamma_s)(\sigma_{nx} - \sigma)}{\beta_n\sigma + (1 - \beta_n)\sigma_{nx}}$$
$$\times \left[\frac{\beta_{n0}^g(1 - \gamma_s^g)}{\beta_n(1 - \gamma_s)} - \frac{\beta_{n1}^g \gamma_s^g}{\beta_n\gamma_s} \right].$$
(A.18)

Equation (A.18) shows that the direction of the effect of a rise in government spending on the consumption ratio depends on the sign of the product of two terms. The bracketed term determines the effect of the rise in G on the price ratio, and the other term, which is proportional to $(\sigma_{nx} - \sigma)$ translates the change in the price ratio into changes in the consumption ratio.

The Effect of a Rise in the World Discount Factor

In this part of the appendix we analyze the effects of a rise in the world discount factor. We assume throughout that the path of government spending remains unchanged.

Differentiating the equilibrium conditions (A.1) and (A.2), expressing them in terms of *total* elasticities, and solving for the dependence of the relative prices of nontradable goods on the discount factor yields

$$\begin{pmatrix} \hat{p}_{n0} \\ \hat{p}_{n1} \end{pmatrix} = \frac{1}{\Delta} \begin{bmatrix} \xi_{n_1\alpha}\xi_{n_0 p_{n1}} - \xi_{n_0\alpha}\xi_{n_1 p_{n1}} \\ \xi_{n_0\alpha}\xi_{n_1 p_{n0}} - \xi_{n_1\alpha}\xi_{n_0 p_{n0}} \end{bmatrix} \hat{\alpha}_{x1}, \tag{A.19}$$

where $\Delta = \xi_{n_0 p_{n0}}\xi_{n_1 p_{n1}} - \xi_{n_0 p_{n1}}\xi_{n_1 p_{n0}}$.

Using (A.5), the total elasticities in equation (A.19) are

$$\xi_{n_0 p_{n0}} = -[(1 - \beta_{n0})\sigma_{nx} + \beta_{n0}\gamma_s\sigma],$$

$$\xi_{n_0 p_{n1}} = \beta_{n1}\gamma_s\sigma,$$

$$\xi_{n_0\alpha} = \gamma_s(\sigma + \mu_1 - 1),$$

$$\xi_{n_1 p_{n0}} = \beta_{n0}(1 - \gamma_s)\sigma, \tag{A.20}$$

$$\xi_{n_1 p_{n1}} = -[(1 - \beta_{n1})\sigma_{nx} + \beta_{n1}(1 - \gamma_s)\sigma],$$

$$\xi_{n_1\alpha} = -[(1 - \gamma_s)\sigma + \gamma_s(1 - \mu_1)],$$

where $\mu_1 = [p_{n1}(\overline{Y}_{n1} - G_{n1}) + (\overline{Y}_{x1} - G_{x1})]/(p_{n1}c_{n1} + c_{x1})$ and where ξ denotes *total* elasticity. For example, the total elasticity of the demand for c_{n0} with respect to p_{n0} is $\xi_{n_0 p_{n0}}$. From (A.1) this elasticity is

$$\xi_{n_0 p_{n0}} = \eta_{n_0 p_{n0}} + \eta_{n_0 z_0}[\beta_{n0} - \eta_{C_0\alpha}\beta_{n0} + \eta_{C_0 w}(\eta_{w p_{n0}} - \beta_{n0})],$$

and in our case the homotheticity assumption implies that $\eta_{n_0 z_0} = \eta_{C_0 w} = 1$. The complete solution is obtained by substituting the expressions in (A.20) into (A.19).

To simplify the exposition, suppose that the expenditure shares do not vary over time. Thus let $\beta_{n0} = \beta_{n1} = \beta_n$. In that case $\Delta = \sigma_{nx}(1 - \beta_n)[\beta_n\sigma + (1 - \beta_n)\sigma_{nx}] > 0$, and the solutions are

$$\hat{p}_{n0} = \left[\frac{\gamma_s\sigma}{\beta_n\sigma + (1 - \beta_n)\sigma_{nx}} + \frac{\gamma_s(\mu_1 - 1)}{(1 - \beta_n)\sigma_{nx}} \right]\hat{\alpha}_{x1}, \qquad (A.21)$$

$$\hat{p}_{n1} = \left[\frac{-(1 - \gamma_s)\sigma}{\beta_n\sigma + (1 - \beta_n)\sigma_{nx}} + \frac{\gamma_s(\mu_1 - 1)}{(1 - \beta_n)\sigma_{nx}} \right]\hat{\alpha}_{x1}. \qquad (A.22)$$

Equations (A.21) and (A.22) show the effects of changes in the discount factor on the domestic relative price of nontradable goods. It is seen that the link between the two operates through two channels: the first term is the intertemporal substitution effect (which is positive in its effect on the current price and negative in its effect on the future price), and the second term is the real wealth effect. The latter is positive if $\mu_1 > 1$—that is, if in the future period GDP (net of government spending) exceeds private spending so that in the current period the private sector runs a trade account deficit—and negative if $\mu_1 < 1$. The magnitudes of both effects (in absolute value) depend negatively on the temporal elasticity of substitution. If the private sector starts with an initial balance in its trade account, then $\mu_1 = 1$, and a rise in α_{x1} (the fall in the rate of interest) raises p_{n0} and lowers p_{n1}.

We turn next to analyze the relation between the discount factor and the intertemporal ratio of consumption of tradable goods. Using equation (A.3), we express the proportional change in c_{x0} as

$$\hat{c}_{x0} = \eta_{x_0 p_{n0}}\hat{p}_{n0} + \hat{P}_0 + \hat{C}_0$$

$$= \beta_n(\sigma_{nx} - 1)\hat{p}_{n0} + \beta_n\hat{p}_{n0} + [-\eta_{C_0\alpha}\beta_n + \beta_n(1 - \gamma_s) - \beta_n]\hat{p}_{n0}$$

$$+ (\eta_{C_0\alpha}\beta_n + \gamma_s\beta_n)\hat{p}_{n1} + (\eta_{C_0\alpha} + \gamma_s\mu_1)\hat{\alpha}_{x1}.$$

Using the Slutsky decomposition (A.5) yields

$$\hat{c}_{x0} = \beta_n(\sigma_{nx} - \gamma_s\sigma)\hat{p}_{n0} + \beta_n\gamma_s\sigma\hat{p}_{n1} + \gamma_s(\sigma + \mu_1 - 1)\hat{\alpha}_{x1}. \qquad (A.12)$$

Using equations (A.21) and (A.22) yields

$$\hat{c}_{x0} = \left\{ \beta_n(\sigma_{nx} - \gamma_s\sigma)\left[\frac{\gamma_s\sigma}{\beta_n\sigma + (1 - \beta_n)\sigma_{nx}} + \frac{\gamma_s(\mu_1 - 1)}{(1 - \beta_n)\sigma_{nx}}\right]\right.$$

$$+ \beta_n\gamma_s\sigma\left[\frac{-(1 - \gamma_s)\sigma}{\beta_n\sigma + (1 - \beta_n)\sigma_{nx}} + \frac{\gamma_s(\mu_1 - 1)}{(1 - \beta_n)\sigma_{nx}}\right]$$

$$+ \left. \gamma_s(\sigma + \mu_1 - 1)\right\}\hat{\alpha}_{x1}.$$

Finally, by collecting terms, we obtain

$$\hat{c}_{x0} = \gamma_s\left[\frac{\sigma_{nx}}{\beta_n\sigma + (1 - \beta_n)\sigma_{nx}}\sigma + \frac{\mu_1 - 1}{1 - \beta_n}\right]\hat{\alpha}_{x1}. \tag{A.23}$$

Following a similar procedure, we note from equation (A.4) that

$$\hat{c}_{x1} = \eta_{x_1p_{n1}}\hat{p}_{n1} + \hat{P}_1 + \hat{C}_1$$

$$= \beta_n(\sigma_{nx} - 1)\hat{p}_{n1} + \beta_n\hat{p}_{n1} + [-\eta_{C_1\alpha}\beta_n + \beta_n(1 - \gamma_s) - \beta_n]\hat{p}_{n0}$$

$$+ (\eta_{C_1\alpha}\beta_n + \gamma_s\beta_n)\hat{p}_{n1} + (\eta_{C_1\alpha} + \gamma_s\mu_1)\hat{\alpha}_{x1}.$$

Using the Slutsky decomposition (A.5), we obtain

$$\hat{c}_{x1} = \beta_n(1 - \gamma_s)\sigma\hat{p}_{n0} + \beta_n[\sigma_{nx} - (1 - \gamma_s)\sigma]\hat{p}_{n1}$$

$$- [(1 - \gamma_s)\sigma - \gamma_s(\mu_1 - 1)]\hat{\alpha}_{x1}.$$

Substituting equations (A.21) and (A.22) into this equation and collecting terms yields

$$\hat{c}_{x1} = \left[\frac{-(1 - \gamma_s)\sigma_{nx}}{\beta_n\sigma + (1 - \beta_n)\sigma_{nx}}\sigma + \frac{\gamma_s(\mu_1 - 1)}{1 - \beta_n}\right]\hat{\alpha}_{x1}. \tag{A.24}$$

Equations (A.23) and (A.24) specify, respectively, the response of current and future consumption of tradable goods to a change in the discount factor.

Finally, subtracting equation (A.24) from equation (A.20), we obtain

$$\hat{c}_{x0} - \hat{c}_{x1} = \left(\frac{\sigma_{nx}\sigma}{\beta_n\sigma + (1 - \beta_n)\sigma_{nx}}\right)\hat{\alpha}_{x1}. \tag{A.25}$$

Equation (A.25) shows that the consumption ratio c_{x0}/c_{x1} is positively related to the discount factor α_{x1}.

Before concluding, we note that in the presence of distortionary taxes the solutions in equations (A.21) through (A.24) for the changes in prices and in the levels of consumption need to be modified to incorporate the real wealth effects induced by the distortions. It is important to emphasize, however, that due to the homotheticity assumption, this modification is not needed for the analysis of the ratios of intertemporal prices and consumption.

In this part of the appendix we determined the effects of changes in the world discount factor on the consumption ratio of exportable goods. This analysis incorporated the requirement that the markets for nontradable goods clear in each period. Implicit in the formulation of the model was the assumption that taxes are nondistortionary. If there were taxes on consumption, then the *effective* domestic discount factor $\hat{\alpha}_{x\tau1}$ differs from the world discount factor $\alpha_{x1} = 1/(1 + r_{x0})$, so that $\hat{\alpha}_{x\tau1} = [(1 + \tau_{c1})/(1 + \tau_{c0})]\alpha_{x1}$, where, as in section 8.1, τ_{c0} and τ_{c1} are the advalorem consumption taxes in periods zero and one. In this case we can replace $\hat{\alpha}_{x1}$ in equation (A.25) by $\hat{\alpha}_{x\tau1}$, and the effects described by the equation also apply to those induced by a change in the *effective* discount factor. This perspective proves useful in our analysis of the effects of a budget deficit. In that analysis the change in the effective discount factor arises from a change in the time profile of taxes, τ_{c0} and τ_{c1}.

V

Overlapping Generations and the
Dynamic Effects of Fiscal Policies

.

10

Budget Deficits with Nondistortionary Taxes: The Pure Wealth Effect

In this chapter we develop an analytical framework for the analysis of the effects of budget deficits in an undistorted economy. In such a framework, it is the induced wealth effects that constitute the primary mechanism by which budget deficits influence the economy. This mechanism supplements the one outlined in chapter 8 where we allowed for distortionary taxes. With such taxes budget deficits influence the economy through temporal and intertemporal substitution effects induced by the distortions.

To conduct a meaningful analysis of budget deficits in the absence of distortions, our analytical framework departs from the pure Ricardian model in which the timing of taxes and government debt issue plays no role as long as the path of government spending is given. We depart from that model by allowing for differences between the time horizons relevant for individual decision making and for the society at large. These differences result in discrepancies between the private and public sectors' costs of borrowing, which in turn implies that the equilibrium is no longer invariant with respect to the timing of taxes. The specification that we use to yield differences between the horizons relevant for the individual and the society relies on the assumption that individuals have finite life. In contrast, the society at large has an infinite horizon due to the continuous entry of newly born generations.

A significant portion of this chapter is devoted to the development of the analytical framework underlying the overlapping-generations model. In this context we specify in detail the procedure by which the individual behavioral functions are aggregated into the corresponding aggregate behavioral functions. This procedure constitutes a key building block which is used in subsequent chapters.

Following the development of the model, we devote the remainder of this chapter to the analysis of the effects of budget deficits on aggregate consumption and debt accumulation in an economy facing given world rates of interest. The wealth effects induced by budget deficits stem from differences between the effective interest rates that individuals use in discounting future taxes and the corresponding market interest rates that govern public sector behavior.

10.1 The Aggregate Consumption Function

We start with a specification of the individual decision problem and derive the individual consumption function. The dynamic character of the overlapping-generations society necessitates great care in the specification of the aggregate behavior. Accordingly, we discuss in detail the procedures underlying the aggregation of the individual consumption functions into the aggregate private-sector consumption function.

Let $c_{a,t}$ denote the level of consumption in period t of an individual of age a, and suppose that the utility function of this individual in period t is

$$U = \frac{1}{1 - \theta} \sum_{v=0}^{\infty} \delta^v c_{a+v,t+v}^{1-\theta}, \tag{10.1}$$

where δ denotes the subjective discount factor and θ is the reciprocal of the intertemporal elasticity of substitution, σ (thus $\theta = 1/\sigma$). Assume that the individual maximizes *expected utility*, which is computed on the basis of his or her probability of survival. We denote the probability that an individual survives from one period to the next by γ, which, in order to facilitate the aggregation, is assumed to be independent of the individual's age. Thus the probability that an individual survives the next v periods is γ^v. Accordingly, the probability as of period t that an individual of age a will be alive in period $t + v$ and enjoy the utility level $[1/(1 - \theta)]c_{a+v,t+v}^{1-\theta}$ is γ^v. Therefore, using equation (10.1), the expected utility can be written as

$$\frac{1}{1-\theta} E_t \sum_{v=0}^{\infty} \delta^v c_{a+v,t+v}^{1-\theta} = \frac{1}{1-\theta} \sum_{v=0}^{\infty} (\gamma\delta)^v c_{a+v,t+v}^{1-\theta}. \tag{10.2}$$

Equation (10.2) is the *certainty equivalent* utility function with an effective discount factor that is equal to $\gamma\delta$. Thus, by reducing the effective discount factor, the probability of death raises the effective subjective discount rate and (in and of itself) tilts consumption toward the present period.

We assume that because of uncertain lifetime, all loans require in addition to regular interest payments a purchase of life insurance. In case of death, the estate is transferred to the life insurance company which, in turn, guarantees to cover outstanding debts. It is assumed that there is a large number of individuals in each cohort so that the frequency of those who survive equals the survival probability, γ. Furthermore we assume that there is competition among insurance companies. Under such circumstances the zero-profit condition ensures that the percentage insurance premium equals the probability of death, $1 - \gamma$. To verify this relation, consider a given population composed of many individuals who, in the aggregate, borrow one dollar. The insurance company's income associated with this loan transaction is the percentage premium, π, which, if invested at the market rate of interest, r, yields at the end of the period $\pi(1 + r)$. On the other hand, since a fraction $(1 - \gamma)$ of this population does not survive, the commitment to cover the outstanding debts costs the company $(1 - \gamma)(1 + r)$ dollars. The zero-profit condition guarantees that $\pi = 1 - \gamma$. An alternative institutional arrangement to the requirement that each loan is associated with a purchase of life insurance is a direct surcharge imposed on the loan. Under such an arrangement it is assumed that in case of death the lender has no claim on the outstanding debt. In this case, in order to secure a safe return, $1 + r$, on a given one-dollar loan, the competitive lender charges $(1 + r)/\gamma$ dollars. Since the fraction of the borrowers who survive to repay the loan is γ, the safe return is $\gamma[(1 + r)/\gamma] = 1 + r$. Thus the *effective* cost of borrowing relevant for individual decision making is $(1 + r)/\gamma$.

Consider an individual who is of age a in period zero. His periodic budget constraints are

$$c_{a,0} = y_0 + b_{a,0} - \left(\frac{1 + r_{-1}}{\gamma}\right) b_{a-1,-1},$$

$$c_{a+1,1} = y_1 + b_{a+1,1} - \left(\frac{1 + r_0}{\gamma}\right) b_{a,0}, \qquad (10.3)$$

$$c_{a+2,2} = y_2 + b_{a+2,2} - \left(\frac{1 + r_1}{\gamma}\right) b_{a+1,1}, \quad \text{etc.,}$$

where the budget constraint applicable to period t is

$$c_{a+t,t} = y_t + b_{a+t,t} - \frac{1 + r_{t-1}}{\gamma} b_{a+t-1,t-1} \qquad (10.3a)$$

and where y_v and $b_{a+v,v}$ are the individual's disposable income and new (one-period) borrowing in period v ($v = 0, 1, \ldots$). The formulation in (10.3) also presumes that disposable income is the same across all individuals regardless of age. This assumption is made to facilitate the aggregation.

Following procedures similar to those in previous chapters, the periodic budget constraints can be consolidated into a single present-value lifetime constraint. For this purpose we define a present-value factor. The present-value factor, which is composed of one-period rates of interest compounded from period zero up to period t, is denoted by α_t, and therefore the ratio α_t/α_{t+1} is the *market* discount factor, which is equal to one plus the market rate of interest in period t (i.e., $1 + r_t$). Accordingly, $\alpha_0 = 1$. Analogously, the market risk factor is $\gamma^t/\gamma^{t+1} = 1/\gamma$. It follows that the *effective* interest factor faced by individuals is $\alpha_t/\gamma\alpha_{t+1}$, and correspondingly the effective interest rate is $[(1 + r_t)/\gamma] - 1$.

Using this notation, the consolidated present-value constraint is

$$\sum_{v=0}^{\infty} \gamma^v \alpha_v c_{a+v,v} = \sum_{v=0}^{\infty} \gamma^v \alpha_v y_v - \frac{1 + r_{-1}}{\gamma} b_{a-1,-1} = w_{a,0}, \qquad (10.4)$$

where $w_{a,0}$ is the wealth of an individual of age a at period zero. Finally, in deriving equation (10.4), we have made use of the solvency requirement that in the limit, as v approaches infinity, the present value of debt commitment is zero. That is,

$$\lim_{v \to \infty} \gamma^v \alpha_v b_{a+v,v} = 0. \qquad (10.5)$$

As seen from the consolidated budget constraint in equation (10.4), the individual's wealth is composed of two components. The first, which is the discounted sum of income, is referred to as *human* wealth, and the second, which is the interest plus principal payments on past debt (which may be positive or negative), is referred to as *financial* (nonhuman) wealth. The key characteristic of human wealth is that it is attached to a specific individual. As a result the individual's human wealth disappears from the system once the individual is not alive.

The individual's problem is to maximize the expected utility, given by equation (10.2), subject to the budget constraint (10.4). Formally, the maximization problem can be written as

$$\max_{\{c_{a+v,v}\}} \frac{1}{1-\theta} \sum_{v=0}^{\infty} (\gamma\delta)^v c_{a+v,v}^{1-\theta} + \lambda\left(w_{a,0} - \sum_{v=0}^{\infty} \gamma^v \alpha_v c_{a+v,v} \right), \tag{10.6}$$

where λ denotes the Lagrange multiplier associated with the budget constraint. The first-order condition of maximization implies that

$$(\gamma\delta)^v c_{a+v,v}^{-\theta} - \lambda(\gamma^v \alpha_v) = 0, \quad \text{for } v = 0, 1, \dots . \tag{10.7}$$

Equation (10.7) shows that the finiteness of life, reflected by γ, influences both the subjective and the market-effective present-value factors, $(\gamma\delta)^v$ and $\gamma^v \alpha_v$, in the *same* manner. It follows therefore that the marginal rates of substitution between the levels of consumption in two consecutive periods equal the *market* (risk-free) discount factor, $1/(1 + r)$, independent of γ. It follows that even though there is a discrepancy between the effective (risk-adjusted) rates of interest applicable to the individual choice and the market (risk-free) rate of interest applicable to the society at large, this discrepancy does not distort the intertemporal allocations of consumption. This property ensures that in the absence of other distortions, the equilibrium obtained is Pareto efficient. In the subsequent discussion we assume that taxes are nondistortionary. As a result the mechanism through which budget deficits influence the real equilibrium does not operate through the distortion effects analyzed in chapter 8. We will return to these issues later on.

Using the budget constraint (10.4) and substituting the solution for $c_{a+v,v}$ from (10.7) yields $w_{a,0} = \sum_{v=0}^{\infty} \gamma^v \alpha_v c_{a+v,v} =$

$\lambda^{-\sigma}\sum_{v=0}^{\infty}\gamma^{v}\alpha_{v}(\delta^{v}/\alpha_{v})^{\sigma}$, where we recall that the elasticity of substitution, σ, is equal to $1/\theta$. Accordingly, the solution for the value of the marginal utility of wealth is

$$\lambda = [(1 - s_0)w_{a,0}]^{-1/\sigma}, \tag{10.8}$$

and the consumption function is

$$c_{a+t,t} = (1 - s_0)\left(\frac{\delta^t}{\alpha_t}\right)^{\sigma} w_{a,0}, \quad \text{for } t = 0, 1, \dots, \tag{10.9}$$

where

$$1 - s_0 = \left\{\sum_{v=0}^{\infty} (\gamma^v\alpha_v)^{1-\sigma}[(\gamma\delta)^v]^{\sigma}\right\}^{-1}.$$

In equation (10.9) the term $(1 - s_0)$ denotes the marginal propensity to consume out of wealth in period zero. Thus for $t = 0$, $c_{a,0} = (1 - s_0)w_{a,0}$. It is seen that, in general, the propensity to consume depends on the *entire path* of effective rates of interest (indicated by the effective present-value factor $\gamma^v\alpha_v$) and on the effective present-value factor $(\gamma\delta)^v$. In the special case for which the utility function is logarithmic, the elasticity of substitution is unity, and the marginal propensity to spend depends only on the effective subjective discount factor, $\gamma\delta$, and not on the path of the effective rates of interest. In that case $1 - s_0 = 1 - \gamma\delta$. This special case may be viewed as intermediate between two extreme cases. In one extreme case the elasticity of substitution is zero, and in the other extreme case the elasticity of substitution is infinite. With no substitution, the marginal propensity to spend depends only on the effective present-value factor $\gamma^v\alpha_v$. In that case consumption is fixed over time (so that the consumption smoothing motive is absolute), and using the budget constraint, the marginal propensity to spend is $1/\sum_{v=0}^{\infty}\gamma^v\alpha_v$. In the other extreme case, with perfect substitution, the marginal propensity to spend is zero if δ^v exceeds α_v, and it is unity if δ^v falls short of α_v. In the general case, as seen from equation (10.9), the spending propensity falls with the rate of interest if the elasticity of substitution exceeds unity, and vice versa if the elasticity of substitution is smaller than unity.

The saving propensity, s_0, is the key parameter linking the value of wealth in period zero with the value of wealth in period one. Analogous to the definition of period-zero wealth of an individual who is of age a at period zero, $w_{a,0}$ (equation 10.4), the value of wealth in period one of the same individual, $w_{a+1,1}$, is defined as

$$w_{a+1,1} = \sum_{v=1}^{\infty} \gamma^{v-1}(1 + r_0)\alpha_v y_v - \frac{1 + r_0}{\gamma} b_{a,0}. \tag{10.10}$$

Using the fact that consumption in period zero is proportional to period zero wealth (with $1 - s_0$ being the proportionality factor), it follows from the definitions of $w_{a,0}$ and $w_{a+1,1}$, and from the budget constraint applicable to period zero (equation 10.3), that

$$w_{a+1,1} = \frac{1 + r_0}{\gamma} s_0 w_{a,0}. \tag{10.11}$$

Equation (10.11) shows that if the individual survives from period zero to period one, then his wealth equals the fraction of wealth not consumed in period zero, $s_0 w_{a,0}$ adjusted by the *effective* rate of interest.

Thus far we have specified the utility-maximizing saving propensity for period zero, s_0, as derived from period-zero maximization problem (10.6). A similar maximization problem can be formulated for an individual of age a in period t. With this formulation the resultant utility-maximizing consumption function for period t, $c_{a,t}$, is

$$c_{a,t} = (1 - s_t)w_{a,t}, \tag{10.12}$$

where

$$1 - s_t = \left\{ \sum_{v=t}^{\infty} \left(\gamma^{v-t} \frac{\alpha_v}{\alpha_t} \right)^{1-\sigma} [(\gamma \delta)^{v-t}]^{\sigma} \right\}^{-1},$$

and

$$w_{a,t} = \sum_{v=1}^{\infty} \gamma^{v-t} \frac{\alpha_v}{\alpha_t} y_v - \frac{1 + r_{t-1}}{\gamma} b_{a-1,t-1}.$$

The spending propensity $1 - s_t$ is the generalization of the expression for period-zero propensity, $1 - s_0$, in equation (10.9), and as is evident, it depends on the entire path of the rates of interest. In general, if the rates of interest vary over time, the saving propensity s_t is not constant, except for the special case in which the elasticity of substitution, σ, is unity. In that case the spending propensity is a constant (equal to $1 - \gamma\delta$). Independent, however, of whether the elasticity of substitution equals to or differs from unity, the spending propensity does not depend on the *age* of the individual. This property (which reflects the assumption that the probability of survival does not depend on age) permits a simple aggregation of the *individual* consumption functions into the *aggregate* consumption function.

We now turn to the derivation of the *aggregate* consumption function. Population is normalized so that at birth every cohort consists of one individual who is assumed to be born without debt. Due to death the size of each cohort of age a becomes γ^a. The equality between the probability of survival of a given cohort and its frequency relative to its initial size stems from the law of large numbers. Since at each period there are γ^a members of a cohort of age a, the (constant) aggregate size of population is

$$\sum_{a=0}^{\infty} \gamma^a = \frac{1}{1 - \gamma}.$$

Aggregate consumption in period t is the sum of consumption of individuals from all cohorts. Since consumption of a cohort of age a is $\gamma^a c_{a,t}$, per-capita aggregate consumption, C_t, is

$$C_t = (1 - \gamma) \sum_{a=0}^{\infty} \gamma^a c_{a,t}. \tag{10.13}$$

Disposable income, y_t, is assumed to be the same across all individuals regardless of age. Therefore the per-capita value of aggregate income, Y_t, is equal to the individual disposable income, y_t. In what follows Y_t is referred to as per-capita income. The per-capita aggregate consumption function (10.13) together with the individual consumption function and the definition of wealth from equation (10.12) yields

$$C_t = (1 - s_t) W_t,$$
(10.14)

where

$$W_t = H_t - (1 + r_{t-1}) B_{t-1}^p,$$

$$H_t = (1 - \gamma) \sum_{a=0}^{\infty} \gamma^a \sum_{v=t}^{\infty} \gamma^{v-t} \frac{\alpha_v}{\alpha_t} y_v = \sum_{v=t}^{\infty} \gamma^{v-t} \frac{\alpha_v}{\alpha_t} y_v,$$

$$B_{t-1}^p = (1 - \gamma) \sum_{v=0}^{\infty} \gamma^{a-1} b_{a-1,t-1}.$$

Equation (10.14) is the per-capita *aggregate* consumption function in which W_t, H_t, and B_{t-1}^p denote, respectively, the per-capita values of aggregate total wealth, aggregate human wealth, and aggregate private sector indebtedness. The per-capita value of aggregate human wealth is defined as the discounted sum of per-capita income computed by using the effective (risk-adjusted) rates of interest. As formulated in equation (10.14), the per-capita value of total aggregate wealth in period t, W_t, equals the value of human wealth in that period net of interest and principal payments on past private-sector per-capita debt. As is evident, the rate of interest applicable to the (per-capita value of) aggregate private-sector debt is the (risk-free) market rate of interest. This should be contrasted with the formulation of the *individual* wealth in equation (10.12) in which the rate of interest applicable to the computation of individual debt service is the (risk-adjusted) effective rate. We also note that as indicated earlier, the invariance of the individual spending propensity with respect to age is reflected in the equality between the individual and the aggregate spending propensities in equations (10.12) and (10.14). Finally, the specification in equation (10.14) defines the per-capita magnitudes of aggregate consumption and wealth. Obviously, as long as the demographic parameter, γ, is given, the size of the population is constant, and therefore the distribution between per-capita and aggregate quantities is inconsequential. In the limit, as γ approaches unity, the magnitude of the aggregate quantities (e.g., population, consumption, and wealth) is boundless, but the per-capita quantities are well defined according to equation (10.14).

10.2 Aggregate Wealth and Its Composition

The analysis of per-capita aggregate consumption specified the behavior of the economy at a point in time as a function of per-capita aggregate wealth. In order to characterize the behavior of the economy over time so as to be able to deal with the dynamic effects of fiscal policies, we need to determine the evolution of per-capita aggregate wealth through time. Since, as will be shown later, the two components of wealth (human and nonhuman wealth) are governed by different laws of motion, we need to study them separately. Throughout, we analyze the evolution of the per-capita aggregate quantities, but, for short, we omit in what follows an explicit mention of the term "per capita." We start with an analysis of the dynamics of human wealth. Lagging the expression for H_t from equation (10.14) by one period yields an analogous expression for H_{t-1} which, together with equation (10.14), yields

$$H_t = \frac{1 + r_{t-1}}{\gamma}(H_{t-1} - Y_{t-1}).$$ (10.15)

Equation (10.15) describes the evolution of aggregate human wealth as a function of the difference between its own lagged value and the lagged value of aggregate income Y_{t-1}. It is important to note that both the definition of aggregate human wealth and its law of motion employ the *effective* rates of interest that include the life insurance premium associated with the probability of death. This feature is specific to the human wealth component and does not play a role in the computation of the other component of wealth to which we turn next.

The evolution of aggregate private debt, B_t^p, can be obtained by aggregating equation (10.3a) across individuals. Accordingly,

$$B_t^p = C_t - Y_t + (1 + r_{t-1})B_{t-1}^p.$$ (10.16)

In contrast with the law of motion governing the accumulation of human wealth (in equation 10.15) and *individual* debt (in equation 10.3a), the accumulation of *aggregate* private debt is governed by the *market* rate of interest $(1 + r_{t-1})$ rather than the *effective* rate of interest $(1 + r_{t-1})/\gamma$. The absence of the life-insurance premium from the law of motion governing aggregate debt accumulation in equation (10.16) stems from the fact that from the perspective of the society at large, the life-insurance premia represent transfers within the society which do not alter the social rates of return.

Having determined the evolution of the human and financial components of wealth, we can now combine the two in order to characterize the evolution of aggregate wealth. Substituting equations (10.15) and (10.16) into the definition of wealth in equation (10.14), and using the consumption function $C_{t-1} = (1 - s_{t-1})W_{t-1}$, we obtain

$$W_t = (1 + r_{t-1})s_{t-1}W_{t-1} + (1 - \gamma)H_t. \tag{10.17}$$

Equation (10.17) expresses the value of wealth in period t in terms of its value in period $t - 1$ and in terms of its human wealth component. The dependence of the path of aggregate wealth on its composition reflects the asymmetry between human and nonhuman wealth. This asymmetry, which arises from the uncertainty concerning the length of life, disappears if the probability of survival is unity. Thus, with $\gamma = 1$, the value of wealth becomes

$$W_t = (1 + r_{t-1})s_{t-1}W_{t-1}. \tag{10.18}$$

In this case the evolution of wealth depends on its *aggregate* value and not on its *composition*.

As indicated by the aggregate consumption function, for any given path of the rate of interest, the evolution of aggregate consumption depends exclusively on the evolution of aggregate wealth. Thus we can use equations (10.14) and (10.17) in order to characterize the evolution of aggregate consumption. Accordingly, the dependence of current consumption on the lagged value thereof is characterized by

$$C_t = s_{t-1}(1 + r_{t-1})\frac{1 - s_t}{1 - s_{t-1}}C_{t-1} + (1 - \gamma)(1 - s_t)H_t. \tag{10.19}$$

Thus, analogously to the characteristics of the evolution of aggregate wealth, aggregate consumption in period t depends on its lagged value as well as on the composition of wealth. In the special case for which $\gamma = 1$, equation (10.19) reduces to

$$C_t = \left[s_{t-1}(1 + r_{t-1}) \frac{1 - s_t}{1 - s_{t-1}} \right] C_{t-1}. \tag{10.19a}$$

In that case (for a given path of the rates of interest) aggregate consumption in period t depends only on its lagged value. The comparison between (10.19) and (10.19a) reveals the role that the finiteness of the individual's horizon plays in determining the dynamics of aggregate consumption. As seen in (10.19a), given the rates of interest, the only variable relevant for predicting future consumption is current consumption. In particular, once current consumption is known, knowledge of wealth is not required for the prediction of future consumption. In the general case, however, as indicated by equation (10.19), once $\gamma < 1$, knowledge of current consumption is not sufficient for the prediction of future consumption, and one needs to know the detailed path of the composition of wealth. In the appendix we modify assumptions underlying equation (10.19) and obtain an empirically estimable form. In the next section we analyze in greater detail the factors governing aggregate consumption. This analysis will then be used in interpreting the effects of fiscal policies.

10.3 Dynamics of Aggregate Consumption

To facilitate the exposition, we assume in this section that the world rate of interest faced by the small economy is stationary so that $r_t = r$. In this case the saving propensity defined in equation (10.12) is constant, and can be written as

$$s = \left(\frac{\gamma}{R} \right)^{1-\sigma} (\gamma\delta)^\sigma = \gamma\delta^\sigma R^{\sigma-1}, \tag{10.20}$$

where $R = 1 + r$. As is evident, the saving propensity is a function of the effective cost of borrowing, γ/R, and the effective subjective discount factor, $\gamma\delta$; the weights of these two factors are $1 - \sigma$ and σ, respectively. In the special case in which the intertemporal elasticity of substitution is unity, the saving propensity equals $\gamma\delta$; in that case the saving propensity is independent of the cost of borrowing.

To determine the dynamics of consumption, we need to characterize the dynamics of wealth. For expositional simplicity suppose that the path of future disposable incomes is stationary so that $Y_t = Y$ for $t > 0$. In that case current and future human capital can be written with the aid of equation (10.14) as

$$H_0 = Y_0 + \frac{\gamma}{R - \gamma} Y,$$

$$H_t = \frac{R}{R - \gamma} Y, \quad \text{for } t > 0.$$

(10.21)

Accordingly, using equations (10.14), (10.19), and (10.21), the levels of current and future consumption are

$$C_0 = (1 - s)\left[\left(Y_0 + \frac{\gamma}{R - \gamma} Y\right) - RB_{-1}^p\right],$$

$$C_t = RsC_{t-1} + (1 - \gamma)(1 - s)\frac{R}{R - \gamma} Y, \quad \text{for } t > 0.$$

(10.22)

The equations in (10.22) characterize the evolution of consumption through time. These consumption dynamics are illustrated in figure 10.1. The schedule $C_{t+1}(C_t)$ plots the values of C_{t+1} as a function of C_t. The equation of this schedule is shown in (10.22). As seen, the slope of the schedule is Rs, and the case drawn in figure 10.1 corresponds to the situation in which $Rs < 1$. In this case the system converges to a steady state with positive consumption. Accordingly, if the initial equilibrium is associated with consumption level C_0 (shown by point A in figure 10.1), the long-run equilibrium is associated with a steady-state level of consumption C (shown by point B in figure 10.1). The arrows in the figure indicate the path along which the level of consumption evolves through time.

To clarify the role played by the finiteness of the horizon, we note that the intercept of the $C_{t+1}(C_t)$ schedule (indicated by point a) depends on the value of γ. Specifically, with infinite lifetime, $\gamma = 1$ and $a = 0$. In that case the $C_{t+1}(C_t)$ schedule emerges from the origin, and the system does not converge to a long-run steady state with positive consumption. In that case the saving propensity is

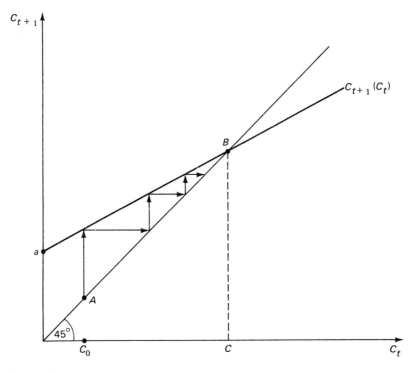

Figure 10.1
Consumption dynamics in the overlapping-generations model: the stable case. Data: $Rs < 1$, $a = (1 - \gamma)(1 - s)[R/(R - \gamma)]Y$, $C_0 = (1 - s)\{Y_0 + [\gamma/(R - \gamma)]Y - RB^p_{-1}\}$, $C = [(1 - \gamma)/(R - \gamma)][(1 - s)/(1 - Rs)]RY$, $C_{t+1} = RsC_t + (1 - \gamma)(1 - s)[R/(R - \gamma)]Y$.

$\delta^\sigma R^{\sigma-1}$, and the slope of the consumption schedule is $(R\delta)^\sigma$. Thus, if $R\delta$ exceeds unity, consumption grows without a bound, and if $R\delta$ falls short of unity, consumption shrinks to zero. It follows that in order to allow for the possibility of a steady-state equilibrium with positive levels of consumption, the model must allow for a finite horizon.

The steady-state trade-balance surplus depends on the discrepancy between output, Y, and consumption C. Using (10.22), the steady-state level of consumption is

$$C = \left(\frac{1-\gamma}{R-\gamma}\right)\left(\frac{1-s}{1-Rs}\right)RY. \tag{10.23}$$

Using this equation along with equation (10.20), the steady-state trade-balance surplus is

$$(Y - C) = \frac{\gamma(R-1)Y}{(R-\gamma)(1-Rs)}[1 - (R\delta)^\sigma].$$

It can be seen that the economy runs a steady-state trade-balance surplus if $R\delta < 1$. This surplus is necessary in order to service the debt accumulated during the transition toward the steady state during which (on average) the economy consumed in excess of its GDP. On the other hand, if $R\delta$ exceeds unity, then the transition toward the steady state is characterized by trade-balance surpluses as the economy produces (on average) in excess of its consumption. In that case the economy reaches the steady state as a net creditor. As a result its steady-state level of consumption exceeds its GDP, and the steady-state trade balance is in deficit.

The foregoing analysis presumed that Rs is smaller than unity so that the economy converges to a long-run equilibrium with a positive level of consumption. To complete the analysis, we show in figure 10.2 the case in which Rs exceeds unity. In that case consecutive increments to the levels of consumption rise over time, and as a result consumption increases without a bound.

The level of consumption can be solved (by forward iteration of equations 10.22) to yield

$$C_t = (Rs)^t(C_0 - C) + C, \tag{10.24}$$

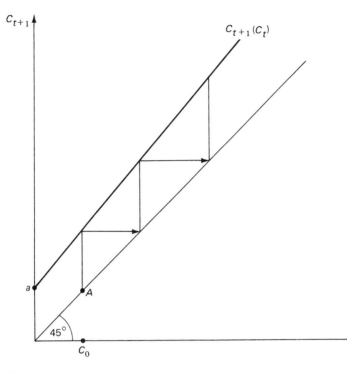

Figure 10.2
Consumption dynamics in the overlapping-generations model: the unstable
case. Data: $Rs > 1$, $a = (1 - \gamma)(1 - s)[R/(R - \gamma)]Y$, $C_0 = (1 - s)\{Y_0 + [\gamma/(r - \gamma)]Y - RB^p_{-1}\}$, $C_{t+1} = RsC_t + (1 - \gamma)(1 - s)[R/(R - \gamma)]Y$.

where C_0 and C are defined in equations (10.22) and (10.23). As seen,
if $Rs < 1$, the first term in equation (10.24) approaches zero with the
passage of time, and consumption converges to its steady-state level
C. On the other hand, if $Rs > 1$, the level of consumption grows
over time without bound since in that case (as indicated by equations 10.22 and 10.23) $C_0 - C$ must be positive.

The foregoing analysis of the dynamics of consumption will prove
useful in the subsequent section where we analyze the effects of
budget deficits.

10.4 Wealth Effects of Budget Deficits

In this section we use the analytical framework of the small open
economy for the analysis of the effects of a budget deficit arising

from a current cut in lump-sum taxes. In order to focus on the essentials underlying aggregate saving and current-account adjustments, we abstract from capital accumulation and from multiple goods. We continue to assume that government spending is financed by taxes or by debt issue. Accordingly, the government budget constraint for period t is

$$G_t = T_t + B_t^g - (1 + r_{t-1})B_{t-1}^g, \tag{10.25}$$

where G_t, T_t, and B_t^g denote, respectively, the per-capita values of government spending, lump-sum taxes, and new government borrowing in period t. As is evident from equation (10.25), in analogy with the evolution of aggregate private debt in equation (10.16), the law of motion governing the accumulation of government debt depends on the *market* rate of interest.

Consolidating the temporal budget constraints (10.25) and imposing the requirement that over time government spending obeys the intertemporal solvency constraint implies that

$$\sum_{v=0}^{\infty} \alpha_v(T_v - G_v) = (1 + r_{-1})B_{-1}^g. \tag{10.26}$$

Equation (10.26) states that the value of government debt commitment (interest plus principal payments) at the beginning of period zero must equal the discounted sum of current and future budget surpluses.

Prior to analyzing the effects of current budget deficits, we note for future use that the sum of private debt, B^p, and government debt, B^g, equals the value of the economy's external debt, B. Hence, using equations (10.16) and (10.25), the evolution of the external debt is governed by the current account position according to

$$B_t - B_{t-1} = (C_t + G_t - Y_t) + r_{t-1}B_{t-1}. \tag{10.27}$$

In order to examine the role of government budget deficits, suppose that the government changes the time pattern of taxes and debt issue while holding the path of spending unchanged. Specifically, consider the situation in which taxes are reduced in period j but are raised in a more distant period u so as to satisfy the government intertemporal solvency constraint. In order to find the effects of the change in the time profile of taxes on the level of current (period-zero) consumption and thereby on the trade balance, we need to determine the change in current wealth, W_0. Since the only component of wealth affected by the tax policy is the current value of human wealth, H_0, it is sufficient to determine the effect of the change in the timing of taxes on current human wealth. Using equation (10.14), current human wealth is

$$H_0 = \sum_{v=0}^{\infty} \gamma^v \alpha_v (Y_v - T_v), \tag{10.28}$$

and the change in current value of human wealth is

$$dH_0 = -(\gamma^j \alpha_j \, dT_j + \gamma^u \alpha_u \, dT_u). \tag{10.29}$$

From the government solvency requirement (10.26) we note that

$$dT_u = \frac{\alpha_j}{\alpha_u} dT_j, \tag{10.30}$$

and therefore the change in current human wealth is

$$dH_0 = -(1 - \gamma^{u-j}) \gamma^j \alpha_j \, dT_j. \tag{10.31}$$

Equation (10.31) shows that a tax cut in period j (followed by a corresponding tax rise in the more distant period, u; i.e., $dT_j < 0$ and $u > j$) raises the current value of human wealth. This positive wealth effect is stronger, the longer the period of time elapsing between the tax cut and the corresponding tax hike. The key factor responsible for the positive wealth effect induced by the tax policy is the finiteness of the individual horizon. At the limit, as γ approaches unity, the wealth effects disappear. In that case the Ricardian proposition reemerges, and once the path of government spending is given, the time pattern of taxes and government debt issue is irrelevant.

The foregoing analysis demonstrated that both a current budget deficit or an anticipated future deficit must raise current period wealth as long as it is financed by a subsequent rise in taxes. The rise in wealth stimulates current period consumption and worsens the trade balance.

The explanation for this result can be given as follows. If the probability of survival, γ, is unity, then the rise in future taxes which is equal in present value to the reduction in current taxes leaves wealth unchanged. On the other hand, the same change in the pattern of taxes raises wealth if each individual knows that there is a positive probability that he or she will not survive to pay these higher future taxes. Under such circumstances the current reduction in taxes constitutes net wealth. Equivalently, the explanation can be stated in terms of the difference between the market and the effective interest factors. For example, in the case of a current tax cut the government solvency requirement implies that changes in current taxes must be made up for by α_u times the offsetting change in future taxes. On the other hand, individuals discount these future taxes by $\gamma^u \alpha_u$. Therefore, as long as $\gamma < 1$, the current budget deficit raises human wealth. Yet another interpretation may be given in terms of a transfer-problem criterion familiar from the theory of international transfers. Accordingly, the budget deficit exerts real effects because it redistributes wealth from those who have not yet been born, and whose marginal propensity to consume current goods is obviously zero, to those who are currently alive, and whose marginal propensity to consume current goods is positive. As a result the budget deficit raises private-sector spending.

The foregoing analysis showed that a change in the time profile of taxes in favor of the present generation raises current consumption and worsens the balance of trade. To characterize the dynamic effects of the tax policy, we use the formulation of section 10.3 and examine the dynamic effects of a current tax cut which is accompanied by a permanent rise in future taxes. Using equation (10.30), the implied changes in current and future disposable incomes are

$$d(Y_0 - T_0) = -\frac{1}{R-1} d(Y - T). \tag{10.32}$$

With such changes in the time profile of disposable income, the change in current consumption (obtained from equation 10.22) is

$$\frac{dC_0}{dT_0} = -\frac{(1-\gamma)(1-s)R}{R-\gamma}. \tag{10.33}$$

Similarly, if the steady state exists (i.e., if $Rs < 1$), then the change in the steady-state level of consumption (obtained from equation 10.23) is

$$\frac{dC}{dT_0} = (R - 1)\frac{(1 - \gamma)(1 - s)R}{(R - \gamma)(1 - Rs)}. \tag{10.34}$$

As is evident from inspection of (10.33) and (10.34), the current budget deficit raises current consumption, C_0, and lowers the long-run level of consumption, C.

The changes in current and future consumption can be illustrated in terms of figure 10.1. Accordingly, a unit rise in current disposable income resulting from a tax cut induces a downward displacement of the $C_{t+1}(C_t)$ schedule by the magnitude $(R - 1)(1 - \gamma)(1 - s)R/(R - \gamma)$. As seen in figure 10.1, such a displacement lowers the long-run level of consumption and displaces the long-run equilibrium point B leftward along the 45° line. In addition, by raising current consumption, the budget deficit displaces the initial equilibrium point, A, rightward along the 45° line. The fall in long-run consumption is necessary in order to finance the larger steady-state debt service resulting from the tilting of the path of consumption in favor of the current generation.

The precise effect of the budget deficit on the level of consumption in any period, t, is obtained from equation (10.24) along with equations (10.33) and (10.34). Accordingly,

$$\frac{dC_t}{dT_0} = -\frac{(1 - \gamma)(1 - s)R}{(R - \gamma)(1 - Rs)}[R(1 - s)(Rs)^t - (R - 1)]. \tag{10.35}$$

As is evident, the current budget deficit raises the levels of consumption in periods that are close to the present, but it lowers the levels of consumption in periods that are more distant from the present. It can be shown from equation (10.35) that the period $\bar{t}$, in which the level of consumption following the tax policy equals the level obtained in the absence of such policy, is

$$\bar{t} = \frac{\log[(R - 1)/(1 - s)R]}{\log Rs}. \tag{10.36}$$

Equation (10.36) shows that a higher saving propensity (induced by a higher value of γ or δ) lowers the length of time during which the level of consumption exceeds the level obtained in the absence of the tax policy. Finally, we note that in the periods immediately following the tax cut, the level of consumption exceeds the level obtained in the absence of such policy, even though disposable income is lower. This consumption pattern reflects the consumption-smoothing motive of the members of the generation enjoying the rise in wealth consequent on the tax cut. Mortality reduces the size of this generation, and birth of new generations implies that the weight in aggregate consumption of the generation benefiting from the tax cut falls over time. Hence aggregate consumption is increasingly dominated by the reduced wealth of the future generations' incurring the rise in taxes, and eventually, after period $\bar{T}$, aggregate consumption falls below the level obtained prior to the tax policy.

10.5 Summary

In this chapter we developed an analytical framework suitable for the analysis of the effects of budget deficits in an undistorted economy. In that framework the principal mechanism through which tax policy influences economic behavior operates through the induced wealth effects. These wealth effects stem from the difference between the *effective* interest rate that individuals use in discounting future taxes and the corresponding *market* interest rates governing government behavior. In the present analysis the specific reason responsible for the difference between the two interest rates arises from differences between the time horizons relevant for private and public-sector decisions. This provides a rationale for our formulation in chapter 7 where we allowed for differences between the private and the public sectors' rates of interest. It is relevant to note that in contrast with the formulation in chapter 8, in which the difference between the intertemporal terms of trade governing the private and the public sectors arises from distortionary taxes, here the interest differential neither reflects nor results in a distortion.

To gain an intuitive feel into the quantitative implications of the finiteness of the horizon, it is instructive to examine the effects of a

Table 10.1
Current-consumption multiplier for alternative length of current tax-cut periods

Length of current tax-cut period	Life expectancy			
	∞ ($\gamma = 1$)	90 ($\gamma = 0.90$)	38 ($\gamma = 0.85$)	20 ($\gamma = 0.80$)
1	0	0.19	0.28	0.36
3	0	0.35	0.49	0.59
5	0	0.48	0.63	0.75
7	0	0.58	0.74	0.84

Note: The multipliers reported are equal to $(1 - \gamma\delta)[(R/(R - \gamma)](1 - \gamma^s)$, where s is one plus the length of the period for which the current tax cut is in effect. Life expectancy of the economic decision maker equals $\sum_{a=1}^{\infty} a\gamma^a = \gamma/(1 - \gamma)^2$. The computations assume that $R = 1.05$ and $\gamma = 0.95$.

current tax cut on current consumption for alternative assumptions concerning the life expectancy of the economic decision maker. Consider a current period unit tax cut lasting for $s - 1$ periods and followed by a permanent rise in taxes that maintains the discounted sum of taxes. The rise in wealth induced by this tax-shift policy equals $[R/(r - \gamma)](1 - \gamma^s)$, and the change in current consumption equals the marginal propensity to consume $(1 - \gamma\delta)$ times this change in wealth. The resulting consumption multiplier is shown in table 10.1 for alternative values of life expectancy and of length of tax-cut period. As is evident, with immortality the multipliers are zero, and the Ricardian proposition emerges. On the other hand, with low life expectancy, for example, twenty years, the multipliers associated with tax cuts lasting one and three periods are, respectively, 0.36 and 0.59. The relatively low life expectancy would seem to correspond to economies in which the average age of the economic decision maker (being roughly the difference between life expectancies at birth and at that age) is relatively high.

An implicit assumption underlying the analytical framework is the absence of a bequest motive. Accordingly, each individual's utility function does not contain as arguments the levels of utility of the subsequent generations. Otherwise, individuals could be thought of as immortal through their offspring up to the indefinite future. In that case the Ricardian proposition reemerges, and budget deficits arising from changes in the time profile of taxes do not alter the real equilibrium. We could of course allow for a bequest motive as long as it does not extend into the indefinite future or, alternatively, as long as there is uncertainty about survival of each dynastic family. In that case the effective life expectancy of the dynastic family decision-making unit may be significantly longer than that of any given individual.

Finally, we note that a similar (nondistorting) mechanism by which budget deficits exert pure wealth effects on the existing generation could also be present under circumstances in which individuals are immortal or, equivalently, are endowed with a bequest motive linking them to their offspring up to the indefinite future. This would be the case if over time there is growth in the number of individuals and entry of new families. Under such circumstances the future tax base is broader, and the burden of the future tax hike associated with the current deficit falls in part on the new members of the society that do not enter into the bequest considerations of the existing families. With this mechanism, the growth-adjusted rates of interest of the society at large (i.e., of the government) is lower than the corresponding rates used by individuals and families.

In case of growth the interest differential depends on the growth rate in a similar manner to its dependence on the mortality rate in the case of finite horizons. In both cases the wealth effects induced by budget deficits are similar.

The analysis in this chapter illustrates the wealth effects induced by changes in the timing of taxes for a given path of the world rates of interest. In the next chapter we use this model to determine the effects of budget deficits on the world rates of interest. Such changes in the world rate of interest constitute the key mechanism for the international transmission of budget deficits in the undistorted world economy.

10.6 Appendix

In this appendix we modify three of the assumptions underlying the consumption equation (10.19) of the text. We allow for an uncertain income stream and for durable goods, and we replace the homothetic utility function by a quadratic function. These modifications yield an empirically estimable form of the consumption equation. Accordingly, the individual's objective function on the right-hand side of equation (10.2) of the text is replaced by

$$E_t \sum_{v=0}^{\infty} (\gamma\delta)^v u(c_{a+v,t+v}), \tag{A.1}$$

where E_t is the conditional-expectation operator reflecting the uncertain income stream. With durable goods, we modify the periodic budget constraint (10.3a) of the text to become

$$c_{a+t,t} = (1 - \phi)c_{a+t-1,t-1} + x_{a+t,t} \tag{A.2a}$$

$$x_{a+t,t} = y_t + b_{a+t,t} - \frac{R}{\gamma}b_{a+t-1,t-1}, \tag{A.2b}$$

where c denotes the *stock* of consumer goods, x denotes the *flow* of consumption purchases, ϕ denotes the rate of depreciation of the stock, and $R = 1 + r_{t-1}$ is assumed to be constant. The flow of income, y_t, is stochastic. Equations (A.2) and (A.2b) reduce to (10.3a) in the special case for which $\phi = 1$ and y_t is deterministic. The utility function is assumed to be quadratic:

$$u(c_{a+v,t+v}) = \alpha c_{a+v,t+v} - \tfrac{1}{2}c^2_{a+v,t+v}, \tag{A.3}$$

where $\alpha > 0$ and $c_{a+v,t+v} < \alpha$. This ensures that the marginal utility of consumption is positive and diminishing. To simplify the notation, we suppress in what follows the subscripts a and v; thus we replace $c_{a+v,t+v}$ by c_t, etc.

The maximization problem can be expressed in dynamic programming terms by the value function v as

$$v\left(y_t - \frac{R}{\gamma}b_{t-1}\right) = \max_{x_t} \left\{ u[x_t + (1 - \phi)c_{t-1}] \right.$$

$$\left. + \gamma\delta E_t v\left[y_{t+1} + \frac{R}{\gamma}\left(y_t - x_t - \frac{R}{\gamma}b_{t-1}\right)\right]\right\}. \tag{A.4}$$

Differentiating the right-hand side of (A.4) and equating to zero yields

$$u'(c_t) - \delta R E_t v'(\cdot) = 0, \tag{A.5}$$

where the primes denote derivatives. Totally differentiating (A.4) yields

$$v'\left(y_t - \frac{R}{\gamma}b_{t-1}\right) = [u'(c_t) - \delta RE_t v'(\cdot)]\frac{dx_t}{dy_t} + \delta RE_t v'(\cdot)$$

$$= \delta RE_t v'(\cdot), \tag{A.6}$$

where use has been made of (A.5). Equations (A.5) and (A.6) imply that

$$u'(c_t) = \delta RE_t u'(c_{t+1}). \tag{A.7}$$

Using the specification in (A.3), we can express (A.7) as

$$\alpha - c_t = \delta RE_t(\alpha - c_{t+1}). \tag{A.8}$$

Expected human wealth is expressed as

$$E_t h_t = E_t \sum_{v=0}^{\infty} \left(\frac{\gamma}{R}\right)^v y_{t+v}. \tag{A.9}$$

From equation (A.9) we obtain

$$y_t = E_t h_t - \frac{\gamma}{R}E_t h_{t+1}. \tag{A.10}$$

For the purpose at hand, it is convenient to define expected (durability-adjusted) wealth as

$$E_t \tilde{w}_t = E_t h_t - \frac{R}{\gamma}b_{t-1} + (1 - \phi)c_{t-1}. \tag{A.11}$$

The constraints (A.2a) and (A.2b), together with (A.10), imply that

$$ac_t = E_t \tilde{w}_t - \left(\frac{\gamma}{R}\right)E_t \tilde{w}_{t+1}, \tag{A.12}$$

where

$$a = 1 - \left(\frac{\gamma}{R}\right)(1 - \phi).$$

We proceed by postulating that the solution to the maximization problem is of the form

$$c_t = \beta_0 + \beta_1 E_t \tilde{w}_t. \tag{A.13}$$

In what follows we show that this is indeed the solution, and we provide explict expressions for the coefficients β_0 and β_1. We first note that equations (A.12) and (A.13) imply that

$$E_t \tilde{w}_{t+1} = \frac{R}{\gamma} [-\beta_0 a + (1 - \beta_1 a) E_t \tilde{w}_t]. \tag{A.14}$$

Substituting (A.13) into (A.8) yields

$$\alpha - (\beta_0 + \beta_1 E_t \tilde{w}_t) = \delta R[\alpha - (\beta_0 + \beta_1 E_t \tilde{w}_{t+1})]. \tag{A.15}$$

Likewise, substituting (A.14) into (A.15) yields

$$\alpha - (\beta_0 + \beta_1 E_t \tilde{w}_t)$$

$$= \delta R \left[\alpha - \left\{ \beta_0 + \beta_1 \frac{R}{\gamma} [-\beta_0 a + (1 - \beta_1 a) E_t \tilde{w}_t] \right\} \right]. \tag{A.16}$$

Rearranging terms in equation (A.16) yields

$$\left\{ (1 - \delta R)\alpha - \left[1 - \delta R \left(1 - \frac{R}{\gamma} \beta_1 a \right) \right] \beta_0 \right\}$$

$$+ \left[-1 + \frac{\delta R^2}{\gamma} (1 - \beta_1 a) \right] \beta_1 E_t \tilde{w}_t = 0. \tag{A.17}$$

The solution specified in equation (A.13) is confirmed if (A.17) holds for all $E_t \tilde{w}_t$. This requirement is fulfilled if each of the bracketed terms in (A.17) equals zero. Thus equating these terms to zero yields

$$\beta_1 = \frac{1}{a} \left(1 - \frac{\gamma}{\delta R^2} \right), \tag{A.18}$$

$$\beta_0 = \alpha \frac{\gamma(1 - \delta R)}{\delta R(R - \gamma)}, \tag{A.19}$$

where from (A.12) the parameter a (and thus β_1) depends on the depreciation coefficient, ϕ. The consumption function (A.13) whose coefficients are given in equations (A.18) and (A.19) is the analogue to the consumption function in equation (10.8).

We turn next to derive a consumption equation suitable for empirical estimations. Using (A.11) in (A.13), aggregating the resultant individual consumption function over all cohorts, and dividing by the size of population yields the per-capita aggregate consumption C_t, where

$$C_t = \beta_0 + \beta_1 \left[E_t \sum_{v=0}^{\infty} \left(\frac{\gamma}{R} \right)^v Y_{t+v} - RB^p_{t-1} + \gamma(1 - \phi)C_{t-1} \right]. \quad \text{(A.20)}$$

Aggregating (A.2b) over all cohorts, the per-capita flow aggregate budget constraint (in period $t - 1$) is

$$B^p_{t-1} = X_{t-1} - Y_{t-1} + RB^p_{t-2}, \quad \text{(A.21)}$$

where X_t denotes aggregate per-capita purchases. This equation is the analogue to equation (10.16). Substituting (A.2a), (A.10), and (A.20) into (A.21) yields

$$B^p_{t-1} = \beta_0 + (\beta_1 - 1)E_{t-1}h_{t-1} + \frac{\gamma}{R}E_{t-1}h_t + R(1 - \beta_1)B^p_{t-2}$$

$$+ \gamma(1 - \phi)(\beta_1 - 1)C_{t-2}. \quad \text{(A.22)}$$

Define

$$E_t \tilde{W}_t = E_t h_t - RB^p_{t-1} + \gamma(1 - \phi)C_{t-1}$$

$$= E_{t-1}h_t - RB^p_{t-1} + \gamma(1 - \phi)C_{t-1} + \varepsilon_t^*, \quad \text{(A.23)}$$

where $\varepsilon^* = (E_t h_t - E_{t-1}h_t)$. Substituting (A.22) into (A.23) yields

$$E_t \tilde{W}_t = (1 - \gamma)E_{t-1}h_t - R\beta_0 - R(\beta_1 - 1)E_{t-1}\tilde{W}_{t-1}$$

$$+ \gamma(1 - \phi)C_{t-1} + \varepsilon_t^*. \quad \text{(A.24)}$$

Equation (A.20) can be rewritten as

$$C_t = \beta_0 + \beta_1 E_t \tilde{W}_t. \quad \text{(A.20a)}$$

Lagging (A.20a) and rearranging yields

$$E_{t-1}\tilde{W}_{t-1} = \frac{1}{\beta_1}(C_{t-1} - \beta_0).$$ (A.25)

Substituting (A.25) into (A.24) yields

$$E_t\tilde{W}_t = (1 - \gamma)E_{t-1}h_t + \gamma(1 \doteq \phi)C_{t-1} - R\beta_0$$

$$- \frac{R(\beta_1 - 1)}{\beta_1}(C_{t-1} - \beta_0) + \varepsilon_t^*,$$ (A.26)

which can be substituted into (A.20a) to yield

$$C_t = \beta_0(1 - R) + \beta_1(1 - \gamma)E_{t-1}h_t$$

$$+ [\gamma(1 - \phi)\beta_1 - R(\beta_1 - 1)]C_{t-1} + \varepsilon_t,$$

where $\varepsilon_t = \beta_1\varepsilon_t^*$ is a stochastic (zero-mean) residual term.

Equation (A.27) is the analogue to equation (10.19). Using the facts that aggregate consumption purchases, X_t, are related to the aggregate stock, C_t, according to $X_t = C_t - (1 - \phi)C_{t-1}$, while $C_{t-1} = \sum_{\tau=0}^{\infty}(1 - \phi)^\tau X_{t-1-\tau}$, we can express (A.27) in terms of the current and the lagged values of *observable* purchases. This form therefore is readily applicable for empirical estimation of the key parameters, particularly, the finite-horizon coefficient γ.

11

An Exposition of the Two-Country Overlapping-Generations Model

In this chapter we extend the overlapping-generations model of chapter 10 to a two-country model of the world economy. We develop a simple diagrammatic exposition which is used in the analysis of the international effects of fiscal policies. The key channel through which the effects of fiscal policies are transmitted internationally is the world rate of interest. As in chapter 10, in the absence of distortionary taxes, the mechanism responsible for the real effects of budget deficit operates through the pure wealth effects. These effects stem from the intergenerational redistribution of income consequent on budget deficits.

The exposition in this chapter is based on the assumption that the utility function is logarithmic. Under this assumption, as shown in chapter 10, the marginal propensity to save is $\gamma\delta$ (where γ denotes the survival probability and δ denotes the subjective discount factor.) Accordingly, the per-capita aggregate consumption function is

$$C_t = (1 - \gamma\delta)W_t, \tag{11.1}$$

where, as before, per-capita aggregate wealth, W_t, equals the sum of human wealth and financial wealth. Human wealth is the discounted sum of disposable income, computed by using the *effective* rates of interest. Since this chapter deals with the interaction between the domestic economy and the rest of the world, we need to specify the behavioral functions of the foreign economy. In what follows variables pertaining to the foreign economy are denoted by an asterisk (*), and it is assumed that the foreign consumption function has the same form as the domestic consumption function.

11.1 World Equilibrium

In this section we analyze the determination of the equilibrium path of world rates of interest in the two-country world economy. As before, we assume that world capital markets are fully integrated and therefore individuals and governments in both countries face the same *market* rates of interest. This feature provides for the key channel through which policies undertaken in one country affect economic conditions in the rest of the world.

World equilibrium requires that in each period the given supply of world output equals the demand. To facilitate the exposition, we divide the horizon into two periods: the present, which is denoted by $t = 0$, and the future ($t = 1, 2, \ldots$). This procedure of time aggregation, which is specified in the appendix, is modified in chapter 12. In aggregating the future into a composite single period, we need to compute the present values of the various flows. Assuming that outputs, government spending, and taxes do not vary across future periods ($t = 1, 2, \ldots$), we define an *average* interest rate, r. This average interest rate, which may be thought of as the yield on current investment lasting up to the indefinite future, represents the entire path of rates of interest that actually *do change* over time. For further reference r may be termed a "constancy-equivalent" interest rate.

The equilibrium conditions include the specification of the initial values of domestic and foreign wealth as well as the requirement that present and future goods-markets clear. These conditions are given in equation (11.2) through (11.5):

$$W_0 = (Y_0 - T_0) + \frac{\gamma}{R - \gamma}(Y - T)$$

$$+ (1 + r_{-1})(B^g_{-1} - B_{-1}), \tag{11.2}$$

$$W_0^* = (Y_0^* - T_0^*) + \frac{\gamma}{R - \gamma}(Y^* - T^*)$$

$$+ (1 + r_{-1})(B^{g^*}_{-1} + B_{-1}), \tag{11.3}$$

$$(1 - \gamma\delta)W_0 + (1 - \gamma\delta^*)W_0^* = (Y_0 - G_0) + (Y_0^* - G_0^*) \tag{11.4}$$

$$\left[\gamma \delta W_0 + \frac{(1-\gamma)}{(R-1)} \frac{R}{(R-\gamma)}(Y-T) \right]$$

$$+ \left[\gamma \delta^* W_0^* + \frac{(1-\gamma)}{(R-1)} \frac{R}{(R-\gamma)}(Y^*-T^*) \right]$$

$$= \frac{1}{R-1}[(Y-G)+(Y^*-G^*)], \tag{11.5}$$

where $R = 1 + r$, and where we have assumed that $\gamma = \gamma^*$.

Equations (11.2) and (11.3) specify the initial equilibrium values of domestic and foreign wealth owned by the existing population. In this specification private wealth is expressed as the sum of the present values of current and future disposable incomes plus the net asset positions. In these equations the term $\gamma/(R-\gamma)$ denotes the present value of an annuity (commencing at period $t = 1$) evaluated by using the effective constancy-equivalent interest rate. These equations also embody the requirement that the home country's initial external indebtedness, B_{-1}, equals the foreign country's initial net creditor position.

Equation (11.4) is the requirement that world demand for goods in period $t = 0$ equal world supply. The left-hand side of this equation shows the sum of domestic and foreign per-capita private sector consumption (as implied by equation 11.1 and its foreign counterpart), and the right-hand side is the sum of per-capita domestic and foreign outputs (Y_0 and Y_0^*) net of government spending. The equality between γ and γ^* ensures that the sizes of the population of the two countries are equal to each other. As a result aggregate world demand and supply can be expressed in terms of an equality between the *unweighted* sum of the individual country per-capita demand and the unweighted sum of the corresponding per-capita supply.

Equation (11.5) specifies the requirement that the discounted sum of per-capita domestic and foreign private demand for future goods equal the discounted sum of per-capita future world outputs net of government spending. These discounted sums are computed as of period $t = 0$ with the aid of the constancy-equivalent interest rate. The interpretation of the various terms follows. Consider the first bracketed term on the left-hand side of equation (11.5). In this expression the term $\gamma \delta W_0$ represents the per-capita savings of the population *present* in $t = 0$; these savings ultimately must be spent on future goods. The second term represents the per-capita wealth of those who will be born in all *future* periods from $t = 1$ onward; this wealth will be spent on future goods. To verify that this is indeed the meaning of the second term, we note that $(Y - T)$ is the disposable income of each individual at the time of birth and its product with $R/(R - \gamma)$ is the present value of such an annuity. Therefore the term $[R/(R - \gamma)](Y - T)$ denotes each individual's wealth at the time of birth, and since by our normalization the size of each cohort at birth is one individual, this term also represents the cohort's wealth at birth. Since in each period in the future there is a new cohort whose wealth at birth is computed similarly, the discounted sum of all future cohorts' wealth (as of period $t = 1$) is obtained by multiplying the term $[R/(R - \gamma)](Y - T)$ by $R/(R - 1)$, which denotes the present value of an annuity (commencing at $t = 1$) evaluated by using the constancy-equivalent interest rate. The resulting expression is then discounted to the present (period $t = 0$) through a division by R. This yields $[R/(R - 1)(R - \gamma)](Y - T)$. Multiplying this term by $(1 - \gamma)$ converts this aggregate wealth into the corresponding per-capita wealth. Equivalently, the first bracketed term on the left-hand side of equation (11.5) can also be obtained as the discounted sum of per-capita consumption, expressed by an equation analogous to equation (10.24). A similar interpretation applies to the second bracketed term on the left-hand side of equation (11.5). Finally, the right-hand side of equation (11.5) is the discounted sum of all future domestic and foreign outputs net of government spending. As a manifestation of Walras's law the system (11.2) through (11.5) is linearly dependent. This property is used in the subsequent analysis.

In addition to equations (11.1) through (11.5) the equilibrium conditions also include the requirements that both governments be solvent. Expressed in terms of the constancy-equivalent interest rate, these requirements are

$$(T_0 - G_0) + \frac{1}{R - 1}(T - G) = (1 + r_{-1})B^g_{-1} \qquad (11.6)$$

and

$$(T_0^* - G_0^*) + \frac{1}{R-1}(T^* - G^*) = (1 + r_{-1})B_{-1}^{g^*}. \tag{11.7}$$

This system of equations can be solved for the equilibrium values of W_0 and W_0^* and R for any given values of the parameters. As shown in the appendix, the solutions obtained for the equilibrium values of wealth, W_0 and W_0^*, are the same as those that may be obtained from the original system (without the specific time aggregation) for which the rates of interest within the future may vary. The use of the constancy-equivalent interest rate thus simplifies the analysis considerably, and it provides complete information about the impact of policies on the precise *current* values of all key variables including wealth, consumption, and debt accumulation, as well as on the average value of the rate of interest (computed as of time zero).

Using the government budget constraints, substituting $C_0/(1 - \gamma\delta)$ for W_0, and omitting equation (11.2) by Walras's law, the complete system of equations can be reduced to two basic market-clearing equilibrium conditions, one for present goods and another for future goods. These conditions are

$$C_0 + (1 - \gamma\delta^*)\left[(Y_0^* - G_0^*) + \frac{\gamma}{R-\gamma}(Y^* - T^*)\right.$$

$$\left. + \frac{1}{R-1}(T^* - G^*) + (1 + r_{-1})B_{-1}\right]$$

$$= [(Y_0 - G_0) + (Y_0^* - G_0^*)], \tag{11.8}$$

$$\left[\frac{\gamma\delta}{(1-\gamma\delta)}C_0 + \frac{(1-\gamma)}{R-1}\frac{R}{(R-\gamma)}(Y - T)\right] + \left\{\gamma\delta^*\left[(Y_0^* - G_0^*)\right.\right.$$

$$\left. + \frac{\gamma}{R-\gamma}(Y^* - T^*) + \frac{1}{R-1}(T^* - G^*) + (1 + r_{-1})B_{-1}\right]$$

$$\left. + \frac{(1-\gamma)}{R-1}\frac{R}{(R-\gamma)}(Y^* - T^*)\right\}$$

$$= \frac{1}{R-1}[(Y - G) + (Y^* - G^*)]. \tag{11.9}$$

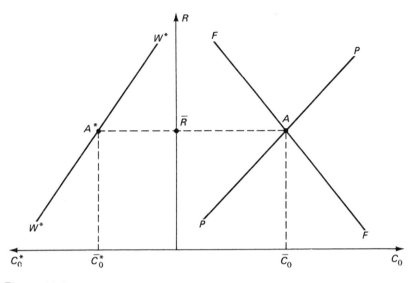

Figure 11.1
Equilibrium consumption and the rate of interest in the world economy

Equation (11.8) is the reduced-form market-clearing condition for present goods, with the left-hand side showing the sum of domestic and foreign private sector demands and the right-hand side showing the world supply of outputs net of government spending. Equation (11.9) is the reduced-form market-clearing condition for future goods, with analogous interpretations applied to the terms on its left and right-hand sides. These market-clearing conditions are used later in the diagrammatic exposition of the world equilibrium.

Throughout we assume that the foreign government follows a balanced-budget policy and that initially the domestic budget is balanced. This ensures that changes in world rates of interest that result from domestic fiscal deficits do not impact on the solvency of the foreign government and therefore do not necessitate secondary changes in fiscal policies.

Figure 11.1 shows the equilibrium of the system. In panel I the PP schedule describes combinations of R and C_0 that maintain equilibrium in the market for *present* goods. It is positively sloped since, as seen from equation (11.8), a fall in the rate of interest raises foreign wealth and induces a rise in foreign spending on present goods;

therefore domestic consumption must fall in order to induce an offsetting reduction in demand. The FF schedule describes combinations of R and C_0 that maintain equilibrium in the market for *future* goods. Its slope is negative since a fall in R creates an excess supply of world future output which is eliminated by an offsetting rise in demand induced by a rise in domestic wealth that is associated with the rise in C_0. Panel II of figure 11.1 portrays the negatively sloped W^*W^* schedule describing the equilibrium relationship between R and C_0^* as implied by the foreign consumption function and by the negative dependence of W^* on R (from equation 11.3). The equilibrium is described by points A and A^* at which the values of the variables are $\bar{C}_0$, $\bar{C}_0^*$, and $\bar{R}$.

11.2 Effects of Current Budget Deficits

In this section we analyze the effects of budget deficits on the world rates of interest and on the levels of domestic and foreign private-sector spending. To focus on the impact of deficits rather than the impact of government spending, we assume that the deficits result from changes in taxes and that the path of government spending is given. Since government spending remains unchanged, solvency requires that current changes in taxes be accompanied by offsetting changes in future taxes. The present value of these tax changes must equal each other. The initial balance in the domestic budget ensures (from equation 11.6) that a change in current taxes, dT_0, must be related to the future change, dT, according to

$$dT_0 = -\frac{1}{R-1}dT, \qquad (11.10)$$

where $1/(R-1) = 1/r$ is the annuity value of a unit tax change commencing from period $t = 1$ and evaluated in period $t = 0$. The rate of interest used in computing this annuity value is the constancy-equivalent rate of interest.

Figure 11.2 is used to determine the effects of a budget deficit. A deficit induced by a current tax cut of $-\Delta T_0$ necessitates (as long as government spending remains unchanged) a corresponding rise in

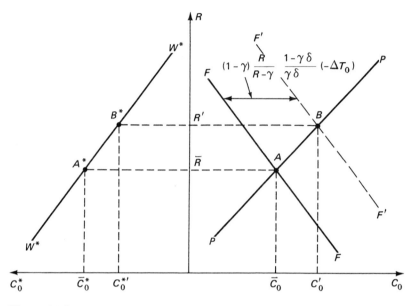

Figure 11.2
The effects of a current budget deficit

future taxes by $(R - 1)\Delta T_0$ according to equation (11.10). These tax changes do not impact on the PP schedule, but as seen from equation (11.9), they induce a fall in demand for future goods. To restore equilibrium at the given rate of interest, W_0 must rise so as to raise demand for future goods. Associated with such a rise in wealth is a rise in current consumption C_0. Thus the FF schedule shifts to the right by $(1 - \gamma)R(1 - \gamma\delta)/[\gamma\delta(R - \gamma)]\Delta T_0$. As a result the new equilibrium is reached at points B and B^* and $C_0' > \bar{C}_0$, $R' > \bar{R}$, and $C_0^{*\prime} < \bar{C}_0^*$.

Thus a budget deficit arising from a reduction in domestic taxes raises the world interest rate. Likewise, the domestic budget deficit raises the equilibrium value of domestic consumption, C_0, and lowers the corresponding value of foreign consumption, C_0^*. It follows that domestic budget deficits are transmitted *negatively* to the rest of the world. The international transmission mechanism is effected through the rate of interest. The rise in the world interest rate lowers foreign wealth and mitigates the initial rise in domestic wealth. These changes in wealth raise domestic spending, lower foreign spending, and worsen the domestic current account of the balance of payments. In the present context the direction of the international transmission is measured in terms of the comovements of current levels of domestic and foreign spending. It is relevant to note, however, that the level of current spending may not be a sufficient indicator for welfare changes. We elaborate on this issue in chapter 12.

As may be seen, if the probability of survival, γ, is unity, then budget deficits do not alter interest rates and consumption. In that case the model yields the familiar Ricardian proposition according to which the timing of taxes, and thereby the timing of deficits, do not influence the real equilibrium of the system as long as the path of government spending remains intact. In terms of figure 11.2, in that case the FF schedule does not shifts in response to such tax changes. In the general case, however, with $\gamma < 1$, budget deficits exert real effects.

11.3 Effects of Current and Future Government Spending

The diagrammatic apparatus developed in the previous section can also be applied to illustrate the effects of government spending. In order to focus on the effect of changes in the level of government spending rather than on the effects of budget deficits, we assume (as in earlier chapters) that government budgets are balanced. The basic mechanism through which balanced-budget changes in government spending influence the economy do not depend, of course, on whether or not the model conforms with the Ricardian equivalence proposition. Accordingly, the results illustrated in this section are similar to those shown in chapter 7. These results are repeated here as a useful application of the diagrammatic apparatus.

Anticipating the results we recall from chapter 7 that, in general, the effects of balanced-budget changes in government spending on private-sector spending and on the world rate of interest depend on the comparison between the time pattern of government spending, as reflected by its saving propensity and the time pattern of domestic private-sector spending, as reflected by its saving propensity. Specifically, if the saving propensity of the government, γ_s^g, exceeds the private-sector saving propensity, γ_s, then a rise in the discounted sum of government spending creates an excess demand for future goods and necessitates a fall in the rate of interest, and vice versa. In the present case the government saving propensity is the fraction of the discounted sum of government spending that falls on future goods. That is,

$$\gamma_s^g = \frac{G/(R-1)}{G_0 + G/(R-1)}. \tag{11.11}$$

Likewise, the corresponding private-sector-saving propensity, γ_s, is the fraction of the discounted sum of private-sector spending that falls on future goods. Using the terms pertaining to domestic private-sector spending from equations (11.4) and (11.5), we obtain

$$\gamma_s = \frac{\gamma \delta W_0 + [(1-\gamma)R]/[(R-1)(R-\gamma)](Y-T)}{W_0 + [(1-\gamma)R]/[(R-1)(R-\gamma)](Y-T)}. \tag{11.12}$$

The expressions in (11.11) and (11.12) define the average saving propensities, while our general principle is stated in terms of a comparison between the *marginal* saving propensities. If, however, the initial levels of debt, government spending, and taxes are zero, if the initial path of output is stationary and if the government maintains balanced budgets then the average and the marginal propensities are equal to each other. In the following exposition we identify the expressions in equations (11.11) and (11.12) with the corresponding marginal saving propensities.

The implications of this general principle are illustrated in figure 11.3 where we analyze the effects of alternative time patterns of government spending. In figure 11.3 the initial equilibrium obtains at points A and A^* at which the levels of domestic and foreign consumption are $\bar{C}_0$ and $\bar{C}_0^*$ and the rate of interest is indicated by $\bar{R}_0$. A transitory balanced-budget rise in *current* government spending of ΔG_0 creates an excess demand for present goods and necessitates a corresponding fall in private-sector spending. As implied by equation (11.8), the PP schedule shifts to the left by ΔG_0 to $P'P'$, and the new equilibrium obtains at points B and B^*. In that case the equilibrium world rate of interest rises and the levels of domestic and foreign private-sector consumption fall. This result conforms

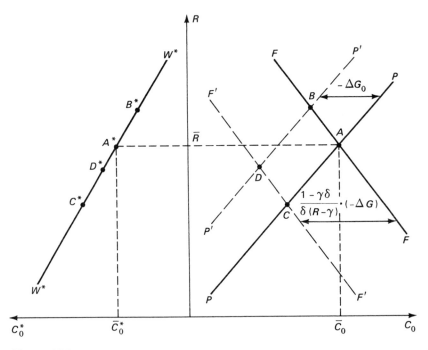

Figure 11.3
The effects of current, future, and permanent government spending on
domestic and foreign consumption and the world rate of interest

with the general principle since, as seen from equations (11.11) and
(11.12), with a transitory rise in current government spending, the
saving propensity of the government, γ_s^g, is zero while the corresponding propensity of the domestic private sector is positive.

Consider next a transitory balanced-budget rise in *future* government spending by ΔG. Such a rise creates an excess demand for
future goods and necessitates a corresponding fall in private-sector
demand for future goods. Such a reduction results from a decline in
wealth that also induces (for any given rate of interest) a corresponding reduction in C_0. As implied by equation (11.9), the FF schedule
shifts to the left by $(1 - \gamma\delta)/[\delta(R - \gamma)]\Delta G$ to the position indicated
by $F'F'$. The new equilibrium obtains at points C and C^*. In that case
the equilibrium world rate of interest falls, domestic private-sector
consumption falls, and foreign consumption rises. This result also
illustrates the general principle since, as seen from equations (11.11)

and (11.12), with a transitory rise in future government spending, γ_s^g is unity while γ_s is smaller than unity.

The foregoing analysis provides the ingredients necessary for determining the effects of a *permanent* balanced-budget rise in government spending. Such a rise in government spending (with $\Delta G_0 = \Delta G$) raises demand for *both* present and future goods and shifts both schedules in figure 11.3 leftward. The impact on the rate of interest depends on the *relative* excess demands in both markets. Diagrammatically, the difference between the horizontal leftward shifts of the *PP* and the *FF* schedules is $(\delta R - 1)/[\delta(R - \gamma)]\Delta G$. Accordingly, if δR falls short of unity, then the leftward shift of the *FF* schedule exceeds that of the *PP* schedule. This situation is shown in figure 11.3 where the new equilibrium obtains at point D and D^*. At this equilibrium the world rate of interest falls, and domestic private-sector consumption falls while foreign consumption rises. If, on the other hand, δR exceeds unity, then the leftward shift of the *PP* schedule exceeds that of the *FF* schedule. In that case the world rate of interest rises and the levels of domestic and foreign private-sector consumption fall.

In interpreting these results, we note that if δR exceeds unity, then the desired level of consumption by individuals in the domestic economy rises over time. In and of itself this contributes to a surplus in the current account of the domestic balance of payments during the early periods. Of course the counterpart to this surplus is a corresponding deficit in the foreign current account of the balance of payments. Thus, if $\delta R > 1$, then (at the margin) the domestic economy is a net saver in the world economy and the permanent rise in government spending raises the world rate of interest. The opposite holds if the domestic economy is a net dissaver in the world economy, that is, if δR falls short of unity.

The dependence of the interest-rate effects of a permanent rise in government spending on whether δR exceeds or falls short of unity conforms with the general principle expressed in terms of a comparison between the domestic private- and public-sector-saving propensities. To verify this conformity, we substitute equation (11.2) for W_0 into equation (11.12); assuming the absence of initial debt as well as balanced budgets and stationary paths of output and government

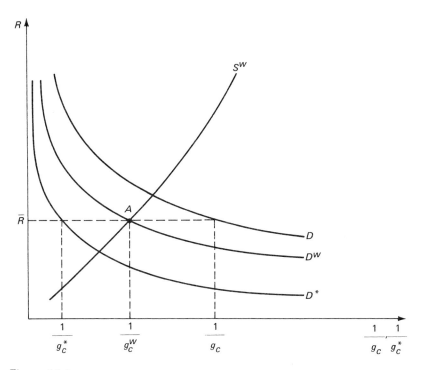

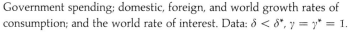

Figure 11.4
Government spending; domestic, foreign, and world growth rates of
consumption; and the world rate of interest. Data: $\delta < \delta^*$, $\gamma = \gamma^* = 1$.

spending, it can be shown that γ_s^g exceeds or falls short of γ_s according to whether δR falls short or exceeds unity.

To gain further insights, we apply the relative demand–relative
supply diagrammatic apparatus of chapter 7 to determine the effects
of balanced-budget changes in government spending on the rates of
growth of domestic and foreign per-capita consumption. Since the
qualitative effects of the analysis do not depend on whether the
survival probability is unity or not, we assume that the value of γ is
unity so that individuals have an infinite horizon. This assumption
permits the use of this diagrammatic device.

Figure 11.4 shows the domestic (D), the foreign (D^*), and the
world (D^w) relative demand schedules as functions of the rate of
interest. In the figure, g_c, g_c^*, and g_c^w denote the ratios of the discounted sum (as of period one) of future consumption to current

consumption of the domestic, the foreign, and the world private sector, respectively. These magnitudes are indicators of the corresponding growth rates of consumption. The model contained in equations (11.1) through (11.5) implies that if $\gamma = 1$ then $g_c = \delta R$ and $g_c^* = \delta^* R$. Hence in the present case the downward-sloping relative demand schedules are rectangular hyperbolas. As in the previous chapters, the D^w schedule is a weighted average of D and D^*. Accordingly,

$$\frac{1}{g_c^w} = \mu \frac{1}{g_c} + (1 - \mu) \frac{1}{g_c^*}, \tag{11.13}$$

where μ is the fraction of the discounted sum of future domestic consumption in the discounted sum of world future output net of government spending.

The S^w schedule in figure 11.4 portrays the ratio of current to (the discounted sum of) future world output net of government spending. This schedule is positively sloped since a rise in the rate of interest lowers the discounted sum of future outputs. The initial equilibrium is shown by point A at which the world relative demand equals the corresponding supply. At this point the equilibrium rate of interest is indicated by $\bar{R}$, and the relative world consumption is indicated by $1/g_c^w$. Associated with this rate of interest, the corresponding values of domestic and foreign relative consumption are indicated by $1/g_c$ and $1/g_c^*$, respectively.

A transitory balanced-budget rise in current government spending lowers the relative supply and induces a leftward displacement of the S schedule. Further the rise in taxes that is necessary to balance the budget lowers private-sector consumption and, as indicated by equation (11.13), reduces the weight of the domestic relative demand in the world relative demand. This induces a displacement of the D^w schedule toward the foreign schedule D^* (whose relative weight has risen). The case shown in figure 11.4 corresponds to the situation in which $\delta < \delta^*$ so that the domestic saving propensity falls short of the foreign one. In that case the domestic schedule D lies to the right of D^*, and the rise in the domestic government spending induces a leftward displacement of the D^w schedule. Specifically, if the relative supply schedule shifts leftward by 1 percent, then the world relative demand schedule shifts leftward by only μ percent. As a result the equilibrium rate of interest rises, and the growth rates of consumption in both countries rise. The same qualitative results apply to the situation in which the saving-propensities condition is reversed so that $\delta > \delta^*$. In that case the D schedule lies to the left of the D^* schedule and the rise in the domestic government induces a rightward shift of the D^w schedule. In that case the rate of interest rises to a larger extent.

A similar analysis applies to the effects of a transitory rise in future government spending. In that case the relative supply schedule shifts to the right, and as before, the world relative demand schedule shifts to a position closer to that of the foreign relative demand schedule. The new equilibrium is associated with a lower rate of interest and a higher growth rate of domestic and foreign consumption. These qualitative results are independent of the relative magnitudes of δ and δ^* since even if the relative world demand shifts in the same direction as the supply, the proportional horizontal displacement of the S schedule, exceeds the corresponding displacement of the D^w schedule.

Finally, a permanent rise in government spending that does not alter the relative share of government spending in world GDP leaves the S schedule intact and displaces the D^w schedule toward the foreign schedule D^*. Hence, if δ exceeds δ^*, the world relative demand schedule shifts to the right, the rate of interest rises, and the growth rates of consumption fall. The opposite holds for the case in which δ falls short of δ^*. Since the equilibrium value of $1/R$ lies in between δ and δ^*, it is evident that the dependence of the effects of a permanent rise in government spending on the saving-propensities condition (i.e., on whether δ exceeds or falls short of δ^*) can be expressed equivalently in terms of whether δR exceeds or falls short of unity. Indeed, the previous analysis in this section was cast in terms of the latter condition.

11.4 Effects of Past Government Spending

We proceed with the exposition in this chapter by applying the diagrammatic apparatus to the analysis of the effects of past balanced-budget rises in government spending. Other things equal, the higher level of past transitory government spending was associated with a worsened past current-account position. Therefore, from the perspective of the current generations, the higher level of past government spending is reflected in a larger size of the initial external debt.

To analyze the effect of the size of the initial external debt position, consider a redistribution of world debt from the home country to the rest of the world. Suppose that this transfer is represented by increasing $(1 + r_{-1})B_{-1}$ by ΔB. This redistribution of world debt lowers domestic demand for both present and future goods and induces a corresponding rise in foreign demand. From equation (11.8) it is seen that the PP schedule shifts to the left by $(1 - \gamma\delta^*)\Delta B$, and from equation (11.9) it is seen that the FF schedule shifts to the left by $(1 - \gamma\delta)(\delta^*/\delta)\Delta B$. From equation (11.3) and the foreign consumption function the transfer also shifts the W^*W^* schedule to the left by $(1 - \gamma\delta^*)\Delta B$. As a result the equilibrium of the system shifts from points A and A^* to points B and B^*.

The effect of the transfer on the new equilibrium rate of interest reflects the usual considerations underlying the transfer-problem criterion. In terms of figure 11.5 the rate of interest falls if the horizontal displacement of the FF schedule exceeds the corresponding displacement of the PP schedule, and vice versa. As can be seen, the difference between the horizontal shifts of the FF and the PP schedules is proportional to $(\delta^* - \delta)/\delta$. If the saving-propensities condition is such that $\delta < \delta^*$, then the transfer raises world savings and necessitates a fall in the rate of interest so as to restore the initial level of world savings. This is the case illustrated in figure 11.5. If, however, $\delta > \delta^*$, then the transfer lowers world savings and induces a rise in the world rate of interest. In general, independent of the direction of the change in the rate of interest, the redistribution of world debt in favor of the foreign country lowers domestic consumption and raises foreign consumption.

11.5 Welfare Aspects

The analysis in the preceeding sections indicated the effects of fiscal policies on interest rates and wealth. Knowledge of these effects was

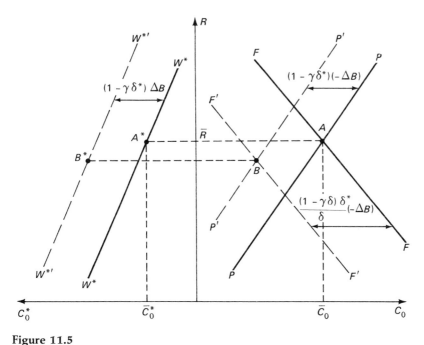

Figure 11.5
Changes in external debt, domestic and foreign consumption, and the world
rate of interest. Data: $\delta < \delta^*$.

sufficient for determining the impact of policies on the paths of
aggregate consumption which, in turn, govern the evolution of the
key economic variables in the world economy. It is obvious, however, that because of the structure of the overlapping-generations
model, the analysis of *normative* questions is much more complex.
Specifically, it is evident that the welfare effects of fiscal policies
cannot be inferred from knowledge of the resulting changes in
aggregate private wealth. In the first place changes in intertemporal
prices (rates of interest) also impact on the level of welfare in addition to their effects on wealth. More important, complexities arise
from the fact that not all generations share equally in the benefits of
tax cuts and in the burdens of tax levies. Furthermore, in designing
optimal fiscal policies, one needs to define a social welfare function.
This raises the conceptual issues concerning the proper weighting of
current and prospective generations in the social welfare function

and the possible implication for the time consistency of government policies.

In this section we illustrate some of these issues by examining the effects of a current budget deficit on the welfare of the population existing in the period of the tax cut. It is convenient to focus the analysis on the individual born in the period of the tax cut, but since the survival probability is the same for all individuals, the direction of the change in welfare is the same for everyone else who is alive during the period of the tax cut. Therefore the qualitative results apply to the entire population that is alive during the period of the deficit. Recalling that each individual is born with no debt and that therefore his wealth consists of the properly discounted value of lifetime disposable income, the per-capita wealth is

$$w_0 = (Y_0 - T_0) + \frac{\gamma}{R - \gamma}(Y - T). \tag{11.14}$$

With the assumed logarithmic utility function, the individual's expected utility is given by

$$\sum_{t=0}^{\infty} (\gamma\delta)^t \log c_t, \tag{11.15}$$

and correspondingly, his consumption (computed with the aid of the constancy-equivalent interest rate) is

$$c_t = (1 - \gamma\delta)(\delta R)^t w_0. \tag{11.16}$$

Using these expressions, it can be shown that the individual's *indirect* expected utility, v, is represented by

$$v = \log \frac{w_0}{R^{-\gamma\delta/(1-\gamma\delta)}} = \log \left[\frac{(Y_0 - T_0) + \gamma/(R-\gamma)(Y-T)}{R^{-\gamma\delta/(1-\gamma\delta)}} \right], \tag{11.17}$$

where the second equality follows from equation (11.14) and $R^{-\gamma\delta/(1-\gamma\delta)}$ is the real-wealth deflator which is the intertemporal price index (in terms of current consumption) appropriate for evaluating the real value of wealth. Thus, utility is a function of *real* wealth. As seen in equation (11.17), current budget deficits impact on the level of utility directly through the effects of the reduction in T_0 and the accompanying rise in T and, indirectly through the effect of changes in the rate of interest. The latter in turn operates through its impact on the present value of future disposable income and on the intertemporal price index. As is evident, in the extreme case with $\gamma = 1$, the direct effects induced by the changes in current and future taxes offset each other (since $dT_0 + dT/[R - 1] = 0$), and since with $\gamma = 1$ the rate of interest does not change, the indirect effect of the tax shift is also zero. Obviously, in that case a budget deficit does not impact on the individual's utility level. In the other extreme for which γ is very small, the individual is concerned mainly with his or her current level of income and consumption and therefore changes in the rate of interest exert small effects on his welfare. In that case the weight, $\gamma\delta/(1 - \gamma\delta)$, of future prices in the real-wealth deflator as well as the weight of future disposable income in w_0 are small, and therefore a current tax cut raises welfare. In general, since the budget deficit raises both the value of wealth and the rate of interest (as shown formally in the appendix), it follows that it raises the level of welfare of the existing population. The preceding analysis examined the impact of current budget deficits on the level of welfare of the existing population. Of course the future rise in taxes and the associated changes in the rates of interest also impact on the utility level of the yet unborn generations.

Turning to the evaluation of foreign welfare, we note that the changes in the rates of interest impact on the welfare of the existing foreign population according to whether the foreign country is a net saver or dissaver. Thus, as far as the existing foreign population is concerned, the direction of changes in their current wealth and consumption (which was emphasized in our preceding positive analysis) is not the relevant indicator for welfare changes. Therefore, in assessing whether the international transmission mechanism is positive or negative, a distinction should be drawn between positive measures of transmission expressed in terms of current consumption and wealth and normative measures expressed in terms of welfare.

In concluding this section, it is relevant to note that throughout the discussion we have not inquired into the motives underlying the adaption of a budget-deficit policy. In this context the possibility that the existing population gains from current deficits raises the question as to what factors limit the introduction of further tax cuts at the expense of future generations, and possibly at the expense of foreigners (if they are net borrowers). In general, considerations that may operate to limit current tax cuts include (1) governments that are also concerned with future generations' welfare, (2) the possibility that the welfare loss imposed on foreigners through the domestic tax cuts may stimulate retaliation and result in a costly "fiscal war," (3) the existence of an upper limit to the feasible rise in future taxes, (4) the existence of distortionary taxes and costly fiscal management that sets an upper limit to the benefits that current tax cuts yield to the existing population, and (5) the possibility that a significant rise in debt introduces the probability of default and may raise the cost of external borrowing. In connection with this final consideration we recall that throughout the analysis individuals were assumed to be mortal, whereas government commitments were implicitly assumed to be immortal. In general, of course, the probability that governments and their commitments survive indefinitely is also less than unity. Under such circumstances the interest-rate differential on private and public sectors' loans, and thereby the impact of budget deficits, is governed by the relation between the default probabilities of individuals and government commitments. It is noteworthy, however, that allowing for the possibility that governments renege on their commitments (in the context of designing optimal policies) introduces to the analysis new dimensions associated with the issues of time-consistent policies.

11.6 Summary

In this chapter we provided an exposition of the two-country overlapping-generations model of the world economy. We developed a simple diagrammatic exposition of the model by focusing on the markets for present and future goods. To reduce the high dimensionality of the model, we have constructed a composite of future goods and defined the concept of a constancy-equivalent rate of interest used in the definition of this composite good. This procedure facilitated the exposition and simplified the analysis considerably without loss of pertinent information.

The diagrammatic apparatus was applied to the analysis of the effects of current budget deficits as well as to the effects of various time patterns of balanced-budget changes in government spending. In this context we focused on the effects of these fiscal policies on the world rate of interest and on the levels and growth rates of domestic and foreign private-sector spending.

The diagrammatic exposition provided in this chapter illustrates the general principles of the various transfer-problem criteria developed in previous chapters. Accordingly, it illustrates that the interest-rate effects of various time patterns of government spending can be determined by simple comparison between the properly defined marginal saving propensities of the domestic private and public sectors. Likewise, the effects of changes in the time profile of taxes are interpreted in terms of a comparison between the marginal spending propensities of current and future generations. Finally, the effects of a redistribution of world debt arising from past balanced-budget changes in government spending depend on the relative magnitudes of the marginal saving propensities of domestic and foreign residents.

We concluded the exposition with a brief analysis of welfare implications of budget deficits. This discussion was cast in terms of the effects of budget deficits on wealth and on the wealth deflator. It was shown that the budget deficit raises the level of welfare of the existing domestic population. The welfare of the foreign population rises if the foreign economy is a net saver in the world economy, and vice versa. In this context we also outlined some of the checks that may limit the incentives for the adoption of budget deficits.

In the next chapter we extend the analysis and focus on the dynamic effects of fiscal policies on rates of interest for various maturities as well as on the time path of short-term rates.

11.7 Appendix

The Time-Aggregation Procedure

The aggregation procedure and the use of the constancy-equivalent rate of interest which underlie equations (11.2) through (11.5) is justified as follows. From equation (10.14) and its foreign-country counterpart, the market-clearing condition for period $t = 0$ is shown in equation (A.1) and the corresponding definitions of wealth are shown in equations (A.2) and (A.3). Thus

$$(1 - s_0)W_0 + (1 - s_0^*)W_0^* = (Y_0 - G_0) + (Y_0^* - G_0^*), \qquad (A.1)$$

$$W_0 = \sum_{t=0}^{\infty} \gamma^t \alpha_t (Y_t - T_t) + (1 + r_{-1})(B_{-1}^g - B_{-1}), \qquad (A.2)$$

$$W_0^* = \sum_{t=0}^{\infty} (\gamma^*)^t \alpha_t (Y_t^* - T_t^*) + (1 + r_{-1})(B_{-1}^{g*} + B_{-1}), \qquad (A.3)$$

where

$$s_0 = 1 - \left\{ \sum_{t=0}^{\infty} (\gamma^t \alpha_t)^{1-\sigma}[(\gamma\delta)^t]^{\sigma} \right\}^{-1},$$

$$s_0^* = 1 - \left\{ \sum_{t=0}^{\infty} [(\gamma^*)^t \alpha_t]^{1-\sigma^*}[(\gamma^*\delta^*)^t]^{\sigma^*} \right\}^{-1}.$$

The value of s_0 is taken from equation (10.9), and s_0^* is the corresponding foreign-country counterpart.

Under the conditions that $Y_t - T_t = Y - T$, $Y_t^* - T_t^* = Y^* - T^*$ (for $t = 1, 2, \ldots$), $\sigma = \sigma^* = 1$, and $\gamma = \gamma^*$, equations (A.1) through (A.3) can be solved for the equilibrium values of W_0, W_0^*, and $\sum_{t=1}^{\infty} \gamma^t \alpha_t$. In the text we define $\sum_{t=1}^{\infty} \gamma^t \alpha_t$ by $\gamma/(R - \gamma)$, where $r = R - 1$ is the constancy-equivalent rate of interest. With these substitutions equations (A.1) through (A.3) become equations (11.2) through (11.4).

It can be readily verified that adding equation (11.5) to the system (11.2) through (11.4) yields a linearly dependent system of equations. Therefore, as a manifestation of Walras's law the *equilibrium* values of W_0, W_0^*, and R can be solved from any subset of three equations from the four-equation system.

The Impact of Budget Deficits

In this part of the appendix we consider the impact of current budget deficits. The quantitative impacts of changes in domestic taxes on R,

W_0, and W_0^*, (evaluated around an initial balanced budget and initial stationary paths of output, taxes, and government spending) can be obtained from any three equations of the system (11.2) through (11.5) along with the implications of the government budget constraint (11.10). These changes are

$$\frac{dW_0}{dT_0} = -(1 - \gamma)(1 - \gamma\delta^*)\lambda^* < 0, \tag{A.4}$$

$$\frac{dW_0^*}{dT_0} = (1 - \gamma)(1 - \gamma\delta)\lambda^* > 0, \tag{A.5}$$

$$\frac{dR}{dT_0} = -(1 - \gamma)\frac{(1 - \gamma\delta)(R - \gamma)^2 \lambda^*}{\gamma(Y^* - G^*)} < 0, \tag{A.6}$$

where λ^* is the relative share of foreign output net of government spending in the corresponding world quantity; that is,

$$\lambda^* = \frac{Y^* - G^*}{Y - G + Y^* - G^*},$$

and where use has been made of the market-clearing condition by which

$$(1 - \gamma\delta)\frac{R}{R - \gamma}(Y - T) + (1 - \gamma\delta^*)\frac{R}{R - \gamma}(Y - T)$$

$$= Y - G + Y^* - G^*.$$

Thus a current budget deficit arising from a reduction of domestic taxes ($dT_0 < 0$) raises the rate of interest and domestic wealth and lowers foreign wealth. Multiplying these changes in wealth by the propensities to consume, $(1 - \gamma\delta)$ and $(1 - \gamma\delta^*)$, yields the corresponding changes in domestic and foreign consumption. These changes vanish if $\gamma = 1$.

12

Fiscal Policies and the Term Structure of Interest Rates

In the previous chapter it was shown that a current budget deficit arising from a cut in current taxes (accompanied by a corresponding rise in future taxes) raises the world rate of interest linking the present period with the future. With nondistortionary taxes the key mechanism responsible for the rise in the rate of interest operates through the pure wealth effects induced by the change in the time profile of taxes. In the absence of such wealth effects—which in our model stem from the finiteness of the horizon—budget deficits that are not accompanied by changes in the level of government spending do not exert real effects. Our analysis was conducted within a framework that consolidated the *entire* future into a single period. Consequently, to ensure solvency, a current budget deficit implies a corresponding rise in future taxes. This procedure of time aggregation does not permit an analysis of the impact of *future* budget deficits that are not accompanied by current changes in taxes but are financed by a rise in taxes in subsequent future periods. In this chapter we examine the dynamic consequences of fiscal policies. These consequences are studied with reference to the effects of future changes in taxes and in government spending on the term structure of interest rates; in addition we study the steady-state implications of cumulative budget deficits.

12.1 Future Budget Deficits and Rates of Interest

To examine the effects of future deficits, we modify in this section the aggregation of the periods. Specifically, we divide the future into two parts: the *near* future and the *distant* future. For simplicity, as in chapter 11, we represent the distant future by a consolidation of the entire period subsequent to that of the near future into a single period. In what follows a subscript 0 designates variables pertaining to the present period, a subscript 1 designates variables pertaining to the near future, and variables that appear without a time subscript pertain to the distant future.

Consider an expected change in taxes occurring in the near future, and suppose that in the present period no taxes are altered. Without changes in present taxes government solvency requires that the near-future tax cut is accompanied by further offsetting changes in the distant future. Thus solvency requires that

$$dT = -(R_1 - 1)\,dT_1,\qquad\qquad(12.1)$$

where $(R_1 - 1)$ is the constancy-equivalent interest rate in the distant future; that is, it is the average one-period rate of interest linking the near future with the distant future. This construct is similar to the one defined in chapter 11. To compute the effects of such future policies, we note that the equilibrium system consists of the following requirements: (1) world output in the present period is demanded, (2) world output in the near future is demanded, (3) world output in the distant future is demanded, and (4) the equilibrium values of domestic and foreign wealth consist of the sums of the present values of disposable incomes in the present, near future, and distant future, adjusted for the initial debt. These requirements are presented, respectively, in equations (12.2) through (12.5):

$$(1 - s_0)W_0 + (1 - s_0^*)W_0^* = (Y_0 - G_0) + (Y_0^* - G_0^*),\qquad(12.2)$$

$$(1 - s_1)[s_0 R_0 W_0 + (1 - \gamma)H_1] + (1 - s_1^*)[s_0^* R_0 W_0^* + (1 - \gamma)H_1^*]$$

$$= (Y_1 - G_1) + (Y_1^* - G_1^*),\qquad\qquad(12.3)$$

$$W_0 = (Y_0 - T_0) + \frac{\gamma}{R_0}H_1 + (1 + r_{-1})(B_{-1}^g - B_{-1}),\qquad(12.4)$$

$$W_0^* = (Y_0^* - T_0^*) + \frac{\gamma}{R_0}H_1^* + (1 + r_{-1})(B_{-1}^{g^*} + B_{-1}),\qquad(12.5)$$

where s_0 and s_1 are the domestic-country marginal propensities to save in the current and in the near-future periods, respectively, s_0^* and s_1^* are the corresponding foreign-country marginal saving propensities, R_0 is (one plus) the interest rate in the present period, and H_1 and H_1^* are, respectively, the domestic- and the foreign-country values of human wealth, evaluated as of the near future (period 1); that is,

$$H_1 = Y_1 - T_1 + \frac{\gamma}{R_1 - \gamma}(Y - T),$$

$$H_1^* = Y_1^* - T_1^* + \frac{\gamma}{R_1 - \gamma}(Y^* - T^*).$$

In specifying the equilibrium conditions (12.2) through (12.5), we have used Walras's law to omit the requirement that in the distant future world output is demanded.

Our analysis in chapter 10 showed that the marginal propensities to save depend on the effective subjective discount factor, $\gamma\delta$, on the path of the effective rates of interest, and on the value of the intertemporal elasticity of substitution. Using the expression in equation (10.12) and incorporating the constancy-equivalent rate of interest, the marginal propensities to save are

$$s_0 = \frac{\gamma R_0^{\sigma-1}\delta^\sigma}{1 + \gamma R_0^{\sigma-1}\delta^\sigma - \gamma R_1^{\sigma-1}\delta^\sigma}, \tag{12.6}$$

$$s_1 = \gamma R_1^{\sigma-1}\delta^\sigma; \tag{12.7}$$

similar expressions, with asterisks added, apply to the foreign-country marginal propensities to save.

To examine the implications of future budget deficits, it is convenient to consider first a bench-mark case in which the utility functions are such that in both countries the intertemporal elasticities of substitution are unity. In that case the domestic and the foreign marginal propensities to save are $\gamma\delta$ and $\gamma\delta^*$, respectively. Hence these saving propensities are independent of the rate of interest and are constant over time. Substituting $\gamma\delta$ and $\gamma\delta^*$, respectively, for s_0 and s_1 and for s_0^* and s_1^* into the system (12.2) through (12.5), it is shown in the appendix that with zero initial debt, taxes, government spending, and stationary outputs,

$$\frac{dR_1}{dT_1} = -(1 - \gamma)\frac{(1 - \gamma\delta)R_1[R_0(R_1 - \gamma) + \gamma R_1]}{(R_1 - \gamma)^2 \gamma R_0 Q^3}, \tag{12.8}$$

where Q denotes world output net of government spending. Equation (12.8) shows that a *future* budget deficit arising from a tax cut in the near future $(dT_1 < 0)$, accompanied by a corresponding rise in taxes in the distant future, raises the *future* rate of interest.

The interpretation of the positive association between the budget deficit and the contemporaneous rate of interest is similar to the one presented in chapter 11. Accordingly, as long as γ falls short of unity, the tax cut in the near future raises wealth and creates an excess demand for goods in the near future (i.e., in the period in which the deficit occurs). To eliminate this excess demand, the future rate of interest (the rate of interest linking the near to the distant future) must rise according to equation (12.8).

Thus far we have examined the relation between future tax policies and the contemporaneous rates of interest. It is shown in the appendix that the effect of the change in future taxes on the current rate of interest is

$$\frac{dR_0}{dT_1} = (1 - \gamma)\frac{(1 - \gamma\delta)(1 - \gamma\delta^*)\gamma[R_0(R_1 - \gamma) + \gamma R_1]\lambda^*}{(R_1 - \gamma)^2 Q}(s - s^*), \tag{12.9}$$

where λ^* is the relative share of foreign output in world output. Equation (12.9) shows that the *effect* of a future budget deficit on the *current* one-period rate of interest depends on the relation between the domestic and the foreign saving propensities. If the foreign saving propensity exceeds the domestic propensity so that $s < s^*$, then the future budget deficit raises the current one-period rate of interest. The opposite holds if $s > s^*$.

In interpreting the impact of the future deficit on the current short-term interest rate, we note that in the present period no government action takes place and therefore the change in the current rate of interest results only from changes in world savings, which in turn stem only from changes in domestic and foreign wealth (since the intertemporal elasticities of substitution are assumed to equal unity). At the prevailing short-term interest rate, foreign wealth falls because of the heavier discounting of future incomes induced by the rise in the future rate of interest while the rise in domestic wealth consequent on the future budget deficit is mitigated by the rise in the future rate of interest. These changes in wealth lower the foreign demand for current goods and raise the domestic demand for these goods. The direction of the induced change in the current rate of interest depends on whether these changes in wealth raise or lower world savings at the prevailing current short-term rates of interest. It is shown in the appendix that once R_1 adjusts so as to clear the market for future goods, then at the prevailing current short-term rate of interest (i.e., for given R_0) the relative magnitude of the changes in domestic and foreign wealth depends on the difference between the saving propensities. If $s = s^*$, the levels of wealth change in opposite directions by the *same* absolute magnitude. In that case the future tax cut leaves *world* equilibrium wealth unchanged, even though it alters its international distribution. Since $s = s^*$, world savings in the current period remain intact, and therefore the prevailing current short-term rate of interest does not change. If, on the other hand, s exceeds s^*, then the rise in domestic current savings (consequent on the future budget deficit) exceeds the corresponding decline in foreign savings so that world saving rises. As a result the current short-term rate of interest falls. The opposite holds if the foreign saving propensity exceeds the domestic propensity so that $s < s^*$.

The foregoing analysis considered the bench-mark case in which, in both countries, the intertemporal elasticity of substitution was unity and, as a result, saving propensities are constant over time. In what follows we consider two additional cases characterized by time-varying saving propensities resulting from two extreme assumptions concerning the value of the domestic intertemporal elasticity of substitution. Accordingly, we consider on the one extreme the case in which the domestic elasticity of substitution is infinite and, on the other extreme, the case in which the domestic substitution elasticity is zero. Throughout the exposition we continue to assume that the foreign elasticity is unity. It is shown that the qualitative results and the general principles obtained for the intermediate case of a unit elasticity of substitution remain intact.

Consider first the case in which the domestic intertemporal elasticity of substitution is infinite. With perfect substitution the existing domestic population consume all their wealth in the first period if the subjective rate of discount exceeds the current rate of interest, that is, if δR_0 falls short of unity. In that case $s_0 = 0$. On the other hand, if δR_0 exceeds unity, domestic residents save all their current income so that $s_0 = 1$. In the subsequent period, if δR_1 falls short of unity, then the entire wealth is consumed in the near future so that $s_1 = 0$. We do not consider the third possibility that all consumption is postponed to the distant future (so that $s_0 = s_1 = 1$), with zero current and near-future consumption, since in this case the near-future budget deficit does not alter the world rates of interest linking the distant future with the other periods.

We start by examining the situation in which $s_0 = 0$ and, as before, $s_0^* = s_1^* = \gamma \delta^*$. Substituting these values into the equilibrium system (12.2) through (12.5), it can be shown that the effects of a near-future budget deficit on the future and current short-term rates of interest are

$$\frac{dR_1}{dT_1} = -(1-\gamma)\frac{R_1 - \gamma}{\gamma Q}, \tag{12.10}$$

$$\frac{dR_0}{dT_1} = -(1-\gamma)\frac{\gamma}{(R_1 - \gamma)Q}. \tag{12.11}$$

Equation (12.10) shows that the near-future budget deficit raises both the future and the current rates of interest.

Prior to interpreting these results, we proceeds by examining the situation in which $s_0 = 1$, $s_1 = 0$, and, as before, $s_0^* = s_1^* = \gamma \delta^*$. Using the equilibrium system (12.2) through (12.5), it can be shown that with these saving propensities the changes in the rates of interest are

$$\frac{dR_1}{dT_1} = -(1-\gamma)\frac{R_1^2}{R_0(R_1 - \gamma)K}, \tag{12.10a}$$

$$\frac{dR_0}{dT_1} = (1 - \gamma)\frac{\gamma R_1}{(R_1 - \gamma)^2 K}, \tag{12.11a}$$

where, as shown in the appendix, K is positive. Equations (12.10a) and (12.11a) show that the near-future budget deficit raises the future rate of interest and lowers the current rate of interest.

These results are similar to those derived previously for the bench-mark case in which the elasticity of substitution was unity. Accordingly, a tax cut occurring in the near-future period (i.e., $dT_1 <$ 0) raises the contemporaneous rate of interest. This is illustrated by equations (12.10) and (12.10a) which are the counterpart to equation (12.8) of the bench-mark case. On the other hand, equations (12.11) and (12.11a) illustrate the principle governing the effect of the future budget deficit on the current rate of interest. Thus, if in the current period the domestic saving propensity, s_0, is smaller than the foreign propensity, s_0^* (as is obviously the case if $s_0 = 0$ and $s_0^* = \gamma\delta^*$), then as illustrated by equation (12.11), the future budget deficit *raises* the current short-term rate of interest. If, on the other hand, the domestic saving propensity exceeds the foreign propensity (as is obviously the case if $s_0 = 1$ and $s_0^* = \gamma\delta^*$), then as illustrated by equation (12.11a), the future budget deficit lowers the current short-term rate of interest. As is evident, this critical role played by the relative magnitudes of the domestic and foreign current saving propensities for the case of domestic perfect substitutabily is also exhibited by equation (12.9) pertaining to the bench-mark case characterized by the unitary elasticity of substitution.

Consider next the other extreme case in which the domestic inter-temporal elasticity of substitution is zero. In that case the saving propensities in equations (12.6) and (12.7) become

$$s_0 = \frac{\gamma R_1}{R_0 R_1 + \gamma(R_1 - R_0)}, \tag{12.6a}$$

$$s_1 = \frac{\gamma}{R_1}. \tag{12.7a}$$

Substituting these values into the equilibrium system (12.2) through (12.5) and recalling that $s_0^* = s_1^* = \gamma\delta^*$, it can be shown that the effects of the future budget deficit on the future and current short-term rates of interest are

$$\frac{dR_1}{dT_1} = -(1 - \gamma)[\gamma\delta^*R_0^2(R_1 - \gamma) + \gamma^2R_1 + (1 - \gamma)v]J, \qquad (12.12)$$

$$\frac{dR_0}{dT_1} = (1 - \gamma)[(R_1 - R_0) + \gamma R_0(1 - \delta^*R_1)]J, \qquad (12.13)$$

where, as shown in the appendix, J and v are positive.

Equation (12.12) demonstrates that analogously to the previous bench-mark case shown in equation (12.8), a tax cut occurring in the near-future period (i.e., $dT_1 < 0$) raises the contemporaneous short-term rate of interest. Equation (12.13) shows that the direction of the change in the current short-term interest rate depends on whether the sum of $(R_1 - R_0)$ and $\gamma R_0(1 - \delta^*R_1)$ is positive or negative. In interpreting this result, it is convenient to consider the case in which in each period the domestic and the foreign saving propensities are equal to each other. In that case the sum of $(R_1 - R_0)$ and $\gamma R_0(1 - \delta^*R_1)$ is zero, and as seen from equation (12.13), the current short-term rate of interest does not change. To verify that the equality between the domestic and foreign current saving propensities implies that the future budget deficit does not alter R_0, suppose that $s_0 = s_0^*$ and that in each country the time profile of income is flat. In that case the time profile of consumption in each country is also flat. Equality between world spending and world income implies that in *each* country separately, income equals spending. The stationary path of foreign consumption implies that the rate of interest equals the foreign subjective rate of time preference or, equivalently, that $1 = \delta^*R_0$. In addition the equality between s_0 and s_0^* implies that $s_0 = \gamma\delta^*$. Using equation (12.6a), it follows that $\gamma\delta^*(R_1 - R_0) = R_1(1 - \delta^*R_0) = 0$, and hence the rate of interest does not change over time so that $R_1 = R_0$. This fixity of the short-term rate of interest implies that the foreign subjective rate of time preference also equals the future short-term rate of interest; that is, $1 = \delta^*R_1$. Therefore in this case the bracketed term in equation (12.13) is zero. It follows that if the domestic and the foreign saving propensities are equal to each other, then a future budget deficit does not alter the current short-term rate of interest. This result obtained for the case in which the domestic elasticity of substitution is zero also conforms with the one shown in equation (12.9) pertaining to the bench-mark case of a unitary elasticity of substitution.

We conclude this discussion by reiterating the results. An anticipated future budget deficit arising from a future tax cut accompanied by a subsequent tax hike raises the future rate of interest. On the other hand, the short-term rate of interest in the current period, a period during which no change in taxes takes place, may rise, remain unchanged, or fall. It was shown that a key factor determining the direction of the change in the current short-term rate of interest is the difference between the domestic and foreign (current) saving propensities. Specifically, as the manifestation of a transfer-problem criterion, the current rate of interest remains unchanged if the domestic and foreign saving propensities are equal to each other. Finally, the effects of budget deficits vanish in the extreme Ricardian case in which the individual horizon is infinite so that $\gamma = 1$, and as a result changes in the timing of taxes do not alter wealth.

12.2 Cumulative Budget Deficits and the Long-Run Rate of Interest

In this section we analyze the long-run effects of budget deficits on the world rate of interest. In general, in the absence of growth, if a steady-state equilibrium for the two-country world economy exists, then the equilibrium rate of interest lies in between the two countries' subjective rates of time preference. On the other hand, if such a steady state does not exist, then in the long run one of the two countries comprises the world economy as a whole and the long-run rate of interest equals its rate of time preference. In the latter case cumulative budget deficits during the transition to the long run obviously do not influence the long-run rate of interest. Therefore we focus in this section on the first case in which the world economy is not reduced in the long run to a closed-economy one-country world. Hence we examine the effects of cumulative budget deficits on the *steady-state* world rate of interest.

To gain insights into the factors governing the steady-state equilibrium, we recall that in the domestic economy at each point in time there are γ^t individuals of age t, and therefore the size of the domestic population is $1/(1 - \gamma)$. The (constant) steady-state value of per-capita disposable income is $(Y - T)$. Each individual is born with no debt, and therefore at birth the individual's wealth consists only of the properly discounted value of lifetime disposable income. In the steady state, with constant interest rate, the wealth of each individual at birth is $w_0 = [R/(R - \gamma)](Y - T)$, where $R - 1$ is the constant steady-state rate of interest, r. At age t the individual's wealth, w_t, is related to his initial wealth, w_0, through the ratio of the saving propensity, s, to the effective discount factor, γ/R. Thus $w_t = (Rs/\gamma)^t w_0$, and correspondingly the wealth of all individuals of age t equals $(Rs)^t w_0$. The assumption that the steady state exists implies that Rs is smaller than unity. Summing over all ages (from zero to infinity), the value of *aggregate* wealth is $\overline{W} = \sum_{t=0}^{\infty} (Rs)^t w_0 = [1/(1 - Rs)]w_0$. Using the preceding expression for w_0, the steady-state level of aggregate domestic consumption $(1 - s)\overline{W}$ is

$$\overline{C} = \frac{1 - s}{1 - Rs} \frac{R}{R - \gamma}(Y - T), \tag{12.14}$$

where $\overline{C}$ denotes the steady-state level of aggregate consumption, $Y - T$ is the steady-state level of per-capita disposable income, and s is the steady-state marginal (and average) propensity to save out of wealth, which, using equation (10.9), can be written as

$$s = \gamma\delta^\sigma R^{\sigma-1}. \tag{12.15}$$

Equation (12.14) is the aggregate analogue to the per-capita steady-state consumption of equation (10.23). Thus the steady-state marginal (and average) propensity to consume out of disposable income is a function of the rate of interest $f(R)$, where

$$f(R) = \frac{1 - \gamma\delta^\sigma R^{\sigma-1}}{1 - \gamma\delta^\sigma R^\sigma} \frac{R}{R - \gamma}. \tag{12.16}$$

Using a similar procedure and denoting the foreign variables by an asterisk, the steady-state level of aggregate foreign consumption is

$$\bar{C}^* = \frac{1 - s^*}{1 - Rs^*} \frac{R}{R - \gamma^*} (Y^* - T^*), \tag{12.17}$$

and the steady-state foreign saving propensity out of wealth is

$$s^* = \gamma^* \delta^{*\sigma^*} R^{\sigma^*-1}, \tag{12.18}$$

where the assumption that the steady state exists implies that Rs^* is smaller than unity. By analogy to equation (12.16), the steady-state foreign propensity to consume out of disposable income is $f^*(R)$, where

$$f^*(R) = \frac{1 - \gamma^* \delta^{*\sigma^*} R^{\sigma^*-1}}{1 - \gamma^* \delta^{*\sigma^*} R^{\sigma^*}} \frac{R}{R - \gamma^*}. \tag{12.19}$$

World equilibrium requires that the sum of domestic and foreign aggregate consumption equals the level of world aggregate output net of governments' spending. Using equations (12.14) through (12.19), the steady-state equilibrium condition is

$$f(R)(Y - T) + f^*(R)(Y^* - T^*) = \frac{Y - G}{1 - \gamma} + \frac{Y^* - G^*}{1 - \gamma^*}, \tag{12.20}$$

where, as before, $Y - G$ denotes domestic per-capita aggregate output net of government spending so that its product with the domestic population size $1/(1 - \gamma)$ yields the corresponding aggregate quantity; a similar interpretation applies to the foreign aggregate quantity $(Y^* - G^*)/(1 - \gamma^*)$.

Equilibrium also requires that both governments be solvent, and thus that in each country the value of government debt equals the sum of the present values of current and future budget surpluses. Thus

$$(T - G) = (R - 1)B^g \tag{12.21}$$

and

$$(T^* - G^*) = (R - 1)B^{g^*}. \tag{12.22}$$

For given values of government debt, B^g and B^{g^*} (which reflect past budget deficits), and for given steady-state values of per-capita government spending, G and G^*, the system (12.20) through (12.22) along with (12.16) and (12.19) can be used to obtain the solutions for the equilibrium steady-state values of the world rate of interest, $R - 1$, and of domestic and foreign per-capita taxes, T and T^*. Finally, the assumption that the steady state exists for the two-country world economy implies that both Rs and Rs^* are smaller than unity. Hence, using equations (12.15) and (12.18) for s and s^*, it follows that in the steady state

$$R < \delta^{-1} \gamma^{-1/\sigma}$$

and   (12.23)

$$R < (\delta^*)^{-1} (\gamma^*)^{-1/\sigma^*}.$$

It is relevant to note that if $\gamma = \gamma^* = 1$, steady-state equilibrium with positive levels of consumption in both countries requires that $\delta = \delta^*$. In that case the equilibrium rate of interest, $R - 1$, equals the common value of the subjective discount rates, $(1 - \delta)/\delta$.

We now examine the effects of past cumulative budget deficits on the long-run values of the rate of interest. A higher cumulative value of past budget deficits in the home country is reflected in a higher steady-state value of government debt, B^g. By differentiating equation (12.20) using the domestic government budget constraint (12.21) and evaluating the derivative around the point of balanced budgets (so that initially $B^g = 0$), we obtain

$$\frac{dR}{dB^g} = \frac{f(R)(R - 1)}{(Y - G)f'(R) + (Y^* - G^*)f^{*\prime}(R)},$$ (12.24)

where $f'(R)$ and $f^{*\prime}(R)$ denote, respectively, the derivative of the domestic and foreign steady-state propensities to consume with respect to the world rate of interest. Inspection of equations (12.16) and (12.19) reveals that the signs of these derivatives are ambiguous. Therefore the effects of a rise in cumulative budget deficits on the long-run rate of interest are not clear cut. The lack of a clear-cut relation between the long-run rate of interest and the size of public debt stems from the fact that a rise in the rate of interest does not exert a clear-cut effect on the steady-state propensities to consume (out of disposable income). Specifically, from equation (12.16) it can be shown that the sign of $f'(R)$ is the same as the sign of h, where

$$h = \sigma s(R - 1)(R - \gamma) + \gamma(1 - Rs)[(\delta R)^{\sigma} - 1]. \qquad (12.25)$$

As examples illustrating the ambiguity of the sign of $f'(R)$, suppose first that δR exceeds unity (so that the world rate of interest exceeds the domestic subjective rate of time preference). In that case $f'(R)$ is positive. As a second example, on the other hand, suppose that the elasticity of substitution, σ, is unitary and δR^2 is smaller than unity. In that case $f'(R)$ is negative. These examples can now be used to illustrate the ambiguity underlying the sign of dR/dB^g in equation (12.24). Accordingly, suppose that the foreign elasticity of substitution is zero. This assumption implies that $f^{*\prime}(R)$ is also zero, and therefore the sign of dR/dB^g depends only on the sign of $f'(R)$. Thus in the first example (for which $\delta R > 1$) a rise in B^g raises the long-run rate of interest, whereas in the second example (for which $\sigma = 1$ and $\delta R^2 < 1$) the same rise in B^g lowers the long-run rate of interest.

It is relevant to note that the short-term effects of budget deficits and the steady-state effects of cumulative deficits are governed by mechanisms that are fundamentally different from each other. In the short run the reduction in taxes raises wealth of the existing population and thereby creates an excess demand for present goods. Market clearing necessitates a rise in the relative price of present in terms of future goods, and thus the rate of interest rises.

On the other hand, when comparing two alternative steady states, the one with a larger government debt (past cumulative deficits) must have higher taxes in order to service the debt. To compensate for the fall in private demand induced by the higher taxes, market clearing necessitates a change in the steady-state rate of interest so as to stimulate steady-state consumption. Depending on the sensitivity of domestic and foreign steady-state consumption to the rate of interest, the latter may rise or fall.

12.3 Government Spending and the Term Structure of Interest Rates

The foregoing analysis dealt with dynamic aspects of tax policies. Throughout it was assumed that the path of government spending was given. In this section we relax this assumption and examine the dynamic effects of government spending on the path of the short- and long-term rates of interest. By focusing on the time path of the rate of interest, we extend the analysis contained in chapter 11 in which, in order to collapse the entire future into a single period, we employed the constancy-equivalent interest rate. This procedure permitted a complete specification of the impact of policies on the current values of the key variables. However, it did not permit a detailed examination of the impact of policies on the paths of the various variables *within* the consolidated future. Since the transmission mechanism operates through the rates of interest, it is instructive to analyze in further detail the impact of government spending on the entire path of these rates. For that purpose we need to return to the complete disaggregated system. To simplify the exposition, we illustrate the analysis with the aid of the bench-mark model in which intertemporal elasticities of substitution are unity. Furthermore, since the qualitative results of the impact of government spending do not depend on the finiteness of the horizon, we assume henceforth that $\gamma = \gamma^* = 1$. As a result the domestic and foreign saving propensities are δ and δ^*, respectively, and the market rates of interest equal the effective rates.

The equilibrium of the world economy is specified in equations (12.26) through (12.29):

$$(1 - \delta)W_0 + (1 - \delta^*)W_0^* = (Y_0 - G_0) + (Y_0^* + G_0^*), \qquad (12.26)$$

$$(1 - \delta)\delta^t W_0 + (1 - \delta^*)\delta^{*t} W_0^* = \alpha_t[(Y_t - G_t)$$

$$+ (Y_t^* - G_t^*)], \quad \text{for } t = 1, 2, \ldots, \qquad (12.27)$$

$$W_0 = \sum_{t=0}^{\infty} \alpha_t(Y_t - G_t) - (1 + r_{-1})B_{-1}, \qquad (12.28)$$

$$W_0^* = \sum_{t=0}^{\infty} \alpha_t(Y_t^* - G_t^*) + (1 + r_{-1})B_{-1}. \qquad (12.29)$$

Equation (12.26) is the requirement that current world demand equals current world output net of government spending. Equation (12.27) corresponds to the same requirement applicable to each future period ($t = 1, 2, \ldots$). In that equation the terms $(\delta^t/\alpha_t)W_0$ and $(\delta^{*t}/\alpha_t)W_0^*$

designate the values of domestic and foreign wealth in period t, and their product with the consumption propensity yields the level of spending. The domestic consumption function is consistent with the one presented in equation (10.9) for the case in which $\sigma = 1$ and $s_0 = \delta$; the foreign consumption function is derived analogously. Equations (12.28) and (12.29) define the equilibrium values of current domestic and foreign wealth. In this specification we substitute goverment spending, G_t and G_t^*, for taxes, T_t and T_t^*, by using the government solvency requirement, and we substitute the value of the initial external debt, B_{-1}, for the sum of the initial values of private and government debt. This system can be solved for the equilibrium values of W_0 and W_0^* and for the present-value factors α_t ($t = 1, 2, \ldots$). From these present-value factors we can then derive the entire path of the equilibrium rates of interest. Obviously, by Walras's law one of the equations in the system can be omitted.

Using this system, the solution for the equilibrium present-value factor is given by

$$\alpha_t = \frac{(\delta^{*t}\sum_{\tau=0}^{\infty}\delta^{\tau}\lambda_{\tau}^* + \delta^t\sum_{\tau=0}^{\infty}\delta^{*\tau}\lambda_{\tau})Q_0 + (\delta^{*t} - \delta^t)(1 + r_{-1})B_{-1}}{(\sum_{\tau=0}^{\infty}\delta^t\lambda_{\tau}^* + \sum_{\tau=0}^{\infty}\delta^{*\tau}\lambda_{\tau})Q_t},$$

(12.30)

where Q_t denotes world output net of government spending in period t—that is, $Q_t = (Y_t - G_t) + (Y_t^* - G_t^*)$, ($t = 0, 1, 2, \ldots$)— and where λ_t denotes the relative share of domestic output net of government spending in Q_t—that is, $\lambda_t = (Y_t - G_t)/Q_t$; analogously, λ_t^* denotes the corresponding foreign share—that is, $\lambda_t^* = (Y_t^* - G_t^*)/Q_t = 1 - \lambda_t$.

We turn to an analysis of the role of the timing of government spending on the term structure as well as on the time path of the rates of interest. Some of the derivations are based on the appendix. We distinguish between transitory and permanent changes, and thereby highlight the dynamic effects of government spending. For this purpose we define the current long-term rate of interest linking the present period with a future period, t, by r_{0t} and recall that the present-value factor, α_t, linking period t with the current period is the compounding of one period discount factors from the present period up to period t; that is, $\alpha_t = [(1 + r_0)(1 + r_1)\ldots(1 + r_{t-1})]^{-1}$. It follows that the long-term rate of interest can be expressed in terms of the present-value factor according to

$$R_{0t} = \alpha_t^{-1/t}, \tag{12.31}$$

where $R_{0t} = 1 + r_{0t}$.

We first examine the effects of fiscal spending on the term structure of interest rates prevailing in the current period (period zero). Consider a *transitory* rise in government spending that takes place in the *current* period. The effect of this change in policy on the term structure of interest rates prevailing in period zero can be obtained from the system (12.26) through (12.29) using the transformation in equation (12.31) (alternatively, this effect could be derived directly from equations 12.30 and 12.31). For ease of exposition we evaluate the various expression around an initial flat time profile of output net of government spending (so that $Q_t = Q$ and $\lambda_t = \lambda$). Accordingly,

$$\frac{dr_{0t}}{dG_0} = \frac{(1 - \delta)(1 - \lambda^*\delta^*)\delta^* + (1 - \delta^*)\lambda^*\delta\delta^{*t}}{(1 - \lambda\delta - \lambda^*\delta^*)\varepsilon_t Q}, \tag{12.32}$$

where $\varepsilon_t = t\alpha_t^{(1+t)/t}$.

As is evident, the right-hand side of equation (12.32) is positive since the term $\lambda\delta + \lambda^*\delta^*$ in the denominator is a weighted average of the subjective discount factors which is smaller than unity. Thus the current transitory rise in government spending raises the entire term structure of interest rates. This rise in the intertemporal relative price of present goods in terms of goods in all other periods is necessary in order to eliminate the excess demand for present goods induced by the current fiscal expansion.

Suppose now that the *transitory* rise in government spending does not occur in the present period but is expected to take place in a *future* period (period s). To determine the impact of this (expected) future policy on the term structure of interest rates prevailing at period zero, we first compute the change in the long-term rate of interest linking the current period with the period in which the fiscal expansion is expected to occur (i.e, period s). Using a similar procedure, we obtain

$$\frac{dr_{0s}}{dG_s} = -\frac{(1-\delta)(1-\delta^*)\alpha_s}{\varepsilon_s Q(1-\lambda\delta-\lambda^*\delta^*)}\left\{\frac{\lambda^*[1-(1-\delta)\delta^s]}{1-\delta}\right.$$

$$+ \left.\frac{1-\lambda^*[1-(1-\delta^*)\delta^{*s}]}{1-\delta^*}\right\}.$$ (12.33)

Equation (12.33) shows a fall in the long-term rate of interest that links the present with the future period in which the transitory fiscal expansion occurs.

We proceed by computing the effect of this transitory rise in government spending on the rates of interest linking the present with all other future periods (other than period s). In this way we obtain the effect of this fiscal change on the entire term structure of interest rates. Accordingly,

$$\frac{dr_{0t}}{dG_s} = \frac{(1-\delta)(1-\delta^*)\lambda^*\alpha_s}{\varepsilon_s Q(1-\lambda\delta-\lambda^*\delta^*)}(\delta^t - \delta^{*t}), \quad \text{for } t \neq s \neq 0.$$ (12.34)

Equation (12.34) shows that the entire term structure of the rates of interest, short- and long-term rates (other than the rate for the particular maturity, r_{0s}) changes in the *same direction*. These rates of interest rise if the domestic marginal propensity to save exceeds the corresponding foreign propensity, and vice versa. The interpretation of this result is given in terms of the familiar transfer-problem criteria. Hence the fall in domestic wealth and the rise in foreign wealth (arising from the change in G_s and r_{0s}) imply that at the prevailing rates of interest for all other maturities ($t \neq s$), the difference between δ and δ^* determines whether world savings is negative or positive, and therefore whether r_{0t} must rise or fall.

The foregoing discussion of the effects of a transitory rise in government spending on the term structure of interest rates is illustrated in figures 12.1 and 12.2 which correspond, respectively, to the cases in which δ exceeds or falls short of δ^*. As seen, a future transitory rise in government spending (which is expected to occur in period $s = 10$) lowers the long-term rate of interest linking the present period with period s. This drop is represented by the move from points A to B in figures 12.1 and 12.2. For all other periods the figures show that the entire term structure of interest rates goes up

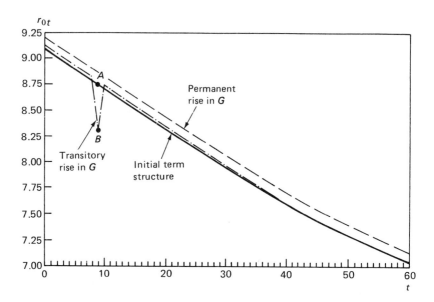

Figure 12.1
The effects of a permanent and transitory rise in government spending in period $t = 10$ on the term structure of interest rates. Data: $\delta = 0.95 > \delta^* = 0.90$, $\lambda_t = \lambda$.

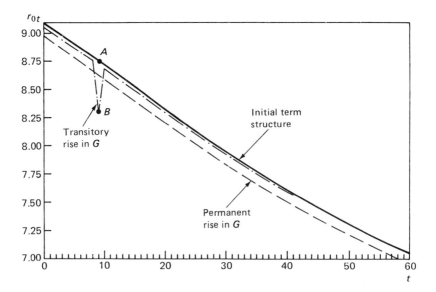

Figure 12.2
The effects of a permanent and transitory rise in government spending in period $t = 10$ on the term structure of interest rates. Data: $\delta = 0.90 < \delta^* = 0.95$, $\lambda_t = \lambda$.

if δ exceeds δ^*, and it goes down if δ falls short of δ^*. In both cases the difference between the new and the old term structure of interest rates diminishes with the term of maturity.

Up to this point we have examined the effects of current and future transitory changes in government spending on the term structure of the rate of interest. We complete this analysis by examining the effects of a *permanent* rise in government spending. Assuming for simplicity that the initial debt position is zero, we note that with a flat time profile of output net of government spending, the equilibrium present-value factor in equation (12.30) can be written as

$$\alpha_t = \frac{\lambda(1 - \delta)\delta^t + \lambda^*(1 - \delta^*)\delta^{*t}}{\lambda(1 - \delta) + \lambda^*(1 - \delta^*)}. \tag{12.30a}$$

Differentiating equation (12.30a) with respect to the level of government spending, G, using the definitions of λ and λ^*, and the transformation in equation (12.31) yields

$$\frac{dr_{0t}}{dG} = \frac{(1 - \delta)(1 - \delta^*)\lambda^*}{\varepsilon_t Q(1 - \lambda\delta - \lambda^*\delta^*)}(\delta^t - \delta^{*t}). \tag{12.35}$$

Equation (12.35) shows that the permanent rise in government spending moves the entire term structure of interest rates in the same direction. If the domestic propensity to save exceeds the foreign propensity, then the rates of interest for all maturities rise, and vice versa. This result, which is also exhibited in figures 12.1 and 12.2, is the analogue to the one obtained in chapter 11 in which the entire future was aggregated into a single period. As before, the dependence of the result on the difference between the domestic and foreign propensity to save can be interpreted in terms of a transfer-problem criterion.

Having analyzed the factors governing the term structure of interest rates prevailing in the current period, we proceed to analyze the effects of transitory and permanent changes in government spending on the *time path* of the *short-term* rates of interest. To avoid repetition, we note that the effects of government spending on the short-term rate of interest in period zero have already been specified in the previous analysis. Therefore, in what follows, we consider the short-term rates of interest prevailing in future periods.

Using the same procedure as before, and recalling that by definition $r_s = (\alpha_s/\alpha_{s+1}) - 1$, the effect of a transitory rise in government spending (occurring in a future period s) on the contemporaneous short-term rate of interest, r_s, is

$$\frac{dr_s}{dG_s} = \frac{[1 - (1 - \delta - \delta r_s)(1 - \delta)\delta^2](1 + r_s)}{(1 - \lambda\delta - \lambda^*\delta^*)Q}$$

$$\times [\lambda(1 - \delta) + \lambda^*(1 - \delta^*)], \quad \text{for } t = s. \tag{12.36}$$

Equation (12.36) shows that the rise in government spending raises the contemporaneous short-term rate of interest. This result is similar to the one obtained in chapter 11. Accordingly, the excess demand stemming from the rise in government spending in period s is eliminated through a rise in the intertemporal price of goods in period s relative to goods in the subsequent period, $s + 1$.

The effects of the transitory future rise in government spending on the short-term rates of interest prevailing in periods other than the contemporaneous one is obtained in a similar manner. Accordingly,

$$\frac{dr_t}{dG_s} = A\alpha_s(\delta - \delta^*), \quad \text{for } t \neq s, t \neq s - 1, \tag{12.37}$$

where

$$A = \frac{\lambda^*(1 - \delta)(1 - \delta^*)[\lambda(1 - \delta) + \lambda^*(1 - \delta^*)]\delta^t\delta^{*t}}{(1 - \lambda\delta - \lambda^*\delta^*)\alpha_{t+1}Q[\lambda(1 - \delta)\delta^{t+1} + \lambda^*(1 - \delta^*)\delta^{*t+1}]} > 0.$$

Thus, analogously to the effects on the long-term rates of interest shown in equation (12.34), the direction of the change in the short-term rates in all periods other than period s (and the period immediately preceding it) depends on the difference between the domestic and foreign propensities to save. If δ exceeds δ^*, then the short-term rates of interest rise in all other periods.

This case is illustrated in figure 12.3 in which it is shown that the transitory rise in government spending in period $s = 10$ raises the short-term rate of interest prevailing in period s (from point A to point B) as well as in all other periods (except for the one immediately preceding period s in which the short-term rate of interest falls

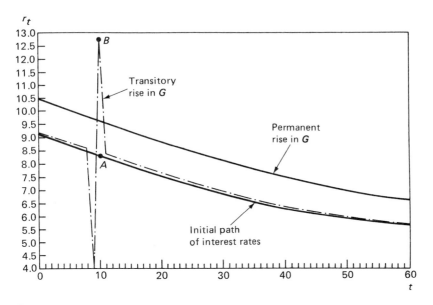

Figure 12.3
The effects of a permanent and transitory rise in government spending in period $t = 10$ on the path of the short-term interest rates. Data: $\delta = 0.95 > \delta^* = 0.90$, $\lambda_t = \lambda$.

sharply). If, on the other hand, δ falls short of δ^*, then the rates of interest in periods other than s falls. This case is illustrated in figure 12.4 in which the short-term rates of interest fall in all other periods (in this case, for the period immediately preceeding period s, the fall in the short-term rate of interest is especially pronounced).

For completeness we also compute the effect of a permanent rise in government spending on the entire time path of the short-term rates of interest. Using a similar procedure and recalling that $dG = dG_t$, it can be shown that

$$\frac{dr_t}{dG} = \frac{A}{(1 - \lambda\delta - \lambda^*\delta^*)}(\delta - \delta^*). \tag{12.38}$$

Thus, as indicated in chapter 11, in the context of a two-period analysis, equation (12.38) shows that depending on whether the domestic propensity to save exceeds or falls short of the corresponding foreign propensity, the entire path of the short-term rates of

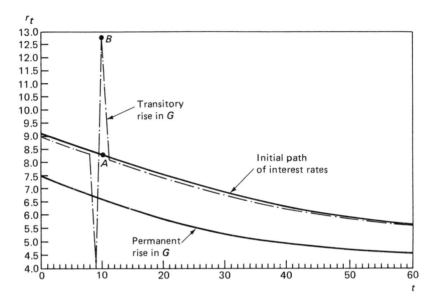

Figure 12.4
The effects of a permanent and transitory rise in government spending in period
$t = 10$ on the path of the short-term interest rates. Data: $\delta = 0.90 < \delta^* = 0.95$,
$\lambda_t = \lambda$.

interest rises or falls. This pattern is also exhibited in figures 12.3 and
12.4. As seen (except for periods s and $s - 1$), the change in the
short-term rates of interest induced by the permanent rise in government spending exceeds the change induced by the transitory rise in
spending (occurring in period s).

The interpretation of this result is similar to the one given previously. Accordingly, the reduction in net domestic output (net
of government spending) alters domestic savings in period t by
$-[dG - (1 - \delta)\,dW_t]$. At the prevailing rates of interest, with a flat
time path of net output, the percentage change in domestic net
output, denoted by μ where $\mu = -dG/(Y - G)$, equals the percentage change in domestic wealth, $-dW_t/W_t$. In that case the incipient
change in domestic savings is $-\mu[(Y - G) - (1 - \delta)W_t]$, where
the term in the brackets measures the value of domestic savings.
Clearly, at the prevailing rates of interest foreign savings do not
change. As is evident, domestic savings are positive if the domestic

marginal propensity to save exceeds the foreign propensity, that is, if $\delta > \delta^*$ (in that case equilibrium requires that initially foreign savings were negative). Conversely, if $\delta < \delta^*$, domestic savings are negative. Thus the permanent rise in domestic fiscal spending lowers world savings and induces a rise in the rates of interest if $\delta > \delta^*$, and vice versa.

12.4 Summary

The analysis in this chapter focused on dynamic aspects of the effects of tax policies and government spending on the equilibrium levels of world rates of interest. We began the analysis by examining the effects of an expected future budget deficit. This deficit arises from an expected cut in future taxes that is financed by a corresponding tax hike in the subsequent future. It was shown that as long as the path of government spending remains intact, such a change in the time profile of future taxes raises the (average of) future rates of interest.

We designed this experiment so as to ensure that in the current period no change in policy occurs. However, the expected future policies alter the current behavior of the forward-looking individuals. As a result the expected future budget deficit may influence the current short-term rate of interest. Our analysis showed that a key factor determining the direction of the change in the current short-term rate of interest is the difference between the domestic and foreign marginal propensities to save. Specifically, in the borderline case in which these two saving propensities are equal to each other, the future budget deficit does not influence the equilibrium value of the current short-term world rate of interest. The analysis suggests the following principle governing the change in the current short-term rate of interest: a future budget deficit raises the current short-term rate of interest if the foreign saving propensity exceeds the corresponding domestic propensity, and vice versa. Stated differently, if the country introducing the future budget deficit runs a deficit in the current account of its balance of payments (so that it is a net dissaver in the world economy), then the current short-term world rate of interest rises. However, if the country runs a surplus in its current account, then the short-term rate of interest falls.

The analysis of the dynamic effects of budget deficits was completed by considering the long-run effects of cumulative budget deficits. Cumulative budget deficits raise the size of the long-run public debt and, as long as government spending does not change, necessitate a corresponding rise in taxes to service the debt. These changes influence the long-run rate of interest through mechanisms that differ fundamentally from those operating in the short run. In addition we showed that the direction of the change in the long-run rate of interest is not clear cut. On the one hand, at unchanged rates of interest, the rise in taxes lowers disposable income and thereby lowers wealth and spending in the long run. This change in spending creates an excess supply of goods that must be offset through an equilibrium change in the long-run rate of interest designed to stimulate long-run spending. The effects of the rate of interest on the long-run level of spending operate through several channels that may exert confliciting influences on spending. The lower rate of interest influences the level of steady-state wealth and spending by altering the rate at which wealth is accumulated through savings. Further, depending on the properties of the saving function, the lower rate of interest may raise or lower the propensity to save out of steady-state wealth. These conflicting effects of the rate of interest on long-run spending imply that the direction of the change in the long-run rate of interest necessary to eliminate the excess supply, induced by the higher level of long-run taxes, is not clear cut.

The chapter concluded with a more detailed analysis of the effects of government spending on the structure of world rates of interest. In this context we examined the effects of transitory (current or future) and permanent changes in government spending on the term structure of interest rates as well as on the time path of short-term rates of interest. It was shown that a transitory rise in government spending occurring in the present period raises the entire term structure of interest rates. If the transitory rise in government spending is expected to occur in a future period, then the rate of interest linking the present period with the period in which the expansion takes place falls. At the same time the rates of interest linking the present with all other future periods rise if the domestic saving propensity exceeds the foreign propensity, whereas these rates of interest fall if the opposite holds. The same saving-propensity condition governs the direction of the change in the rates of interest for all maturities if the rise in current government spending is permanent rather than transitory.

Concerning the effects of government spending on the time path of short-term rates of interest, we showed that a transitory rise in government spending raises the contemporaneous short-term rate of interest, although its effect on short-term rates in all other periods depends on the saving-propensity condition. As with the term structure, the same saving-propensity condition determines the direction of the change in short-term rates of interest in all periods if the current rise in government spending is permanent rather than transitory.

12.5 Appendix A: Effects of Near-Future Budget Deficits

In this appendix we derive some of the expressions presented in the text.

Case 1: $\sigma = \sigma^* = 1$ $(s_0 = s_1 = \gamma\delta, s_0^* = s_1^* = \gamma\delta^*)$

Differentiating the system (12.2) through (12.5) of the text and evaluating the solutions around an initial equilibrium with zero debt, taxes, government spending, and stationary outputs yields

$$\frac{dR_1}{dT_1} = -\frac{(1-\gamma)}{A}\frac{(1-\gamma\delta)\gamma R_1 J}{R_0^2(R_1-\gamma)^2} < 0, \tag{A.1}$$

$$\frac{dR_0}{dT_1} = \frac{(1-\gamma)}{A}\frac{(1-\gamma\delta)(1-\gamma\delta^*)\gamma^3 R_1 Y^*}{R_0(R_1-\gamma)^3}(s-s^*) \gtrless 0, \tag{A.2}$$

$$\frac{dW_0}{dT_1} = -(1-\gamma)\frac{\gamma R_1(1-\gamma\delta^*)Y^*}{R_0(R_1-\gamma)[(1-\gamma\delta)Y+(1-\gamma\delta^*)Y^*]} < 0, \tag{A.3}$$

$$\frac{dW_0^*}{dT_1} = (1-\gamma)\frac{\gamma R_1(1-\gamma\delta)Y^*}{R_0(R_1-\gamma)[(1-\gamma\delta)Y+(1-\gamma\delta^*)Y^*]} > 0, \tag{A.4}$$

where

$$A = [(1 - \gamma\delta)Y + (1 - \gamma\delta^*)Y^*]\frac{\gamma^2}{R_0^2(R_1 - \gamma)^2}$$

$$\times \{(1 - \gamma\delta)[\gamma\delta(R_0R_1 + \gamma R_1 - \gamma R_0) + (1 - \gamma)R_1]Y$$

$$+ (1 - \gamma\delta^*)[\gamma\delta^*(R_0R_1 + \gamma R_1 - \gamma R_0) + (1 - \gamma)R_1]Y^*\} > 0$$

and

$$J = (1 - \gamma\delta)[(1 - \gamma)R_1 + \gamma\delta R_0(R_1 - \gamma) + \gamma^2\delta R_1]Y$$

$$+ (1 - \gamma\delta^*)[(1 - \gamma)R_1 + \gamma\delta^* R_0(R_1 - \gamma) + \gamma^2\delta R_1]Y^* > 0.$$

To obtain the solutions presented in the text, we manipulate equations (A.1) through (A.4) as follows. First, from equations (12.2), (12.4), and (12.5), together with the assumptions that initially debt, government spending, and taxes are zero and that outputs are stationary, we obtain

$$(1 - \gamma\delta)Y + (1 - \gamma\delta^*)Y^* = \frac{R_0(R_1 - \gamma)}{R_0(R_1 - \gamma) + \gamma R_1}(Y + Y^*). \qquad (A.5)$$

Second, from equations (12.3) through (12.5), together with the same assumptions, we obtain

$$[\gamma\delta R_0(R_1 - \gamma) + (1 - \gamma)R_1 + \gamma^2\delta R_1](1 - \gamma\delta)Y$$

$$+ [\gamma\delta^* R_0(R_1 - \gamma) + (1 - \gamma)R_1 + \gamma^2\delta^* R_1](1 - \gamma\delta^*)Y^*$$

$$= (R_1 - \gamma)(Y + Y^*). \qquad (A.6)$$

Substituting (A.5) and (A.6) into (A.1) and (A.2) and recalling that $\gamma\delta^* = s^*$ yields equations (12.8) and (12.9) of the text.

We now show that once R_1 adjusts so as to clear the market for future goods, then, at the prevailing current short-term rate of interest (i.e., for given R_0), the direction of change in world savings depend only on the saving-propensity condition. For this purpose we use the system (12.3) through (12.5) of the text and ignore the current-period equation (12.2). Using this subsystem and solving for dW_0/dT_1 and for dW_0^*/dT_1, we obtain

$$\frac{dW_0}{dT_1} + \frac{dW_0^*}{dT_1}$$

$$= \frac{\gamma^2(1 - \gamma)Y^*(1 + s + s^*)}{R_0(R_1 - \gamma)\{(\gamma s^* + 1 - \gamma)Y^* + [\gamma s + (1 - \gamma)]\}Y}(s - s^*).$$

(A.7)

Equation (A.7) show that if $s > s^*$, then world wealth rises, and vice versa. It also shows that if $s = s^*$, then current world savings remains unchanged, and thereby R_0 need not change. Similar reasoning shows that if $s > s^*$, then $(s\,dW_0 + s^*\,dW_0^*)/dT_1 > 0$. To eliminate the rise in savings, R_0 must fall. The opposite holds if $s < s^*$. This rationalizes the sign of dR_0/dT_1 in equaton (A.2) which corresponds to equation (12.9).

Case 2: $\sigma = \infty$ (the case with $s_0 = 1, s_1 = 0$) and $\sigma^* = 1$ $(s_0^* = s_1^* = \gamma\delta^*)$

The solutions obtained from the system (12.2) through (12.5) summarized in equations (12.10a) and (12.11a) are

$$\frac{dR_1}{dT_1} = -(1 - \gamma)\frac{R_1^2}{R_0(R_1 - \gamma)K} < 0,$$

(A.8)

$$\frac{dR_0}{dT_1} = (1 - \gamma)\frac{\gamma R_1}{(R_1 - \gamma)^2 K} > 0,$$

(A.9)

where

$$K = \gamma Y_0 + \left[\frac{R_1}{R_0(R_1 - \gamma)^2}(1 + \gamma(R_0 - 1)) + \gamma\frac{R_1}{R_1 - \gamma}\right]\gamma Y$$

$$+ [(1 - \gamma\delta^*)(R_1 - \gamma)(R_0 + \gamma) + \gamma(1 - \gamma\delta^*)](1 - \gamma\delta^*)Y^* > 0$$

Case 3: $\sigma = 0$ and $\sigma^* = 1$ $(s_0 = \gamma R_1/[R_0 R_1 + \gamma(R_1 - R_0)]$, $s_1 = \gamma/R_1, s_0^* = s_1^* = \gamma\delta^*)$

The solutions obtained from the system (12.2) through (12.5) summarized in equations (12.12) and (12.13) are

$$\frac{dR_1}{dT_1} = -(1 - \gamma)[\gamma\delta^* R_0^2(R_1 - \gamma) + \gamma^2 R_1 + (1 - \gamma)v]J < 0, \quad \text{(A.10)}$$

$$\frac{dR_0}{dT_1} = (1 - \gamma)[(R_1 - R_0) + \gamma R_0(1 - \delta^* R_1)]J \gtrless 0, \quad \text{(A.11)}$$

where

$$J = \frac{R_1(1 - \gamma\delta^*)(R_1 - \gamma)^2}{\gamma(1 - \gamma\delta^*)^2[\gamma\delta^* v + (1 - \gamma)R_1]v Y^{*2}} > 0$$

and

$$v = R_0 R_1 + \gamma(R_1 - R_0) > 0.$$

12.6 Appendix B: Effects of Government Spending

Transitory Government Spending

Differentiating equations (12.26), (12.27), and (12.29) (omitting equation 12.28 by Walras's law) with respect to G_0 and evaluating the solutions around an initial flat time path of output net of government spending, the effects of a *current* transitory rise in government spending are

$$\frac{d\alpha_t}{dG_0} = -\frac{(1 - \delta)(1 - \delta^*\lambda^*)\delta^t + (1 - \delta^*)\delta\lambda^*\delta^{*t}}{(1 - \delta)(1 - \delta^*)\Delta Q} < 0, \quad \text{(A.12)}$$

$$\frac{dW_0}{dG_0} = -\frac{1 - \delta^*\lambda^*}{(1 - \delta)(1 - \delta^*)\Delta} < 0, \quad \text{(A.13)}$$

$$\frac{dW_0^*}{dG_0} = -\frac{\lambda^*\delta}{(1 - \delta)(1 - \delta^*)\Delta} < 0, \quad \text{(A.14)}$$

where

$$\Delta = \frac{1 - \lambda\delta - \lambda^*\delta^*}{(1 - \delta)(1 - \delta^*)} > 0.$$

Similarly, suppose now that the transitory change in fiscal spending is expected to take place in the future (i.e., $s \neq 0$). To solve for the effect of dG_s on the path of the present-value factors, α_t, we first differentiate equation (12.27) and use (12.28) of the text to obtain

$$\frac{d\alpha_t}{dG_s} = (1 - \delta^*)\frac{\delta^{*t} - \delta^t}{Q}\frac{dW_0^*}{dG_s} + \gamma_{t,s}\frac{\alpha_t}{Q}, \tag{A.15}$$

where

$$\gamma_{t,s} = \begin{cases} 1, & \text{for } t = s, \\ 0, & \text{for } t \neq s. \end{cases}$$

We then differentiate the foreign wealth equation (12.29) of the text and obtain

$$\frac{dW_0^*}{dG_s} = \sum_{t=0}^{\infty} (Y^* - G^*)\frac{d\alpha_t}{dG_s}. \tag{A.16}$$

Substituting (A.15) into (A.16) yields after some manipulations

$$\frac{dW_0^*}{dG_s} = \frac{\alpha_s \lambda^*}{(1 - \delta^*)\Delta} > 0. \tag{A.17}$$

Since Q is given, domestic and foreign wealth must change in opposite directions so as to ensure an unchanged value of world consumption in period zero. Thus from equation (12.26) and from (A.17) it follows that

$$\frac{dW_0}{dG_s} = -\frac{\alpha_s \lambda^*}{(1 - \delta)\Delta} < 0. \tag{A.18}$$

Finally, substituting equation (A.17) into (A.15) yields the solution for the change in the present-value factor:

$$\frac{d\alpha_t}{dG_s} = \frac{(1 - \delta^*)\alpha_s \lambda^*}{\Delta Q}(\delta^{*t} - \delta^t) \gtreqless 0, \quad \text{for } t \neq s \neq 0, \tag{A.19}$$

and

$$\frac{d\alpha_s}{dG_s} = \frac{\alpha_s}{\Delta Q}\left\{\frac{\lambda^*[1 - (1 - \delta)\delta^s]}{(1 - \delta)} \right.$$

$$\left. + \frac{1 - \lambda^*[1 - (1 - \delta^*)\delta^{*s}]}{(1 - \delta^*)}\right\} > 0, \quad \text{for } s \neq 0. \tag{A.20}$$

Permanent Government Spending

The expression for the permanent change in government spending on the current value of wealth can be computed from the previous expressions. For example, the effect of a permanent change in fiscal spending (dG) on foreign wealth is equivalent to the sum of the effects of all current (dG_0) and future transitory changes (dG_s) of equal magnitudes. Thus adding (A.14) to the sum of the expression in (A.17), for $t = 1, 2, \ldots$, yields the effect of an equivalent permanent change, as in (A.21):

$$\frac{dW_0^*}{dG} = \frac{dW_0^*}{dG_0} + \sum_{t=1}^{\infty} \frac{dW_0^*}{dG_t} = \frac{\lambda^*}{\Delta} \sum_{t=1}^{\infty} (\alpha_t - \delta^t),$$

$$= \frac{\lambda^{*2}}{\Delta(1 - \delta)(1 - \delta^*)(1 - \lambda\delta - \lambda^*\delta^*)} (\delta^* - \delta) \gtrless 0. \qquad \text{(A.21)}$$

where in deriving the last equality in (A.21) we made use of equation (12.30a) of the text. Thus the direction of change of foreign wealth depends on the saving-propensity condition.

Differentiating equation (12.26) of the text and using (A.21) yields

$$\frac{dW_0}{dG} = -\frac{[\lambda^*(1 - \delta^*) + \lambda(1 - \delta) + \lambda\lambda^*(\delta - \delta^*)]}{[(1 - \delta)(1 - \delta^*)\Delta]^2} < 0, \qquad \text{(A.22)}$$

where the inequality in (A.22) follows from the fact that the minimum value of the bracketed term (as δ^* approaches unity) is positive. Thus the permanent rise in government spending lowers domestic wealth.

To determine the effect of the permanent rise in government spending on α_t, we differentiate equation (12.30a) with respect to G noting that $\lambda = 1 - \lambda^* = (Y - G)/Q$. Thus

$$\frac{d\alpha_t}{dG} = \frac{\lambda^*}{Q\Delta(1 - \lambda\delta - \lambda\delta^*)} (\delta^{*t} - \delta^t) \gtrless 0. \qquad \text{(A.23)}$$

Thus the direction of change in the present-value factor depends on the saving-propensity condition.

Finally, the effects of transitory and permanent government

spending on the current rates of interest of various maturities can be obtained by applying the transformation

$$1 + r_{0t} = \alpha_t^{-1/t} \tag{A.24}$$

to the derivatives of the present-value factors. Likewise, the effects of transitory and permanent government spending on the time path of the short-term rates of interest can be obtained by applying the transformation

$$1 + r_t = \frac{\alpha_t}{\alpha_{t+1}} \tag{A.25}$$

to the derivatives of the present-value factors.

13

Budget Deficits, Lump-Sum Taxes, and Real Exchange Rates

The analytical framework developed in chapters 10 through 12 focused on the pure wealth effects of budget deficits. To highlight the essential mechanisms, the analysis employed a broad and unrefined commodity aggregation. In this chapter we extend the analysis by allowing for a more refined commodity aggregation distinguishing between tradable and nontradable goods. The incorporation of nontradable goods into the model permits a reexamination of the consequences of budget deficits on the real exchange rate as they operate through the mechanism of the pure wealth effect. The analysis of this mechanism (assuming lump-sum taxes and a finite horizon) supplements the one carried out in chapter 9 where we allowed for distortionary taxes and thereby focused on the substitution effects of budget deficits.

The exposition is divided into two main parts. In the first we examine the small-country case with special emphasis on the dynamics of the real exchange rate. In the second part we examine the two-country case with special emphasis on the consequences of budget deficits for the cross-country comovements of real exchange rates. This extension provides an additional dimension to the analysis of the international transmission mechanism of budget deficits.

13.1 Real Exchange-Rate Dynamics: The Small-Country Case

In this section we extend the analysis of the small-country case provided in chapter 10 to an economy producing and consuming internationally tradable and nontradable goods. The focus of the analysis is on the dynamics of the real exchange rate (the relative price of tradable goods in terms of nontradable goods). To facilitate

the exposition, we do not repeat the detailed derivations underlying the aggregation procedures and rely on the general principles
employed in chapter 10. Furthermore we simplify the analysis by
assuming that the utility function is logarithmic so that the saving
propensity does not depend on the path of the real exchange rate.
We also assume that the world rate of interest, r_x (measured in terms
of tradable goods) faced by the small economy is constant.

With this specification aggregate private-sector spending in period
t, Z_t, is related to private-sector wealth, W_t, according to

$$Z_t = (1 - s)W_t, \tag{13.1}$$

where s denotes the constant saving propensity and where spending
and wealth are measured in terms of tradable goods. The value of
wealth can be expressed as

$$W_t = \frac{R}{R - \gamma}\overline{Y}_x + \sum_{v=0}^{\infty}\left(\frac{\gamma}{R}\right)^v p_{n,t+v}\overline{Y}_n$$

$$- \sum_{v=0}^{\infty}\left(\frac{\gamma}{R}\right)^v T_{t+v} - RB_{t-1}^p. \tag{13.2}$$

Equation (13.2) defines wealth as the discounted sum of disposable
income net of debt commitment. As seen, GDP in period t (measured
in terms of tradable goods) is $\overline{Y}_x + p_{nt}\overline{Y}_n$, where $\overline{Y}_x$ and $\overline{Y}_n$ are,
respectively, the fixed levels of production of tradable and nontrad-
able goods, and p_{nt} is the relative price of nontradable goods—
the inverse of the real exchange rate. Disposable income is simply
GDP minus taxes. As in the previous chapters, the discounted sum
of disposable income is obtained by employing the effective discount
factor γ/R, where $R = 1 + r_x$.

Before proceeding, we recall in passing that with the assumed
logarithmic utility function the saving propensity equals $\gamma\delta$. In the
more general case the saving propensity is

$$s_t = 1 - \left\{\sum_{v=t}^{\infty}\left[\left(\frac{\gamma}{R}\right)^{v-t} P(p_{n,v})\right]^{1-\sigma} [(\gamma\delta)^{v-t}]^\sigma\right\}^{-1}$$

where $P(p_{n,v})$ is the price index expressed as a function of the relative
price of nontradable goods. This formulation is the extension of

equation (10.12). As is evident, though the saving propensity generally depends on the path of the real exchange rate, this dependency is eliminated in the logarithmic case in which the intertemporal elasticity of substitution in unity.

Total private-sector spending is composed of purchases of tradable and nontradable goods. Thus $Z_t = C_{xt} + p_{nt}C_{nt}$, where C_{xt} and C_{nt} denote, respectively, consumption of tradable and nontradable goods. The assumed form of the utility function implies that these quantities are proportional to total spending according to

$$C_{xt} = (1 - \beta_n)Z_t, \tag{13.3}$$

$$p_{nt}C_{nt} = \beta_n Z_t, \tag{13.4}$$

where β_n denotes the expenditure share of nontradable goods.

Equilibrium in the market for nontradable goods requires that in each period, t, private-sector demand for nontradable goods equals the value of output net of government purchases of these goods, G_{nt}. Thus, using equations (13.1) and (13.4), the equilibrium condition is

$$(1 - s)\beta_n W_t = p_{nt}(\overline{Y}_n - G_{nt}). \tag{13.5}$$

Private-sector debt in each period reflects the debt commitment in the recent past plus the flow of new debt arising from the excess of spending over disposable income. Accordingly, using equations (13.1) and (13.5), the dynamic evolution of private-sector debt implies that

$$B_t^p = RB_{t-1}^p + \frac{1}{\beta_n}p_{nt}(\overline{Y}_n - G_{nt}) - (\overline{Y}_x + p_{nt}\overline{Y}_n - T_t). \tag{13.6}$$

For given paths of government spending and taxes, the system of equations (13.2), (13.5), and (13.6) supplemented by the solvency condition (according to which in the limit all debt is repaid) can be solved to yield the equilibrium paths of the real exchange rate of private-sector debt. Once these paths are known, the rest of the model can be solved to yield the equilibrium paths of spending on tradable and nontradable goods as well as for the evolution of the current account of the balance of payments.

We show in the appendix (equations A.20 and A.21) that the

equilibrium paths of the price of nontradable goods (the inverse of the real exchange rate) and of private-sector debt are

$$p_{nt} = \bar{p}_n + \bar{v}(B^p_{-1} - B^p)\lambda^t_1 \qquad (13.7)$$

and

$$B^p_t = B^p + (B^p_{-1} - B^p)\lambda^{t+1}_1, \qquad (13.8)$$

where, as shown in the appendix, λ_1 is a positive fraction and $\bar{v}$ is a negative expression. The magnitudes of λ_1, $\bar{v}$, $\bar{p}_n$, and B^p depend on the parameters of the model. To facilitate the subsequent analysis of budget deficits, we assume that the conditions necessary for the existence of a steady-state equilibrium are satisfied. In that case, as shown in the appendix, $\bar{p}_n$ is positive and the sign of B^p depends on whether δR exceeds or falls short of unity. Suppose that δR falls short of unity. In that case the economy is a net debtor in the steady state. If the initial debt B^p_{-1} is smaller than the steady-state debt, then, as indicated by equation (13.8), the economy keeps on borrowing along the path to the steady state until its net debtor position reaches B^p. Along this path, as indicated by equation (13.7), the relative price of nontradable goods falls monotonically until it reaches the steady-state level, $\bar{p}_n$. The monotonic rise in the economy's net-debtor position lowers wealth and reduces spending. As a result, along the path, the current account of the balance of payments improves. The reduced demand for nontradable goods consequent on the reduced wealth reflects itself in a downward trend of the relative price of these goods, that is, a rise in the real exchange rate.

The foregoing analysis concludes the specification of the dynamics of the key economic variables in the small open economy. We turn next to analyze the dynamic response of these variables to a budget deficit resulting from an unanticipated change in the time profile of taxes. Consider an initial steady state disturbed by a tax cut, occurring in period zero, that is accompanied by a corresponding tax hike in period one, and suppose that in all other future periods taxes remain at their initial level of zero. Following the usual mechanism, the current-period budget deficit raises the existing population's wealth and stimulates spending. This raises the relative price of nontradable goods. On the other hand, once the rise in period-one taxes occurs, the wealth of the population existing in period one falls. The level of wealth in period one is lower since the segment of the population that enjoyed the initial tax cut raised its spending in period zero and thereby consumed part of its wealth while the newly born segment of the population inherited a larger tax liability. The reduction in period-one wealth induces a fall in spending and lowers the relative price of nontradable goods. Finally, throughout the periods subsequent to period one, the relative weight of these two segments in the total population declines due to mortality while at the same time the relative weight of the newly born not subject to the higher taxes of period one rises. The changes in the composition of the population occurring with the passage of time are associated with an upward trend in aggregate wealth, spending, and the relative price of nontradable goods. Ultimately, since the relative weight of those subject to the change in the tax profile approaches zero, the initial steady-state equilibrium is restored.

The pattern of response discussed here is illustrated in figure 13.1 which shows the dynamic effects that an unanticipated fall in taxes in period zero accompanied by a fully anticipated corresponding rise in taxes in period one exert on the relative price of nontradable goods and on consumption. This figure is one of the diagrammatic counterparts to the precise solutions for the general cases shown in the appendix. We also note that since total spending is related positively to the relative price of nontradable goods, the general pattern exhibited by the path of p_n also applies to the path of spending in figure 13.1.

In figure 13.2 we show the path of the economy's external debt. Since by assumption government debt in the initial equilibrium was zero, and since the tax profile ensures that from period two onward government debt is also zero, it follows that during these periods private-sector debt, B_t^p, coincides with the economy's external debt, B_t. In this context we note that since the steady-state value of the economy's external debt remains intact, the discounted sum of current and prospective trade surpluses (adjusted for the initial debt commitment)—all evaluated at the long run—also remains unchanged. Further, since the levels of output are fixed, it follows that

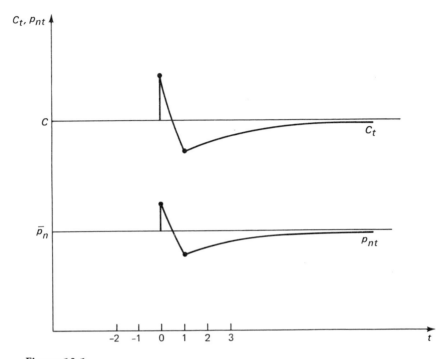

Figure 13.1
The dynamic effects of an unanticipated government-budget deficit on the
relative price of nontradable goods and on consumption

the discounted sum of current and future consumption—evaluated
at the same long run—also remains intact. It follows that if we
truncate the path of consumption in figure 13.1 at any arbitrary
period short of the steady state, the discounted sum of the postdeficit consumption exceeds the corresponding quantity obtained
along the benchmark path with no taxes.

Having analyzed the path of debt during period two and onward,
we return to elaborate on the evolution of the economy's external
debt during periods zero and one—the periods during which the tax
policy is in effect. In period zero the rise in total spending consequent on the budget deficit must be financed through external borrowing as reflected in the increased size of the economy's external
debt. This change in the economy's net-debtor position reflects pri-
marily the rise in government debt necessary to finance the budget

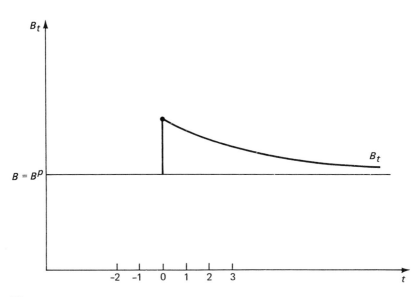

Figure 13.2
The dynamic effects of an unanticipated government-budget deficit on the
economy's external debt

deficit. In fact private-sector debt in period zero falls (since only
a fraction of the rise in wealth is spent). The rise in government
debt exceeds the reduction in private-sector debt, and therefore the
economy's external debt in period zero rises.

In period one the economy's external debt can be written as

$$B_1 = R^2 B_{-1} + (1 - \beta_n)(RZ_0 + Z_1) - (R\overline{Y}_x + \overline{Y}_x). \qquad (13.9)$$

Equation (13.9) expresses the value of external debt in period one as
the present value of the initial debt commitment plus the excess of
consumption of tradable goods over the production of these goods,
all evaluated in present values as of period one. Our previous arguments imply that the postdeficit external debt in period one (a period
that falls short of the steady state) exceeds the corresponding value
along the bench-mark path with no taxes since the value of $RZ_0 +
Z_1$ along the postdeficit path exceeds the corresponding quantity
along the bench-mark path with no taxes. This completes our analysis of the dynamic effects of budget deficits as they operate in the
small open economy.

13.2 Budget Deficits and Real Exchange Rates: The Two-Country World

In this section we extend the analysis to the two-country case. As in previous chapters such an extension illuminates the nature of the international transmission mechanism of tax policies. In our analysis we continue to assume that all taxes are nondistortionary. As a result the mechanism responsible for the real consequences of budget deficits operates through the wealth effects. We adopt the general features of the model outlined in chapter 11 but modify the classification of commodities so as to allow for the existence of nontradable goods at home and abroad. This extension introduces the domestic and foreign real exchange rates as key variables adjusting to the budget deficits. Thus, by emphasizing the wealth effects of tax policies, the present analysis supplements the one presented in chapter 9 in which due to distortionary taxes the intertemporal substitution effects were emphasized.

To simplify the exposition, we follow a similar procedure as in chapter 11 and divide the horizon into two: the current period and the future period. All quantities pertaining to the current period are indicated by a zero subscript, and the paths of the exogenous variables are assumed stationary across future periods.

Equilibrium necessitates that in the current period world output of tradable goods is demanded and the discounted sum of future outputs of tradable goods equals the discounted sums of future domestic and foreign demands. Likewise, in each country current and future period outputs of nontradable goods must be demanded. In what follows we outline the complete two-country model. The aggregate consumption functions at home and abroad are $Z_t = (1 - s)W_t$ and $Z_t^* = (1 - s^*)W_t^*$, where as before the propensities to save, s and s^*, are equal to $\gamma\delta$ and $\gamma\delta^*$ (where the survival probability, γ, is assumed to be equal across countries). Domestic and foreign wealth are defined as

$$W_0 = (\bar{Y}_{x0} + p_{n0}\bar{Y}_{n0} - T_0) + \frac{\gamma}{R - \gamma}(\bar{Y}_x - p_n\bar{Y}_n - T)$$

$$+ (1 + r_{x,-1})(B_{-1}^g - B_{-1}) \qquad (13.10)$$

and

$$W_0^* = (\overline{Y}_{x0}^* + p_{n0}^* \overline{Y}_{n0}^* - T_0^*) + \frac{\gamma}{R - \gamma}(\overline{Y}_x^* + p_n^* \overline{Y}_n^* - T^*)$$

$$+ (1 + r_{x,-1})(B_{-1}^{*g} + B_{-1}).$$ (13.11)

As seen, equations (13.10) and (13.11) express wealth as the sum of the present values of current and future disposable incomes plus net asset positions. Also it is recalled that in these equations the term $\gamma/(R - \gamma)$ denotes the present value of an annuity (commencing at period $t = 1$) evaluated by using the discount factor relevant for private decision making, γ/R.

The market-clearing conditions for the domestic nontradable goods require that

$$\beta_n(1 - s)W_0 = p_{n0}[\overline{Y}_{n0} - \beta_n^g(1 - \gamma_s^g)G]$$ (13.12)

and

$$\beta_n\left[sW_0 + \frac{1 - \gamma}{R - 1}\frac{R}{R - \gamma}(\overline{Y}_x + p_n\overline{Y}_n - T)\right]$$

$$= \frac{1}{R - 1}[p_n\overline{Y}_n - \beta_n^g\gamma_s^g G],$$ (13.13)

where, as before, G denotes the discounted sum of government spending and where β_n^g and γ_s^g indicate the government's temporal and intertemporal spending patterns. Equation (13.12) specifies the equilibrium condition in the current-period market, and equation (13.13) states that the discounted sum of domestic demand for future nontradable goods equals the discounted sum of future supply net of government absorption.

Analogously, equations (13.14) and (13.15) describe the corresponding equilibrium conditions in the foreign markets for nontradable goods.

$$\beta_n^*(1 - s^*)W_0^* = p_{n0}^*\overline{Y}_{n0}^* - \beta_n^{*g}(1 - \gamma_s^{*g})G^*$$ (13.14)

and

$$\beta_n^* \left[s^* W_0^* + \frac{1-\gamma}{R-1} \frac{R}{R-\gamma} (\overline{Y}_x^* + p_n^* \overline{Y}_n^* - T^*) \right]$$

$$= \frac{1}{R-1} [p_n^* \overline{Y}_n^* - \beta_n^{*g} \gamma_s^{*g} G^*]. \tag{13.15}$$

Finally, the equilibrium conditions in the *world* market for tradable goods are specified in equations (13.16) and (13.17), where the first of the two pertains to the current period and the second pertains to the discounted sums of demand and supply in all future periods:

$$(1 - \beta_n)(1 - s) W_0 + (1 - \beta_n^*)(1 - s^*) W_0^*$$

$$= \overline{Y}_x - (1 - \beta_n^g)(1 - \gamma_s^g) G + \overline{Y}_x^* - (1 - \beta_n^{*g})(1 - \gamma_s^{*g}) G^* \tag{13.16}$$

and

$$(1 - \beta_n) \left[s W_0 + \frac{1-\gamma}{R-1} \frac{R}{R-\gamma} (\overline{Y}_x + p_n \overline{Y}_n - T) \right]$$

$$+ (1 - \beta_n^*) \left[s^* W_0^* + \frac{1-\gamma}{R-1} \frac{R}{R-\gamma} (\overline{Y}_x^* + p_n^* \overline{Y}_n^* - T^*) \right]$$

$$= \frac{1}{R-1} [\overline{Y}_x - (1 - \beta_n^g) \gamma_s^g G + \overline{Y}_x^* - (1 - \beta_n^{*g}) \gamma_s^{*g} G^*]. \tag{13.17}$$

The system of equations (13.10) through (13.17) can be solved for the equilibrium values of the domestic and foreign current-period wealth, W_0 and W_0^*, current and future prices of nontradable goods (the inverse of the corresponding real exchange rates), p_{n0}, p_{n0}^*, p_n, p_n^*, and for the world rate of interest, $R - 1$. As usual, the eight-equation system (13.10) through (13.17) is linearly dependent, and thus, by Walras's law, one of these equations can be left out. In what follows we leave out equation (13.10) specifying the equilibrium value of domestic wealth.

Analogously to our analysis in chapter 11, we can reduce the complete model to two basic equilibrium conditions. These conditions state that the world markets for tradable goods clear in both the current period as well as in the (consolidated) future period.

These equations, derived explicitly in the appendix, are reduced-form equations—they incorporate the requirement that in each country and in all periods the markets for nontradable goods clear. Accordingly,

$$(1 - \beta_n)(1 - \gamma\delta)W_0 + (1 - \beta_n^*)(1 - \gamma\delta^*)W_0^* = \overline{Y}_x + \overline{Y}_x^*, \quad (13.18)$$

$$(1 - \beta_n)\left[\gamma\delta W_0 + \frac{(1 - \gamma)R}{(R - 1)(R - \gamma)} I(R, W_0, T) \right]$$

$$+ (1 - \beta_n^*)\left[\gamma\delta^* W_0^*(R) + \frac{(1 - \gamma)R}{(R - 1)(R - \gamma)} I^*(R) \right]$$

$$= \frac{1}{R - 1}(\overline{Y}_x + \overline{Y}_x^*), \quad (13.19)$$

where we replaced s and s^* by $\gamma\delta$ and $\gamma\delta^*$, respectively.

Equation (13.18) states that the sum of world private demand for current tradable goods equals world supply. In this equation $(1 - \beta_n)(1 - \gamma\delta)W_0$ is the home country's private demand, and $(1 - \beta_n^*)(1 - \gamma\delta^*)W_0^*$ is the corresponding foreign demand. The foreign wealth is expressed as a negative function of the rate of interest reflecting the role of the latter in discounting future incomes and in influencing the real exchange rate used to evaluate the income streams. It is noteworthy that this reduced-form functional dependence of wealth on the rate of interest is not shown explicitly for the domestic wealth since we have omitted the explicit domestic-wealth equation (13.10) by Walras's law. This choice makes the equilibrium determination of domestic wealth (along with the world rate of interest) the focus of the subsequent analysis.

The second reduced-form equation (13.19) states that the discounted sum of domestic and foreign demands for future tradable goods equals the discounted sum of future world supply. The first term is the product of the consumption share of tradable goods $(1 - \beta_n)$ and total domestic future consumption. The latter equals the sum of the savings of those alive in period zero, $\gamma\delta W_0$, and the discounted sum of the demand for future goods of those who will be born in the future and whose disposable income in each period is I. This reduced-form future disposable income (in terms of tradable goods) is expressed as a negative function of future taxes, T, and a positive function of the future relative price of nontradable goods. The latter in turn depends negatively on R (through its effect on future wealth of those yet unborn) and positively on W_0 (through its effect on the demand of those alive). An analogous interpretation applies to the foreign disposable income, I^*. The dependence of I^* on R only reflects the assumption that foreign taxes are zero and incorporates the negative dependence of W_0^* on R. Before proceeding, it is relevant to note that in the absence of nontradable goods, $\beta_n = \beta_n^* = 0$, $I(R, W_0, T) = Y - T$, $I^*(R) = Y^*$, $\overline{Y}_n = \overline{Y}_n^* = 0$, and $W^*(R) = Y^* + Y^*/(R - 1) + R(B_{-1}^g + B_{-1})$. Thus in this special case equations (13.18) and (13.19) reduce to equations (11.8) and (11.9).

Equations (13.18) and (13.19) yield the equilibrium values of the home country's initial wealth, W_0, and the world rate of interest, $r_x = R - 1$, for any given values of the parameters. In equilibrium the demand for nontradable goods $\beta_n(1 - \gamma\delta)W_0$ equals the value of the supply, $p_{n0}\overline{Y}_n$. Hence the equilibrium price (the inverse of the real exchange rate) is

$$p_{n0} = \frac{\beta_n(1 - \gamma\delta)W_0}{\overline{Y}_n}. \tag{13.20}$$

The equilibrium of the system is analyzed by means of figure 13.3. The PP schedule drawn in panel I of figure 13.3 shows combinations of r_x and p_{n0} that clear the market for present tradable goods. It is positively sloped since a rise in the rate of interest lowers foreign demand (by lowering W_0^*), and a rise in p_{n0} raises domestic demand (by raising W_0). The future tradable-goods market clears along the FF schedule. This schedule is negatively sloped since a rise in the rate of interest creates an excess demand for future tradable goods which must be offset by a fall in W_0 (and therefore p_{n0}). Panel II of the figure shows the negative relation between the equilibrium rate of interest and the foreign relative price of nontradable goods. This relation is based on equation (13.21) which is the foreign-country analogue to equation (13.20):

$$p_{n0}^* = \frac{\beta_n^*(1 - \gamma\delta^*)}{\overline{Y}_n} W_0^*(R). \tag{13.21}$$

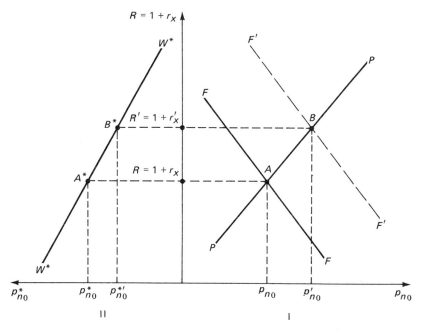

Figure 13.3
Budget deficits, the real exchange rate, and the real rate of interest

The equilibrium of the system is shown by point A in panel I and point A^* in panel II of figure 13.3. Accordingly, the current equilibrium relative price of domestic tradable goods is p_{n0}, the foreign equilibrium relative price is p_{n0}^*, and the corresponding equilibrium rate of interest is r_x. In what follows we analyze the effects of a domestic budget deficit on the world rate of interest and on the equilibrium real exchange rates. The formal derivations of the results are contained in the appendix.

A domestic budget deficit arising from a current tax cut necessitates a corresponding rise in future taxes, T. As seen from equation (13.19), the rise in future taxes lowers future domestic disposable income, I, and thereby lowers the demand for future goods. For a given world rate of interest the fall in demand can be eliminated by a rise in W_0. As implied by equation (13.20) the rise in W_0 is associated with a rise in p_{n0}. Thus the FF schedule shifts to the right to $F'F'$. As is evident the horizontal shifts of the FF schedule is proportional to $(1 - \gamma)$; if $\gamma = 1$ the position of the schedule as well as the characteristics of the initial equilibrium remain intact (the Ricardian equivalence case). In general, as indicated in panel I, the new equilibrium obtains at point B with a *higher rate of interest, a higher domestic relative price of nontradable goods, p_{n0}, and a higher level of domestic wealth and consumption. The new equilibrium is indicated in panel II by point B^*, where it is seen that the higher rate of interest lowers foreign wealth and consumption and reduces the foreign relative price of nontradable goods.* Thus on the basis of the correlations between domestic and foreign private-sector spending and between domestic and foreign real exchange rates, *the international transmission of the budget deficit is negative.* As an interpretation we note that the wealth effects induced by the domestic budget deficit creates an excess demand for present tradable goods resulting in a rise in their *intertemporal* relative price—the rate of interest. Likewise, it creates an excess demand for domestic nontradable goods and an excess supply of foreign nontradable goods. These excess demands and supplies alter the *temporal* relative price of these goods—the real exchange rates.

13.3 Summary

In this chapter we analyzed the consequences of budget deficits on the real exchange rate operating through the mechanism of the pure wealth effect. To focus on this mechanism rather than the mechanism of substitution effects, we assumed that all taxes are nondistortionary. In that case the finiteness of the horizon implies that budget deficits induce a positive wealth effect.

Our analysis of the small-country case focused on the dynamic consequences of budget deficits. In general, alterations in the time profile of taxes induce modifications of the intertemporal patterns of private-sector spending that reflect themselves in the time profile of the real exchange rate. Specifically, a budget deficit arising from a current tax cut that is accompanied by a subsequent tax hike raises current wealth, stimulates current consumption, and lowers the relative price of tradable goods—the real exchange rate. The corresponding tax hike that follows exerts the opposite influence: it lowers private-sector spending and raises the real exchange rate.

The changes in consumption and debt accumulation occurring during the period of the tax hike more than offset the changes occurring during the period of the tax cut. As a result the stage is set for the dynamics of private-sector spending as well as the real exchange rate. These dynamic effects influence all of the subsequent periods. Accordingly, throughout the period following the tax hike, the path of private-sector spending lies below the path obtained in the absence of the tax policy, but over time it converges back to the initial path. Correspondingly, throughout the period following the tax hike, the path of the real exchange rate lies above the path obtained in the absence of the tax policy, but it converges to it over time.

These dynamic effects of the budget deficit illustrate a general principle: the consequences of temporary tax policies stretch beyond the period during which the temporary policy is in effect. The counterpart to these dynamic implications is the rise in the economy's external debt induced by the budget deficit; the service of this debt stretches into the indefinite future.

Our analysis of the two-country case focused on the consequences of budget deficits on the domestic and the foreign real exchange rates. In this case the international transmission mechanism operates through the effects of the budget deficit on the world rate of interest. Accordingly, the wealth effect induced by the budget deficit raises the domestic demand for present-period goods, and thereby lowers the domestic real exchange rate and raises the world rate of interest. The rise in the world rate of interest transmits the effects of the domestic deficit to the rest of the world: it lowers foreign spending and raises the foreign real exchange rate. Accordingly, the budget deficit induces negative cross-country correlations between the levels of private-sector spending as well as between the real exchange rates.

The pattern of the cross-country correlations between real exchange rates and the effects of budget deficits on the world rate of interest reflect the mechanism of the pure wealth effect set in place in the absence of distortionary taxes. These results should be contrasted with those obtained in chapters 8 and 9 where it was shown that with distortionary taxes the effects of budget deficits depend on the specific taxes that are altered. In this context we also note that the interest-rate and real exchange-rate effects of a balanced-budget rise in government spending (analyzed in chapter 9) carry over to the infinite-horizon model used here.

Finally, as remarked in chapter 9, the analysis can be reinterpreted by viewing leisure as the nontradable good and the real wage as the reciprocal of the real exchange rate. With such a reinterpretation the analysis in this chapter yields insights into the effects of budget deficits on real-wage dynamics, and on cross-country correlations of real wages.

13.4 Appendix A: Real Exchange-Rate Dynamics for the Small Country

Here we present the formal model and derive the equilibrium conditions contained in section 13.1. The equilibrium value of wealth is

$$W_t = \frac{R}{R - \gamma} \overline{Y}_x + \sum_{v=0}^{\infty} \left(\frac{\gamma}{R}\right)^v p_{n,t+v} \overline{Y}_n$$

$$- \left[\sum_{v=0}^{\infty} \left(\frac{\gamma}{R}\right)^v T_{t+v} + RB_{t-1}^p \right]. \tag{A.1}$$

Equation (A.1), which reproduces equation (13.1), specifies the value of wealth, W_t, as the sum of the present values of current and future production of tradable goods and nontradable goods minus the sum of the present values of current taxes, future taxes, and the initial debt commitment.

The equilibrium condition in the market for nontradable goods is

$$(1 - s)\beta_n W_t = p_{nt} \overline{Y}_n, \tag{A.2}$$

which reproduces equation (13.5) under the assumption that government spending is zero. Under the same assumption the evolution of the private-sector debt is

$$B_t^p = RB_{t-1}^p + \frac{1}{\beta_n} p_{nt} \overline{Y}_n - (\overline{Y}_x + p_{nt} \overline{Y}_n - T_t), \tag{A.3}$$

where use has been made of equation (A.2) and the fact that $p_{nt} \overline{Y}_{nt} =$

$\beta_n Z_t$. This equation corresponds to (13.6). Finally, the model is closed by the solvency condition,

$$\lim_{t \to 0} \left(\frac{1}{R}\right)^t B_t^p = 0, \tag{A.4}$$

which supplements equation (13.6).

To solve the model, we define the discounted sum of the values of future output of nontradable goods (in terms of tradable goods) by Q_n. Accordingly,

$$Q_{nt} = \sum_{v=0}^{\infty} \left(\frac{\gamma}{R}\right)^v p_{n,t+1+v} \overline{Y}_n. \tag{A.5}$$

Using (A.5) to define $Q_{n,t-1}$ and subtracting $(\gamma/R)Q_{nt}$ yields

$$p_{nt} \overline{Y}_n = Q_{n,t-1} - \frac{\gamma}{R} Q_{nt}. \tag{A.6}$$

Substituting equation (A.5) into equation (A.1), and equation (A.6) into equation (A.2), and combining the resulting expressions yields

$$Q_{nt} = \frac{R}{\gamma} \left\{ [1 - (1-s)\beta_n]Q_{n,t-1} - (1-s)\beta_n \frac{R}{R-\gamma} \overline{Y}_x \right.$$

$$\left. + (1-s)\beta_n \sum_{v=0}^{\infty} \left(\frac{\gamma}{R}\right)^v T_{t+v} + (1-s)\beta_n R B_{t-1}^p \right\}. \tag{A.7}$$

Similarly, substituting equation (A.6) into equation (A.3) yields

$$B_t^p = R B_{t-1}^p + \frac{1 - \beta_n}{\beta_n} \left(Q_{n,t-1} - \frac{\gamma}{R} Q_{nt} \right) - (\overline{Y}_x - T_t). \tag{A.8}$$

Using equation (A.7) for Q_{nt} in equation (A.8) and collecting terms yields

$$B_t^p = [1 - (1-\beta_n)(1-s)]R B_{t-1}^p + (1-\beta_n)(1-s)Q_{n,t-1}$$

$$- \left[1 - (1-\beta_n)(1-\beta)\frac{R}{R-\gamma} \right] \overline{Y}_x$$

$$+ T_t - (1-\beta_n)(1-s) \sum_{v=0}^{\infty} \left(\frac{\gamma}{R}\right)^v T_{t+v}. \tag{A.9}$$

Equations (A.7) and (A.9) can be expressed in a matrix form as follows:

$$\begin{pmatrix} Q_{nt} \\ B_t^p \end{pmatrix} = A \begin{pmatrix} Q_{n,t-1} \\ B_{t-1}^p \end{pmatrix} + a\bar{Y}_x + D_t, \tag{A.10}$$

where

$$A = \begin{bmatrix} [1 - (1-s)\beta_n]\dfrac{R}{\gamma} & (1-s)\beta_n\dfrac{R^2}{\gamma} \\[2ex] (1-\beta_n)(1-s) & [1 - (1-\beta_n)(1-s)]R \end{bmatrix},$$

$$a = \begin{bmatrix} -\dfrac{\beta_n(1-s)R^2}{\gamma(R-\gamma)} \\[3ex] (1-\beta_n)(1-s)\dfrac{R}{R-\gamma} - 1 \end{bmatrix},$$

and

$$D_t = \begin{bmatrix} \dfrac{(1-s)\beta_n R}{\gamma} \displaystyle\sum_{v=0}^{\infty} \left(\dfrac{\gamma}{R}\right)^v T_{t+v} \\[3ex] T_t - (1-\beta_n)(1-s) \displaystyle\sum_{v=0}^{\infty} \left(\dfrac{\gamma}{R}\right)^v T_{t+v} \end{bmatrix}.$$

We first solve the system of equations (A.10) for the case in which there are no taxes. Accordingly, the solution is

$$\begin{pmatrix} Q_{nt} \\ B_t^p \end{pmatrix} = \bar{Y}_x(I-A)^{-1}a + A^{t+1}\begin{pmatrix} Q_{n,-1} \\ B_{-1}^p \end{pmatrix}, \tag{A.11}$$

where I is the identity matrix. The first expression on the right-hand side of equation (A.11) is

$$\begin{pmatrix} Q \\ B^p \end{pmatrix} \equiv \bar{Y}_x(I-A)^{-1}a = -\frac{\bar{Y}_x}{\Delta}\begin{pmatrix} \dfrac{\beta_n(1-s)(1-\gamma)R^2}{\gamma(R-\gamma)} \\[3ex] 1 - \delta R \end{pmatrix},$$

where

$$\Delta = \frac{1}{\gamma}[\beta_n R(1-s)(1-\gamma) - (1-sR)(R-\gamma)].$$

To compute the second expression on the right-hand side of (A.11), we recall from the rules of matrix algebra that

$$A^{t+1} = V\Omega^{t+1}V^{-1}, \tag{A.13}$$

where Ω is the diagonal matrix with the eigenvalues of A on its diagonal and V is the matrix of the corresponding eigenvectors. That is,

$$\Omega = \begin{pmatrix} \lambda_1 & 0 \\ 0 & \lambda_2 \end{pmatrix} \quad \text{and} \quad V = \begin{pmatrix} v_1 & v_2 \\ 1 & 1 \end{pmatrix},$$

where we have normalized the second component of each of the eigenvectors to unity. Computing the expressions for the eigenvalues of A yields

$$\lambda_i = \frac{R}{2}[\mu + (-1)^i \sqrt{\mu^2 - 4\delta}], \quad i = 1, 2, \tag{A.14}$$

where

$$\mu = (1 - \beta_n)\left(\frac{1}{\gamma} + s\right) + \beta_n(1 + \delta).$$

Similarly, the first components of the eigenvectors in V are

$$v_i = \frac{\lambda_i - R[1 - (1 - \beta_n)(1 - s)]}{(1 - \beta_n)(1 - s)}, \quad i = 1, 2. \tag{A.15}$$

Now that we have the expressions for the matrices Ω and V, we can compute A^{t+1} in equation (A.12). Substituting the resulting expression along with equation (A.12) into equation (A.11) yields

$$Q_{nt} = Q + \frac{1}{v_2 - v_1}\{[v_2(Q_{n,-1} - Q) - v_1 v_2(B^p_{-1} - B^p)]\lambda_2^{t+1}$$

$$- [v_1(Q_{n,-1} - Q) - v_1 v_2(B^p_{-1} - B^p)]\lambda_1^{t+1}\}, \tag{A.16}$$

$$B^p_t = B^p + \frac{1}{v_2 - v_1}\{[(Q_{n,-1} - Q) - v_1(B^p_{-1} - B^p)]\lambda_1^{t+1}$$

$$- [(Q_{n,-1} - Q) - v_2(B^p_{-1} - B^p)]\lambda_2^{t+1}\}. \tag{A.17}$$

Observing from (A.14) that $\lambda_2 > R$ and applying the solvency condition (A.4) to equation (A.17) yields the restriction

$$Q_{n,-1} = Q + v_1(B^p_{-1} - B^p). \tag{A.18}$$

This restriction nails down the initial value of $Q_{n,-1}$, and from equation (A.6) it also determines the initial value of $p_{n_0}\bar{Y}_n$. Substituting equation (A.18) into equations (A.16) and (A.17) yields

$$Q_{nt} = Q + v_1(B^p_{-1} - B^p)\lambda_1^{t+1}, \tag{A.19}$$

$$B^p_t = B^p + (B^p_{-1} - B^p)\lambda_1^{t+1}. \tag{A.20}$$

Finally, to obtain the solution for $p_{nt}\bar{Y}_n$, we substitute equations (A.19) and (A.20) into equation (A.6). Accordingly,

$$p_{nt} = \frac{1}{\bar{Y}_n}\left[\frac{R-\gamma}{R}Q + \left(\frac{R-\lambda_1\gamma}{R}\right)v_1(B^p_{-1} - B^p)\lambda_1^t\right]$$

$$= \bar{p}_n + \bar{v}(B^p_{-1} - B)\lambda_1^t. \tag{A.21}$$

Equations (A.19) and (A.20), or alternatively (A.20) and (A.21), constitute the solution to the system (A.10) for the case in which there are no taxes ($D_t = 0$). As is evident, since $\lambda_1 < 1$, the condition for the existence of steady-state equilibrium is that $Q > 0$. Using equation (A.12), this condition requires that $\beta_n R(1 - \gamma\delta)(1 - \gamma) < (1 - \gamma\delta R)(R - Y)$. For example, if $\gamma\delta R < 1$ and $\beta_n < (1 - \gamma\delta R) \times (R - \gamma)/(1 - \gamma\delta)(1 - \gamma)$, then the steady state exists. Likewise, if R approaches unity, then the steady-state equilibrium also exists. In the steady state the country is a net debtor if $1 > \delta R$, and vice versa.

We turn next to develop a procedure of solving the system shown in equation (A.11) for the case in which the government follows a tax policy so that ($D_t \neq 0$).

Assume now that the government raises period-zero taxes by the amount T. To balance its intertemporal budget, future taxes must be lowered. Suppose that in period-one taxes are lowered by the amount RT, whereas in all other periods they are set at zero. This tax structure is then applied to equation (A.10) to get the general solution of the equilibrium system.

The time-dependent vector D_t in equation (A.10) is

$$D_0 = \begin{bmatrix} D_0^1 \\ D_0^2 \end{bmatrix} = \begin{bmatrix} \dfrac{R}{\gamma} \beta_n (1-s)(1-\gamma) \\[2ex] [1 - (1-\beta_n)(1-s)(1-\gamma)] \end{bmatrix} \cdot T,$$

$$D_1 = \begin{bmatrix} D_1^1 \\ D_1^2 \end{bmatrix} = \begin{bmatrix} -\dfrac{R^2}{\gamma} \beta_n (1-s) \\[2ex] -R[1 - (1-\beta_n)(1-s)] \end{bmatrix} \cdot T,$$

(A.22)

and

$$D_t = 0, \quad t = 2, 3, \ldots.$$

Since from period two onward taxes are zero, we can apply the solution stated in equations (A.19) and (A.20) to this period for any given value of B_1^p. An equation of the type shown in (A.18) implies that there is a corresponding equilibrium value Q_{n1}. Accordingly,

$$Q_{n1} = Q + v_1 (B_1^p - B^p).$$ (A.23)

We now iterate backward, using equations (A.10) and (A.22) to find the general-equilibrium path for the initially given value of debt B_{-1}^p. Rearranging (A.10) yields

$$\begin{bmatrix} Q_{n0} \\ B_0^p \end{bmatrix} = \begin{bmatrix} A^{11}(Q_{n1} - a_1 \bar{Y}_x - D_1^1) + A^{12}(B_1^p - a_2 \bar{Y}_x - D_1^2) \\ A^{21}(Q_{n1} - a_1 \bar{Y}_x - D_1^1) + A^{22}(B_1^p - a_2 \bar{Y}_x - D_1^2) \end{bmatrix},$$

(A.24)

$$\begin{bmatrix} Q_{n,-1} \\ B_{-1}^p \end{bmatrix} = \begin{bmatrix} A^{11}(Q_{n0} - a_1 \bar{Y}_x - D_0^1) + A^{12}(B_0^p - a_2 \bar{Y}_x - D_0^2) \\ A^{21}(Q_{n0} - a_1 \bar{Y}_x - D_0^1) + A^{22}(B_0^p - a_2 \bar{Y}_x - D_0^2) \end{bmatrix},$$

(A.25)

where A^{ij} is the ijth component of the inverse of the A matrix and a_i is the ith component of the a vector. Expressed explicitly, using $s = \gamma\delta$, these terms are

$$A^{11} = \frac{1}{\delta R} [1 - (1-\beta_n)(1-\gamma\delta)] > 0,$$

$$A^{12} = -\frac{(1-\gamma\delta)}{\gamma\delta} \beta_n < 0,$$

$$A^{21} = -\frac{1}{\delta R^2}(1 - \beta_n)(1 - \gamma\delta) < 0,$$

$$A^{22} = \frac{1}{\gamma\delta R}[1 - \beta_n(1 - \gamma\delta)] > 0,$$

$$a_1 = -\frac{R^2\beta_n(1 - \gamma\delta)}{(R - \gamma)\gamma} < 0,$$

$$a_2 = \frac{R}{R - \gamma}(1 - \beta_n)(1 - \gamma\delta) - 1, \qquad (A.26)$$

where it is noted that $A^{11} > \gamma/R$.

Solving for (Q_{n0}, B_0^p) and substituting the resulting solutions into (A.25) yields

$$Q_{n,-1} = M + [A^{11}(A^{11}v_1 + A^{12}) + A^{12}(A^{21}v_1 + A^{22})]B_1^p$$

$$- (1 - \gamma)\frac{(1 - \gamma\delta)\beta_n}{\gamma\delta}T, \qquad (A.27)$$

where

$$M = A^{11}[A^{11}(Q - v_1B^p - a_1\bar{Y}_x) - A^{12}a_2\bar{Y}_x - a_1\bar{Y}_x]$$

$$+ A^{12}[A^{21}(Q - v_1B^p - a_1\bar{Y}_x) - A^{22}a_2\bar{Y}_x - a_2\bar{Y}_x],$$

and

$$B_{-1}^p = N + [A^{21}(A^{11}v_1 + A^{12}) + A^{22}(A^{21}v_1 + A^{22})]B_1^p$$

$$+ (1 - \gamma)\frac{1}{\gamma\delta R}(1 - \beta_n)(1 - \gamma\delta)T, \qquad (A.28)$$

where

$$N = A^{21}[A^{11}(Q - v_1B^p - a_1\bar{Y}_x) - A^{12}a_2\bar{Y}_x - a_1\bar{Y}_x]$$

$$+ A^{22}[A^{21}(Q - v_1B^p - a_1\bar{Y}_x) - A^{22}a_2\bar{Y}_x - a_2\bar{Y}_x].$$

Solving for B_1^p from equation (A.28) and substituting the result into equations (A.27). (A.23), and (A.24) yields

$$Q_{n,-1} = M - \frac{A^{11}(A^{11}v_1 + A^{12}) + A^{12}(A^{21}v_1 + A^{22})}{A^{21}(A^{11}v_1 + A^{12}) + A^{22}(A^{21}v_1 + A^{22})}N$$

$$+ \frac{A^{11}(A^{11}v_1 + A^{12}) + A^{12}(A^{21}v_1 + A^{22})}{A^{21}(A^{11}v_1 + A^{12}) + A^{22}(A^{21}v_1 + A^{22})} B^p_{-1}$$

$$- (1 - \gamma)\frac{(1 - \gamma\delta)}{\gamma\delta R}$$

$$\times \left[\frac{A^{11}(A^{11}v_1 + A^{12}) + A^{12}(A^{21}v_1 + A^{22})}{A^{21}(A^{11}v_1 + A^{12}) + A^{22}(A^{21}v_1 + A^{22})} \right.$$

$$\left. \times (1 - \beta_n) - R\beta_n \right] T. \tag{A.29}$$

$$Q_{n0} = A^{11}(Q - v_1 B^p - a_1 \overline{Y}_x) - A^{12}a_2 \overline{Y}_x$$

$$- \frac{A^{11}v_1 + A^{12}}{A^{21}(A^{11}v_1 + A^{12}) + A^{22}(A^{21}v_1 + A^{22})} N$$

$$+ \left[\frac{A^{11}v_1 + A^{12}}{A^{21}(A^{11}v_1 + A^{12}) + A^{22}(A^{21}v_1 + A^{22})} \right] B^p_{-1}$$

$$- (1 - \gamma)\frac{(1 - \beta_n)(1 - \gamma\delta)}{\gamma\delta R}$$

$$\times \left[\frac{A^{11}v_1 + A^{12}}{A^{21}(A^{11}v_1 + A^{12}) + A^{22}(A^{21}v_1 + A^{22})} \right] T, \tag{A.30}$$

$$Q_{n1} = \left[Q - v_1 B^p - \frac{v_1 N}{A^{21}(A^{11}v_1 + A^{12}) + A^{22}(A^{21}v_1 + A^{22})} \right]$$

$$+ \left[\frac{v_1}{A^{21}(A^{11}v_1 + A^{12}) + A^{22}(A^{21}v_1 + A^{22})} \right] B^p_{-1}$$

$$- (1 - \gamma)\frac{(1 - \beta_n)(1 - \gamma\delta)}{\gamma\delta R}$$

$$\times \left[\frac{v_1}{A^{21}(A^{11}v_1 + A^{12}) + A^{22}(A^{21}v_1 + A^{22})} \right] T, \tag{A.31}$$

where it is noted from the previous expressions that the bracketed terms multiplying T in equations (A.30) and (A.31) are negative.

We are now in a position to calculate the equilibrium values of the output of nontradable goods. Using equations (A.6) and (A.29) through (A.31) yields

$$p_{n0}\,\overline{Y}_n = P_0$$

$$+ \left[\frac{A^{11}(A^{11}v_1 + A^{12}) + A^{12}(A^{21}v_1 + A^{22}) - \gamma/R(A^{11}v_1 + A^{12})}{A^{21}(A^{11}v_1 + A^{12}) + A^{22}(A^{21}v_1 + A^{22})} \right] B^p_{-1}$$

$$- \frac{(1-\gamma)(1-\gamma\delta)}{\gamma\delta R}$$

$$\times \left\{ \frac{[A^{11} - (\gamma/R)](A^{11}v_1 + A^{12}) + A^{12}(A^{21}v_1 + A^{22})}{A^{21}(A^{11}v_1 + A^{12}) + A^{22}(A^{21}v_1 + A^{22})} \right.$$

$$\left. \times (1-\beta_n) - R\beta_n \right\} T, \tag{A.32}$$

where

$$P_0 = M - \frac{N\{[A^{11} - (\gamma/R)](A^{11}v_1 + A^{12}) + A^{12}(A^{21}v_1 + A^{22})\}}{A^{21}(A^{11}v_1 + A^{12}) + A^{22}(A^{21}v_1 + A^{22})}$$

$$- \frac{\gamma}{R}[A^{11}(Q - v_1 B^p - a_1 \overline{Y}_x) - A^{12}a_2 \overline{Y}_x],$$

and

$$p_{n1}\,\overline{Y}_n = P_1 + \left[\frac{A^{11}v_1 + A^{12} - \gamma v_1/R}{A^{21}(A^{11}v_1 + A^{12}) + A^{22}(A^{21}v_1 + A^{22})} \right] B^p_{-1}$$

$$- (1-\gamma)\frac{(1-\beta_n)(1-\gamma\delta)}{\gamma\delta R}$$

$$\times \left[\frac{A^{11}v_1 + A^{12} - \gamma v_1/R}{A^{21}(A^{11}v_1 + A^{12}) + A^{22}(A^{21}v_1 + A^{22})} \right] T, \tag{A.33}$$

where

$$P_1 = A^{11}(Q - v_1 B^p - a_1 \overline{Y}_x) - A^{12}a_2 \overline{Y}_x - \frac{\gamma}{R}(Q - v_1 B^p)$$

$$- \frac{H[A^{11}v_1 + A^{12} - (\gamma/R)v_1]}{A^{21}(A^{11}v_1 + A^{12}) + A^{22}(A^{21}v_1 + A^{22})}.$$

Using the facts that $A^{11} > \gamma/R$ and $v_1 < 0$ and using the expressions in (A.10), (A.12), (A.14), and (A.15), it is possible to sign the tax coefficients in equations (A.32) and (A.33). These signs are, respectively, positive and negative. The foregoing analysis was based on the assumption that current taxes are raised and future taxes are lowered. It follows that a deficit, arising from a current tax cut (accompanied by a tax hike in the subsequent period), raises p_{n0} and lowers p_{n1}. To determine the induced changes in consumption, we recall that $p_{n0}\,\overline{Y}_n = \beta_n Z_0$ and $p_{n1}\,\overline{Y}_n = \beta_n Z_1$. It follows that Z_0 rises, and Z_1 falls.

Finally, for the sake of completeness we also report the equilibrium values of production of nontradable goods in all other future periods. In our framework this provides the characterization of the paths of the (inverse of the) real exchange rate and of consumption. Accordingly, we use equation (A.19) for the periods in which taxes have not changed (i.e., from the second period onward), and we note that from the perspective of the second period, the initial debt position is B_1^p. Thus

$$Q_{n,t} = Q + v_1(B_1^p - B^p)\lambda_1^{t-1}, \quad t = 1, 2, 3, \ldots . \tag{A.34}$$

The value of B_1^p in equation (A.34) is obtained from the solution of equation (A.28); this yields

$$B_1^p = \frac{1}{J}\left[B_{-1}^p - N - (1 - \gamma)\frac{(1 - \beta_n)(1 - \gamma\delta)}{\gamma\delta R}T \right], \tag{A.35}$$

where

$$J = A^{21}(A^{11}v_1 + A^{12}) + A^{22}(A^{21}v_1 + A^{22}).$$

Substituting equation (A.34) into (A.6) (for $t = 2, 3, \ldots$) yields

$$p_{nt}\overline{Y} = \frac{R - \gamma}{R}Q + v_1\left(\frac{R - \lambda_1\gamma}{R}\right)(B_1^p - B^p)\lambda_1^{t-2}, \quad t = 2, 3, \ldots . \tag{A.36}$$

Equation (A.36) supplements (A.32) and (A.33) in specifying the path of the value of production of nontradable goods, and thereby the paths of the real exchange rate and consumption.

We conclude this part of the appendix by noting that from equation (A.20) the path of the private-sector debt for all periods, $t = 2$, $3, \ldots$, is

$$B_t^p = B^p + (B_1^p - B^p)\lambda_1^{t-1}, \quad t = 1, 2, 3, \ldots, \tag{A.37}$$

where B_1^p is specified in equation (A.35). Under the assumed specification of the time profile of taxes this path of private-sector debt coincides with the economy's external debt since the initial debt of the government as well as its debt from period two onward is zero.

13.5 Appendix B: Real Exchange Rates in a Two-Country World

In this appendix we first derive the reduced-form equations (13.18) and (13.19). Throughout we omit equation (13.10) by Walras's law. Using equations (13.13) and (13.5) and solving for the future values of production of nontradable goods yields

$$p_n \overline{Y}_n = A[(R - 1)sW_0 + \frac{(1 - \gamma)R}{R - \gamma}(\overline{Y}_x - T)], \tag{A.38}$$

$$p_n^* \overline{Y}_n^* = A^*[(R - 1)s^* W_0^* + \frac{(1 - \gamma)R}{R - \gamma}(\overline{Y}_x^* - T^*)], \tag{A.39}$$

where

$$\theta = \frac{\beta_n^g \gamma_s^g G}{p_n \overline{Y}_n}, \quad \theta^* = \frac{\beta_n^{*g} \gamma_s^{*g} G^*}{p_n^* \overline{Y}_n^*}$$

$$A = \frac{\beta_n}{(1 - \theta) - \beta_n(1 - \gamma)R/(R - \gamma)},$$

$$A^* = \frac{\beta_n^*}{(1 - \theta^*) - \beta_n^*(1 - \gamma)R/(R - \gamma)}.$$

The requirement that in equilibrium there is positive consumption of nontradable goods that command a positive price imposes the feasibility condition according to which

$$A \geq 0, \quad A^* \geq 0. \tag{A.40}$$

Substituting (A.39) and equation (13.14) into equation (13.11) yields

$$W_0^* = D^* \left[\overline{Y}_x^* - T_0^* + \frac{\gamma}{R - \gamma} \left(1 + A^* \frac{(1 - \gamma)R}{R - \gamma} \right) (\overline{Y}_x^* - T^*) \right.$$

$$\left. + (1 + r_{x,-1})(B_{-1}^{*g} + B_{-1}) \right], \tag{A.41}$$

where

$$D^* = (1 - \theta^*) \left\{ (1 - \theta^*) \right.$$

$$\left. - \beta_n^* \left[\frac{(R - 1)\gamma s^*}{(1 - \theta^*)(R - \gamma) - \beta_n^*(1 - \gamma)R} + \frac{1 - s^*}{1 - \theta^*} \right]^{-1} \right\}.$$

The requirement that in equilibrium wealth is positive imposes the additional feasibility constraint according to which

$$D^* \geq 0. \tag{A.42}$$

Substituting equation (A.41) into equation (13.16) yields

$$(1 - \beta_n)(1 - s)W_0 + (1 - \beta_n^*)D^* \left\{ \overline{Y}_x^* - T_0^* \right.$$

$$+ \frac{\gamma}{R - \gamma} \left[1 + A^* \frac{(1 - \gamma)R}{R - \gamma} \right] (\overline{Y}_x^* - T^*)$$

$$\left. + (1 + \tilde{r}_{x,-1})(B_{-1}^{*g} + B_{-1}) \right\}$$

$$= \overline{Y}_x - (1 - \beta_n^g)(1 - \gamma_s^g)G + \overline{Y}_x^* - (1 - \beta_n^{*g})(1 - \gamma_s^{*g})G^*. \tag{A.43}$$

Substituting equations (A.38) and (A.39) for $p_n \overline{Y}_n$ and $p_n^* \overline{Y}_n^*$ into equation (13.17) yields

$$(1 - \beta_n) \left[sW_0 + \frac{(1 - \gamma)R}{(R - 1)(R - \gamma)} \right.$$

$$\times \left\{ A(R - 1)sW_0 + \left[1 + A \frac{(1 - \gamma)R}{R - \gamma} \right] (\overline{Y}_x - T) \right\} \right]$$

$$+ (1 - \beta_n^*) \left[s^* W_0^* + \frac{(1 - \gamma)R}{(R - 1)(R - \gamma)} \right.$$

$$\times \left\{ A^*(R-1)s^*W_0^* + \left[1 + A^*\frac{(1-\gamma)R}{R-\gamma}\right](\bar{Y}_x^* - T^*) \right\} \right]$$

$$= \frac{1}{R-1}[\bar{Y}_x - (1 - \beta_n^g)\gamma_s^g G + \bar{Y}_x^* - (1 - \beta_n^{*g})\gamma_s^{*g}G^*]. \qquad (A.44)$$

The system of equations (A.41), (A.43), and (A.44) can be used to solve for the equilibrium values of W_0, W_0^*, and R.

To derive the more compact formulation of the reduced-form equilibrium conditions of the text, we focus on the role of domestic tax policy by assuming that $G = G^* = T^* = 0$. We first note that for a given value of the parameters the equilibrium value of foreign wealth shown in equation (A.41) can be expressed implicitly as

$$W_0^* = W_0^*(R), \quad \frac{\partial W_0^*}{\partial R} < 0. \qquad (A.45)$$

Equation (A.45) expresses foreign current wealth as a negative function of the rate of interest. This reduced-form relationship incorporates the equilibrium conditions in the markets for current and future nontradable goods. The negative dependence on the rate of interest reflects the role of the rate of interest in discounting future incomes and in influencing the real exchange rates used to evaluate the income streams. Next we define the domestic and foreign reduced-form future disposable incomes

$$I(R, W_0, T) = (R-1)A\gamma\delta W_0 + \left[1 + \frac{(1-\gamma)RA}{R-\gamma}\right](\bar{Y}_x - T) \qquad (A.46)$$

and

$$I^*(R) = (R-1)A^*\gamma\delta^*W_0^*(R) + \left[1 + \frac{(1-\gamma)RA^*}{R-\gamma}\right]\bar{Y}_x^*. \qquad (A.47)$$

Equation (A.46) expresses disposable income (in terms of tradable goods) as a negative function of future taxes, T, and a positive function of the relative price of nontradable goods, p_n. The latter in turn depends negatively on R (through its effect on future wealth of those yet unborn) and positively on W_0 (through its effect on the demand of those alive). An analogous interpretation applies to the foreign disposable income, I^*, where in (A.47) we incorporate the functional dependence of W_0^* on R and the assumption that foreign taxes are zero.

Substituting equations (A.46) and (A.47) into (A.43) and (A.44) together with the assumption that $G = G^* = T^* = 0$ yields

$$(1 - \beta_n)(1 - \gamma\delta)W_0 + (1 - \beta_n^*)(1 - \gamma\delta^*)W_0^*(R) = \bar{Y}_x + \bar{Y}_x^*,$$

(A.48)

$$(1 - \beta_n)\left[\gamma\delta W_0 + \frac{(1 - \gamma)R}{(R - 1)(R - \gamma)}I(R, W_0, T)\right]$$

$$+ (1 - \beta_n^*)\left[\gamma\delta^* W_0^*(R) + \frac{(1 - \gamma)R}{(R - 1)(R - \gamma)}I^*(R)\right]$$

$$= \frac{1}{R - 1}(\bar{Y}_x + \bar{Y}_x^*).$$

(A.49)

Equations (A.48) and (A.49) are the reduced-form equilibrium conditions (13.18) and (13.19). These equations underlied the diagrammatical analysis of the next.

We turn next to a more formal analysis of the comparative statics results reported in the text. For this purpose we return to the complete model outlined in equations (13.10) through (13.16), omitting equation (13.17) by Walras's law. We continue to assume that $G = G^* = T^* = 0$. Substituting (A.28) and equation (13.12) into equation (13.11) yields

$$W_0 = D\left\{\bar{Y}_x - T_0 + \frac{\gamma}{R - \gamma}\left[1 + A\frac{(1 - \gamma)R}{R - \gamma}\right](\bar{Y}_x - T)\right.$$

$$\left. + (1 + r_{x,-1})(B_{-1}^g - B_{-1})\right\},$$

(A.50)

where

$$D = \left\{1 - \beta_n\left[\frac{(R - 1)\gamma^2\delta}{(R - \gamma) - \beta_n(1 - \gamma)R} + (1 - \gamma\delta)\right]\right\}^{-1}.$$

Likewise, with zero foreign govenment spending and taxes equation (A.41) becomes

$$W_0^* = D^* \left\{ \bar{Y}_x^* + \frac{\gamma}{R - \gamma} \left[1 + A^* \frac{(1 - \gamma)R}{R - \gamma} \right] \bar{Y}_x^* \right.$$

$$\left. + (1 + r_{x,-1})(B_{-1}^{*g} + B_{-1}) \right\}, \tag{A.51}$$

where

$$D^* = \left\{ 1 - \beta_n^* \left[\frac{(R - 1)\gamma^2 \delta^*}{(R - \gamma) - \beta_n^*(1 - \gamma)R} + (1 - \gamma\delta^*) \right] \right\}^{-1},$$

and feasibility requires that $D \geq 0$ and $D^* \geq 0$. Finally, using equation (13.16), we get

$$(1 - \beta_n)(1 - \gamma\delta)W_0 + (1 - \beta_n^*)(1 - \gamma\delta^*)W_0^* = \bar{Y}_x + \bar{Y}_x^*. \tag{A.52}$$

The system of equations (A.50) through (A.52) solves for the equilibrium values of W_0, W_0^*, and R. Differentiating this system, and noting that from the government budget constraint $dT_0 = -[1/(R - 1)]dT$, yields

$$\frac{dW_0}{dT} = -(1 - \gamma)\frac{J_1 J_2}{\Delta}(1 - \beta_n^*)(1 - \gamma\delta^*) > 0, \tag{A.53}$$

$$\frac{dW_0}{dT} = (1 - \gamma)\frac{J_1 J_2}{\Delta}(1 - \beta_n)(1 - \gamma\delta) < 0, \tag{A.53}$$

$$\frac{dR}{dT} = -(1 - \gamma)\frac{J_2}{\Delta}(1 - \beta_n)(1 - \gamma\delta) > 0, \tag{A.54}$$

where

$$\Delta = - \left\{ (1 - \beta_n^*)^2(1 - \gamma\delta^*)\frac{\gamma[1 - \beta_n^*(1 - \gamma)]\bar{Y}_x^* D^{*2}}{[(R - \gamma) - \beta_n^*(1 - \gamma)R]^2} \right.$$

$$\left. + (1 - \beta_n)^2(1 - \gamma\delta)\frac{\gamma[1 - \beta_n(1 - \gamma)]\bar{Y}_x D^2}{[(R - \gamma) - \beta_n(1 - \gamma)R]^2} \right\} < 0,$$

$$J_1 = \frac{(1 - \beta_n^*)\gamma[1 - \beta_n^*(1 - \gamma)]\bar{Y}_x^* D^{*2}}{[(R - \gamma) - \beta_n^*(1 - \gamma)R]^2} > 0,$$

$$J_2 = \frac{(1 - \beta_n)RD}{(R - 1)[(R - \gamma) - \beta_n(1 - \gamma)R]} > 0.$$

Using (A.53) and (A.54) together with equation (13.20) and (13.21) yields

$$\frac{dp_{no}}{dT} = -(1 - \gamma)\frac{J_1 J_2}{\Delta \overline{Y}_n}\beta_n(1 - \gamma\delta)(1 - \beta_n^*)(1 - \gamma\delta^*) > 0, \qquad (A.56)$$

$$\frac{dp_{no}^*}{dT} = (1 - \gamma)\frac{J_1 J_2}{\Delta \overline{Y}_n^*}\beta_n^*(1 - \gamma\delta^*)(1 - \beta_n)(1 - \gamma\delta) < 0. \qquad (A.57)$$

The results reported in (A.53) through (A.57) justify the diagrammatic analysis of the text. They show that a current budget deficit (necessitating a future rise in taxes so that $dT > 0$) raises domestic wealth, lowers foreign wealth, raises the world rate of interest, lowers the domestic current real exchange rate (the reciprocal of p_{no}), and raises the foreign current real exchange rate. All of these real effects vanish if the value of γ approaches unity. In that case the pure wealth effects of budget deficits do not exist.

A similar computation reveals that the effects of the budget deficit on the future value of the real exchange rates are ambiguous. This ambiguity reflects the conflicting forces exercised by the wealth and substitution effects induced by the change in the rate of interest that in the home country supplements the direct wealth effects of the tax policy. It can be shown, however, that the budget deficit decelerates the rate of increase of the foreign real exchange rate between the present and the future period.

VI

Exchange-Rate Regimes and Tax Policies

14

Exchange-Rate Regimes and Intertemporal Monetary Considerations

Our previous analysis from chapter 5 onward abstracted from monetary considerations. This abstraction enabled us to focus entirely on the temporal and the intertemporal implications of fiscal policies. In this chapter we extend the analytical framework by incorporating some monetary considerations. The purpose is not to provide a complete framework for monetary analysis. Rather, we introduce the minimal building blocks necessary to examine the implications that alternative monetary environments have for the analysis of fiscal policies. A critical issue that needs to be addressed in specifying the monetary environment of the interdependent world economy concerns the exchange-rate regime. Accordingly, much of the analysis in this chapter is devoted to a detailed specification of the monetary mechanisms associated with alternative exchange-rate regimes. The framework developed here is used in the next chapter in the analysis of the relationships between exchange-rate policies and fiscal policies.

14.1 The Analytical Framework

The analytical framework is specified in the simplest possible form that still captures the main features necessary for the incoporation of monetary considerations. In this vein we assume a two-period model in which domestic and foreign goods are internationally tradable and are perfect substitutes in consumption. For convenience we adopt the cash-in-advance formulation. Accordingly, purchases of goods require cash payments which are assumed to be carried out in terms of the seller's currency. Thus goods produced abroad are purchased with foreign currency, and domestically produced goods are purchased with domestic currency.

At the *beginning* of each period individuals transact in the financial markets and obtain the desired portfolio composition. The desired holdings of domestic and foreign currencies reflect the pattern of planned purchases of domestic and foreign goods that take place *during* the period. The counterpart to these purchases are the sales of goods by firms. Accordingly, during each period domestic firms accumulate domestic currency and foreign firms accumulate foreign currency. At the *end* of the each period (which coincides with the beginning of the subsequent period) domestic firms redistribute the proceeds of their sales to domestic individuals in the form of wages and dividends. Analogously, at the end of each period foreign firms also redistribute their proceeds to foreign individuals in the form of wages and dividends.

The first-period budget constraints applicable to domestic individuals consist of three equations. The first one is

$$M_{H0} + e_0 M_{F0} = P_{-1} Y_{x,-1} - \tilde{T}_0 + \tilde{B}^p_{H0} + e_0 \tilde{B}^p_{F0}$$

$$- \tilde{R}_{H,-1} \tilde{B}^p_{H,-1} - e_0 \tilde{R}_{F,-1} \tilde{B}^p_{F,-1}, \tag{14.1}$$

where M_H and M_F are, respectively, the domestic holdings of domestic and foreign currencies, e is the exchange rate, the price of foreign currency in terms of domestic currency, and $\tilde{B}^p_H$ and $\tilde{B}^p_F$ denote the domestic private-sector issue of one-period nominal bonds denominated in units of domestic and foreign currency, respectively. In addition P is the domestic-currency price of domestic output (Y_x), and $\tilde{R}_H$ and $\tilde{R}_F$ are the nominal returns (one plus the nominal rate of interest) on the domestic and foreign-currency denominated one-period bonds. A subscript 0 corresponds to period zero, and a subscript -1 corresponds to the previous period, -1. Equation (14.1) states that at the beginning of the first period (period zero) the value of domestic currency holdings equals the proceeds from sales by domestic firms during the previous period, $P_{-1} Y_{x,-1}$, plus new private-sector nominal borrowing, $\tilde{B}^p_{H0} + e_0 \tilde{B}^p_{F0}$, minus debt commitment on past borrowing.

The other first-period budget constraints, representing the cash-in-advance formulation, are

$$P_0 C_{x0} = M_{H0},$$ (14.2)

$$P_0^* C_{m0} = M_{F0}.$$ (14.3)

Equation (14.2) states that the holdings of domestic currency at the beginning of the period equals planned spending on these goods during the period; in the equation C_x denotes planned consumption of domestically produced goods. Analogously, equation (14.3) specifies the holdings of foreign currency (at the beginning of the period) in terms of planned spending on imported (foreign goods) C_m, whose (foreign currency) price is P^*. Implicit in the formulation of the cash-in-advance constraints of equations (14.2) and (14.3) is the assumption that all currency is held only for transaction purposes. In this formulation, as long as the nominal rates of interest are positive, currencies do not perform the store-of-value function since they are dominated in the portfolio by interest-earning bonds.

The second-period budget constraints analogous to equations (14.1) through (14.3) are

$$M_{H1} + e_1 M_{F1} = P_0 Y_{x0} - \tilde{T}_1 - \tilde{R}_{H0} \tilde{B}_{H0}^p - e_1 \tilde{R}_{F0} \tilde{B}_{F0}^p,$$ (14.4)

$$P_1 C_{x1} = M_{H1},$$ (14.5)

$$P_1^* C_{m1} = M_{F1}.$$ (14.6)

The only point worth noting with respect to the second-period budget constraints is that during this last period the solvency requirement implies that debt commitments are honored while no new debt is incurred.

It is assumed that the world markets for goods and financial assets are fully integrated and that individuals have unrestricted access to these markets. As a result the arbitrage conditions are

$$P_t = e_t P_t^*, \qquad t = 0, 1,$$ (14.7)

$$\tilde{R}_{Ht} = \frac{e_{t+1}}{e_t} \tilde{R}_{Ft}, \qquad t = -1, 0.$$ (14.8)

Equation (14.7) is the purchasing-power-parity relation. It represents the law of one price (reflecting the perfect substitutability between domestic and foreign goods). Likewise, equation (14.8) is the interest-rate parity relation. It represents the law of one return (reflecting the perfect substitutability between domestic- and foreign-currency denominated bonds, expressed in common currency units).

Money-market equilibrium in the domestic economy implies that

$$P_t Y_{xt} = M_t, \tag{14.9}$$

where M denotes the domestic money supply.

The left-hand side of equation (14.9) represents the (reduced-form) world demand for domestic currency. It represents the sum of the domestic demand, M_{Ht}, and the foreign demand, M_{Ht}^*. In view of the cash-in-advance constraints the sum of these demands can be written as $P_t(C_{xt} + C_{xt}^*)$, where C_{xt}^* denotes the foreign purchase of the domestically produced good. The reqiurement that the world demand for the domestic good equals the level of domestic output implies that $C_{xt} + C_{xt}^* = Y_{xt}$. Hence $P_t Y_{xt}$ is the world demand for the domestic currency. Equivalently, the interpretation of the left-hand side of equation (14.9) could also be given by noting that money is used only for transactions involving the purchase of domestic output; hence, if all output is purchased, the world demand for domestic money equals the value of domestic output. In equilibrium this quantity equals the existing supply of money. In this context we note in passing that in the simple formulation of equation (14.9), since money serves only as a medium of exchange, the income velocity of circulation is unitary.

The supply of money in any given period equals the supply prevailing in the previous period augmented by the net flow of a new currency arising from public-sector deficits. In order to focus on the role of exchange-rate management, we assume for simplicity that the monetary authorities do not engage in active open-market operations but rather confine their activities to sustain the exchange-rate regime. For the same reason we also assume that the government does not finance its current operations by debt issue. In addition, since we focus in this chapter on the monetary considerations, we simplify the exposition and assume that government purchases are zero.

In specifying the public-sector budget constraints, it is convenient to separate between transactions involving the domestic currency and transactions involving the foreign currency. With the simplifying assumptions the budget constraint associated with the domestic-currency account of the public sector is

$$\tilde{X}_t = \tilde{T}_t + D_t, \tag{14.10}$$

where $\tilde{X}_t$ denotes the domestic-currency value of public-sector outlays incurred by the purchases of foreign exchange associated with the management of the exchange rate. As specified by equation (14.10) these outlays are financed through taxes, $\tilde{T}_t$, and through the new issue of domestic currency, D_t. Accordingly, the money supply, $M_t = M_{t-1} + D_t$, is represented by

$$M_t = M_{t-1} + \tilde{X}_t - \tilde{T}_t. \tag{14.11}$$

The foreign-currency account of the public sector consists of transactions involving foreign exchange. The unique characteristic of these transactions is that in contrast with those involving the domestic currency, they can not be financed through the issue of currency. Accordingly, with our simplifying assumptions, the budget constraints associated with the foreign-currency account of the public sector during the two periods are

$$\tilde{R}_{F,-1}\tilde{B}^g_{F,-1} = \tilde{B}^g_{F0} + \frac{1}{e_0}\tilde{X}_0, \tag{14.12}$$

$$\tilde{R}_{F0}\tilde{B}^g_{F0} = \frac{1}{e_1}\tilde{X}_1, \tag{14.13}$$

where $\tilde{B}^g_{F0}$ denotes government borrowing for the purpose of exchange-rate management. These borrowings, which are expressed in units of foreign currency, consist of government issue of one-period nominal bonds. As with the private sector, solvency requires that in the last period all debt commitments are settled and no new borrowing takes place.

This completes the simple analytical framework. We turn next to a specification of the monetary mechanisms associated with alternative exchange-rate regimes starting with the flexible exchange-rate system.

14.2 The Flexible Exchange-Rate Regime

Under a flexible exchange-rate regime the authorities do not intervene directly in the foreign-exchange market. As a result the flow of currency associated with the management of the exchange rate is zero, and likewise, public-sector debt incurred in the process of managing the rate is also zero so that $\tilde{X} = \tilde{B}^g_{F0} = 0$. In this case the exchange-rate adjusts freely so as to clear the market for currencies.

To characterize the behavior of the private sector under such an exchange-rate regime, it is useful to specify the consumption-possibility set that is available to individuals in equilibrium. We first substitute the cash-in-advance constraints of equations (14.2) and (14.3) into the first-period budget constraint (14.1), and using the parity conditions (14.7), for $t = 0$, and (14.8), for $t = -1$, we obtain

$$P_0 C_0 = P_{-1} Y_{x,-1} - \tilde{T}_0 + \tilde{B}_0 - \tilde{R}_{H,-1}\tilde{B}_{-1}, \tag{14.14}$$

where, recalling that the two goods are perfect substitutes, $C = C_x + C_m$ denotes total domestic consumption and, recalling that the two nominal bonds are perfect substitutes, $\tilde{B}^p = \tilde{B}^p_H + e\tilde{B}^p_F$ denotes total domestic private-sector borrowing. Since by our assumption government debt is zero, we replace in equation (14.14) the term $\tilde{B}^p_t$ by the economy's external debt, $\tilde{B}_t$. Applying the same procedure to the second-period budget constraint (14.4), we use the corresponding cash-in-advance equations (14.5) and (14.6) and the parity conditions (14.7), for $t = 1$, and (14.8), for $t = 0$, to obtain

$$P_1 C_1 = P_0 Y_{x0} - \tilde{T}_1 - \tilde{R}_{H0}\tilde{B}_0. \tag{14.15}$$

Using the money-market equilibrium condition (14.9)—applied to $t = -1$—we substitute M_{-1} for $P_{-1}Y_{x,-1}$, and using equation (14.11)—applied to $t = 0$—we substitute M_0 for $M_{-1} - \tilde{T}_0$; we then use the money-market equilibrium condition and substitute the term $P_0 Y_{x0}$ for M_0. This yields

$$P_0 C_0 = P_0 Y_{x0} + \tilde{B}_0 - \tilde{R}_{H,-1}\tilde{B}_{-1}. \tag{14.16}$$

Likewise, substituting into equation (14.15) the terms M_0 for $P_0 Y_{x0}$,

M_1 (from 14.11) for $(M_0 - T_1)$, and $P_1 Y_{x1}$ for M_1 yields

$$P_1 C_1 = P_1 Y_{x1} - \tilde{R}_{H0} \tilde{B}_0. \tag{14.17}$$

Finally, dividing (14.17) by $\tilde{R}_{H0}$, adding the resultant equation to (14.16), and dividing the outcome by P_0 yields

$$C_0 + \frac{1}{R_0} C_1 = Y_{x0} + \frac{1}{R_0} Y_{x1} - R_{-1} B_{-1}, \tag{14.18}$$

where $R_{-1} = (P_{-1}/P_0)\tilde{R}_{H,-1}$ and $R_0 = (P_0/P_1)\tilde{R}_{H0} = (P_0^*/P_1^*)\tilde{R}_{F0}$ denote the real return (i.e., one plus the world common real rates of interest) on bonds, and $B_{-1} = (1/P_{-1})\tilde{B}_{-1}$ denotes the real value of the economy's external debt inherited from period $t = -1$.

Equation (14.18) expresses the equilibrium consumption-possibility set available to the private sector in terms of the equality between the discounted sum of consumption and the discounted sum of GDP net of external debt commitment. As is evident, this equation is analogous to equation (5.6) which was derived for a barter economy without a public sector. This similarity is noteworthy in view of the fact that the present chapter allows for the monetary sector. However, due to the Ricardian characteristics of the model, the monetary sector is fully internalized by the private sector, and therefore does not manifest itself in the consumption-possibility set.

We conclude that with the assumptions of perfect capital markets, flexible market-clearing prices, no distortions and no difference between the time horizons of the private and the public sectors, the introduction of money and a flexible exchange-rate regime do not impact on the real equilibrium, and thus in that case money is a veil.

Finally, we note that the exchange rate associated with the equilibrium of the system can be obtained from the conditions of equilibrium in the world currency markets. Accordingly, using equations (14.9) together with its foreign-currency counterpart (i.e., $P_t^* Y_{mt} = M_t^*$), and taking account of the purchasing-power-parity relation of equation (14.7) yields

$$e_t = \frac{M_t}{M_t^*} \frac{Y_{mt}}{Y_{xt}}. \tag{14.19}$$

Equation (14.19) specifies the equilibrium exchange rate as the product of the ratios of money supplies and (real) money demands. As is evident, the (absolute values of the) elasticities of the equilibrium exchange rate with respect to money and output are unitary. Further the constant velocity specification implies that in this formulation the nominal exchange rate does not depend on the rates of interest. Finally, the assumption that all the goods are internationally tradable is responsible for the fact that the real exchange rate does not appear explicitly in the nominal exchange-rate equation.

This completes the analytical framework applicable to the analysis of the flexible exchange-rate regime. We turn next to analyze the alternative regime in which the exchange rate is fixed.

14.3 The Fixed Exchange-Rate Regime

Under a fixed exchange-rate regime the authorities intervene in the foreign-exchange market and peg the rate at a prespecified level, $\bar{e}$. In that case $e_0 = e_1 = \bar{e}$. With the fixed exchange rate the parity conditions (14.7) and (14.8) imply that the ratio of domestic to foreign prices is fixed so that $P_t/P_t^* = \bar{e}$, and that the rates of interest on securities of different currency denominations are equalized so that $\tilde{R}_{Ht} = \tilde{R}_{Ft}$.

The intervention in the foreign-exchange market induces changes in the money supply. These changes are the counterpart to the change in international reserves used up in the process of pegging the rate of exchange. The surplus in the overall balance of payments is the sum of the surpluses in the current and the capital accounts of the balance of payments. These surpluses in turn correspond to the excess supply of foreign exchange induced by the international transactions at the prevailing exchange rate, $\bar{e}$. To prevent changes in this peg, the authorities must absorb this quantity and supply in exchange domestic currency. Hence the periodic expansions in the domestic money supply associated with the pegging operations are

$$\tilde{X}_0 = [M_{H0}^* + \tilde{R}_{H,-1}\tilde{B}_{H,-1}^{*p} - \tilde{B}_{H0}^{*p}]$$

$$- \bar{e}[M_{F0} + \tilde{R}_{F,-1}\tilde{B}_{F,-1}^{p} - \tilde{B}_{F0}^{p}], \tag{14.20}$$

$$\tilde{X}_1 = [M_{H1}^* + \tilde{R}_{H0}\tilde{B}_{H0}^{*p}] - \bar{e}[M_{F1} + \tilde{R}_{F0}\tilde{B}_{F0}^p]. \tag{14.21}$$

Equation (14.20) expresses the monetary injections in terms of the (domestic-currency value of the) monetary flows associated with international transactions in period zero. The first bracketed term shows the monetary inflows induced by foreign residents and the second bracketed term shows the monetary outflows induced by domestic residents. The former consists of foreign demand for domestic money, M_{H0}^*, plus principal and interest payments on past domestic debt held by foreigners, $\tilde{R}_{H,-1}\tilde{B}_{H,-1}^{*p}$, minus new issue by foreigners of domestic-currency-denominated bonds, $\tilde{B}_{H0}^{*p}$. Analogously, the second bracketed term consists of domestic demand for foreign currency, M_{F0}, plus interest and principal payments on past domestic holdings of foreign-currency-denominated bonds, $\tilde{R}_{F,-1}\tilde{B}_{F,-1}^p$, minus new issue by domestic residents of foreign-currency-denominated bonds, $\tilde{B}_{F0}^p$, all expressed in units of the domestic currency.

Equivalently, the right-hand side of equation (14.20) can be expressed as the sum of the surpluses in the trade account, TA, the service account, SA, and the capital account, CA, of the balance of payments. Accordingly,

$$\tilde{X}_0 = \bar{e}[(TA)_0 + (SA)_0 + (CA)_0], \tag{14.20a}$$

where, using the cash-in-advance constraints (14.5) and (14.6) along with their foreign-country counterparts,

$$(TA)_0 = P_0^*(C_{x0}^* - C_{m0}) = \frac{1}{\bar{e}}M_{H0}^* - M_{F0},$$

$$(SA)_0 = (\tilde{R}_{-1} - 1)\left(\frac{1}{\bar{e}}\tilde{B}_{H,-1}^{*p} - \tilde{B}_{F,-1}^p\right),$$

$$(CA)_0 = (\tilde{B}_{F0}^p - \tilde{B}_{F,-1}^p) - \frac{1}{\bar{e}}(\tilde{B}_{H0}^{*p} - \tilde{B}_{H,-1}^{*p}),$$

where due to interest-rate equalization, $\tilde{R}_{-1} = \tilde{R}_{H,-1} = \tilde{R}_{F,-1}$. An analogous interpretation applies to equation (14.21) which reflects the solvency requirement that in the last period no new debt is issued and all past debt commitments are settled.

The consequences of the fixed exchange-rate regime for the behavior of the private sector can be analyzed using a similar procedure to the one followed in the previous section. Accordingly, as before, we determine the consumption-possibility set. Using the private-sector budget constraints (14.1) and (14.4), the parity conditions, the money-supply rules (14.11), and the money-market equilibrium condition, we perform identical substitutions as in the previous section and obtain

$$P_0 C_0 = P_0 Y_{x0} - \tilde{X}_0 + \tilde{B}_0^p - \tilde{R}_{H,-1} \tilde{B}_{-1}^p, \qquad (14.22)$$

$$P_1 C_1 = P_1 Y_{x1} - \tilde{X}_1 - \tilde{R}_{H0} \tilde{B}_0^p. \qquad (14.23)$$

Finally, substituting equations (14.12) and (14.13)—the foreign-currency accounts of the public sector—into equations (14.22) and (14.23), respectively, consolidating the resulting two equations, and expressing in real terms yields

$$C_0 + \frac{1}{R_0} C_1 = Y_{x0} + \frac{1}{R_0} Y_{x1} - R_{-1} B_{-1}, \qquad (14.24)$$

where $B = B^p + B^g$ denotes the economy's external debt.

As is evident the consumption-possibility set characterized by equation (14.24) for the fixed exchange-rate regime is *identical* to the one characterized by equation (14.18) for the flexible exchange-rate regime. This identity reflects the Ricardian structure of the model along with the assumptions of perfect capital markets, flexible prices, and the absence of distortionary taxes.

Before concluding this section, it is noteworthy that the responsibility for fixing the rate of exchange imposes a constraint on the conduct of macroeconomic policies. To highlight the implications of this constraint, we consolidate the public-sector equations (14.10)—for $t = 0$ and $t = 1$—with equations (14.12) and (14.13), making use of the fact that with fixed exchange rates the rates of interest are equalized. This yields

$$\left(D_0 + \frac{1}{R_0} D_1 \right) + \left(\tilde{T}_0 + \frac{1}{R_0} \tilde{T}_1 \right) = \bar{e} R_{-1} \tilde{B}_{F,-1}^g. \qquad (14.25)$$

Equation (14.25) shows that the payments of principal and interest on the initial public-sector debt commitment are financed through monetary expansions and through taxes, whose discounted sums must equal the domestic-currency value of the debt commitment. As a result, given the government commitment to the fixed exchange rate, an independently given tax policy—reflected in the discounted sum $\tilde{T}_0 + (1/R_0)\tilde{T}_1$—necessitates a specific monetary adjustment—reflected in the discounted sum $D_0 + (1/R_0)D_1$; and conversely, an independently given monetary policy necessitates a specific tax adjustment.

14.4 Summary

In this chapter we developed a minimal framework for the incorporation of money into the intertemporal model of the world economy. The framework was designed to yield a bench-mark formulation characterized by the properties that money is a veil. As a result the detailed monetary mechanisms implied by the adoption of alternative exchange-rate regimes do not influence the real equilibrium. The key characteristics yielding this neutrality result are perfect capital markets, flexible market-clearing prices, the absence of distortionary taxes and other distortions, and an identical time horizon governing private and public-sector decisions. Some of these assumptions are relaxed in the next chapter in which we identify key mechanisms associated with the management of the exchange rate with equivalent tax policies.

15

Exchange-Rate Management Viewed as Tax Policies

The analysis in the preceding chapter demonstrated the intimate connection between monetary and fiscal policies. The interdependence between these policies stems from the budget constraints of the public sector. Hence changes in the money supply arising from exchange-rate management necessitate corresponding compensating changes in monetary or tax policies designed to ensure public-sector solvency. The specific combination of these monetary and tax policies was immaterial in the frictionless undistorted bench-mark model. In that model the time distribution of lump-sum taxes and of monetary policy does not alter the real equilibrium. Hence, as was shown, the real equilibrium was neutral with respect to the nominal exchange-rate regime.

In this chapter we modify the bench-mark model by introducing key features that break the strong neutrality results. The main purpose is to design a framework within which the management of exchange rates exerts significant effects on the economic system. We then use the extended model to demonstrate that the various forms of exchange-rate management are equivalent to corresponding tax policies analyzed in previous chapters. This equivalence serves to clarify the precise mechanisms through which exchange-rate policies influence the economic system. The features of exchange-rate management that are equivalent to taxes provide the rationale for viewing exchange-rate policies as part of the broader issue of fiscal management.

15.1 The Analytical Framework

In this section we present an analytical framework suitable for the analysis of real effects of exchange-rate management in the context of a small-country model, and we build on the basic structure of the model developed in chapter 14. To highlight the salient issues, we consider specific categories of exchange-rate policies. Thus we supplement the two regimes discussed in the previous chapter with an additional regime—the dual exchange rate regime. Such a regime allows for separate exchange rates for commercial and for financial transactions.

In introducing the analytical framework, it is convenient to start with a specification of the policy actions undertaken in managing the dual exchange-rate regime. In this context government transactions can be separated into two accounts: a domestic-currency account and a foreign-currency account. We assume that the government sets the paths of the two exchange rates (the commercial and the financial rates) and allows free mobility of capital. In period t the monetary expansion induced by government foreign exchange intervention in pegging the *financial* exchange rate is $\bar{s}_t(\hat{B}_t^p - \tilde{R}_F \hat{B}_{t-1}^p)$, where $\bar{s}_t$ denotes the pegged financial exchange rate, $\tilde{R}_F$ denotes the world (fixed) nominal rate of interest on foreign-currency denominated bonds, and $\hat{B}^p$ denotes private-sector debt expressed in units of foreign exchange (in contrast with $\tilde{B}^p$ used in chapter 14 to denote private-sector debt expressed in units of domestic currency). In addition the monetary expansion in period t associated with pegging the *commercial* exchange rate at the level $\bar{e}_t$ is $\bar{e}_t P_t^*(Y_x - C_t)$, where $(Y_x - C_t)$ is the (per-capita aggregate) real trade balance—the excess of production (which is assumed to be fixed) over spending. Thus the monetary injections associated with foreign exchange interventions are

$$\tilde{X}_t = \bar{e}_t p_t^*(Y_x - C_t) + \bar{s}_t(\hat{B}_t^p - \tilde{R}_F \hat{B}_{t-1}^p). \tag{15.1}$$

It is noteworthy that in this formulation we have assumed for convenience that the exchange rate applicable to debt service is the financial exchange rate. The key results of this chapter do not depend on this assumption.

An alternative specification generating a dual exchange-rate regime assumes that the government imposes a binding quota on the volume of private-sector net international borrowing and pegs the commercial exchange rate. In this formulation the financial exchange rate, s, is determined in the free market. We denote the quota by $\overline{B}_t^p$. Accordingly, equation (15.1) becomes

$$\tilde{X}_t = \overline{e}_t p_t^*(Y_x - C_t) + s_t(\overline{B}_t^p - \tilde{R}_F \overline{B}_{t-1}^p). \tag{15.2}$$

The two alternative formulations of the monetary consequences of exchange-rate interventions reflect themselves in the money supply as shown by equation (14.11), and the condition for money-market equilibrium is the same as in equation (14.9).

The private sector is assumed to consist of overlapping generations as in chapters 10 through 13. This assumption introduces into the model a finite horizon, and thereby it constitutes an additional modification of the bench-mark model of chapter 14. The budget constraint of an individual of age a at time t is

$$\overline{e}_t P_t^* c_{a,t} = \overline{e}_{t-1} P_{t-1}^* Y_x + s_t \hat{b}_{a,t} - \tilde{T}_t - \frac{\tilde{R}_F}{\gamma} s_t \hat{b}_{a-1,t-1}, \tag{15.3}$$

where $\hat{b}$ is the debt of the individual expressed in units of foreign currency. This constraint is analogous to the one shown by equation (10.3) but is modified to incorporate the cash-in-advance–dual-exchange-rate elements. Accordingly, $\overline{e}_t P_{t-1}^* Y_x$ represents the sales by domestic firms during period $t - 1$, whose proceeds are distributed to individuals at the beginning of period t. The last term on the right-hand side of equation (15.3) represents the debt commitments. As is evident, the relevant effective rate of interest is $(\tilde{R}_F/\gamma) - 1$, reflecting the risk associated with mortality. The unique feature of the dual exchange-rate regime is reflected by the two exchange rates appearing in equation (15.3). The domestic price level, $P_t = \overline{e}_t P_t^*$, is governed by the commerical exchange rate through the purchasing-power-parity relation. On the other hand, debt commitments are settled through the financial exchange rate, s_t. Strictly speaking, equation (15.3) applies to the formulation under which the financial exchange rate, s_t, is determined in the free market. With the alternative formulation, under which the path of the financial exchange rate is also pegged, the term s_t is replaced by $\overline{s}_t$.

Equation (15.3) is the budget constraint applicable to period t. It is shown in the appendix that consolidating the periodic constraints into a single lifetime constraint and making use of the requirement that in the limit as time approaches infinity the present value of debt commitment (computed using the effective rate of interest) is zero yields

$$\sum_{t=0}^{\infty} \frac{\overline{e}_t P_t^*}{s_t} d_t c_{a+t,t} = \sum_{t=0}^{\infty} \frac{\overline{e}_{t-1} P_{t-1}^*}{s_t} d_t Y_x - \sum_{t=0}^{\infty} d_t \frac{\tilde{T}_t}{s_t} - \frac{\tilde{R}_{F,-1}}{\gamma} \hat{b}_{a-1,-1}$$

$$= \hat{w}_{a,0}, \qquad (15.4)$$

where $d_t = (\gamma/\tilde{R}_F)^t$.

This constraint defines the initial value of wealth, $\hat{w}_{a,0}$, expressed in units of first-period foreign currency. The economic interpretation of the various terms follows. Consider, for example, the coefficients of $c_{a,0}$ and $c_{a+1,1}$ on the left-hand side of equation (15.4). These coefficients are $\overline{e}_0 P_0^*/s_0$ and $(\overline{e}_1 P_1^*/s_1)(\gamma/\tilde{R}_F)$, respectively. The domestic relative price of consumption in period one in terms of consumption in period zero is $[(\overline{e}_1/\overline{e}_0)/(s_1/s_0)][(P_1^*/P_0^*)/(\tilde{R}_F/\gamma)]$. This relative price is the product of two terms: the real effective *world* discount factor (shown by the second bracketed term) and the differential rates of depreciation of the commercial and the financial exchange rates (shown by the first bracketed term). This latter component, which represents the contribution of exchange-rate management to the overall real rate of return on investment in financial assets, translates the world real effective discount factor into the corresponding domestic discount factor. That is, the capital gain on an investment in assets denominated in foreign currency is (s_1/s_0), and its product with $(\overline{e}_0/\overline{e}_1)$ translates the return into units of foreign-currency-denominated goods. A similar interpretation applies to the coefficients multiplying the rates of consumption in other periods. As is evident, divergencies between the domestic and the foreign real rates of interest stem from the terms involving exchange-rate changes in the dual exchange-rate regime. It is important to note that these divergencies arise only from *differences* in the percentage rates of depreciations of the commerical and financial exchange rates. In the absence of such a difference, the domestic and foreign real rates of interest are equalized.

The present-value factors multiplying the levels of output on the right-hand side of equation (15.4) differ from those used to evaluate the sequence of consumption. The difference arises from the underlying cash-in-advance assumption, according to which nominal proceeds from sales of output are distributed with a one period lag. The next term on the right-hand side of equation (15.4) represents the discounted sum of nominal taxes. The final term is the individual's debt commitment $(\bar{R}_{F,-1}/\gamma)\hat{b}_{a-1,-1}$. To express these quantities in units of period-zero consumption, we need to multiply the various coefficients by $s_0/(\bar{e}_0 P_0^*)$. As a result for any given initial foreign price, the real value of wealth also depends on the ratio of the two exchange rates in period zero, $s_0/\bar{e}_0$.

To evaluate the real effects of exchange-rate management, we need to determine the equilibrium value of wealth. The foregoing discussion dealt with the factors governing the pricing of consumption in various periods, under the conditions of a dual exchange-rate regime. To complete the analysis of the determinants of consumption, we need to determine the dependence of the equilibrium level of wealth on the exchange-rate regime. Accordingly, we incorporate the equilibrium conditions into the individual equation (15.4) which is then aggregated over individuals. As shown in the appendix, this procedure yields

$$\hat{W}_0 = \sum_{t=0}^{\infty} \frac{\bar{e}_t P_t^*}{s_t} d_t Y_x + \sum_{t=0}^{\infty} \left(\frac{\bar{e}_t}{s_t} - \gamma \frac{\bar{e}_{t+1}}{s_{t+1}} \right) d_t \hat{B}_t$$

$$- (1 - \gamma) \sum_{t=0}^{\infty} d_t \hat{B}_t^p - \frac{\bar{e}_0}{s_0} \tilde{R}_{F,-1} \hat{B}_{-1}, \tag{15.5}$$

where $\hat{W}_0$ denotes the (per-capita) aggregate value of equilibrium wealth expressed in units of period-zero foreign exchange.

The pertinent characteristics of equation (15.5) are discussed in the subsequent sections. Prior to this discussion it is relevant to remark that the pricing coefficients of output, $(\bar{e}_t P_t^*/s_t)d_t$, are the same as the pricing coefficients of consumption shown in equation (15.4).

In *equilibrium* the lagged payments reflecting the cash-in-advance convention have no effect on the pricing of outputs.

In interpreting the salient features of the equilibrium-wealth equation (15.5), it is useful to consider special cases. The analysis of these special cases highlights the basic mechanisms through which exchange-rate management influences the economic system. A revealing bench mark is the case in which the authorities do not intervene at all in the foreign-exchange market and allow for free international mobility of capital. In that case $\bar{e}_t = s_t$, and $\hat{B}_t^p = \hat{B}_t$ (since in the absence of intervention and open-market operations public-sector debt is zero). Hence equation (15.5) becomes

$$\hat{W}_0 = \sum_{t=0}^{\infty} P_t^* d_t Y_x - \tilde{R}_{F,-1} \hat{B}_{-1}. \tag{15.6}$$

In this bench-mark case the equilibrium value of wealth is the discounted sum of GDP net of initial external debt commitment. This expression (which is the analogue to the expression on the right-hand side of equation 14.18) reveals that the consumption-opportunity set is the same as the one obtained in the undistorted barter economy. This illustrates the point made earlier in chapter 10—that the finiteness of the horizon, in and of itself, does not introduce a distortion into the economic system.

In the next section we consider a departure from the bench-mark case and examine the pure effects of the dual exchange-rate regime.

15.2 Dual Exchange Rates as Distortionary Taxes

In order to focus on the unique mechanism associated with the dual exchange-rate policies, consider the infinite-horizon case in which $\gamma = 1$. To facilitate the exposition, we suppose that the foreign price is fixed and normalized to unity; that is, we let $P_t^* = 1$. In that case $\tilde{R}_F = R$, and since $\gamma = 1$, we replace the present-value factor d_t by $\alpha_t = R^{-t}$. Further we express (15.5) in units of first-period consumption—by multiplying each term by $(s_0/\bar{e}_0)$—and note that the real value of wealth spans the consumption-opportunity set. Accordingly,

$$\sum_{t=0}^{\infty} \Pi_t \alpha_t C_t = \sum_{t=0}^{\infty} \Pi_t \alpha_t Y_x + \sum_{t=0}^{\infty} \alpha_t (\Pi_t - \Pi_{t+1}) B_t - R_{-1} B_{-1}$$

$$= W_0, \tag{15.7}$$

where $\Pi_t = (s_0/\bar{e}_0)/(s_t/\bar{e}_t)$.

We define the dual exchange-rate *premium* by the percentage discrepancy between s and $\bar{e}$; that is, the premium is $(s/\bar{e}) - 1$. Accordingly, Π_t reflects the *evolution* of the dual exchange-rate premium over time. A rise in the premium is associated with a decline in Π_t. The discounted sum of consumption shown in equation (15.7) differs from the one obtained in the undistorted Ricardian model (as illustrated by equation 12.28) by one important property: it is influenced by the time path of the dual exchange-rate premium. Indeed, if the premium is constant for all time then the consumption-possibility set characterized by equation (15.7) coincides with the one obtained in the undistorted barter economy.

In general, the evolution (rather than the level) of the dual exchange-rate premium influences the consumption-possibility set by distorting the prices governing the intertemporal allocation of consumption (and of output if investment is allowed for) and by influencing wealth. The distortionary effect on the intertemporal prices arises from the wedge that the dual exchange-rate system introduces between the effective domestic and world rates of interest. An additional channel through which the dual exchange-rate premium influences wealth operates through the interaction between the evolutions of the premium and of the external debt, as reflected by the term

$$\sum_{t=0}^{\infty} \alpha_t (\Pi_t - \Pi_{t+1}) B_t. \tag{15.8}$$

To illustrate this mechanism, consider, for example, the coefficient of B_0, $\{1 - [(s_0/\bar{e}_0)/(s_1/\bar{e}_1)]\}$. With positive net external debt, B_0, this coefficient represents the "subsidy rate" induced by the evolution of the premium, and B_0 is the "subsidy base." The subsidy rate represents the percentage rate of the reduction in the value of the debt measured in terms of domestic goods. Accordingly, if s_1 exceeds s_0, then the foreign-currency value of the debt incurred in period zero depreciates. Adjusting this depreciation for the rise in domestic prices (indicated by $\bar{e}_1/\bar{e}_0$) yields the subsidy in real terms. Accordingly, the expression in (15.8) can be viewed as the discounted sum of the products of the periodic subsidy rates and the periodic subsidy bases.

The two effects of the dual exchange-rate system (the intertemporal-price effect and the wealth effect) are equivalent to those arising from the imposition of distortionary taxes on international borrowing. Since in our formulation the exchange rate applicable to debt service is the financial rate, this dual exchange-rate system is equivalent to a system of taxes on international borrowing in which debt service is not exempt from the tax. Alternatively, a dual exchange-rate system, in which the exchange rate applicable to the debt service is the commerical rate, is equivalent to the system of taxes on international borrowing, analyzed in chapter 8, in which debt service is exempt from the tax.

We conclude this section by characterizing the effects of dual exchange-rate policy, cast as a distortionary tax on international borrowing, on the real equilibrium. Assuming a logarithmic utility function—so that the consumption function is $C_t = (1 - \delta)W_t$—and recalling that from the national income accounts that $C_t - Y_t = B_t - RB_{t-1}$, we can solve for the time path of external debt. Accordingly,

$$B_t = \frac{C_0}{\alpha_t} \sum_{\tau=0}^{t} \frac{\delta^\tau}{\Pi_\tau} - \sum_{\tau=0}^{t} \frac{Y_x}{\alpha_{t-\tau}} + \frac{R_{-1}B_{-1}}{\alpha_t}. \tag{15.9}$$

Equation (15.9) states that the economy's external debt is the difference between the sums of the present values of past (including the present) consumption and outputs adjusted for the initial debt commitment (in present value as of period t).

Using the economywide solvency requirement that in the limit (as time goes to infinity) the present value of external debt, evaluated using the world real rate of interest, equal zero, equation (15.9) can be written as

$$C_0 = \frac{\sum_{t=0}^{\infty} \Pi_t \alpha_t Y_x - R_{-1}B_{-1}}{\sum_{t=0}^{\infty} (\delta^t/\Pi_t)}. \tag{15.10}$$

Equation (15.10) shows that a future deceleration in the rate of change of the dual exchange-rate premia (i.e., a rise in Π_t) raises current consumption. This rise reflects the increased value of wealth consequent on the reduction in the effective domestic rate of interest.

Equations (15.9) and (15.10) constitute a system that can be solved to yield the equilibrium path of the external debt and the equilibrium value of C_0 for the case in which the dual exchange-rate regime is implemented through pegging the exchange-rate premium, thereby determining the path of Π_t. Alternatively, if the dual exchange-rate regime is implemented through the imposition of a binding quota on the private sector's external borrowing, then the same system of equations (together with the specification of the path of government debt) can be solved for the path of the dual exchange-rate premium and for the equilibrium value of consumption.

In view of the equivalence between the dual exchange-rate policy and the policy of imposing taxes on international borrowing, the general issues raised in our analysis of distortionary taxes in chapter 8 are also applicable here.

15.3 Exchange-Rate Management as Lump-Sum Taxes

In this section we depart from the bench-mark case of equation (15.6) and examine the pure wealth effects of exchange-rate management. Thereby we determine the circumstances under which exchange-rate policies can be cast as being equivalent to lump-sum tax policies. In order to focus on the pure wealth effect associated with exchange-rate management, we introduce the finite horizon by assuming that the value of γ is less than unity, and we assume that the authorities peg the exchange rate without separating between the commercial and the financial rates. In this unified exchange-rate regime the management of the rate is nondistortionary, and its impact on the real economic system operates only through the pure wealth effect.

Using the assumptions that the exchange-rate regime is unified (i.e., $e_t = s_t$) and that the fixed foreign price P^* is normalized to unity, we express the consumption-opportunity set of equation (15.5) as

$$\sum_{t=0}^{\infty} d_t C_t = \sum_{t=0}^{\infty} d_t Y_x + (1 - \gamma) \sum_{t=0}^{\infty} d_t B_t^g - R_{-1} B_{-1}, \qquad (15.11)$$

where we have used the definitions of $B^g = B - B^p$ and $d_t = (\gamma/R)^t$.

The only element that distinguishes between the consumption-opportunity set shown in equation (15.11) and the set obtained in the barter economy (embodied in the expression for wealth in equation 10.14) is the second term on the right-hand side of equation (15.11). It follows that in contrast with the consequences of dual exchange rates, the unified rate results in undistorted intertemporal prices. For example, as shown on the left-hand side of equation (15.11), the relative price of consumption in period one in terms of consumption in period zero is the world real discount factor, $1/R$.

In our pure monetary model without government spending, the term $(1 - \gamma)\sum_{t=0}^{\infty} d_t B_t^g$ is governed by the movement of international reserves induced by the pegging of the exchange rate (as illustrated by equations 14.12 and 14.13). Accordingly, unless the government designs its tax and monetary policy so as to always meet (at the given peg) changes in the demand for money, the pegging operations are reflected in the evolution of government debt.

As is evident, changes in the stock of government debt influence the real equilibrium by altering the value of wealth. The extent to which government debt influences private-sector wealth depends on the difference between private and social rates of discount. This difference reflects the finiteness of the individual's expected horizon. This is the same mechanism responsible for the real effects of lump-sum taxes analyzed in chapters 10 through 12. Thus the effects of unified exchange-rate management are equivalent to those exerted by lump-sum tax cum transfer policies.

15.4 Summary

This chapter demonstrated the equivalence between exchange-rate management and tax policies. For this purpose we used the minimal monetary framework and have not attempted to provide a complete analysis of the broader issues associated with monetary and exchange-rate policies in the world economy. To establish the key propositions, we modified the bench-mark model characterized by perfect capital markets, flexible market-clearing prices, no distortions, and no difference between the time horizons of the private and the public sector in various directions. We showed that dual exchange-rate policies can be usefully cast as distortionary taxes on international borrowing, and unified pegged exchange-rate policies can be usefully cast as lump-sum tax cum subsidy policies. The equivalence between the various characteristics of exchange-rate management and tax management justifies the inclusion of exchange-rate analysis into the broader framework of the analysis of fiscal policies.

15.5 Appendix: Derivation of Equilibrium Wealth

In this appendix we derive the equilibrium value of wealth. We first consolidate the periodic budget constraints for the individual. As shown in equation (15.3), the budget constraint of an individual of age a at time t is

$$\bar{e}_t P_t^* c_{a,t} = \bar{e}_{t-1} P_{t-1}^* Y_x + s_t \hat{b}_{a,t} - \tilde{T}_t - \left(\frac{\tilde{R}_F}{\gamma} \right) s_t \hat{b}_{a-1,t-1}. \tag{A.1}$$

In more detail these constraints can be written as

$$\bar{e}_0 P_0^* c_{a,0} = \bar{e}_{-1} P_{-1}^* Y_x + s_0 \hat{b}_{a,0} - \tilde{T}_0 - \left(\frac{\tilde{R}_F}{\gamma} \right) s_0 \hat{b}_{a-1,-1}, \tag{A.1a}$$

$$\bar{e}_1 P_1^* c_{a+1,1} = \bar{e}_0 P_0^* Y_x + s_1 \hat{b}_{a+1,1} - \tilde{T}_1 - \left(\frac{\tilde{R}_F}{\gamma} \right) s_1 \hat{b}_{a,0}, \tag{A.1b}$$

$$\bar{e}_2 P_2^* c_{a+2,2} = \bar{e}_1 P_1^* Y_x + s_2 \hat{b}_{a+2,2} - \tilde{T}_2 - \left(\frac{\tilde{R}_F}{\gamma} \right) s_2 \hat{b}_{a+1,1}, \quad \text{etc.}$$
$$\tag{A.1c}$$

Multiplying (A.1c) by $(s_1/s_2)(\gamma/\tilde{R}_F)$ and adding to (A.1b) yields

$$\bar{e}_1 P_1^* c_{a+1,1} + \frac{\bar{e}_2 P_2^* s_1}{s_2} \frac{\gamma}{\tilde{R}_F} c_{a+2,2}$$

$$= \bar{e}_0 P_0^* Y_x + \frac{\bar{e}_1 P_1^* s_1}{s_2} \frac{\gamma}{\tilde{R}_F} Y_x + s_1 \frac{\gamma}{\tilde{R}_F} \hat{b}_{a+2,2}$$

$$- \tilde{T}_1 - \frac{s_1}{s_2} \frac{\gamma}{\tilde{R}_F} \tilde{T}_2 - s_1 \frac{\tilde{R}_F}{\gamma} \hat{b}_{a,0}. \tag{A.1d}$$

Multiplying (A.1d) by $(s_0/s_1)(\gamma/\tilde{R}_F)$, adding to (A.1a), and dividing the resulting equation by $\bar{e}_0 P_0^*$ yields

$$c_{a,0} + \frac{\bar{e}_1 P_1^*}{\bar{e}_0 P_0^*} \frac{s_0}{s_1} \frac{\gamma}{\tilde{R}_F} c_{a+1,1} + \frac{\bar{e}_2 P_2^*}{\bar{e}_0 P_0^*} \frac{s_0}{s_2} \left(\frac{\gamma}{\tilde{R}_F}\right)^2 c_{a+2,2}$$

$$= \left[\frac{\bar{e}_{-1} P_{-1}^*}{\bar{e}_0 P_0^*} + \frac{s_0}{s_1} \frac{\bar{e}_0 P_0^*}{\bar{e}_0 P_0^*} \frac{\gamma}{\tilde{R}_F} + \frac{\bar{e}_1 P_1^*}{\bar{e}_0 P_0^*} \frac{s_0}{s_2} \left(\frac{\gamma}{\tilde{R}_F}\right)^2 \right] Y_x$$

$$+ \frac{s_0}{\bar{e}_0 P_0^*} \left(\frac{\gamma}{\tilde{R}_F}\right)^2 b_{a+2,2}$$

$$- \left[\frac{\tilde{T}_0}{\bar{e}_0 P_0^*} + \frac{s_0 \tilde{T}_1}{s_1 \bar{e}_0 P_0^*} \left(\frac{\gamma}{\tilde{R}_F}\right) + \frac{s_0 \tilde{T}_2}{s_2 \bar{e}_0 P_0^*} \left(\frac{\gamma}{\tilde{R}_F}\right)^2 \right]$$

$$- \left(\frac{\tilde{R}_F}{\gamma}\right) \frac{s_0}{\bar{e}_0 P_0^*} \hat{b}_{a-1,-1}. \tag{A.1e}$$

Applying a similar procedure for all periods yields

$$\sum_{t=0}^{\infty} \frac{\bar{e}_t P_t^*}{s_t} d_t c_{a+t,t} = \sum_{t=0}^{\infty} \frac{\bar{e}_{t-1} P_{t-1}^*}{s_t} d_t Y_x - \sum_{t=0}^{\infty} d_t \frac{\tilde{T}_t}{s_t}$$

$$- \left(\frac{\tilde{R}_F}{\gamma}\right) \hat{b}_{a-1,-1} = \hat{w}_{a0}, \tag{A.2}$$

where $d_t = (\gamma/\tilde{R}_F)^t$. Equation (A.2) is equation (15.4).

To compute the equilibrium value of wealth, we need to incorporate the equilibrium conditions into the expression of wealth in equation (A.2). The monetary mechanism, shown in equations (14.11) and (15.2), is reproduced here as

$$M_t = M_{t-1} + \tilde{X}_t - \tilde{T}_t, \tag{A.3}$$

$$\tilde{X}_t = \bar{e}_t P_t^*(Y_x - C_t) + s_t(\hat{B}_t^p - \tilde{R}_F \hat{B}_{t-1}^p). \tag{A.4}$$

The equilibrium condition is shown by equation (14.9) and is reproduced here as

$$M_t = \bar{e}_t P_t^* Y_x. \tag{A.5}$$

Expressing (A.3) as $M_{t-1} - \tilde{T}_t = M_t - \tilde{X}_t$, and using (A.5), for

$t - 1$, we can write equation (A.2) as

$$\hat{w}_{a0} = \sum_{t=0}^{\infty} \frac{1}{s_t} d_t (M_t - \tilde{X}_t) - \frac{\tilde{R}_F}{\gamma} \hat{b}_{a-1,-1}. \tag{A.6}$$

Finally, using (A.5) for M_t, the equilibrium individual wealth is

$$\hat{w}_{a0} = \sum_{t=0}^{\infty} \frac{\overline{e}_t P_t^*}{s_t} d_t Y_x - \sum_{t=0}^{\infty} d_t \frac{\tilde{X}_t}{s_t} - \frac{\tilde{R}_F}{\gamma} \hat{b}_{a-1,-1}. \tag{A.7}$$

To obtain the per-capita value of aggregate wealth, we follow the procedure developed in chapter 10. Accordingly, applying the aggregation operator $(1 - \gamma)\sum_{a=0}^{\infty} \gamma^a$ to both sides of (A.7), the per-capita wealth, $\hat{W}_0$, is

$$\hat{W}_0 = \sum_{t=0}^{\infty} \frac{\overline{e}_t P_t^*}{s_t} d_t Y_x - \sum_{t=0}^{\infty} d_t \frac{\tilde{X}_t}{s_t} - \tilde{R}_F \hat{B}_{-1}^p. \tag{A.8}$$

Using (A.4) for $\tilde{X}$ and recalling from the balance-of-payments accounting that $P_t^*(Y_x - C_t) = -(\hat{B}_t - \tilde{R}_F \hat{B}_{t-1})$, the second term on the right-hand side of (A.8) can be written as

$$-\sum_{t=0}^{\infty} d_t \frac{\tilde{X}_t}{s_t} = \sum_{t=0}^{\infty} d_t \frac{\overline{e}_t(\hat{B}_t - \tilde{R}_F \hat{B}_{t-1}) - s_t(\hat{B}_t^p - \tilde{R}_F \hat{B}_{-1}^p)}{s_t}$$

$$= \sum_{t=0}^{\infty} d_t \frac{\overline{e}_t}{s_t}(\hat{B}_t - \tilde{R}_F \hat{B}_{t-1}) + \tilde{R}_{F,-1} \hat{B}_{-1}^p - (1 - \gamma) \sum_{t=0}^{\infty} d_t \hat{B}_t^p$$

$$= \sum_{t=0}^{\infty} \left(\frac{\overline{e}_t}{s_t} - \gamma \frac{\overline{e}_{t+1}}{s_{t+1}} \right) d_t \hat{B}_t + \tilde{R}_{F,-1} \hat{B}_{-1}^p$$

$$- (1 - \gamma) \sum_{t=0}^{\infty} d_t \hat{B}_t^p - \frac{\overline{e}_0}{s_0} \tilde{R}_{F,-1} \hat{B}_{-1}. \tag{A.9}$$

Finally, substituting (A.9) into (A.8) yields

$$\hat{W}_0 = \sum_{t=0}^{\infty} \frac{\overline{e}_t P_t^*}{s_t} d_t Y_x + \sum_{t=0}^{\infty} \left(\frac{\overline{e}_t}{s_t} - \gamma \frac{\overline{e}_{t+1}}{s_{t+1}} \right) d_t \hat{B}_t$$

$$- (1 - \gamma) \sum_{t=0}^{\infty} d_t \hat{B}_t^p - \frac{\overline{e}_0}{s_0} \tilde{R}_{F,-1} \hat{B}_{-1}, \tag{A.10}$$

which is equation (15.5).

VII

Epilogue

16

Empirical and Theoretical Overview

In this book we have attempted to develop a unified conceptual framework suitable for the analysis of the effects of government expenditure and tax policies on key macroeconomic aggregates in the interdependent world economy. The analysis was motivated by the major developments occurring in the world economy during the first half of the 1980s: changes in national fiscal policies were unsynchronized, real rates of interest were high and volatile, and real exchange rates exhibited diverging trends and were subject to large fluctuations. Furthermore large fiscal imbalances resulted in drastic changes in public debt and were associated with large imbalances in current-account positions and with significant changes in the international allocations of debt. Though these real-world developments provide the impetus for the analysis, the orientation of the book is theoretical. It aims at clarifying the complex economic mechanisms underlying the international transmission of the effects of macroeconomics policies. An empirical implementation of the theory developed throughout the book is highly complex. Without attempting to launch on such a challenging endeavor, we provide in section 16.1 some illustrative computations of the intertemporal model and compare the results with the actual data. Section 16.2 highlights key differences between the income-expenditure and the intertemporal models as reflected in the economic mechanisms underlying the main channels of the international transmission of fiscal policies. Finally, section 16.3 contains a brief discussion of suggested extensions.

16.1 An Illustrative Computation

In this section we use the analytical model developed in section 13.2 to compute the predicted paths of domestic and foreign consumption that are implied by the actual paths of the exogenous macroeconomic variables. We then compare these predicted paths of consumption with the paths that have actually been followed. In addition we compute the correlations between the predicted paths of consumption and the actual paths of the other variables and compare these correlations with those actually observed in the data. Though these computations should not be viewed as the empirical counterpart to the theoretical model, they nevertheless are suggestive of the potential applicability of the theoretical approach.

The illustrations used in this section center around the paths of consumption since the comovements of these paths with the other key economic variables were the focus of the theoretical analysis. In performing the computations, we have assumed specific values for the key parameters. These parameter values along with the actual paths of the exogenous variables were substituted into the model yielding the solution paths of the endogenous variables.

Tables 16.1 and 16.2 report the actual and the predicted annual growth rates of private-sector consumption in the United States and in the rest-of-the-world for the period 1956 to 1984. For this illustration the rest-of-the-world is defined as the Group of Seven major industrial countries excluding the United States. This group comprises Canada, France, Italy, Japan, the United Kingdom, and West Germany. The computation of the model necessitates the conversion of all data for various countries into common currency units. In view of the sharp changes in exchange rates that have occurred during the sample period, the choice of the common numeraire may have significant consequences for the relations among the various time series. Therefore, to allow for this possibility, we have computed all series for two alternatives. The first expresses the data in constant German prices, and the second in constant U.S. prices.

The growth rates reported in both tables exhibit considerable correlation between the actual and the predicted time series. For

Table 16.1
Predicted and actual U.S. consumption: 1956–1984 (annual percentage growth rates)

Year	In constant German prices		In constant U.S. prices	
	Actual	Predicted	Actual	Predicted
1956	2.21	1.97	3.21	1.89
1957	3.26	−1.30	1.99	−1.46
1958	1.00	−7.96	0.30	−6.30
1959	6.23	8.74	6.25	7.97
1960	2.94	5.91	3.03	6.61
1961	−3.29	−8.45	1.95	−0.95
1962	2.17	−1.22	4.76	1.96
1963	2.34	3.66	3.96	5.03
1964	4.37	7.38	5.62	8.91
1965	4.01	5.46	5.62	6.89
1966	4.30	−1.63	4.66	−1.14
1967	3.68	−4.95	2.52	−6.47
1968	7.51	3.44	4.97	1.18
1969	4.72	6.23	2.72	6.97
1970	−4.33	−8.42	0.95	1.40
1971	−1.88	−5.11	3.65	2.50
1972	−5.30	0.82	5.81	11.27
1973	−14.69	−2.08	3.75	16.69
1974	−0.95	−6.65	−1.43	−5.29
1975	−1.34	−5.63	0.68	−3.60
1976	8.50	14.36	4.83	9.93
1977	−1.15	2.95	4.20	8.81
1978	−6.02	2.93	3.82	14.58
1979	−1.97	0.57	0.62	5.78
1980	4.07	2.56	−2.53	−0.34
1981	25.97	23.23	0.41	−4.07
1982	9.06	0.29	1.19	−8.20
1983	10.10	12.09	5.07	6.41
1984	16.73	15.80	4.06	2.86
Mean	2.84	2.24	2.99	3.10
Standard deviation	7.40	7.62	2.23	6.36
RMSE	5.25		5.21	
Correlation	0.75		0.61	

Note: In aggregating the six non-U.S. countries into the rest-of-the-world we have used two alternative methods. The first expressed all quantities in German marks deflated by the German GDP deflator; the second expressed all quantities in U.S. dollars deflated by the U.S. GDP deflator. The parameters used in forming the predicted series are $\gamma = \gamma^* = 0.99$, $\delta = \delta^* = 0.95$, $\varepsilon_n = \varepsilon_n^* = \beta_n = \beta_n^* = 0.40$ and $\theta = \theta^* = 0.25$.

Table 16.2
Predicted and actual rest-of-the-world consumption: 1956–1984 (annual percentage growth rates)

Year	In constant German prices		In constant U.S. prices	
	Actual	Predicted	Actual	Predicted
1956	6.14	2.84	7.13	2.55
1957	5.23	−0.38	3.96	−0.75
1958	2.05	−5.74	1.36	−4.20
1959	1.72	9.39	1.73	8.30
1960	7.76	7.17	7.85	7.57
1961	1.73	−7.04	6.97	0.33
1962	5.27	−0.12	7.86	2.90
1963	6.76	4.49	8.38	5.67
1964	6.45	8.28	7.70	9.60
1965	6.02	6.98	7.63	8.20
1966	5.08	0.70	5.44	0.98
1967	5.78	−2.17	4.62	−3.91
1968	4.45	6.01	1.91	3.41
1969	6.42	8.32	4.43	8.62
1970	0.15	−5.84	5.43	3.57
1971	3.49	−2.21	9.02	5.02
1972	5.43	3.20	16.54	13.25
1973	−1.82	−1.55	16.62	16.57
1974	1.06	−7.30	0.58	−5.98
1975	5.12	−5.54	7.14	−3.52
1976	3.54	13.18	−0.14	9.38
1977	2.02	3.66	7.37	9.78
1978	6.43	3.46	16.27	14.88
1979	1.31	−2.57	3.90	1.95
1980	5.75	−2.66	−0.86	−6.72
1981	11.85	18.54	−13.71	−8.01
1982	−1.60	−2.02	−9.47	−10.46
1983	4.24	8.96	−0.78	3.32
1984	7.92	16.41	−4.74	3.93
Mean	4.34	2.63	4.49	3.32
Standard deviation	2.99	6.87	6.73	6.88
RMSE	5.73		5.11	
Correlation	0.61		0.72	

Note: The rest-of-the-world comprises a weighted average of the non-U.S. G-7 countries (Canada, France, Italy, Japan, the United Kingdom, and West Germany). See the note to table 16.1.

example, the actual mean annual growth rate of U.S. private-sector consumption (in constant German prices) is 2.84 percent with a standard deviation of 7.4 percent, whereas the predicted mean and standard deviation are 2.24 percent and 7.60 percent, respectively. The correlation between the predicted and actual rates of growth of consumption is 0.75. A similar pattern (with a somewhat lower correlation) emerges for the series that are based on constant U.S. prices. In that case the means of the actual and of the predicted growth rates are reasonably close to each other, being 2.99 and 3.10 percent, respectively, but the standard deviations of the two series are further apart from each other, being 2.23 and 6.36 percent, respectively. The correlation coefficient corresponding to these two series is 0.61.

The relation between the actual and the predicted growth rates of private-sector consumption in the rest-of-the-world is shown in table 16.2. When expressed in constant U.S. prices, the mean and the standard deviation of the actual series are 4.49 and 6.73 percent, respectively, whereas the corresponding mean and standard deviation of the predicted data are 3.32 and 6.88, respectively. The correlation between the actual and the predicted series is also significant, being 0.72. When the data are expressed in constant German prices, the correlation between the two series is also relatively high (even though somewhat less pronounced), being 0.61.

The correlations between the growth rates of private-sector consumption and the growth rates of the key economic variables are shown in tables 16.3 and 16.4. In these tables we report the correlations between the *actual* growth rates of consumption and the other macroeconomic variables and compare these correlations with the corresponding correlations between the *predicted* growth rates of consumption and the same macroeconomic variables. As is evident, especially for growth rates of series expressed in constant German prices, there is considerable similarity between the actual and the predicted correlations. This similarity which is exhibited by figures pertaining to U.S. consumption (in table 16.3) and to the rest-of-the-world consumption (in table 16.4) is reflected in both the relative magnitudes and signs of the various correlations.

Overall, the computations reported in tables 16.1 through 16.4

Table 16.3
Correlations between annual growth rates of U.S. consumption and key economic variables: 1956–1984

Actual growth rates in	In constant German prices		In constant U.S. prices	
	Actual	Predicted	Actual	Predicted
Y	0.98	0.81	0.84	0.69
I	0.81	0.90	0.81	0.76
C	1.00	0.75	1.00	0.61
G	0.93	0.53	0.03	−0.47
T	0.84	0.75	0.37	0.39
WPI/CPI	−0.50	−0.23	−0.18	0.27
Y^*	0.62	0.73	0.32	0.65
I^*	0.30	0.48	0.32	0.62
C^*	0.57	0.57	0.39	0.61
G^*	0.50	0.39	0.11	0.45
T^*	0.35	0.29	0.05	0.45
WPI*/CPI*	−0.40	−0.28	−0.24	0.04
$C + C^*$	0.97	0.78	0.62	0.71

Note: See the note to table 16.1.

Table 16.4
Correlations between annual growth rates of rest-of-the-world consumption and key economic variables: 1956–1984

Actual growth rates in	In constant German prices		In constant U.S. prices	
	Actual	Predicted	Actual	Predicted
Y	0.60	0.76	0.36	0.73
I	0.58	0.92	0.33	0.78
C	0.57	0.70	0.39	0.72
G	0.53	0.47	0.01	−0.33
T	0.65	0.73	0.20	0.40
WPI/CPI	−0.27	−0.28	0.37	0.21
Y^*	0.92	0.75	0.98	0.74
I^*	0.69	0.55	0.90	0.72
C^*	1.00	0.61	1.00	0.72
G^*	0.81	0.34	0.94	0.53
T^*	0.49	0.24	0.82	0.51
WPI*/CPI*	−0.48	−0.28	0.01	−0.02
$C + C^*$	0.75	0.75	0.96	0.83

Note: See the note to table 16.2.

indicate considerable conformity between the actual and predicted growth rates. They exhibit similar patterns of correlations between the actual growth rates of consumption and of key macroeconomic variables, on the one hand, and between the predicted growth rates of consumption and the same variables, on the other hand. These results indicate the potential usefulness of the analytical framework developed in this book. It is important to reiterate, however, that the purpose of these computations has only been illustrative and should not be viewed as a substitute for a thorough empirical implementation of the model.

16.2 Interest Rates and Terms of Trade: Differences between Models

In this section we highlight some of the key differences between the predictions of, and the economic mechanisms underlying, the income expenditure model and the intertemporal model. The integration of both goods and capital markets in the world economy implies that the key channels through which the effects of fiscal policies are transmitted internationally are the temporal and the intertemporal prices—that is, the world rates of interest and the commodity terms of trade. Accordingly, in what follows we choose to illustrate the differences between the two approaches developed in the preceeding chapters by focusing on, and summarizing, the interest-rate and the terms-of-trade effects of fiscal policies. The different predictions of the two alternative models concerning the effects of fiscal policies on the current world rate of interest and on the current terms of trade are summarized, respectively, in tables 16.5 and 16.6.

The interest-rate effects are shown in table 16.5. The results pertaining to the income-expenditure model are based on the analysis in chapter 4 and those pertaining to the intertemporal model are based on the analysis in chapter 9 extended (on the basis of chapters 10 through 13) to allow for a finite horizon. The key characteristics emerging from table 16.5 are the significant differences in the predictions of the various models. Furthermore, for those cases in which a given policy may either raise or lower the rate of interest, the key factors governing the actual outcome differ drastically across the two models. In the income-expenditure model these key factors

Table 16.5
The effects of fiscal policies on the current rate of interest: the income-expenditure and the intertemporal models

Effects of	Income-expenditure model		Intertemporal model	
	Fixed exchange rates	Flexible exchange rates	Tradable goods	Nontradable goods
Debt-financed rise in government spending				
Current	+	+	+	+ (for $\sigma_{nx} > \sigma$) − (for $\sigma_{nx} < \sigma$)
Future	0	0	−	− (for $\sigma_{nx} > \sigma$) + (for $\sigma_{nx} < \sigma$)
Permanent	+	+	+ (for $CA > 0$) − (for $CA < 0$)	$\left. \begin{matrix} + \\ - \end{matrix} \right\} a$
Tax-financed rise in government spending				
Current	+ (for $A > 0$) − (for $A < 0$)	0	+	+ (for $\sigma_{nx} > \sigma$) − (for $\sigma_{nx} < \sigma$)
Future	0	0	−	− (for $\sigma_{nx} > \sigma$) + (for $\sigma_{nx} < \sigma$)
Permanent	+ (for $A > 0$) − (for $A < 0$)	0	+ (for $CA > 0$) − (for $CA < 0$)	$\left. \begin{matrix} + \\ - \end{matrix} \right\} a$
Current tax cut	+	+	+	+

Note: A rise in the world rate of interest is indicated by a +, and a fall by a −. The signs corresponding to the income-expenditure model are based on the assumption that exchange-rate expectations are static and that there are no revaluation effects; those pertaining to the intertemporal model presume that taxes are nondistortionary. $A = s/M_y - s^*/M_{y^*}^*$, CA denotes the current account position, and a indicates that the result depends on the interactions between the current account position and the sign of the difference between the intertemporal elasticity of substitution, σ, and the temporal elasticity of substitution, σ_{nx}.

Table 16.6
The effects of fiscal policies on the current terms of trade: the income-expenditure and
the intertemporal models

Effects of	Income-expenditure model	Intertemporal model
Debt-financed rise in government spending		
Current	$+$ (for $\tilde{B} > 0$) $-$ (for $\tilde{B} < 0$)	$+$ (for $J > 0$) $-$ (for $J < 0$)
Future	0	$-$
Permanent	$+$ (for $\tilde{B} > 0$) $-$ (for $\tilde{B} < 0$)	$\left.\begin{array}{c}+\\-\end{array}\right\} a$
Tax-financed rise in government spending		
Current	$+$	$+$ (for $J > 0$) $-$ (for $J < 0$)
Future	0	$-$
Permanent	$+$	$\left.\begin{array}{c}+\\-\end{array}\right\} a$
Current tax cut	$+$ (for $\tilde{D} > 0$) $-$ (for $\tilde{D} < 0$)	0

Note: A rise in the relative price of importables in terms of exportables is indicated
by a $+$, and a fall by a $-$. The signs corresponding to the income expenditure model are
based on the assumptions that the exchange rate is flexible, that exchange-rate expectations
are static, and that there are no revaluation effects. The signs pertaining to the intertemporal model are based on the assumption that all goods are internationally trad-
able. $\tilde{B} = e_t(M_y/M_r)[\tilde{a}^* + \tilde{s}^*(1 - a^g)] - (M_{y^*}^*/M_{r^*}^*)[\tilde{a} + \tilde{s}a^g]$, $\tilde{D} = e_t(M_y/M_r)(\tilde{a}^* + \tilde{s}^*) -$
$(M_{y^*}^*/M_{r^*}^*)\tilde{a}$, $J = \beta_m^g - \beta_m(1 - \gamma_s)$, and a indicates that the result depends on the interactions
between the current-account position and the sign of the difference between the shares of
importables of the private sector, β_m, and of the government, β_m^g.

reflect relative magnitudes of parameters measuring the effects of changes in income on spending and on money demand. In contrast, in the intertemporal model the key factors reflect intertemporal parameters, both the temporal/intertemporal substitution elasticities and the current-account positions. It is also relevant to note that for the cases in which the *directions* of predicted interest-rate changes do not differ across the two models, the *magnitudes* of the changes may differ sharply since the mechanisms that operate in the two models are not the same.

A similar inference applies to the comparison of the predictions of the two models concerning the terms-of-trade effects of fiscal policies, shown in table 16.6. Due to the assumed fixity of GDP deflators in the income-expenditure model, the changes in the terms of trade pertaining to this model arise from exchange-rate changes (under the flexible exchange-rate regime) and are based on the analysis in chapter 4. The results pertaining to the intertemporal model are based on those analyzed in chapter 7 extended (on the basis of chapters 10 through 12) to allow for a finite horizon. As examples of the difference, consider the effects of a debt-financed rise in current government spending on the current terms of trade. Both models imply that the current terms of trade may either rise (deteriorate) or fall (improve). However, the factors determining the actual outcome differ significantly. In the income-expenditure model the actual result depends on the relative sensitivities of the domestic and the foreign rates of interest to income changes (arising from the fiscal policy). These relative sensitivities underly the sign of the parameter $\tilde{B}$. In contrast, in the intertemporal model the actual result depends on the difference between the government and private-sector's propensity to spend on current importables out of wealth. These propensities underly the sign of the parameter J.

The examples shown in tables 16.5 and 16.6 were based on simplified versions of the models chosen to highlight differences between some of their predictions. The more complex versions analyzed in the preceding chapters allow for mechanisms and factors that may generate additional differences. These include debt revaluation effects arising from terms-of-trade changes, exchange-rate expectations in the income-expenditure model of chapter 4, details of the nominal exchange rate regime underlying the inter-temporal model of chapter 15, and distortionary taxes. The latter factor is of special interest since it plays a unique role in determining the effects of tax policy in the intertemporal model. Specifically, as shown in chapter 8, the various types of taxes can be classified into those for which a current tax cut raises the world rate of interest (e.g., as a value-added tax) and those for which a current tax cut lowers the world rate of interest (e.g., an income tax).

For ease of exposition, the summary provided in tables 16.5 and 16.6 considers only the effects of policies on the *current* values of the interest rate and the terms of trade. As such it focuses on the current channels of the international transmission of fiscal policies. Through-out the discussion in this book we emphasized that current policies also have profound effects on the *future* values of the interest rates and the terms of trade. The two models also differ sharply in their predictions of these future values. The differences reflect the funda-mental distinction between the models. The intertemporal model is based on forward-looking behavior of individuals and governments whose current and future decisions must obey intertemporal budget constraints. No such features characterize the dynamics of the income-expenditure model.

Finally, the analysis in this book also highlights differences be-tween the models that are not summarized in tables 16.5 and 16.6. These differences are reflected in the current and the future levels (and growth rates) of domestic and foreign private-sector consump-tion, investment, outputs, and real exchange rates.

16.3 Suggested Extensions

We conclude this epilogue with a brief outline of suggested extensions that could usefully be incorporated into the analytical framework developed in this book. One of the important features of the inter-temporal approach is that it allows a proper welfare analysis. Being based on individual utility maximization, this approach is suitable for the normative evaluation of the consequences of macroeconomic policies. Most of this book, however, was devoted to a positive analysis. Absent market failures, the equilibrium obtained is efficient. Under such circumstances, policy interventions in the international capital markets constitute protectionism that reduces the gains from intertemporal trade in the same way as standard protectionism caused by policy interventions that restrict the free international flow of goods in a static setting reduce the gains from temporal trade. With this in mind it would be desirable to evaluate the welfare implications of some of the policy experiments carried out in the various chapters of this book. In this context, in the absence of nondistortionary taxes, it would be relevant to determine explicitly the dynamic path of the (second-best) optimal tax structure along with the optimal temporal and intertemporal allocations of government spending.

Throughout, we analyzed the effects of alternative timings of taxes and the public-debt issue. An extension would shift the emphasis away from issues involving budget deficits and surpluses toward issues involving the temporal composition of taxes. In this context a relevant question would examine the effects of various revenue-neutral tax reforms on the key macroeconomic variables in the world economy.

The book focused on the international dimensions of fiscal policies. As such, monetary considerations were given a minimal role. On the occasions in which monetary considerations were incorporated, the rationale for money holdings was exclusively based on transaction demand. The limited function assigned to money stems from the assumption of complete information and full certainty. A useful extension would modify these assumptions and would thereby render additional motives for holding money (precautionary and store-of-value motives). Such an extension would permit a more complete analysis of macroeconomic policies, including monetary and exchange-rate policies. It would provide a framework for the positive as well as the normative analysis of the international dimensions of the mix of these policy instruments.

The incorporation of uncertainty and the lack of complete information would then raise additionally relevant issues such as bankruptcy and default. In this context a relevant task would be the clarification of the effects of various measures of fiscal policies on the likelihood of bankruptcies and defaults in the international capital markets.

An additional extension could modify the demographic structure of the overlapping generations model so as to allow for life-cycle characteristics of saving behavior. The differences in the saving propensities across age groups, resulting from the life-cycle model, imply that changes in the age distribution of income alter the aggregate saving behavior. This provides for an additional channel through which age-dependent tax or transfer policies influence the world economy. Such an extension could modify some of the interest-rate effects of fiscal policies.

The overlapping-generations model could be extended further so as to include a bequest motive linking different generations. If consumers have *operative* altruistic bequest motives, then they behave as if their horizon is infinite. In such a case changing the timing of lump-sum taxes has no effect on the equilibrium allocations. In practice, however, under the existing institutional structure, no one can effectively appropriate future labor income of his descendents. Thus the minimum amount of bequest is constrained to be zero (i.e., negative bequests are not allowed). Those individuals who would choose to leave negative bequests are therefore constrained in their consumption-savings choices. Accordingly, a bequest motive must be sufficiently strong in order to be operative. The individuals who are bequest constrained favor tax policies that increase their lifetime income at the expense of future generations, even when the present value of the tax change is zero. Domestic tax policies influence the world economy if for some individuals the bequest motive is not operative.

Our analysis of the dynamic effects of government purchases and taxes abstracted from the distinction between durable and non-durable goods. An extension that allows for such a distinction, and incorporates durable goods into the model, breaks the synchronization between the flow of services and the flow of purchases. Whereas the desired flow of services is governed by the consumption-smoothing effects, the time pattern of purchases depends, among other things, on the rate of depreciation. Since the demand for, and thereby the purchases of durable goods, do not reflect only the consumption-smoothing and the consumption-tilting effects (which govern the desired flow of services), the allowance for durable goods may also modify the interest-rate effects of government purchases and taxes.

Yet another extension would modify the assumption of complete wage and price flexibility. With uncertainty and with incomplete and asymmetric information, it is likely that economic agents would find it optimal to enter into contracts that might yield some endogenously (and voluntarily) determined wage and price rigidities. Such (contract-based) rigidities would incorporate elements similar to those present in the income-expenditure model into the intertemporal model and would allow for the Keynesian features underlying the determination of output and employment.

Throughout this book we assumed that the foreign government followed a balanced-budget policy. This assumption was adopted to ensure that changes in world rates of interest that result from domestic fiscal policies do not affect the solvency of the foreign government. If the foreign government does not follow a balanced-budget policy, then interest-rate changes would necessitate secondary changes in foreign spending or taxes in order to restore solvency. An extension of the analysis would relax the foreign balanced-budget assumption and would allow for the necessary adjustment of foreign fiscal management.

A more major extension would recognize that the interdependencies among the various open economies provide incentives for strategic behavior by individual countries. Such a strategic behavior could then be incorporated into a more elaborate game-theoretic framework. The complex structure of overlapping cohorts introduces, however, conceptual difficulties in specifying the relevant weights assigned to different generation in the social welfare functions, and in general, these social welfare functions may not result in time-consistent policies. Further the interdependencies and the strategic behavior could result in inefficient outcomes from a global perspective that may call for harmonization of fiscal policies. On the other hand, if within a country, taken as a single unit, there are conflicts of interest among various groups (labor, employers, the government, etc.), then international coordination among governments may result in outcomes inferior to those obtained in the absence of such co-ordination. In such an extended framework, which incorporates the incentives for strategic behavior, government spending and the timing of taxes would become endogenous variables that are determined in the context of world equilibrium.

16.4 Appendix

In this appendix we elaborate on the computations underlying tables 16.1 through 16.4. The basic two-country model used in the computations is reported in appendix B of chapter 13. In tables 16.3 through 16.4, Y denotes GNP, I denotes investment, C denotes private-sector consumption, G denotes government purchases, T denotes tax revenue, WPI denotes the wholesale price index, CPI denotes the consumer price index, and an asterisk designates variables pertaining to the rest of the world. Additional variables used in solving the model are government debt (denoted by B^g) and the economy's external debt (denoted by B).

The key parameters used in the computations are γ, the survival probability; δ, the subjective discount factor; β_n, the expenditure share of nontradable goods in private-sector spending; and θ, the proportion of the output of nontradable goods absorbed by government purchases. The relative share of nontradable goods output in GNP, ε_n, is assumed to equal the expenditure share, β_n. Similar notations (with an added asterisk) designate the parameters pertaining the rest-of-the-world. In choosing the parameter values, we select a relatively large value of γ. With the implied long life expectancy of the dynastic families, the model used in the computations is close to being Ricardian. The source for all the data is the IMF, *International Financial Statistics* (IFS). The values of the various variables (measured in current prices) are taken from the following lines of the IFS data source: G, line 91f; C, line 96f; Y, line 99a; I, line 93e; T, line 81; WPI, line 63; and CPI, line 64.

As indicated earlier the rest-of-the-world comprises the G-7 countries, excluding the United States (Canada, France, Italy, Japan, the United Kingdom, and West Germany). In aggregating the data for these six countries, we first converted all individual country series into a common currency by using the relevant period's average exchange rate. The resulting series were then deflated by the GDP deflator of the country representing the numeraire currency, thereby yielding the constant price (real) time series. An exception was the consumption series for which the (numeraire currency) CPI was used. The sum of the individual country series (excluding the United States) constitutes the rest-of-the-world series.

In view of the sharp changes in the U.S. dollar exchange rate that have taken place during the sample period (1956 through 1984), we have adopted two alternatives: in the first, all series were expressed in constant German prices (computed with the aid of the DM exchange rate and the West German GDP deflator); in the second, all series were expressed in constant U.S. prices (computed with the aid of the U.S. dollar exchange rate and the U.S. GDP deflator). The two alternative rest-of-the-world and U.S. series, converted into the corresponding percentage annual growth rates, underly the statistical computations in tables 16.1 through 16.4.

Implicit in the specification of the model is the assumption that the future variables (income and taxation) underlying the computation of human capital are expected to be stationary. To implement this assumption, we have calculated a simple average of the remaining future values of each of the series (due to the finite sample this means that the series length is declining over time). The resulting simple averages were used as measures of permanent future income and future taxes. Since in our model investment is taken as exogenous, the GNP series are netted out of current investments.

The external-debt series for each country (not readily available) was constructed by cumulating current account deficits starting from 1952.

In performing the simulations, we use equation (13.16) and express W_0 in terms of W_0^*. Using this expression, and noting that

$$(1 + r_{x, -1})B_{-1}^{*g} = T_0^* - G_{x0}^* - \theta_0^* p_{n0}^* Y_{n0}^*$$

$$+ \frac{1}{R - 1}(T^* - G_x^* - \theta^* p_n^* Y_0^*),$$

where

$$G_{x0}^* = (1 - \beta_n^*)(1 - \gamma_s^{*g})G^*, \quad G_x^* = (1 - \beta_n^*)\gamma_s^{*g}G^*,$$

$$\theta_0^* = \frac{\beta_n^*(1 - \gamma_s^{*g})G^*}{p_{n0}^* Y_{n0}^*}, \qquad \theta^* = \frac{\beta_n^*\gamma_s^{*g}G^*}{p_n^* Y_n^*},$$

equations (13.11), (13.13), (13.15), and (13.17) become

$$(1 - \beta_n^*)(1 - \gamma^*\delta^*)W_0^* = (Y_{x0}^* - G_{x0}^*) + \frac{\gamma}{R - \gamma}(Y_x^* - T^* + p_n^* Y_n^*)$$

$$+ \frac{1}{R - 1}(T^* - G_x^* - \theta^* p_n^* Y_n^*)$$

$$+ (1 + r_{x,-1})B_{-1}, \tag{A.1}$$

$$(1 - \theta^*)p_n^* Y_n^* = \beta_n^*\gamma^*\delta^*(R - 1)W_0^*$$

$$+ \frac{\beta_n^*(1 - \gamma^*)R}{R - \gamma^*}(Y_x^* - T^* + p_n^* Y_n^*), \tag{A.2}$$

$$(1 - \theta)p_n Y_n = \frac{\beta_n\gamma\delta}{(1 - \beta_n)(1 - \gamma\delta)}\left[Y_{x0} - G_{x0} + Y_{x0}^* \right.$$

$$- G_{x0}^* - (1 - \beta_n^*)(1 - \gamma^*\delta^*)(R - 1)W_0^*$$

$$\left. + \frac{\beta_n(1 - \gamma)R}{R - \gamma}(Y_x - T + p_n Y_n) \right], \tag{A.3}$$

$$(Y_x - G_x + Y_x^* - G_x^*) = \frac{\gamma\delta(R - 1)}{1 - \gamma\delta}[Y_{x0} - G_{x0} + Y_{x0}^* - G_{x0}^*$$

$$- (1 - \beta_n^*)(1 - \gamma^*\delta^*)W_0^*]$$

$$+ \frac{(1 - \beta_n)(1 - \gamma)R}{R - \gamma}(Y_x - T + p_n Y_n)$$

$$+ (1 - \beta_n^*)\gamma^*\delta^* W^*(R - 1)$$

$$+ \frac{(1 - \beta_n^*)(1 - \gamma^*)R}{R - \gamma^*}(Y_x^* - T^* + p_n^* Y_n^*). \tag{A.4}$$

Equations (A.1) through (A.4) were used to obtain the solution for

W_0^*, p_n^*, p_n, and R. We use these solutions together with equation (13.16) to solve for W_0; we then use equations (13.12) and (13.14) to obtain the solutions for p_{n0} and p_{n0}^* (which are the reciprocals of the real exchange rates in period zero). Given the solutions for W_0 and W_0^*, domestic and foreign consumption are computed with the aid of the consumption functions $C_0 = (1 - \gamma\delta)W_0$ and $C_0^* = (1 - \gamma^*\delta^*)W_0^*$.

The procedure used for dividing (the exogenously given levels of) output and government spending into tradable and nontradable goods employed the following definitions $Y_{nt} = \varepsilon_n(Y_t - I_t)$, $Y_{xt} = (1 - \varepsilon_n)(Y_t - I_t)$, $G_{nt} = \theta\varepsilon_n(Y_t - I_t)$, $G_{xt} = G_t - \theta\varepsilon_n(Y_t - I_t)$, where Y_t and I_t denote real GNP and real investment in period t.

In simulating the system, we used the nonlinear equation solution procedure based on Powell's hybrid algorithm for the Newton-type iteration method.

17

Bibliographical Notes

Throughout this book we have not dealt with the large body of literature bearing on the subjects covered in the various chapters. In this chapter we provide selected bibliographical notes. We do not present a comprehensive survey of the voluminous work underlying the development of economic thought and analysis of fiscal policies in the world economy. Rather, our purpose is to indicate some linkages between the ideas and concepts developed in this book and the work that precedes it. We do not refer here to our own earlier work which is cited in the preface to the book.

17.1 Selected Notes on the Literature

Part II of the book is devoted to the presentation of traditional approaches to international macroeconomics, with special emphasis given to the role of fiscal policies. It opens with a model of international economic interdependence which is based on the Keynesian analysis of the foreign-trade multiplier as developed, among others, by Metzler (1942a), Machlup (1943), and Robinson (1952).

Throughout the book we analyze the international mechanism of adjustment in terms of the transfer-problem criterion. This criterion was developed originally in the context of post-World War I discussions about the German reparations, and it was debated among Keynes (1929), Ohlin (1929), and Rueff (1929). This concept was further clarified by Metzler (1942b), Meade (1951), Samuelson (1952), Johnson (1956), and Mundell (1960).

The basic model used throughout our analysis of the traditional approach to international macroeconomics is the income-expenditure model. In specifying this model, we have employed elements from the absorption approach to the balance of payments, as developed by Alexander (1952), and from the monetary approach to the balance of payments, as presented by Polak (1957), Johnson (1958), Prais (1961), Mundell (1964), Frenkel and Johnson (1976), and IMF (1977). Our analysis of the full employment (classical) version of the income-expenditure model in chapter 3 is related to that of Mundell (1968, chap. 8).

The increased integration of world capital markets led to the development of models in which international capital mobility plays a pivotal role. A pioneering treatment of international capital mobility appears in Iversen (1935). The incorporation of capital movements into the main corpus of international macroeconomics was carried out in a series of classic articles in the 1960s by Mundell (collected in Mundell 1968 and 1971), and by Fleming (1962). The so called Mundell-Fleming model is still the main workhorse of traditional open-economy macroeconomics. This model has been extended in several directions. Among them is a long-run analysis by Rodriguez (1979); a stock (portfolio) specification of capital mobility by McKinnon (1969), Floyd (1969), Branson (1970), and Frenkel and Rodriguez (1975); an analysis of the debt-revaluation effects induced by exchange-rate changes by Boyer (1977) and Rodriguez (1979); and an analysis of expectations and exchange-rate dynamics by Kouri (1976) and Dornbusch (1976). A critical evaluation of the Mundell-Fleming model is provided by Purvis (1985).

Expositions of the income-expenditure models for alternative exchange-rate regimes and for different degrees of international capital mobility are presented in Swoboda and Dornbusch (1973) and Mussa (1979). The diagrammatic analysis used in chapters 2 through 4 builds in part on these two expositions.

Surveys of various issues covered by the traditional approaches to open-economy macroeconomics are contained in Frenkel and Mussa (1985), Kenen (1985), Marston (1985), and Obstfeld and Stockman (1985), and a comprehensive treatment is provided in Dornbusch (1980).

Part III of the book (chapters 5 and 6) provides an exposition of the basic elements of intertemporal macroeconomics. The intertemporal approach extends Fisher's (1930) analysis to the entire spectrum of macroeconomic decision making, including saving, investment, and labor. Examples of such extensions, in the context of consumption-savings decisions are Modigliani and Brumberg (1954), Friedman (1957), and Hall (1978). Examples in the context of investment theory are Lucas (1967), Uzawa (1968), Tobin (1969), Lucas and Prescott (1971), Abel (1979), Hayashi (1982), and Abel and Blanchard (1986). Other examples in the context of dynamic labor supply and demand are Lucas and Rapping (1969), Heckman (1974), Ghez and Becker (1975), and Sargent (1978). Integrations of the various elements into a general equilibrium model of closed-economy business-cycle theory are contained in Barro (1981a) and Lucas (1981).

Elements of the intertemporal approach that we develop in chapter 5 have been used in the context of open economies, with special emphasis given to the theory of international borrowing and the current account of the balance of payments. Examples of writings in this approach are Bruno (1976, 1982), Eaton and Gersovitz (1981), Sachs (1981, 1984), Razin (1984), and Penati (1987). In chapter 6 we develop the relations between temporal and intertemporal prices and their effects on the time profile of spending and the current account. This analysis is based on Obstfeld (1982), Dornbusch (1983), and Svensson and Razin (1983), who in turn reexamine the older problem of the effects of changes in the terms of trade on savings as analyzed by Harberger (1950) and Laursen and Metzler (1950).

The intertemporal approach to fiscal policies in the world economy is presented in part IV of the book (chapters 7 through 9). Our analysis of the effects of government spending in chapters 7 and 9 builds on a model embodying the Ricardian neutrality property, according to which intertemporal shifts of lump-sum taxes do not influence the economic system. Typically, this proposition is ascribed to Ricardo, even though, as documented by O'Driscoll (1977), Ricardo himself while anticipating its logic denied its practical validity. Analyses of elements underlying the Ricardian proposition originate in Buchanan (1958), Modigliani (1961), Bailey (1962), and Patinkin (1965), and its modern revival is due to Barro (1974).

Early discussion of the long-term effects of fiscal policies in a Keynesian closed-economy context is contained in Blinder and Solow (1973). In the context of the intertemporal approach Barro (1981a) highlights the distinction between permanent and transitory government spending.

Our discussion of distortionary taxes in chapters 8 and 9 is related to the earlier research emphasizing intertemporal considerations in a closed-economy framework. Examples of such research are Barro (1974, 1979, 1981b), Feldstein (1974, 1977), Kydland and Prescott (1980), Brock and Turnovsky (1981), King (1983), Lucas and Stokey (1983), and Judd (1987). In the international context examples of analyses of various aspects of distortionary taxes are found in Razin and Svensson (1983), Aschauer and Greenwood (1985), Greenwood and Kimbrough (1985), Kimbrough (1986), and van Wijnbergen (1986).

Part V of the book (chapters 10 through 13) deals with the dynamic effects of fiscal policies in models of overlapping generations. The first formulation of the model in a closed economy context is due to Samuelson (1958), and the detailed analysis of public debt and capital accumulation within this model is found in Diamond (1965). Examples of open-economy applications of this model are Buiter (1981), Dornbusch (1985), and Persson and Svensson (1985). Aspects of welfare are highlighted in Fried (1980) and Persson (1985). In chapters 10 and 11 we adopt another formulation of the overlapping generations model, based on Yaari (1965) and due to Blanchard (1985). In this model the finiteness of the horizon stems from lifetime uncertainty. An application of the model to a two-country framework is found in Buiter (1987). The role of population growth in overlapping families models is treated by Weil (1987).

Chapters 12 and 13 are devoted to the analysis of the effects of current and anticipated future fiscal policies on the term structure of world rates of interest and the dynamics of real exchange rates. Examples of related work dealing with similar issues are Blanchard (1984), Branson (1986), Dantas and Dornbusch (1986), and Helpman and Razin (1987), whose model is used in parts of chapter 13. Dynamic patterns of real exchange rates induced by resource changes rather than fiscal policies are analyzed in the context of the so called "Dutch disease." Early examples of such analyses are Gregory (1976), Corden and Neary (1982), and Purvis and Neary (1985).

The issue of exchange-rate regimes and tax policies is examined in part VI of the book (chapters 14 and 15). The exposition adopts a cash-in-advance payments convention introduced by Clower (1967) and developed into a rigorous general-equilibrium framework by Lucas (1980). The intertemporal considerations relevant for comparisons among exchange-rate regimes are analyzed in Helpman and Razin (1979) and Kareken and Wallace (1981). In chapter 14 we highlight these considerations. Examples of previous applications of the cash-in-advance convention to the analysis of exchange-rate regimes are contained in Stockman (1980), Helpman (1981), Lucas (1982), Greenwood (1983), Persson (1984), and Helpman and Razin (1984). The distortions associated with multiple exchange-rate systems and capital controls are analyzed in chapter 15. Examples of related analyses are Lanyi (1975), Flood (1978), Marion (1981), Adams and Greenwood (1985), Aizenman (1985), Dornbusch (1986), Greenwood and Kimbrough (1986), and Obstfeld (1986). The (lump-sum) tax equivalence of exchange-rate management is also examined in chapter 15. The formulation used is based on Helpman and Razin (1987) which extends Blanchard (1985) to the cash-in-advance monetary framework.

Chapter 16 in part VII of the book is devoted to an empirical implementation and a discussion of proposed extensions. The data used in this chapter (as well as in chapter 1 of part I of the book) are from the International Monetary Fund, *International Financial Statistics* and *World Economic Outlook*, various issues.

Empirical analyses of the effects of fiscal policies on private-sector spending are ample. Examples are Kochin (1979), Barro (1981), Feldstein (1982), Kormendi (1983), Aschauer (1985), Aschauer and Greenwood (1985), and Leiderman and Razin (1987). A survey of key issues relevant for empirical testing is Leiderman and Blejer (1987). Simulations of models based on consumers with finite horizons are found in Blanchard and Summers (1984), Hubbard and Judd (1986), and Poterba and Summers (1986). The intertemporal approach to macroeconomics has also been subjected to numerous empirical tests. Examples are Hall (1978), MaCurdy (1981), Altonji (1982), and Mankiw, Rothemberg, and Summers (1985).

Kydland and Prescott (1982) simulate a theoretical dynamic model, using assumed parameter values, and are able to generate behavior that closely resembles economic time series. The illustrative example in chapter 16 applies this method to a two-country equilibrium model of the world economy.

The proposed extensions outlined in chapter 16 cover issues that have received some attention in the literature. In what follows we list some examples of writings relevant for such extensions. The lack of precautionary and store-of-value motives of money holdings in the cash-in-advance modeling has been addressed and dealt with by Helpman and Razin (1982) and Svensson (1986), among others. The role of bankruptcies and defaults in the international capital markets is analyzed by Eaton and Gersovitz (1981), Sachs (1984), and Aizenman (1986). A modification of the saving behavior allowing for life-cycle characteristics is contained in Auerbach and Kotlikoff (1987) and Modigliani (1987). A further modification of the saving behavior arising from an altruistic bequest motive that is not operative is examined by Barro (1974), Drazen (1978), and Feldstein (1986). An analysis of the dynamic effects of government purchases that allows for durable goods, which is sketched in the appendix to chapter 10, is provided by Mankiw (1987). A contract-based wage rigidity is analyzed by Gray (1976), Fischer (1977), Azariadis (1978), and Aizenman and Frenkel (1985).

The constraints on the conduct of fiscal policies may give rise to difficulties associated with time inconsistency of government actions. Such issues are dealt with in Calvo (1978), Kydland and Prescott (1977), Lucas and Stokey (1983), Calvo and Obstfeld (1988), and Persson and Svensson (1986). A related issue concerns the formulation of a positive theory of government policy, as analyzed by Barro and Gordon (1983) in the context of a closed economy. Accordingly, in situations for which policymakers are unable to commit their course of future actions, the game-theoretic equilibrium may be suboptimal relative to outcomes where commitments are permitted.

The interdependencies among countries provides incentives for strategic behavior by individual countries. Analysis of the implications of such strategic behavior is contained in Hamada (1976, 1985). The interdependencies among countries may call for harmonization and coordination of economic policies. Early analyses of these issues are contained in Cooper (1968, 1985). Examples of analyses of this issue within a game-theoretic framework are Oudiz and Sachs (1984), Rogoff (1984, 1986), Canzoneri and Gray (1983), and Conzoneri and Henderson (1987).

17.2 Selected References

Abel, Andrew B. 1979. *Investment and the Value of Time.* New York: Garland.

Abel, Andrew B., and Blanchard, Olivier. 1983. The Present Value of Profits and Cyclical Movements in Investment. *Econometrica* 51 (May): 675–692.

Adams, Charles, and Greenwood, Jeremy. 1985. Dual Exchange Rate Systems and Capital Controls: An Investigation. *Journal of International Economics* 18 (February): 43–63.

Aizenman, Joshua. 1985. Adjustment to Monetary Policy and Devaluation under Two-Tier and Fixed Exchange Rate Regimes. *Journal of Development Economics* 18 (May/June): 153–169.

Aizenman, Joshua. 1986. Country Risk, Asymmetric Information, and Domestic Rules. NBER Working Paper Series No. 1880, April.

Aizenman, Joshua, and Frenkel, Jacob A. 1985. Optimal Wage Indexation, Foreign Exchange Intervention, and Monetary Policy. *American Economic Review* 75 (June): 402–423.

Alexander, Sidney S. 1952. Effects of a Devaluation on a Trade Balance. *IMF Staff Papers* 2, No. 2, (April): 263–278.

Altonji, Joseph G. 1985. The Intertemporal Substitution Model of Labor Market Fluctuations: An Empirical Analysis. *Review of Economic Studies* 49, no. 5 (special issue on unemployment), 783–824.

Aschauer, David A. 1985. Fiscal Policy and Aggregate Demand. *American Economic Review* 75 (March): 117–127.

Aschauer, David A., and Greenwood, Jeremy. 1985. Macroeconomic Effects of Fiscal Policy. In *The 'New Monetary Economics,' Fiscal Issues and Unemployment,* edited by Karl Brunner and Allan H. Meltzer. Carnegie Rochester Conference Series on Public Policy 23, Autumn, 91–138.

Auerbach, Alan J., and Kotlikoff, Laurence J. 1987. *Dynamic Fiscal Policy.* London: Cambridge University Press.

Azariadis, Costas. 1978. Escalator Clauses and the Allocation of Cyclical Risks. *Journal of Economic Theory* 18 (June): 119–155.

Bailey, Martin J. 1962. *National Income and the Price Level.* New York: McGraw-Hill.

Barro, Robert J. 1974. Are Government Bonds Net Wealth? *Journal of Political Economy* 82 (November/December): 1095–1117.

Barro, Robert J. 1979. On the Determination of Public Debt. *Journal of Political Economy* 87 part 1 (October): 940–971.

Barro, Robert J. 1981a. Output Effects of Government Purchases. *Journal of Political Economy* 89 (December): 1086–1121.

Barro, Robert J. 1981b. *Money, Expectations, and Business Cycles: Essays in Macroeconomics*. New York: Academic Press.

Barro, Robert J., and Gordon, David B. 1983. A Positive Theory of Monetary Policy in a Natural Rate Model. *Journal of Political Economy* 91 (August): 589–610.

Blanchard, Olivier J. 1984. Current and Anticipated Deficits, Interest Rates and Economic Activity. *European Economic Review* 25 (June): 7–27.

Blanchard, Olivier J. 1985. Debt, Deficits, and Finite Horizons. *Journal of Political Economy* 93 (April): 223–247.

Blanchard, Olivier J., and Summers, Lawrence H. 1984. Perspectives on High World Interest Rates. *Brookings Papers on Economic Activity* 2: 273–333.

Blinder, Alan S., and Solow, Robert M. 1973. Does Fiscal Policy Matter? *Journal of Public Economics* 2 (November): 319–337.

Boyer, Russell S. 1977. Devaluation and Portfolio Balance. *American Economic Review* 67 (March): 54–63.

Branson, William H. 1970. Monetary Policy and the New View of International Capital Movements. *Brookings Papers on Economic Activity* 2: 235–262.

Branson, William H. 1986. Causes of Appreciation and Volatility of the Dollar. In *The U.S. Dollar-Recent Developments, Outlook, and Policy Options*. Kansas City: Federal Reserve Bank of Kansas City, 33–52.

Brock, William, and Turnovsky, Stephen. 1981. The Analysis of Macroeconomic Policies in Perfect Foresight Equilibrium. *International Economic Review* 84 (February): 179–209.

Bruno, Michael. 1976. The Two-Sector Open Economy and the Real Exchange Rate. *American Economic Review* 66 (September): 566–577.

Bruno, Michael. 1982. Adjustment and Structural Change under Raw Material Price Shocks. *Scandinavian Journal of Economics* 84: 199–221.

Buchanan, James M. 1958. *Public Principles of Public Debt*. Homewood: Irwin.

Buiter, Willem H. 1981. Time Preference and International Lending and Borrowing in an Overlapping-Generations Model. *Journal of Political Economy* 89 (August): 769–797.

Buiter, Willem H. 1987. Fiscal Policy in Open Interdependent Economies. In *Economic Policy in Theory and Practice*, edited by Assaf Razin and Efraim Sadka. London: Macmillan, 101–144.

Calvo, Guillermo A. 1978. On the Time Consistency of Optimal Policy in a Monetary Economy. *Econometrica* 46 (November): 1411–1428.

Calvo, Guillermo A., and Obstfeld, Maurice. 1988. Optimal Time-Consistent Fiscal Policy with Finite Lifetimes. *Econometrica*, forthcoming.

Canzoneri, Matthew, and Gray, Jo Anna. 1985. Monetary Policy Games and the Consequences of Noncooperative Behavior. *International Economic Review* 26 (October): 547–564.

Canzoneri, Matthew, and Henderson, Dale. 1987. *Strategic Aspects of Macroeconomic Policy Making in Interdependent Economies*. Unpublished manuscript. Georgetown University.

Clower, Robert W. 1967. A Reconsideration of the Microfoundations of Monetary Theory. *Western Economic Journal* 6 (December): 1–8.

Cooper, Richard N. 1968. *The Economics of Interdependence*. New York: McGraw-Hill.

Cooper, Richard N. 1985. Economic Interdependence and Coordination of Economic Policies. In *Handbook of International Economics*, Vol. 2, edited by Ronald W. Jones and Peter B. Kenen. Amsterdam: North Holland, 1195–1234.

Corden, W. Max, and Neary, J. Peter. 1982. Booming Sector and De-Industrialization in a Small Open Economy. *Economic Journal* 92 (December): 825–848.

Dantas, Daniel V., and Dornbusch, Rudiger. 1984. Anticipated Budget Deficits and the Term Structure of Interest Rates. NBER Working Paper Series No. 1518, December.

Diamond, Peter A. 1965. National Debt in a Neoclassical Growth Model. *American Economic Review* 55 (December): 1126–1150.

Dornbusch, Rudiger. 1976. Expectations and Exchange Rate Dynamics. *Journal of Political Economy* 84 (December): 1161–1176.

Dornbusch, Rudiger. 1980. *Open Economy Macroeconomics*. New York: Basic Books.

Dornbusch, Rudiger. 1983. Real Interest Rates, Home Goods, and Optimal External Borrowing. *Journal of Political Economy* 91 (February): 141–153.

Dornbusch, Rudiger. 1985. Intergenerational and International Trade. *Journal of International Economics* 18 (February): 123–139.

Dornbusch, Rudiger. 1986. Special Exchange Rates for Capital Account Transactions. *The World Bank Economic Review* 1 (September): 3–33.

Drazen, Allan. 1978. Government Debt, Human Capital, and Bequests in a Life-Cycle Model. *Journal of Political Economy* 86 (June):505–516.

Eaton, Jonathan, and Gersovitz, Mark. 1981. Poor-Country Borrowing in Private Financial Markets and the Repudiation Issue. *Princeton Studies in International Finance* 47 (June).

Feldstein, Martin S. 1974. Tax Incidence in a Growing Economy with Variable Factor Supply. *Quarterly Journal of Economics* 88 (November):551–573.

Feldstein, Martin S. 1977. The Surprising Incidence of a Tax on Pure Rent: A New Answer to an Old Question. *Journal of Political Economy* 85 (April):349–360.

Feldstein, Martin S. 1982. Government Deficits and Aggregate Demand. *Journal of Monetary Economics* 9 (January):1–20.

Feldstein, Martin S. 1986. The Effects of Fiscal Policies When Incomes Are Uncertain: A Contradiction to Ricardian Equivalence. NBER Working Paper Series No. 2062, November.

Fischer, Stanley. 1977. Long-Term Contracting, Sticky Prices, and Monetary Policy: A Comment. *Journal of Monetary Economics* 3 (July):317–323.

Fisher, Irving. 1930. *Theory of Interest.* New York: Macmillan.

Fleming, J. Marcus. 1962. Domestic Financial Policies under Fixed and under Floating Exchange Rates. *IMF Staff Papers* 9 (November):369–379.

Flood, Robert P. 1978. Exchange Rate Expectations in Dual Exchange Markets. *Journal of International Economics* 8 (February):65–78.

Floyd, John E. 1969. International Capital Movements and Monetary Equilibrium. *American Economic Review* 59, part 1 (September):472–492.

Frenkel, Jacob A., and Johnson, Harry G., eds. 1976. *The Monetary Approach to the Balance of Payments.* London: Allen & Unwin.

Frenkel, Jacob A., and Mussa, Michael L. 1985. Asset Markets, Exchange Rates and the Balance of Payments. In *Handbook of International Economics*, Vol. 2, edited by Ronald W. Jones and Peter B. Kenen. Amsterdam: North Holland, 680–747.

Frenkel, Jacob A., and Razin, Assaf. 1985a. Government Spending, Debt and International Economic Interdependence. *Economic Journal* 95 (September):619–639.

Frenkel, Jacob A., and Razin, Assaf. 1985b. Fiscal Expenditures and International Economic Interdependence. *International Economic Policy Coordination*, edited by Willem H. Buiter and Richard C. Marston. Cambridge: Cambridge University Press, 37–73.

Frenkel, Jacob A., and Razin, Assaf. 1986a. The International Transmission and Effects of Fiscal Policies. *American Economic Review* 76 (May):330–335.

Frenkel, Jacob A., and Razin, Assaf. 1986b. Fiscal Policies in the World Economy. *Journal of Political Economy* 94, part 1 (June): 564–594.

Frenkel, Jacob A., and Razin, Assaf. 1986c. Real Exchange Rates, Interest Rates and Fiscal Policies. *The Economic Studies Quarterly* 37 (June): 99–113.

Frenkel, Jacob A., and Razin, Assaf. 1986d. The Limited Viability of Dual Exchange-Rate Regimes. NBER Working Paper Series No. 1902, April.

Frenkel, Jacob A., and Razin, Assaf. 1986e. Fiscal Policies and Real Exchange Rates in the World Economy. NBER Working Paper Series No. 2065, November.

Frenkel, Jacob A., and Razin, Assaf. 1986f. Deficits with Distortionary Taxes: International Dimensions. NBER Working Paper Series No. 2080, November.

Frenkel, Jacob A., and Razin, Assaf. 1987a. The International Transmission of Fiscal Expenditures and Budget Deficits in the World Economy. In *Economic Policy in Theory and Practice*, edited by Assaf Razin and Efraim Sadka. London: Macmillan, 51–96.

Frenkel, Jacob A., and Razin, Assaf. 1987b. The Mundell-Fleming Model: A Quarter Century Later. *IMF Staff Papers*, forthcoming.

Frenkel, Jacob A., and Razin, Assaf. 1987c. Spending, Taxes and Deficits: International Intertemporal Approach. *Princeton Studies in International Finance*, forthcoming.

Frenkel, Jacob A., and Razin, Assaf. 1987d. Exchange-Rate Management Viewed as Tax Policies. Unpublished manuscript.

Frenkel, Jacob A., and Rodriguez, Carlos A. 1975. Portfolio Equilibrium and the Balance of Payments: A Monetary Approach. *American Economy Review* 65 (September): 674–688.

Fried, Joel. 1980. The Intergenerational Distribution of the Gains from Technical Change and from International Trade. *Canadian Journal of Economics* 13 (February): 65–81.

Friedman, Milton. 1957. *A Theory of the Consumption Function*. Princeton: Princeton University Press.

Ghez, Gilbert R., and Becker, Gary S. 1975. *The Allocation of Time and Goods over the Life Cycle*. New York: Columbia University Press.

Gray, Jo Anna. 1976. Wage Indexation: A Macroeconomic Approach. *Journal of Monetary Economics* 2 (April): 221–235.

Greenwood, Jeremy. 1983. Expectations, the Exchange Rate and the Current Account. *Journal of Monetary Economics* 12 (November): 543–569.

Greenwood, Jeremy, and Kimbrough, Kent P. 1985. Capital Controls and Fiscal Policy in the World Economy. *Canadian Journal of Economics* 18 (November): 743–765.

Greenwood, Jeremy, and Kimbrough, Kent P. 1986. An Investigation in the Theory of Foreign Exchange Controls. Duke University, Working Paper, No. 86 (13).

Gregory, R. G. 1976. Some Implications of the Growth of the Mineral Sector. *The Australian Journal of Agricultural Economics* 20 (August): 71–91.

Hall, Robert E. 1978. Stochastic Implications of the Life Cycle–Permanent Income Hypothesis: Theory and Evidence. *Journal of Political Economy* 86 (December): 971–987.

Hamada, Koichi. 1976. Strategic Analysis of Monetary Interdependence. *Journal of Political Economy* 84, part 1 (August): 677–700.

Hamada, Koichi. 1985. *The Political Economy of International Monetary Interdependence*, Cambridge: MIT Press.

Harberger, Arnold C. 1950. Currency Depreciation, Income and the Balance of Trade. *Journal of Political Economy* 58 (February): 47–60.

Hayashi, Fumio. 1982. Tobin's Marginal q and Average q: A Neoclassical Interpretation. *Econometrica* 50 (January): 213–224.

Heckman, James J. 1974. Shadow Prices, Market Wages and Labor Supply. *Econometrica* 42 (July): 679–694.

Helpman, Elhanan. 1981. An Exploration in the Theory of Exchange Rate Regimes. *Journal of Political Economy* 89 (October): 865–890.

Helpman, Elhanan, and Razin, Assaf. 1979. Towards a Consistent Comparison of Alternative Exchange Rate Regimes. *Canadian Journal of Economics* 12 (August): 394–409.

Helpman, Elhanan, and Razin, Assaf. 1982. A Comparison of Exchange Rate Regimes in the Presence of Imperfect Capital Markets. *International Economic Review* 23 (June): 365–388.

Helpman, Elhanan, and Razin, Assaf. 1984. The Role of Saving and Investment in Exchange Rate Determination Under Alternative Monetary Mechanisms. *Journal of Monetary Economics* 13 (May): 307–325.

Helpman, Elhanan, and Razin, Assaf. 1987. Exchange Rate Management: Intertemporal Tradeoffs. *American Economic Review* 77 (March): 107–123.

Hubbard, R. Glenn, and Judd, Kenneth L. 1986. Liquidity Constraints, Fiscal Policy, and Consumption. *Brookings Paper on Economic Activity* 1: 1–50.

International Monetary Fund. 1977. *The Monetary Approach to the Balance of Payments*. Washington, D.C.: International Monetary Fund.

International Monetary Fund. *International Financial Statistics*. Washington, D.C.: International Monetary Fund, various issues.

International Monetary Fund. *World Economic Outlook*. Washington, D.C.: International Monetary Fund, various issues.

Iversen, Carl. 1935. *Aspects of the Theory of International Capital Movements*. London: Oxford University Press.

Johnson, Harry G. 1956. The Transfer Problem and Exchange Stability. *Journal of Political Economy* 59 (June):212–225.

Johnson, Harry G. 1958. Towards a General Theory of the Balance of Payments. In *International Trade and Economic Growth*, by Harry G. Johnson, London: Allen & Unwin, 153–168.

Judd, Kenneth L. 1987. A Dynamic Theory of Factor Taxation. *American Economic Review* 77 (May):42–48.

Kareken, John, and Wallace, Neil. 1981. On the Indeterminacy of Equilibrium Exchange Rates. *Quarterly Journal of Economics* 96 (May):202–222.

Kenen, Peter B. 1985. Macroeconomic Theory and Policy: How the Closed Economy Was Opened. In *Handbook of International Economics*, Vol. 2, edited by Ronald W. Jones and Peter B. Kenen. Amsterdam: North Holland, 625–677.

Keynes, John M. 1929. The German Transfer Problem. *Economic Journal* 39 (March):1–7.

Kimbrough, Kent P. 1986. Foreign Aid and Optimal Fiscal Policy. *Canadian Journal of Economics* 17 (February):35–61.

King, Mervin A. 1983. The Economics of Saving. NBER Working Paper Series No. 1247, October.

Kochin, Levis. 1974. Are Future Taxes Discounted by Consumers? *Journal of Money, Credit, and Banking* 6 (August):385–394.

Kormendi, Roger. 1983. Government Debt, Government Spending, and Private Sector Behavior. *American Economic Review* 73 (December):994–1010.

Kouri, Pentti J. K. 1976. The Exchange Rate and the Balance of Payment in the Short Run and in the Long Run: A Monetary Approach. *Scandinavian Journal of Economics* 78 (May):280–304.

Kydland, Finn E., and Prescott, Edward C. 1977. Rules Rather Than Discretion: The Inconsistency of Optimal Plans. *Journal of Political Economy* 85 (June):473–491.

Kydland, Finn E., and Prescott, Edward C. 1980. A Competitive Theory of Fluctuations and the Feasibility and Desirability of Stabilization Policy. In *Rational Expectations and Economic Policy*, edited by Stanley Fischer. Chicago: University of Chicago Press, 169–198.

Kydland, Finn E., and Prescott, Edward C. 1982. Time to Build and Aggregate Fluctuations. *Econometrica* 50 (September): 1345–1370.

Lanyi, Anthony. 1975. Separate Exchange Markets for Capital and Current Transactions. *IMF Staff Papers* 22 (November): 714–749.

Laursen, Svend, and Metzler, Lloyd A. 1950. Flexible Exchange Rates and the Theory of Employment. *Review of Economics and Statistics* 32 (November): 281–299.

Leiderman, Leonardo, and Blejer, Mario I. 1987. Modelling and Testing Ricardian Equivalence: A Survey. Washington, D.C.: International Monetary Fund, Fiscal Affairs Department.

Leiderman, Leonardo, and Razin, Assaf. 1987. Testing Ricardian Neutrality with an Intertemporal Stochastic Model. Foerder Institute Working Paper No. 2-87, Tel-Aviv University, January (forthcoming in *Journal of Money Credit and Banking*, 1988).

Lucas, Robert E., Jr. 1967. Optimal Investment Policy and the Flexible Accelerator. *International Economic Review* 8 (February): 78–85.

Lucas, Robert E., Jr. 1980. Equilibrium in a Pure Currency Economy. *Economic Inquiry* 18 (April): 203–220.

Lucas, Robert E., Jr., 1981. *Studies in Business-Cycle Theory*. Cambridge: MIT Press.

Lucas, Robert E., Jr. 1982. Interest Rates and Currency Prices in a Two-Country World. *Journal of Monetary Economics* 10 (November): 335–359.

Lucas, Robert E., Jr., and Prescott, Edward C. 1971. Investment under Uncertainty. *Econometrica* 39 (September): 659–681.

Lucas, Robert E., Jr., and Rapping, Leonard A. 1969. Real Wages, Employment and Inflation. *Journal of Political Economy* 77 (September/October): 721–754.

Lucas, Robert E., Jr., and Stokey, Nancy L. 1983. Optimal Fiscal and Monetary Policy in an Economy Without Capital. *Journal of Monetary Economics* 12: 55–93.

Machlup, Fritz. 1943. *International Trade and the National Income Multiplier*. Philadelphia: Blakiston.

MaCurdy, Thomas E. 1981. An Empirical Model of Labor Supply in a Life Cycle Setting. *Journal of Political Economy* 89 (December): 1059–1085.

Mankiw, Gregory N. 1987. Government Purchases and Real Interest Rates. *Journal of Political Economy* 95 (April): 407–419.

Mankiw, Gregory N., Rotemberg, Julio J., and Summers, Lawrence H. 1985. Intertemporal Substitution in Macroeconomics. *Quarterly Journal of Economics* 100 (February): 225–251.

Marion, Nancy P. 1981. Insulation Properties of a Two-Tier Exchange Market in a Portfolio Balance Model. *Economica* 48 (February): 61–70.

Marston, Richard C. 1985. Stabilization Policies in Open Economies. In *Handbook of International Economics*, Vol. 2, edited by Ronald W. Jones and Peter B. Kenen. Amsterdam: North Holland, 859–916.

McKinnon, Ronald I. 1969. Portfolio Balance and International Payments Adjustment. In *Monetary Problems of the International Economy*, edited by Alexander K. Swoboda and Robert A. Mundell. Chicago: University of Chicago Press, 199–234.

Meade, James E. 1951. *The Theory of International Economic Policy: The Balance of Payments*, Vol. 1. London: Oxford University Press.

Metzler, Lloyd A. 1942a. Underemployment Equilibrium in International Trade. *Econometrica* 10 (April): 97–112.

Metzler, Lloyd A. 1942b. The Transfer Problem Reconsidered. *Journal of Political Economy* 50 (June): 397–414.

Modigliani, Franco. 1961. Long-Run Implications of Alternative Fiscal Policies and the Burden of the National Debt. *Economic Journal* 71 (December): 730–755.

Modigliani, Franco. 1987. The Economics of Public Deficits. In *Economic Policy in Theory and Practice*, edited by Assaf Razin and Efraim Sadka. London: Macmillan, 3–44.

Modigliani, Franco, and Brumberg, Richard. 1954. Utility Analysis and the Consumption Function: An Interpretation of Cross Section Data. In *Post-Keynesian Economics*, edited by Kenneth K. Kurihara. New Brunswick: Rutgers University Press, 383–436.

Mundell, Robert A. 1960. The Pure Theory of International Trade. *American Economic Review* 50 (March): 67–110.

Mundell, Robert A. 1964. A Reply: Capital Mobility and Size. *Canadian Journal of Economics and Political Science* 30 (August): 421–431.

Mundell, Robert A. 1968. *International Economics*. New York: Macmillan.

Mundell, Robert A. 1971. *Monetary Theory*. Pacific Palisades: Goodyear.

Mussa, Michael L. 1979. Macroeconomic Interdependence and the Exchange Rate Regime. In *International Economic Policy: Theory and Evidence*, edited by Rudiger

Dornbusch and Jacob A. Frenkel. Baltimore: John Hopkins University Press, 160–204.

Neary, J. Peter, and Purvis, Douglas D. 1982. Sectoral Shocks in a Dependent Economy: Long-Run Adjustment and Short-Run Accommodation. *Scandinavian Journal of Economics* 84:229–253.

O'Driscoll, Gerald P. 1977. The Ricardian Nonequivalence Theorem. *Journal of Political Economy* 85 (February):207–210.

Obstfeld, Maurice. 1982. Aggregate Spending and the Terms of Trade: Is There a Laursen-Metzler Effect? *Quarterly Journal of Economics* 97 (May):251–270.

Obstfeld, Maurice. 1986. Capital Controls, the Dual Exchange Rate and Devaluation. *Journal of International Economics* 20 (February):1–20.

Obstfeld, Maurice, and Stockman Alan C. 1985. Exchange Rate Dynamics. In *Handbook of International Economics*, Vol. 2, edited by Ronald W. Jones and Peter B. Kenen. Amsterdam: North Holland, 917–977.

Ohlin, Bertil. 1929. The Reparation Problem: A Discussion. *Economic Journal* 39 (June):172–178.

Oudiz, Gilles, and Sachs, Jeffrey D. 1985. International Policy Coordination in Dynamic Macroeconomic Models. In *International Economic Policy Coordination*, edited by Willem H. Buiter and Richard C. Marston, Cambridge: Cambridge University Press, 274–319.

Patinkin, Don. 1965. *Money, Interest and Prices*. Rev. ed. New York: Harper & Row.

Penati, Alessandro. 1987. Government Spending and the Real Exchange Rate. *Journal of International Economics* 22 (May):237–256.

Persson, Torsten. 1984. Real Transfers in Fixed Exchange Rate Systems and the International Adjustment Mechanism. *Journal of Monetary Economics* 13 (May):349–369.

Persson, Torsten. 1985. Deficits and Intergenerational Welfare in Open Economies. *Journal of International Economics* 19 (August):1–19.

Persson, Torsten, and Svensson, Lars E. O. 1985. Current Account Dynamics and the Terms of Trade: Harberger-Laursen-Metzler Two Generations Later. *Journal of Political Economy* 93 (February):43–65.

Polak, Jacques J. 1957. Monetary Analysis of Income Formation and Payments Problems. *IMF Staff Papers* 6 (November):1–50.

Poterba, James M., and Summers Lawrence H. 1986. Finite Lifetimes and the Crowding-Out Effects of Budget Deficits. NBER Working Paper Series No. 1955.

Prais, S. J. 1961. Some Mathematical Notes on the Quantity Theory of Money in an Open Economy. *IMF Staff Papers* 8 (May): 212–226.

Purvis, Douglas D. 1985. Public Sector Deficits, International Capital Movements, and the Domestic Economy: The Medium-Term Is the Message. *Canadian Journal of Economics* 18 (November): 723–742.

Razin, Assaf, and Svensson, Lars E. O. 1983. The Current Account and the Optimal Government Debt. *Journal of International Money and Finance* 2 (August): 215–224.

Razin, Assaf. 1984. Capital Movements, Intersectoral Resource Shifts and the Trade Balance. *European Economic Review* 26 (October/November): 135–152.

Razin, Assaf, and Sadka, Efraim, eds. 1987. *Economic Policy in Theory and Practice: Essays in Memory of Abba P. Lerner.* London: Macmillan.

Robinson, R. 1952. A Graphical Analysis of the Foreign Trade Multiplier. *Economic Journal* 62 (September): 546–564.

Rodriguez, Carlos A. 1979. Short- and Long-Run Effects of Monetary and Fiscal Policies Under Flexible Exchange Rates and Perfect Capital Mobility. *American Economic Review* 69 (March): 176–182.

Rogoff, Kenneth. 1985. Can International Policy Coordination be Counterproductive? *Journal of International Economics* 18 (May): 199–217.

Rogoff, Kenneth. 1986. Reputational Constraints on Monetary Policy. NBER Working Paper Series No. 1986, July.

Rueff, Jacques. 1929. Mr Keynes' Views on the Transfer Problem: A Criticism. *Economic Journal* 39 (September): 388–399.

Sachs, Jeffrey D. 1981. The Current Account and Macroeconomic Adjustment in the 1970's. *Brookings Papers on Economic Activity* 1: 201–268.

Sachs, Jeffrey D. 1984. Theoretical Issues in International Borrowing. *Princeton Studies in International Finance* 54 (July).

Samuelson, Paul A. 1952. The Transfer Problem and Transport Costs: The Terms of Trade When Impediments Are Absent. *Economic Journal* 62 (June): 278–304.

Samuelson, Paul A. 1958. An Exact Consumption-Loan Model with or without the Social Contrivance of Money. *Journal of Political Economy* 66 (December): 467–482.

Sargent, Thomas J. 1978. Estimation of Dynamic Labor Demand Schedules under Rational Expectations. *Journal of Political Economy* 86 (December): 1009–1044.

Stockman, Alan C. 1980. A Theory of Exchange Rate Determination. *Journal of Political Economy* 88 (August): 673–698.

Svensson, Lars E. O. 1986. Sticky Goods Prices, Flexible Asset Prices, Monopolistic Competition, and ·Monetary Policy. *Review of Economic Studies* 53 (July): 385–405.

Svensson, Lars E. O., and Razin, Assaf. 1983. The Terms of Trade and the Current Account: The Harberger-Laursen-Metzler Effect. *Journal of Political Economy* 91 (February):91–125.

Swoboda, Alexander K., and Dornbusch, Rudiger. 1973. Adjustment, Policy, and Monetary Equilibrium in a Two-Country Model. In *International Trade and Money*, edited by Michael G. Connolly and Alexander K. Swoboda. London: Allen & Unwin, 225–261.

Tobin, James. 1969. A General Equilibrium Approach to Monetary Theory. *Journal of Money, Credit, and Banking* 1 (February):15–29.

Uzawa, Hirofumi. 1969. Time Preference and the Penrose Effect in a Two-Class Model of Economic Growth. *Journal of Political Economy* 77, part 2 (July/August): 628–652.

Van Wijnbergen, Sweder. 1986. On Fiscal Deficits, the Real Exchange Rate and the World Rate of Interest. *European Economic Review* 30 (October):1013–1023.

Weil, Philippe 1987. Overlapping Families of Infinitely Lived Agents. *Quarterly Journal of Economics*, forthcoming.

Yaari, Menahem E. 1965. Uncertain Lifetime, Life Insurance, and the Theory of the Consumer. *Review of Economic Studies* 32 (April):137–50.

Index